HYPNOSIS
and
BEHAVIORAL MEDICINE

HYPNOSIS
and
BEHAVIORAL MEDICINE

Daniel P. Brown
The Cambridge Hospital

Erika Fromm
The University of Chicago

LAWRENCE ERLBAUM ASSOCIATES PUBLISHERS
Hillsdale, New Jersey　　　　　　　London

Lawrence Erlbaum Associates, Inc., Publishers
365 Broadway
Hillsdale, New Jersey 07642

Printed in the United States of America by
Braun-Brumfield, Inc., Ann Arbor, Michigan

Library of Congress Cataloging-in-Publication Data

Brown, Daniel P., 1948–
    Hypnosis and behavioral medicine.

    Includes bibliographies and indexes.
    1. Hypnotism—Therapeutic use. 2. Medicine and
psychology. 3. Behavior therapy. I. Fromm, Erika.
II. Title. [DNLM: 1. Behavior Therapy. 2. Hypnosis.
WM 415 B877h]
RC495.B78   1987   616.89′142   86-19961
ISBN 0-89859-925-3

10 9 8 7 6 5 4 3

Contents

List of Figures

Foreword

Hypnosis and Behavioral Medicine integrates advances in behavioral medicine with recent scientific findings and theories of clinical hypnosis. It is written by two experienced clinicians, one a foremost hypnoanalyst, the other the director of a behavioral medicine clinic in a teaching hospital affiliated with the Harvard Medical School. The book represents their distillation of years of experience in the use of hypnosis and behavioral medicine interventions to treat patients with psychophysiological disorders and behavioral problems. The authors' perspective reflects the growing sophistication of behavioral medicine interventions used by practitioners. They also illustrate how our understanding of hypnosis has advanced over the past twenty years. Yet, curiously, the clinical and research literature both in behavioral medicine and in hypnotherapy have developed largely independently of each other. Each of these clinical areas typically has ignored the major advances in the other field. To bridge the gap between the practice of hypnosis and the practice of behavioral medicine, the authors have written this book to help educate the behavioral medicine audience to the usefulness of hypnosis as part of a comprehensive treatment program and also to educate the clinical hypnosis audience to the major advances in behavioral medicine. The book is written for practitioners in both fields.

Hypnosis and Behavioral Medicine is set within the context of contemporary trends in behavioral medicine. Previous hypnosis books that have attempted to integrate behavior modification and hypnosis into some form of hypnobehavioral therapy have had only a limited focus: Behavior modification has been cast primarily in terms of conditioning models of learning and systematic desensitization. The authors of *Hypnosis and*

Behavioral Medicine have expanded the scope of clinical behaviorism to include recent neobehaviorist trends. They emphasize the movement of contemporary behaviorist thinking beyond the restricted confines of conditioning models (classical and operant conditioning) to a self-regulation model of behavioral change and have likewise broadened the horizon of behaviorism to incorporate new theoretical developments in environmental control, cognitive-behaviorism, social modeling, and coping theory. Along with an increased appreciation of the complexity of human behavior and related theoretical advances, behavioral clinicians have developed an armamentarium of sophisticated clinical procedures, some of which have been substantiated by clinical outcome studies: self-monitoring, stimulus control, self control of internal states, behavioral self-regulation and contingency management, skill in internal perception, systematic desensitization, cognitive therapy, and relapse prevention. Chapter 1 presents a selective review of the field of behavioral medicine. Beginning with a discussion of the historical development of behavioral medicine as a new field, it reviews some of the major theoretical advances, explains a number of standard treatment procedures, discusses treatment goals, and concludes with a section on assessment of the many complex factors that contribute to a psychophysiological disorder or behavioral problem.

This book is also set within the context of a contemporary understanding of hypnotic phenomena. Chapter II presents a selective review of scientific and clinical knowledge of hypnosis. The domain of hypnosis is defined as comprising at least three important dimensions: expectations regarding hypnotic effects; an altered state of consciousness, or trance; and a special hypnotic relationship. The effects of hypnosis are in part determined by the idiosyncratic meaning that the hypnotic situation has for the particular patient and the specific expectation of change attributed to hypnotic procedures. Hypnosis is, however, conceived as something more than a placebo phenomenon. It is seen as involving an altered state of consciousness characterized by cognitive, sensory, and perceptual changes. Hypnosis is also seen as a special type of patient–therapist relationship, in which the patient is more receptive to the suggestions of the hypnotherapist, more receptive to internal physiological events in the stream of consciousness as structured by the hypnotic situation, and more influenced by the hypnotic transference. The authors argue that the clinical efficacy of hypnosis and self-hypnosis in behavioral medicine lies in the ability to directly effect sensory/physiological changes and cognitive/perceptual changes in the service of greater bodily self-regulation, improved coping capacity, and the control of behavior.

The balance of the book integrates hypnosis and behavioral medicine into a systematic framework for the treatment of a variety of psychophysiological disorders (chronic pain, headache, hypertension, asthma, gastrointestinal disorders, skin conditions, and immune-related disorders) and habit and behavioral disorders (smoking, obesity, substance and alcohol abuse, sexual dysfunctions, and sleep disorders). The major contribution of the volume is its presentation of detailed and comprehensive clinical protocols for the treatment of a variety of psychophysiological and habit disorders—detailed in its spelling out each step of the treatment procedure and comprehensive in its integration of a variety of treatment procedures and theoretical perspectives into a single treatment plan (with a decision tree for determining which aspects of the overall treatment protocol need to be emphasized for a particular patient). The authors have tried to integrate well-established, state-of-the-art clinical procedures, along with new developments, into their treatment protocols. The book can be said to be a clinical manual of sorts in behavioral medicine. Even if hypnosis were not emphasized as its primary treatment perspective, the book could serve as a useful guide to practitioners of behavioral medicine who were less familiar with hypnosis.

Each section of the clinical manual is presented in roughly the same framework. The section on headache, for example, begins with a discussion of assessment, both psychiatric and behavioral. Next, the authors discuss the psychobiological mechanisms that contribute to the cause and maintenance of the headache. Then the authors discuss the typical medical and pharmacological treatment of headache and go on to introduce a multimodal hypnobehavioral protocol for the treatment of headache. The systematic protocol includes: direct hypnotic suggestions for symptom relief; daily self-monitoring of the vicissitudes of symptoms; analysis of which situations alleviate and exacerbate headache symptoms; stimulus control; behavioral self-regulation; hypnotic relaxation; hypnosis, biofeedback and combined hypnosis/biofeedback for the development of voluntary control over specific physiological processes contributing to the disorder; hypnotic suggestions for altering the cognitive factors that maintain the symptoms (e.g. attitudes, beliefs, self-statements); use of group hypnotherapy when indicated; hypnotic suggestions for skill development and symptom challenge; recommendations for life style rehabilitation; procedures for relapse prevention and maintenance of treatment effects; hypnotic suggestions to deal with the acute exacerbation of symptoms; and adjunctive life style interventions. The authors also offer recommendations for the use of short-term hypnotherapy and hypnoanalysis for those patients who are unresponsive to the hypnobehavioral treatment, but suggest that the reader consider their other recent book, *Hypnotherapy and Hypnoanalysis,* for a more detailed account of these procedures.

Each treatment protocol ends with a discussion of clinical outcome.

Although the authors recognize that outcome studies on hypnotherapy are sparse and inconclusive, they remain optimistic. Most poor outcomes, they speculate, are the result of asking the wrong research questions, not of the ineffectiveness of hypnosis. They argue that it is too simple to evaluate simply whether or not hypnosis is effective in behavioral medicine. Rather, outcome studies must consider the type of presenting problem, the characteristics of the patient and the therapist, the quality of the therapeutic relationshp, the conditions under which the treatment is being conducted, the approach taken toward the hypnosis, the style of hypnotic induction, and the specific nature of the hypnotic suggestions given. Clearly, a multidimensional, systems approach to research and practice is called for.

The emphasis of the book, and its main strength, lies in its presentation of a multidimensional perspective in which various systems of treatment are integrated. The authors believe that illness development is complex and that most presenting problems are a mixture of a number of contributing factors, some causing, some maintaining the condition. Behavioral assessment and treatment consist of "partialling out the variance" in an attempt to determine the relative weight of each factor contributing to the psychophysiological disorder or habit disorder and then to develop a treatment plan that addresses each component. According to the authors, these disorders have multiple causes. In addition, a number of factors—conditioning, illness behaviors, medication overuse—maintain the disorder apart from what caused it. The task of the clinician is to assess the relative contribution of each of the contributing factors and to individualize the treatment plan accordingly. The authors also recognize distinct subgroups of patients within the population of, say, headache patients, for whom certain single treatment strategies may be effective, for example, direct hypnotic suggestions, self-monitoring, and the like. At the same time, they recommend a comprehensive, multimodal, and individualized treatment plan that meets the needs of a heterogeneous patient population and increases the probability of successful outcome in a wide range of patients.

In many ways, this book is integrative and refreshing. Psychologists, physicians, and nurses interested in clinical hypnosis and behavioral medicine should find this book rewarding.

Gary E. Schwartz, Ph.D.

Preface

This book was written in response to the needs of many professionals who are actively treating patients who have psychophysiological disorders or behavioral problems associated with medical illness. We have tried to fold into a single volume a synopsis of the modern scientific understanding of hypnosis and a comprehensive review of clinical procedures and research in behavioral medicine. The book represents fifteen years of collaboration by its authors on clinical hypnosis and, in the last eight years, an attempt to apply our knowledge of clinical hypnosis to the field of behavioral medicine as part of the Program in Behavioral Medicine at The Cambridge Hospital/Harvard Medical School and as part of a group private practice specializing in hypnosis and behavioral medicine. Over these years we have gained clinical experience with large numbers of patients presenting with the problems typical of a behavioral medicine clinic; have had the opportunity to teach hypnosis and behavioral medicine to psychology interns, psychiatric residents and medical residents and to mental health and health professionals; and have been able to engage in clinical research on hypnosis and behavioral medicine.

While the book represents what the authors have learned from each other, it also represents what we have learned from others. No work is written in a vacuum. We have tried to build upon the scientific understanding of hypnosis, and in this sense our work shows the influence of Ernest R. and Josephine Hilgard and others. We have also tried to build upon our understanding of the advances in the rapidly developing field of behavioral medicine, and our work shows the influence many leading experts in the field. The discussions at the annual meetings of the Conference on the Voluntary Control of Internal States (Council Grove

Conference), the Society of Clinical and Experimental Hypnosis, and the Society of Behavioral Medicine have given us the opportunity to learn of the newest developments in the field and of state-of-the-art clinical interventions. In particular, our understanding of asthma has been shaped by the work of Thomas Creer, Ph.D., of sleep disorders by that of Ralph Turner, Ph.D., and of weight problems by Kelly Bronwell, Ph.D., through their presentations of workshops at the Society of Behavioral Medicine. We especially wish to acknowledge our debt to Steve Fahrion, Ph.D., of The Menninger Foundation. Our understanding of behavioral interventions in hypertension was shaped by discussions with him. Dr. Fahrion was generous enough to share his clinical protocols with us, and our chapter clearly shows the influence of his excellent unpublished paper, "Etiology and intervention in essential hypertension: A biobehavioral approach." Likewise, our understanding of behavioral interventions in cancer was shaped by discussions with Pat Norris, Ph.D., also of The Menninger Foundation.

We are thankful not only to our teachers but to our associates who have worked closely with us in the development of our ideas, notably, Jean Kristeller, Ph.D., who helped in the initial development of the Behavioral Medicine Program at The Cambridge Hospital, and Deborah Hulihan, Psy.D., the current Associate Director of that program; and to the associates in our group practice, with whom we have had many rich discussions of cases in hypnosis and behavioral medicine: Howard Berens, M.D., Deborah Block, M.A., Deborah Hulihan, Psy.D., Stephanie Jones, M.Ed., Steve Kahn, Ph.D., Harris McCarter, M.A., Dee Dee Pike, Psy.D., and Lena Theodorou, Psy.D. We are also thankful to our many patients and students, from whom we have learned so much. For each of us there has been no greater joy than to watch a patient utilize hypnosis to discover coping resources and develop a sense of genuine mastery over symptoms, or to watch a clinical student or professional discover the phenomena of hypnosis, assimilate hypnosis into his or her clinical behavioral medicine practice, and then grow to become a seasoned practitioner. In this respect, we hope that this work will serve a new generation of clinical students and their patients.

A work like this could not have been written without the hard work of many others who assisted us at various stages of the process. We are grateful to our research assistants. Michael Dysart and Stephanie Morgan did an enormous amount of work collecting the many hypnosis and behavioral medicine papers reviewed in this book. Mary Hallowitz, Betty Johnson, Lisa Lombard, and Stephan Kahn were of considerable help in critically reading the manuscript in its near-final stages. We are especially grateful to Sarah Skinner for her preparation of the various drafts of the manuscript on the word processor. Her dedication, insightful editorial comments, critical judgment, and conscientious diligence helped produce presentable and readable drafts. We are also especially grateful to Estelle Keren, who faithfully tackled the tedious task of putting the extensive references on the word processor, and checking and rechecking them for accuracy. She also coordinated each stage of the project and facilitated smooth communication between the authors and the editor. We also want to thank Marushka Glissen for her help in checking the reference list against the original published works and for proofreading. We especially want to thank Eleanor Starke Kobrin for her consistently reliable editing and for expediting the publication schedule. Last, we want to express our deepest appreciation and gratitude to our families and friends for their patience and tolerance while we were so deeply immersed in writing this book.

1 Behavioral Medicine

HISTORY OF BEHAVIORAL MEDICINE

Behavioral medicine is a new field in which clinical methods and theories derived from the behavioral sciences are applied to the treatment and prevention of medical illness. Since the early 1970s, behavioral medicine has emerged as a scientific and clinical discipline in its own right. Behavioral medicine developed, in part, out of a growing dissatisfaction by medical practitioners with consultation/liaison psychiatry and its roots in psychosomatic medicine, whose beginnings were in the 1940s, with psychodynamic explanations of specific illnesses (Alexander & French, 1948) and the search for personality factors associated with specific illnesses (Dunbar, 1943). After nearly two decades of research, which for the most part yielded negative results, interest in psychodynamically based psychosomatic medicine began to wane in other ways. Consultation/liaison psychiatry, however, remained useful to medical practitioners in the diagnosis of mental illness in patients who also were physically ill, in treatment by therapeutic and pharmacological means, and in sensitizing clinicians to the need to refine interviewing skills. Although psychotherapeutic and pharmacological interventions were useful to the physician in treating certain psychiatric patients, these methods simply did not address the general needs of the physician confronted in everyday practice with large numbers of patients who had a significant behavioral component associated with their medical illness. These methods disregarded, for example, compliance with treatment regimens associated with chronic illness, the effects of attitudes and beliefs on illness, illness behavior, psychophysiological disorders, and the impact of health-risk factors in a person's lifestyle on generating and preventing disease.

Over the same interval behavioral scientists, predominantly psychologists, began collaborating with physicians. One area in which behavioral scientists in the last 25 years have offered procedures directly relevant to medical practitioners is biofeedback. Since the now classic work of Miller (1969) and his associates on operant conditioning of physiological processes, behaviorally oriented clinicians have begun to develop methods of applying these principles directly to the treatment of a wide range of psychophysiological disorders: pain, headache, cardiovascular disease,

1

asthma, and gastrointestinal disorders. As biofeedback procedures gained more and more popularity, professional societies began to form (for example, the Biofeedback Society of America), and annual reviews of the growing clinical studies now regularly appear in the literature.

At the same time, there appeared a surge of scientific interest in altered states of consciousness (Tart, 1969). In the 1960s and 70s, hypnosis became an area of legitimate scientific inquiry, largely through the works of Ernest Hilgard (1965) at Stanford and Martin Orne (1959, 1977) at the Psychiatric Institute of the University of Pennsylvania. New investigations began into mental imagery and daydreaming—once an area disdained by the conventional scientific community (Holt, 1964). Clinical applications—the so-called imagery therapies—began to proliferate by the mid-1970s (see Jerome Singer's *Imagery and Daydreaming Methods in Psychotherapy and Behavior Modification,* 1974). Scientists, both experimental and clinical, also began to assimilate Eastern meditative methods (Carrington, 1977; Shapiro, 1978) into the growing repertoire of what are now called self-control strategies.

The integration of independent contributions from research on altered states of consciousness and on biofeedback began in 1970, with the annual conference on the Voluntary Control of Internal States and were sponsored by the Green family at the Menninger Foundation. The conferences were attended by those in the forefront of research on altered states of consciousness (hypnosis, meditation, drug-induced states, imagery, and nontraditional healing) as well as by the researchers on biofeedback. From these dialogues, biofeedback researchers began to realize the important contribution of the patient's internal state to the outcome of biofeedback training. Paralleling these developments, imaginal and meditative methods began to find their way into clinical practice.

During the 1960s and 1970s, behaviorism also underwent a significant revision. Behaviorism had traditionally been associated with conditioning and learning. The classical conditioning model of Pavlov (1927) and the operant conditioning model of Skinner (1953) both assume that punishment and reward are the main means of changing behavior. The early clinical procedures based on a conditioning model were largely aversive procedures, such as eliminating a behavior problem like smoking or alcoholism by inducing nausea and vomiting. As outcome studies began to accumulate, it became clear that positive reinforcement of healthy and desirable behaviors was more effective than negative reinforcement of problem behaviors. These results necessitated a shift from an eliminative model to a constructional model of behavior modification (Delprato, 1981). Behavioral therapists began to think less about the elimination of specific maladaptive behaviors and more about the generation of new adaptive repertoires.

Behaviorists also began to approach the complexity of human behavior. The attempt of early behavioral interventions was to isolate specific, easily identifiable problem behaviors or target behaviors. The focus was on behavior per se, independent of the context in which it occurred. Behaviorists began to focus now on behavioral-environmental interactions (Kanfer, 1977). Major advances in the treatment of weight problems (Stuart, 1967) and insomnia (Bootzin, 1977) occurred with this treatment strategy.

Beginning to appreciate the complexity of human behavior, behavioral scientists began also to focus on the patient's internal resources rather than only on behavioral change. Emphasis on discrete problem behaviors were superseded by emphasis on general coping resources applicable across many situations and types of problems. Lazarus (1966) was the first to emphasize the importance of assessing the range and adequacy of coping strategies available to patients in times of stress. In addition, behaviorists began to shift to an understanding of cognitive processes. Interest in a pure stimulus-response model of learning was replaced by an interest in covert processes as mediators of behavior change. As cognitive psychology began to emerge as a legitimate field of inquiry within psychology in the mid-1970s, behaviorists also began to soften their historic rejection of the importance of internal processes in behavioral change. The *Annual Review of Behavior Therapy* considered 1976 as the "Year of Cognition" (Wilson, 1980) for behavioral therapists, and a new generation of cognitive-behaviorists emerged in the writings of Beck (1976) and Meichenbaum (1974). Ellis (1962) had already worked towards this goal years earlier.

While the theoretical underpinnings of behavioral therapy were undergoing a radical revision in the 1970s, behaviorists were making consistent gains in clinical research methodology. Clinical outcome studies of psychodynamic therapy had earlier been notoriously poorly designed and had not provided control cases. Behaviorally oriented clinicians had learned from these mistakes. The outcome studies on behavior modification of anxiety, phobias, weight, and smoking were carefully controlled and had more sophisticated designs. Advocates of behavior modification succeeded where dynamically oriented therapists had failed: they were able to substantiate and measure treatment gains. Since medical training emphasizes the use of measurement in routine medical diagnosis and treatment (e.g. laboratory data), behavioral therapists who emphasized outcome measures were able to put their clinical findings in a form more familiar, credible, and relevant to physicians than had been the case with the contributors from consultation/liaison psychiatry.

All of these independent and concurrent trends came together in the mid-1970s. The *Zeitgeist* had changed. The time had ripened for the emergence of a new discipline, behavioral medicine, a term that can be traced to an anthology of early biofeedback papers called *Biofeedback: Behavioral Medicine,* in which the editor, Lee Birk (1973) tried to reassess the behavioral science underpinnings of biofeedback. But the field did not blossom into a full fledged discipline until the leading scientists converged to discuss and articulate the basic questions and concepts that ultimately came to define the field. Their dialogues began in 1969, with the Banff International Conference on Behavior Modification. The 1976 Banff Conference on Behavioral Self-Management in particular addressed the changing field of behavior therapy.

The first formal definition of behavioral medicine was presented at the 1977 Yale Conference on Behavioral Medicine in which invited scientists came together to articulate the dimensions of this developing field of inquiry. According to the Yale conference, behavioral medicine was defined as follows:

> Behavioral Medicine is the field concerned with the development of behavioral science knowledge and techniques relevant to the understanding of physical health and illness and the application of this knowledge and these techniques to prevention, diagnosis, treatment and rehabilitation (Schwartz & Weiss, 1978, p. 7)

That meeting constituted an official statement of the new discipline. Since then, the signs of the discipline's obvious development have included the formation of an Academy of Behavioral Medicine Research and The Society of Behavioral Medicine, and the appearance of new journals, for example, the *Journal of Behavioral Medicine, Behavioral Medicine Abstracts, Health Psychology* and *Advances.* Departments of behavioral medicine have been established in most major academic and medical institutions. The majority of hospitals and health maintenance organizations now include behavioral medicine interventions in their repertoire of treatment strategies. A later revision of the definition of behavioral medicine by the Academy of Behavioral Medicine Research emphasized the interdisciplinary nature of behavioral medicine and the integration of behavioral and biomedical knowledge and practice (Schwartz & Weiss, 1980). The current practice of behavior medicine is an integration of behavioral therapy, an understanding of physiological processes, cognitive therapy, self-control strategies, and an understanding of altered states of consciousness and biofeedback.

What we present in this book is written in the hope of strengthening the fusion of the many disparate threads that have come to define the discipline of behavioral medicine. The contributions of clinical hypnosis have not yet been fully integrated with the major advances behavioral medicine has made over the past decade. In fact, the discipline of behavioral medicine and the advances in clinical hypnosis have evolved nearly independent of each other over this period. On the one hand with some important but rare exceptions, few practitioners of behavioral medicine have utilized hypnosis extensively with their clients, nor have scientists-practitioners conducted nearly as many outcome studies with hypnosis as have been conducted with progressive muscle relaxation, stimulus-control, self-monitoring, cognitive therapy, and the like. Even where hypnosis is used by practitioners of behavioral medicine, their approach does not show a sophisticated understanding of the many advances made in clinical hypnosis during the last 25 years (Fromm, 1986). On the other hand, clinical literature on hypnosis, as reported in the major journals ((*American Journal of Clinical Hypnosis, International Journal of Clinical and Experimental Hypnosis,* and *British Journal of Medical Hypnotism*) seldom cite the major advances in behavioral medicine. Some attempts have been made to integrate hypnosis with behavioral therapy (Dengrove, 1976; Kroger & Fezler, 1976). However, these so-called hypnobehavioral therapies take into account neither the significant theoretical revisions and major advances in clinical methods made by behavioral therapists over the past decade, nor the increasing sophistication of their research design.

It is our belief that practitioners and researchers of both clinical hypnosis and behavioral medicine could benefit from an integration between the two disciplines. Each has something to offer to the other. It is also our belief that such an integration represents one of the cutting edges of clinical hypnosis. (The other, we believe, is dynamic hypnotherapy and hypoanalysis [see Brown & Fromm, 1986]). Rodolfa et al. (1985) recently surveyed some 500 members of the American Society of Clinical Hypnosis to assess current and future trends in hypnosis. The survey showed that practitioners agreed that behavioral medicine was "the general area with the most promising future for the application of hypnosis" (p. 24).

THE CLINICAL CONTRIBUTIONS OF BEHAVIORAL MEDICINE

Behavioral medicine offers procedures for the treatment of a wide range of clinical problems. These methods are directly relevant to the majority of patients seen by physicians, because many medical problems seen by physicians have some behavioral component. Behavioral medicine has made significant advances in the treatment of psychophysiological disorders: acute and chronic pain; headache; cardiovascular disease such as hypertension, Raynaud's Syndrome, tachycardia and other coronary heart syndromes; asthma and chronic obstructive pulmonary disease; gastrointestinal disorders; skin disorders; immune-related disorders (autoimmune diseases, allergies, and cancer) and genitourinary disorders. Behavioral medicine also has made significant contributions to the treatment of various behavioral and habit disorders, such as smoking, overweight, ideopathic sleep disturbances, and sexual dysfunctions. Furthermore, it has contributed to preventive medicine through the identification and counteraction of the health-risk factors involved in smoking, overweight, stress, type A behavior, alcohol or substance abuse, and too much or too little physical activity. Behavioral medicine is designed to assess lifestyle and identify factors that contribute to health or risk of illness, as well as to develop interventions to alter lifestyle in the direction of health. Concerned only with symptom relief, traditional medical practices failed to take into account the contribution of lifestyle to the etiology of disease (Schwartz, 1979). We now know that nearly half of all mortalities are directly attributable to lifestyle problems (Milsum, 1980).

Behavioral medicine is also concerned with areas traditionally canvassed by psychosomatic medicine and consultation/liaison psychiatry. These include the treatment of anxiety disorders, phobias (particularly agoraphobia), and the somatizing and hypochondriacal disorders. Behavioral medicine addresses itself to the learned and behavioral components of the disorders that cannot be helped by medication alone. In addition, behavioral medicine is concerned with the development of treatment strategies for the behavioral and psychological components associated with chronic physical illness. They include: noncompliance with treatment regimens, for example, the diabetic's diet and medication; failure to integrate chronic illness into one's self-concept; or the impact of the family system on the etiology and maintenance of symptoms. Although the scope of behavioral medicine has expanded considerably, this book concerns itself with those areas which have generated the bulk of clinical literature in behavioral medicine, namely psychophysiological disorders and habit and behavioral disorders.

THE BASIC PRINCIPLES OF BEHAVIORAL CHANGE

Conditioning and Learning

Classical conditioning or respondent conditioning was first derived by Pavlov (1927) from his studies of salivation in dogs. Dogs were presented with an unconditioned stimulus (UCS) to which they responded with salivation, an unconditioned response (UCR). Pavlov then demonstrated some of the basic principles of learning by pairing a neutral conditioning stimulus (CS)—the sound of a bell or a tuning fork—with the UCS, or sight of the food. Through repeated trials pairing UCS and CS, he discovered that presentation of the CS alone (the bell) elicited the UCR (salivation). The dog had learned to produce the physiological response to the previously neutral stimulus. In this manner, adaptive and maladaptive behaviors can be learned through their association with an unconditioned stimulus and an unconditioned response. For example, the nausea and vomiting commonly associated with chemotherapy may be a consequence of classical conditioning. The drugs (UCS) typically used in chemotherapy cause nausea and vomiting (UCR). After four or five sessions, certain patients learn to associate previously neutral stimuli with the unconditioned stimulus. The sight of the hospital, the examining room, or the doctor (CS) may produce the nausea and vomiting (UCR) before the actual administration of the next drug trial. The patient now has conditioned anticipatory nausea and vomiting.

Operant, or instrumental, conditioning was devised by Skinner (1953). Whereas classical conditioning pertains to the associative link between the unconditioned stimulus and the conditioned stimulus, operant conditioning pertains to the consequences of behavior. Any behavior may produce its own positive or negative reinforcers, depending on the nature of the response contingencies and the schedule of reinforcing responses. The type of learning that occurs depends on the environmental consequences that shape the behavior. Through operant learning mechanisms, some patients learn chronic insomnia. Patients may experience an acute disruption in sleep for any number of reasons—depression, worry about a pending examination, anticipation of a vacation. They respond to the acute sleep disturbance by drastically altering sleep routines. They may ordinarily read difficult material or watch exciting television in bed. By bringing these activities into the bedroom, patients no longer utilize sleep stimuli like the bedroom and bed as discriminatory cues to trigger the sleep-onset mechanism. Instead, they carry waking activities into the sleep-onset period and thereby maintain the sleep disturbance (Bootzin, 1977). In a similar fashion, insomniac patients who regularly take sleeping pills and headache patients who routinely take Ergot medication learn to produce chronic instability of the physiological mechanisms underlying sleep-onset and vasomotor response, respectively. Operant learning plays a large role in the maintenance of many maladaptive psychophysiological disorders and in the acquired maladaptive lifestyles that contribute to illness (Schwartz, 1977).

Many techniques devised by behavioral scientists to treat various disorders are based on a mixture of classical and operant learning theories

(Keefe & Blumenthal, 1982). Whereas animals have been used to develop classical as well as operant conditioning models in pure form, human behavior is so complex that it is best understood and treated by means of a combination of classical and operant methods (Kanfer & Phillips, 1970). The relative contributions of classical and operant conditioning to the etiology and maintenance of psychophysiological symptoms may be difficult to assess. Both may be important, as in the development and maintenance of anticipatory asthma (Creer, 1979). It is perhaps more accurate to speak of the conditioning of symptoms and of treatment as deconditioning or desensitization. Deconditioning or systematic desensitization (Wolpe, 1958) and contingency management (Pomerleau & Brady, 1979) are the main tools used for therapy by behavioral scientists.

Social Modeling

Much learning occurs by following another's example. Sometimes we are more likely to repeat the exemplified behavior if we are rewarded for following the example of others. We may spontaneously imitate another's example without practice. These examples of observational learning (Gilmore, 1968) are quite relevant to the clinician (Kanfer & Phillips, 1970).

Cognitive-Behavioral Learning

Behavioral scientists have become increasingly aware of the role of cognitive processes as mediators of behavioral change. Irrational beliefs (Ellis, 1962), cognitive distortions (Beck, 1976), and negative self-talk (Mahoney & Mahoney, 1976; Meichenbaum, 1974) all contribute to the development of maladaptive emotional states and behaviors ranging from anxiety, problematic eating and smoking, to depression. Normally covert cognitive processes however, can come under the scrutiny of the patient's awareness and the therapist's observations. The patient learns to recognize cognitive patterns as they occur in the stream of consciousness and as they pertain to the development and maintenance of his symptoms and problem behaviors. Patients learn to restructure cognitive processes directly and thereby develop healthy adaptive behaviors.

THE STANDARD TOOLS OF THE BEHAVIOR THERAPIST

Self-Monitoring

Self-monitoring, the systematic self-observation of behavior (Kazdin, 1974; McFall, 1977; Nelson, 1977), is an effective treatment strategy at the onset of treatment (although, according to Kazdin (1974), it does not effectively maintain behavioral change. The patient, given instructions to keep daily records of the fluctuations of symptoms, thus is enlisted as an active collaborator in the treatment process. He systematically records the time any change in a symptom occurs and notes its context—what he is doing, thinking, and feeling at the time the symptom changes; whether he is alone or in the presence of others, at home or at work. The patient thus sharpens self-observational skills and becomes more consciously aware of the character of his symptoms. Self-monitoring is a way of observing daily behavior in a thorough and comprehensive manner. It is especially effective after the patient has learned to monitor a few very specific behaviors, recording the change in behavior precisely when it is noted (McFall, 1977). Patients learn the principles of self-control, which are very important to behavioral change and its maintenance.

Through self-monitoring, the patient receives immediate feedback on which factors contribute to an increase and which to a decrease of symptoms. He may discover certain high risk times, times when symptoms are more likely to occur; and he may discover certain high risk situations in which the symptoms typically occur. Through self-monitoring, the patient also develops internal performance standards that guide behavioral change. Sometimes self-monitoring alone—without any additional treatment intervention—helps to alleviate the symptoms. This phenomenon, known as reactivity, is more apparent in the earlier stages of treatment.

Stimulus Control

Through learning, otherwise neutral events—certain behavioral routines or the nature of the physical surroundings or objects in the environment—can become stimuli for maladaptive behaviors. We are conditioned daily by the very environment we live in. Stimulus control is the method by which the patient learns to identify which cues in the environment foster maladaptive or adaptive behaviors and then alter the environment and the behavioral routines accordingly (Kanfer & Phillips, 1970). For example, habitually leaving food around the house may trigger maladaptive eating habits. In therapy, patients learn to become better "environmental engineers" (Mahoney & Mahoney, 1976), that is, to modify their behavioral routines and eliminate environmental cues which maintain behavioral problems.

Self-Control of Internal Stats and Skill Training

Behavioral scientists have employed a variety of means to gain access to and develop control over internal states. Jacobson (1938), who pioneered progressive muscle relaxation, systematically taught patients to tense and relax each of the main muscle groups of the body. Regular practice of progressive muscle relaxation results in deep relaxation, which is subjectively convincing and is accompanied by distinct physiological changes (Paul, 1969)—notably decreased sympathetic arousal (Stoyva & Budzynski, 1974), especially if the patient is able to develop an internal representation of the relaxed state (Stilson et al., 1980). Some have gone so far as to consider the relaxation response to be the "final common pathway" of the treatment of psychophysiological disorders (Silver & Blanchard, 1978).

Hypnosis and self-hypnosis are yet different ways to gain access to and control of internal states. Hypnosis often does involve relaxation, but it is more than that. It also characteristically involves cognitive and perceptual alterations (Frankel, 1976; Orne, 1977). There are considerable individual differences in hypnotic responsiveness. People who are hypnotizable may upon suggestion produce significant sensory and physiological changes. Imagery (Singer, 1974) and visualizations (Epstein 1986) are increasingly being used in medical treatment to aid both in diagnosis and assessment of the course of the illness (Achterberg & Lawlis, 1978) and in its cure (Epstein, 1986; Simonton et al., 1978). These methods are especially powerful for people with a talent for imaginative processes. Meditation is a self-control method (Shapiro, 1978) that uses skillful and sustained deployment of focused attention (Brown & Engler, 1980) and has led to the development of a variety of clinical techniques (Carrington, 1977; Shapiro, 1978). Breathing exercises directly produce beneficial physiological and psychological states (Stone & DeLeo, 1976). Biofeedback uses technology to enhance internal control over physiological processes based on operant conditioning (Miller, 1969; Wentworth–Rohr, 1984).

Outcome studies comparing these strategies for self-control of internal states have yielded equivocal results. When large numbers of subjects are compared, no differences show up regardless of whether progressive muscle relaxation, hypnosis, imagery, meditation, breathing, or biofeedback was used for the attainment of self-control. All are equally effective for the control of internal states; not all, however, are equally effective for the same patient. Highly hypnotizable patients respond better to hypnosis; good visualizers, to imagery and visualization. Various meditation and breathing exercises are better suited to those individuals who are able to concentrate. Although progressive muscle relaxation and biofeedback are generally applicable to most people, there are marked differences in the rate at which these techniques are developed as skills. We recommend careful assessment to determine which method for developing self-control is best suited to a given patient.

Behavioral Self Regulation, Contingency Management, and Self-Management

Behavioral self-regulation is the means by which the patient decreases the likelihood of continuing maladaptive behaviors and increases the probability of promoting healthy behaviors through self-monitoring, developing accurate means of self-appraisal, establishing appropriate self-imposed performance criteria, and setting up means of self-reinforcement (Kanfer & Phillips, 1970). The patient first learns self-regulation by following the therapist's model and then takes on an increasingly active role in the treatment, eventually becoming able to maintain self regulation without the presence or aid of the therapist. Through self-monitoring, patients learn to become skillful analysts of maladaptive and adaptive behaviors (Kanfer, 1977) and their respective reinforcement contingencies. Behavioral self-regulation can be applied to the analysis of various types of behaviors, as well as to the degree to which the behavior is engaged in and its frequency of occurrence (quality, quantity, and frequency). The patient learns to set a realistic schedule of behavioral change and to identify specific goals and accomplishments. For example, in order to gain control over maladaptive eating habits, the patient may establish a schedule that can help him modify poor eating patterns, by altering the quality and quantity of food consumed and the frequency of consumption until the desired weight-loss goal is reached. To stop smoking the patient can schedule a systematic reduction of the number of cigarettes smoked each day until the desired goal of quitting smoking is achieved. Patients also learn to become good problem solvers. They learn, for example, to analyze patterns of problematic eating such as snacking or the habitual, almost unconscious "lighting up" that smokers often indulge in.

Systematic Desensitization

Systematic desensitization (Wolpe, 1958) entails the progressive exposure to stimuli or feared situations. The patient first learns to relax deeply, and a hierarchy of less-to-more feared stimuli is then constructed. In imagery scenes and while in a relaxed state, the patient is systematically presented with these less-to-more feared stimuli until he can maintain the relaxation even while imaging the formerly feared stimulus (*in vitro* desensitization). He may also construct a hierarchy of less-to-more real-life situations or events. Eventually, the therapist instructs the patient to encounter the feared events in real life (*in vivo* exposure). In this way, the patient learns to produce a response antagonostic to anxiety (a relaxation response) in the presence of the anxiety-provoking stimulus. He is systematically counterconditioned.

Skill Development Regarding Internal Perception

There are great individual differences in the capacity to perceive internal changes (Pennebaker, 1982). Most people are poor discriminators of all but general and pervasive physiological changes or not very specific, localized physiological events (Pennebaker, 1982). Certain classes of patients are notoriously poor discriminators, for example, patients with obesity, asthma, or irritable bowel syndrome. The capacity to distinguish among a variety of internal sensory changes and classes of internal experiences is known as visceral perception (Brener, 1977). Obese patients are very poor visceral perceptors. They cannot easily tell whether they are hungry or are feeling an emotion (Schachter & Singer, 1962). Individuals vary considerably in their ability to determine whether internal sensations are to be considered symptoms or normal bodily events. They need to be taught symptom perception. Some patients, notably those with irritable bowel syndrome, are especially inaccurate in deciding whether perceived bowel activity at any given moment is normal or symptomatic of the illness. They behave as if there were some dysfunction between actual bowel activity and subjective experience (Latimer, 1983). The ability to identify the sequence of internal changes that culminates in the full manifestation of symptoms is known as syptom discrimination (Creer, 1979). Asthmatics, for example, are poor symptom discriminators; they report asthma symptoms when objective respiratory functioning is within normal limits and feel normal when objective respiratory function indicates a high risk of attack (Rubinfeld & Pain, 1977a, 1977b). These related abilities in sensory perception—visceral perception, symptom perception, and symptom discrimination—are considered together as examples of what has been called internal sensory perception (Mason, 1961).

Skills training in internal perception is a newly emerging tool of behavioral scientists. Behavioral scientists have developed methods to train patients who are deficient in internal sensory perception. Patients can learn the skills of visceral perception. For instance, an obese patient can learn to recognize, discriminate, and label a multitude of internal states and, most important, to distinguish between hunger and a variety of emotional states. Patients can also learn to tell the difference between experiencing normal physiological events and symptomatic sensations. Patients with irritable bowel syndrome can be taught to monitor bowel activity in order to discriminate between normal activity and an underactive or overactive bowel. Asthmatic patients can learn skills to detect the sequence of events leading up to an asthma attack, from the subtle changes in breathing or the just noticeable tightness in the chest, to the recognition of an impending attack, to the actual attack. By differentiating each link in the chain of events culminating in the attack, the asthamtic learns to utilize coping strategies to cut off the attack early in the sequence.

Cognitive Therapy

Cognitive therapy deals with the maladaptive types of thinking a patient habitually engages in. The patient's attitudes may be faulty: He may not have an aversive enough attitude towards harmful behaviors, for example, smoking, and may not develop positive attitudes towards beneficial health behaviors (Spiegel & Spiegel, 1978). Patients may also harbor irrational beliefs, especially about emotionally arousing situations (Ellis, 1962). Most people carry on an internal dialogue, consisting largely of negative statements to themselves. These negative self-statements, often not fully in awareness, defeat the patient's attempt at healthy behavioral change (Mahoney & Mahoney, 1976; Meichenbaum, 1974, 1978). Some patients show serious distortions in their thinking (Beck, 1976). Assuming that one lacks the ability to effect change (lack of efficacy expectations) also significantly hinders behavioral change (Bandura, 1977).

Using cognitive therapy, the therapist helps the patient to identify the negative attitudes, irrational beliefs, cognitive distortions, and inadequate efficacy expectations that result in maladaptive behaviors and the inability to effect behavioral change. The patient must learn to change them to more positive ones.

Cognitive therapy also deals with the design of adequate coping strategies (Lazarus, 1966). The therapist assesses the patient's current repertoire of coping strategies and helps the patient to strengthen them and develop new ones appropriate to the management of his behavioral problems and symptoms.

In addition, cognitive therapists concern themselves with the representations of health and illness. Patients often evidence distortions in body image and self-concept associated with their symptoms. The therapist helps the patient to identify and correct these distortions and develop a healthy body image and self-concept. In the case of obesity and smoking, it is unlikely that the treatment gains will be maintained unless the patient is able to alter his self-concept and body image in the course of treatment—to develop an internal representation of himself as a nonsmoker or as a thin person. In the case of chronic illness, the work entails the integration of the chronic illness into the self image (Nerenz & Leventhal, 1983).

THE TREATMENT GOALS OF BEHAVIORAL MEDICINE

The goals of treatment are largely dependent on the model of behaviorism used to guide the treatment. The behavioral therapies represent a variety of techniques that are not integrated into a consistent theoretical framework or even a single learning theory (Kanfer & Phillips, 1970). Although behavioral scientists might agree that the overall goal of treatment is to change behavior, approaches to behavioral change have become more diverse as the field has grown, and so there are now many perspectives on what it means to change behavior. From the perspective of operant learning and contingency management, the goal of behavioral intervention is to eradicate maladaptive (often pleasurable) behaviors and to cultivate adaptive gratifying ones in their stead. Delprato (1981), for example, speaks of eliminative versus constructional models of behavioral therapy wherein problem behaviors are eliminated through negative reinforcement and new healthy behaviors are established through positive reinforcement. Others have made similar distinctions between strategies for treating maladaptive and adaptive behaviors; for example, Kanfer and Grimm (1977) talk about extinction of behavioral excesses and fostering behaviors in areas where there are behavioral deficits. These behavioral therapists stress that elimination of harmful behaviors alone does not necessarily lead to healthy functioning. Health is not simply the absence of illness. Sometimes it is necessary to target unhealthy behaviors with the goal of reducing their occurrence, for example, smoking, problematic eating, and overuse of substances conditioned by anticipatory panic reactions regarding symptom onset. Sometimes it is necessary to define and cultivate healthy behaviors that are absent, for example, self-monitoring, the ability to relax, physical exercise, compliance with the treatment regimen. With most patients, *both* approaches are indicated, and the subtotal of eliminating the maladaptive behaviors and cultivating adaptive behaviors is the establishment of a healthy lifestyle. Furthermore, inasuch as the neobehaviorist is usually sensitive both to the context in which behavior occurs and to the internal state of the patient, the treatment plan is also likely to include stimulus-control and cognitive therapy.

Because of the shift away from conditioning models of behavioral change towards cognitive models, neobehavioral treatment goals are often conceptualized in terms of some variation on the theme of self-regulation. Kanfer (1977) reconceptualizes behavior modification as a self-regulation model. He emphasizes the importance of the patient's own self-generated behavior and the capacity for self-reinforcement as the vehicle of behavioral change. According to Kanfer, the patient presents with well-learned and entrenched maladaptive behaviors. Once these are disrupted by such methods as self-monitoring and stimulus-control, and the practice of positive self-statements, self-regulatory processes become activated. The patient begins to become his own behavior analyst, to solve his own problems, to set the criteria by which to measure his performance, and to provide his own positive reinforcement for the behavioral change, for example, the intrinsic satisfaction that comes with successful performance.

While Kanfer's (1977) theory of self regulation is still set within the context of a reinforcement model of behavioral change, Schwartz (1977, 1979) advocates a cybernetic information-processing model for bodily functioning that more definitely departs from the conditioning models of learning. Schwartz sees the human organism as an automatic, self-regulating system that uses complex feedback from various levels of functioning to stabilize and correct the operations within the bodily system. In this sense, the body is its own health care system. Illness occurs when there is "disregulation" within the system, that is, when the organism fails to attend to important feedback anywhere in the system. Biofeedback training is one way to provide the patient with necessary biological information so that bodily functioning can correct itself. Whatever version of self-regulation theory is espoused, neobehaviorists have shifted the locus of responsibility for the treatment gains from the doctor to the patient: Compliance with the doctor's treatment is superseded by adherence to a plan mutually shaped and agreed upon by the doctor and the patient; the patient enacts it with greater and greater autonomy, toward the attainment of complex, individualized goals.

Still others have conceptualized the goal as the fostering of coping skills and related beliefs about these skills. Lazarus (1966) pioneered the view that health is related to adequacy of coping, and illness to ineffective coping. The goal of treatment is to develop the patient's coping skills, first by assessing and strengthening available coping resources and then by teaching the patient new coping skills, for example, relaxation skills, so the patient can cope competently. Like the ego psychologists (Hart, 1961; Rapaport, 1967), Lazarus sees coping as a passive response to a stressful situation imposed on the patient. The patient who copes effectively takes an active role in shaping events. Lazarus has also moved away from earlier notions of coping as a general trait toward an understanding of coping episodes. Neobehaviorists try to help patients evaluate their coping responses in specific situations and analyze the conditions under which coping is adequate or inadequate in these situations. Goldfried (1977), for example, has reconceptualized progressive muscle relaxation as a form of training in coping skills. He believes that progressive muscle relaxation is effective not so much because the patient relaxes, but because he has developed a coping skill that he can effectively use to reduce anxiety when encountering an anxiety-provoking situation. The emphasis on coping episodes has also become the basis for current important clinical research on relapse prevention (Marlatt & Gordon, 1980).

If coping is an important goal of behavioral treatment, then the patient's subjective appraisal of coping is equally important. In his concept of self efficacy, Bandura (1977) emphasizes the patient's beliefs in his own coping skills. Self-efficacy is the patient's perception of his ability to effect change within himself. Bandura believes that self-efficacy is essential to any therapeutic change, and he has substantiated this claim by clinical research. One goal of treatment, then, is to foster the patient's sense of self-efficacy by setting a series of realistically attainable goals, the mastery of which enhances self-efficacy, which, in turn, can have a salutary effect on one's self-evaluation—what Lazarus calls competence in coping. A related goal of treatment is to foster what Antonovsky (1979) has called a sense of coherence, by which he means:

> The sense of coherence is a global orientation that expresses the extent to which one has a pervasive, enduring, though dynamic feeling of confidence that one's internal and external environments are predictable and that there is a high probability that things will work out as well as can reasonably be expected. (p. 123)

The self-perception of competence in specific situations may generalize to one's general outlook on life.

Another goal of behavioral medicine treatment is the long-term maintenance of treatment gains. Relapse is a significant problem. Most people who intentionally lose significant amounts of weight, gain it all back, sometimes more, within 1 or 2 years after treatment. Nearly 75% of people who quit smoking relapse by the end of the first year after quitting (Hunt et al., 1971). The relapse rates are similar for other habit and addictive disorders, notably substance abuse and alcoholism—so similar that Hunt and his associates believe that there are general mechanisms underlying relapse across disorders. While relapse rates are typically lower for treatment of psychophysiological disorders like headaches or hypertension, they are, nevertheless, still substantial enough that the phenomenon of relapse needs to be taken seriously. The data accumulated on relapse rates has necessitated a shift in treatment emphasis in the field of behavioral medicine. Contemporary practitioners are as concerned with relapse prevention as with treatment itself. In fact, relapse prevention is correctly considered an essential component of the initial treatment plan (Marlatt & Gordon, 1980, 1985).

Marlatt and Gordon's important book, *Relapse Prevention,* represents the most thorough clinical research on relapse prevention. They advocate a situational approach to relapse. They teach patients to become accurate analysts of the relapse behavior in its context. Whether treating smoking, weight problems, substance abuse, or alcoholism, they first train patients to self-monitor all incidences of slips and relapses in order to understand better the exact conditions under which relapse occurs. The research findings are consistent across disorders. Patients are at high risk of relapse when the following conditions are met:

1. They encounter high risk situations specific to that individual.
2. They do not have adequate coping resources.
3. They experience low self-efficacy, that is, they do not feel that they have control over the situation.

4. They have learned to have often unrealistically positive expectations about the use of the cigarette, food, or substance as a solution to the difficult situation at hand.

Most high risk situations fall into two categories: (a) difficulty managing emotional states; and (b) interpersonal influences, for example, others' modeling the maladaptive behavior, or using the behavior as a response to interpersonal conflicts. Whereas the initial strategy in relapse prevention is to identify the situational and cognitive determinants of relapse specific to the individual, the primary emphasis in relapse prevention is to help the patient develop adequate coping strategies and cognitions appropriate to the maintenance of treatment gains. The therapist helps the patient develop a number of skills to cope successfully with *each* of the situations for which he is most likely to be at risk of relapse. Consequently, patients terminate treatment with a set of coping tools available to them in advance of the situations they are likely to encounter that would otherwise lead to relapse. Interventions specifically designed to decrease the probability of relapse increase the likelihood that treatment effects will be maintained long after treatment is terminated.

Regardless of the relative emphasis given in any treatment to the elimination of maladaptive behaviors or the development of adaptive behaviors in their context, fostering self-regulation, or developing coping skills and the related sense of self efficacy and coherence, we believe that they *all* are necessary ingredients of successful treatment, the prevention of illness, and the maintenance of health.

A MULTIPLE CAUSATION MODEL FOR THE DEVELOPMENT OF ILLNESS

Causative and Maintenance Factors

The etiology of psychophysiological disorders and behaviorally related illnesses is exceedingly complex. We are accustomed to thinking of emotional disorders as stemming from a single cause, but in reality a number of factors are likely to contribute to the development of a disorder. Factors that may have been important originally in the evolution of the disorder may become less influential over time; other factors may take over the central role in maintaining the disorder once it has become established. A disorder may seem to take on a life of its own almost dissociated from those factors which originally contributed to its development. In this sense, we speak of a disorder as being progressive, not always in the sense of having a degenerative course but as accumulating an impressive array of aspects that make the disorder increasingly complex and serve to sustain it (Bakal, 1982). Alcoholism perhaps demonstrates the most obvious example of the difference between causative factors and maintenance factors in the progression of a disease. The position taken here is that most psychophysiological disorders—chronic pain, headache, hypertension, asthma, and the like—and most health-related behavioral disorders, for example, smoking and over-weight conform to a model wherein the complex factors contributing to the development of the disorder are not necessarily the same factors that maintain it.

Multiple Causation

Our current understanding of psychophysiological disorders is a good illustration of a theory of multiple causation. In certain instances, genetic factors may be important: Some people may be genetically predisposed to develop certain autoimmune diseases (Fauci, 1981), cancer (Knudson, 1977), certain skin diseases (Behrman et al., 1978), and possibly migraines and hypertension. Other factors may also contribute to a biological predisposition toward such illnesses although it is not exactly clear why individuals become predisposed to develop one type of illness rather than another. Traditional psychosomatic medicine espoused the so called "weak organ theory" of psychophysiological disorders. An individual was believed to be more prone to develop a certain type of psychophysiological disorder than any other because one of his organ systems was more vulnerable or more liable to malfunction than others.. One person may be vulnerable to migraines; another, to asthma. Many developmental and situational factors contribute to the specific biological vulnerability in question. Early nutritional patterns may affect fat cell metabolism and predispose some individuals to weight problems. A plethora of infectious diseases may cause tissue damage; for example, early childhood pneumonia may sensitize the bronchial passages and increase the probability of developing asthma. Over the course of their development, certain people may develop a sensitivity to certain drugs or various allergies. Aspirin sensitivity, for example, contributes to the onset of asthma in some people. Viral infections may alter tissue structure, as in the case of virus-mediated skin diseases like warts and herpes lesions. Acute injuries may also cause tissue damage. Minor tissue damage accompanying an injury may produce intense acute pain, and, for some people, the pattern of extreme physical inactivity in response to this pain may contribute to a chronic pain syndrome. Hormonal changes accompanying menstruation and pregnancy can exacerbate psychophysiological symptoms, such as migraines, headaches, breast cancer, and the like, in women (MacMahon et al., 1973). In other words, there are a great variety of sometimes unrelated factors any combination of which may predispose a person to a psychophysiological disorder.

The role of stress in these conditions has been thoroughly investigated. However, the number of different categories of stress factors subsumed under the rubric of stress has grown so substantially that some people have begun to question the use of the term stress. Early work on stress emphasized the role of "stressful life events" in the etiology of illness (Holmes & Rahe, 1967). Major changes in life circumstances, either positive or negative—for example, loss of an important relationship, marriage, loss of a job, a promotion, or chronic financial worries—are associated with increased risk of illness. The more changes over a given period of time and consequently the greater destabilization of daily living patterns, the higher the risk of illness. Current work on stress has shifted the emphasis away from major life events toward those situations which most people find stressful on an everyday basis. The daily hassles a person experiences also increase the probability of illness (Kanner et al., 1981), for example, waiting in traffic or experiencing frustration over some blocked work goal.

Some researchers have focused on the environment as a source of potential stress, such as noise pollution. Extreme temperature change, especially exposure to cold, is a powerful stressor, in particular to the cardiovascular and immune systems. Barometric changes, changes in the weather, and altitude changes are likely to increase the chance of illness or exacerbate existing conditions in some people. Exposure to toxic substances, radiation, and certain toxic foodstuffs are also associated with illness. Inhaling irritating fumes, such as cigarette smoke, automobile exhaust, or air contaminated by factory incinerators, likewise stress the organism. In some people, they trigger migraine attacks and asthma episodes.

The nature of the social environment can also be a major source of stress. Extremes of isolation and chronic loneliness, on one hand, and overcrowding and lack of solitude, on the other, contribute to the development of illness. Persons who lack adequate support systems are at high risk; conversely, healthy social supports are to some extent a buffer against a person's contracting illness.

Some stress researchers have placed less emphasis on the external situation or physical/social factors associated with risk of illness than on focus within the individual. Not all people react in the same way to the same situation or environment; what is stressful for one may not be stressful for another. Therefore, it is more accurate to speak of perceived stress rather than of a stressful situation per se. The degree to which an event is or is not perceived and reacted to as stressful depends to a large extent on the scope and adequacy of coping resources available to the person (Roskies & Lazarus, 1980) and the degree to which the person believes he has the resources to cope with the situation (Bandura, 1977) or perceives he has control over it (Marlatt & Gordon, 1980). There is, for example, a fairly extensive research literature on chronic coping failures, particularly coping with social isolation and patterns of emotional expression, as they pertain to the etiology of illness. Chronic failures in the capacity to experience and express certain emotions in healthy ways, notably anger, have been implicated in the etiology or exacerbation of migraines, inflammatory bowel disease, and some forms of cancer, at least for certain people.

The extent to which emotional stress has an impact on psychophysiological disorders is not yet clear. Emotional stress played a central role in the early psychodynamic and psychosomatic theories of these disorders, but its influence was, perhaps, exaggerated. Today, we know that emotional stress is a factor in psychophysiological disorders only for certain patients, although it may exacerbate existing conditions in other patients.

Certain persistent personality traits and patterns of behavior may also contribute to illness. At least in the area of cardiovascular disease, there is solid evidence of the existence of a personality configuration associated with cardiovascular risk (Price, 1982). The so-called Type A personality describes a person who is competitive, aggressive, and time-pressured. A chronically aggressive and hurried lifestyle puts a consistently excessive demand on the cardiovascular system and increases the likelihood of cardiovascular disease.

A chronic pattern of physical inactivity also increases risk of illness and is critical in weight problems. Dietary problems also promote illness, for example, excessive sodium intake, which can elevate blood pressure. Such "behavioral excesses" (Kanfer & Grimm, 1977) as smoking, being chronically overweight, and habitually using substances like caffeine, amphetamines, and alcohol play a major role in asthma, hypertension, and vascular headaches respectively.

As behavioral scientists learn more about the roles of stress and coping, personality, and behavioral styles in the evolution and exacerbation of psychophysiological illnesses, we come to the unfortunate conclusion that the human body is becoming less and less fit to live in the kind of environment, and to survive the kind of lifestyle, that we have constructed for ourselves.

As the categories of stress factors associated with illness have grown in number and diversity, we have learned to understand their effects on the human organism better: various stress factors all contribute to a general or specific disregulation of the organism (Schwartz, 1977, 1979). One of the main types of disregulation is that of the autonomic nervous system. The various patterns of stress impinging on the individual over time contribute to destabilization of autonomic functioning. A common outcome is hyperactivity of the autonomic nervous system, especially sympathetic hyperactivity, as well as loss of integration of the balance between sympathetic and parasympathetic functioning (Gellhorn, 1967). Chronic patterns of stress may sensitize the receptor sites of the cells in the autonomic nervous system, thereby increasing their potential to become activated in response to stressful stimuli.

The autonomic nervous system directly mediates a number of organ systems: the cardiovascular response (regional vasomotor response and cardiac output), the activity of the striate muscles, the activity of the bronchial passages, gastrointestinal activity, and sweat and sebaceous gland activity. Indirectly, it affects other systems as well, notably the immune system. Chronic disregulation of autonomic functioning may cause disregulation or malfunctioning of one or a number of organ systems, any one of which may play a central role in the development of a particular psychophysiological disorder—hypertension, headaches, asthma, peptic ulcer disease, irritable bowel syndrome, skin disorders, and immune-related disorders, depending on the particular organ system affected. For example, chronic patterns of cardiovascular disregulation play an important role in vascular headaches and hypertension; over reactivity of the smooth muscle tissue of the bronchial passages in the case of asthma; and so forth. In each instance, the normal physiological response pattern to ongoing stimuli has been altered. One typical consequence is that the organ responds in an extreme and highly irregular way. For example, the frontalis muscles of the forehead may become too hyperactive in response to everyday stress, and the person becomes headache prone.

Because the response of these organ systems controlled by the autonomic nervous system is mediated by a variety of humoral agents, we can also speak of autonomic disregulation at the biochemical level. One aspect of the stress response pertains to the release of a variety of humoral agents in response to acute stress, and to the long-term effects of the humoral agents on the metabolism. Acute stress results in the immediate release of a variety of catecholamines (a catecholamine cascade) and corticosteroids. These, in turn, mediate a number of important changes such as smooth muscle response, which affects the size of the blood vessels in hypertension and that of the airways in asthma, respectively; the histamine-mediated local inflammatory response in headaches, inflammatory bowel disease, certain skin diseases, and asthma; and the pain threshold in pain and headache syndromes. The long-term effects of the disregulation of the humoral system is only just now beginning to be understood. Humoral agents released during stress and not effectively metabolized can accumulate in the tissue and alter its structure. Coronary heart disease is, in part, mediated by catecholamine release and the extent to which these substances weaken the heart tissue. Recent evidence (McKinney et al. 1984) suggests also that the disregulated release of humoral agents may affect the receptor sites of the cell walls of blood vessels and increase the binding of free fatty acids to these sites as in artherosclerosis. Continuous disregulated release of humoral agents in response to stress may cause chronic depletion of humoral substances, which further increases the likelihood of illness.

The Levels of Development of Illness

It is useful to understand the development of psychophysiological disorders on a number of hierarchically related levels: causative factors; autonomic disregulation; disregulation of specific organ systems; disregulaton of the humoral system; and secondary maintenance factors. Besides biological predisposition, a variety of causative factors can give rise to a disregulation of the psychophysiological functioning of the organism. The particular causative factors are diverse and highly specific to the individual. Because a number of causative factors operate over time, it is very difficult to ascertain for any given patient exactly what the factors are and how significant each has been in the overall development of the disorder. By no means the least among these causative factors is stress, stress not so much in the psychological or emotional sense as in the physiological sense. Stress pertains to any of a wide variety of external situations and environmental agents, as well as to internal coping ability, personality factors, and behavioral styles that contribute to autonomic disregulation. A level of disregulation is that of specific organ systems, such as the striate musculature or the cardiovascular system. An even more refined and microscopic view of the biological stress response is disregulation of the humoral system. Each of these levels represents a particular perspective taken on understanding the disregulation of the organism with regard to psychophysiological disorders in general and the psychophysiology of the stress response pattern in particular.

Additional factors come into operation to maintain the disorder once it has developed. It is in the maintenance of the psychophysiological and behavioral disorders, rather than in the causation, that learning plays a role. For example, the asthmatic response, once established, can become conditioned. Early in the course of the illness, the patient may develop bronchial spasms to a specific allergen. Once the bronchial spasm has been produced in a variety of situations, neutral stimuli may become associated with the bronchospastic response. In this manner, the patient learns to produce bronchospasms to to neutral stimuli. He may become asthmatic even in the absence of the allergens. Or the patient who experiences intense pain may become increasingly inactive. The pattern of inactivity itself then becomes the basis of further disregulation of the pain perception mechanisms, since normal pain perception is in part, based on feedback from normal muscle activity (Melzack, 1973), particularly the larger muscle groups of the body. In this case, the altered activity reinforces the disregulation of pain perception and increases the probability that the pain will be sustained. Furthermore, the chronic pain patient learns a number of bracing postures by which to avoid exacerbating the pain. The habitual use of these postures causes secondary pain in other areas of the body. Secondary conditioning is an important factor operating in many psychophysiological disorders.

A related phenomenon is anticipatory anxiety and panic. The patient who, on the basis of previous experience, dreads the onset of symptoms and becomes anxious may actually produce the symptoms. The anticipatory anxiety reaction is itself an acute stress. The sympathetic discharge characteristic of an anxiety response may cause further physiological disregulation. For instance, an asthmatic may misperceive normal bodily sensations as if they were early warning signs of an impending attack. In certain asthmatic patients, the ensuing anxiety can cause bronchial spasms. Some hypersensitive patients, likewise, become so worried about having their blood pressure taken that they give unusually high readings in the doctor's office. The headache-prone patient may dread a migraine coming on. The anticipatory anxiety may disregulate the vasomotor response and actually produce the vascular headache.

Another closely related phenomenon is illness-behavior. The chronic pain patient learns to perform a variety of rituals in an attempt to cope with the pain, for example, lying down for long periods or adopting unusual postures. Such pain behaviors, once learned, tend to take on a life of their own, whether or not the patient is actually experiencing pain at the moment. Similarly, the patient with a skin disorder such as acne or dermatitis, learns a variety of picking behaviors in response to the altered sensory thresholds that accompany the skin condition. These also take on a life of their own. The picking causes further irritation to the skin and serves to maintain the condition.

Overuse of a treatment, too, can sustain a disorder. For instance, a pattern of frequent dieting and relapse promotes continued weight gain (Kolata, 1986). Overuse of inhalents can exacerbate symptoms in asthmatic patients by disregulating the activity of the muscles that make up the airways. Migraine sufferers, who learn to use Cafergot as soon as the onset of symptoms is evident, may continue to use it even at the slightest hint of a headache. Cafergot has a powerful vasoconstrictive action on the blood vessels of the head and cuts off the vasomotor changes that are characteristic of the full headache response. By excessive use of medication, migraine patients cause frequent alterations in the vasomotor system and thereby actually train it to become less stable.

Addictive behavior also is a factor in the maintenance of disorders, especially smoking, substance abuse, alcoholism, and sometimes problem eating. In each case, the behavioral problem is associated with physiological or psychological withdrawal symptoms, or both: the psychological craving, anxiety, and depression that often accompany substance or alcohol withdrawal; the psychological craving and emotional reactions accompany dieting. The patient maintains the behavior not so much for its pleasurable qualities as to prevent these unpleasant withdrawal symptoms. To make matters worse, there are complex interactions among various addictive disorders. It is not uncommon for a recovered alcoholic to revert to the smoking behavior he gave up years before or for a substance abuser to increase smoking during detoxification.

Cognitive processes also further the disorder. A defeatist, catastrophizing style of thinking may distract a patient from drawing on available coping resources to alleviate symptoms. Some headache patients passively resign to the onset of headache symptoms; they fail to utilize the headache-reducing coping skills they learned to use in the therapist's office. Or the problematic eater slips during a holiday and foregoes all the gains made over months of behavior modification for weight loss. Negative self-statements, crises in self-efficacy, and body and self-image distortions have powerful effects upon behavior. As long as the person who has successfully quit smoking still sees himself as a smoker and has not integrated a new self-image as a nonsmoker into his overall self concept, he is still at risk of relapse. Likewise, body image distortions as being fat and ugly impede the maintenance weight loss.

Psychological conflict can nourish illness too, particularly when the symptoms take on a special meaning in the patient's unconscious or within the family system. A man may not quit smoking because of unresolved intrapsychic conflicts associated with his father's dying of lung cancer as a consequence of smoking. A child may have continuous asthma attacks in order to maintain the equilibrium within the family system.

There are also strong social influences that support illness. Maladaptive behaviors can be modeled and reinforced through advertising. People often smoke or engage in problematic eating behaviors because they see others doing the same and because these behaviors are being consistently reinforced in a subtle way through advertising. Within the family arena, the maladaptive behaviors of other family members—a spouse's smoking, family food rituals—exert a powerful influence on the patient to continue his own maladaptive behaviors. In the case of psychophysiological disorders, the social ostracism that often accompanies, for example, a skin disorder or asthma, may contribute to further physiological disregulation and maintain the condition.

Lifestyle is another contributor to the persistence of a disorder. Risk factors such as lack of exercise, time pressure, and inability to find ways and times to relax, all create stress and serve as the necessary reinforcers to sustain maladaptive behaviors and symptoms.

ASSESSMENT AND TREATMENT IN BEHAVIORAL MEDICINE

Partialing Out the Variance of an Illness

It should be apparent from the foregoing discussion of illness development that a patient who presents with a psychophysiological symptom or a habit disorder of any significant duration presents the clinician with a complex interplay of factors that have caused and maintained the condition. Clinicians often fail to realize the multitude of factors that make up an illness. The task of the clinician is to identify as accurately as possible all the factors operating in the development of the condition and to assess the relative contribution of each to the current symptom picture. Figure 1.1 lists the typical causative and maintenance factors. Conditioning, anticipatory anxiety, the development of illness behaviors, misuse of medication, addictive behavior, maladaptive cognitions, social influence, and lifestyle influences—the factors that maintain an illness are as important to the understanding of an illness as those that contributed to its cause. In other words, both the development and the maintenance of illness have a strong behavioral component. It is easy to understand, then, why behavioral medicine, which directly addresses this dimension of illness, has come into its own as a discipline relevant to the work of physicians.

Assessment

Many patients present with clearcut, circumscribed symptoms, such as pain, headache or ulcers. It is tempting to focus solely on the symptoms, develop a behavioral treatment plan, and formulate treatment goals in terms of alleviating symptoms only. We, however, recommend a comprehensive evaluation of the patient, which includes a detailed history and mental status examination, as well as an assessment of the presenting behavioral complaint. One objective of this assessment is to ascertain the nature of the psychopathology and the patient's coping resources. The

CAUSATIVE FACTORS

predisposing biological factors
genetic predisposition
developmental/situational
   early nutritional patterns
   tissue damage through infection
   acquired drug sensitivity
   acute injury
   extreme physical inactivity
hormonal changes associated with menstruation & pregnancy

psychosocial and stress factors
stressful life events
daily hassles
environmental factors
   noise pollution
   exposure to extreme temperatures
   barometric, weather and altitude changes
   exposure to toxic substances, radiation, toxic foodstuffs
social environment
   isolation
   overcrowding
personality traits e.g. Type A behavior
inadequate coping resources
life style factors
   chronic physical inactivity
   diet
   behavioral excesses e.g. smoking, problematic eating, substance abuse

MAINTENANCE FACTORS

secondary conditioning
anticipatory anxiety & panic
adoption of illness behaviors
overuse of treatment, especially medications
addictive behavior; attempts to prevent withdrawal
maladaptive cognitions
   negative self-statements
   lack of self-efficacy
   body image and self-image problems
conflict
   intrapsychic
   systemic (family, health provider)
social influence
   persuasion, negative modeling, & advertising
reinforcing life style influences

FIG. 1.1. Causative & Maintenance Factors in the Development of Illness

clinician should alertly listen for indications of major mental illness, substance or alcohol abuse, character pathology, posttraumatic stress syndromes, depression, and so forth. Seemingly clearcut psycho-physiological and physical symptoms, such as headaches, may mask more serious or pervasive problems that are more amenable to psychotherapy or pharmacotherapy than to the methods of behavioral medicine. The clinician should also use the case history as a means to develop a dynamic formulation of the primary conflicts and maladaptive patterns of rela-tionships that manifest themselves repeatedly in a variety of ways throughout the patient's course of life. The clinician must be sensitive to the particular conflicts and transference distortions that might complicate the behavioral treatment. In taking the history, the clinician should pay particular attention to the current context of the patient's life in order to ascertain whether or not the symptom functions as part of a wider sys-tem's conflict. Is the symptom, for example, functioning to maintain equilibrium within the family or the marriage relationship? Is the symp-tom related to an impasse in treatment with a primary-care physician or a therapist? When symptoms are related to systems conflicts, behavioral treatment becomes complicated.

The purpose of the behavioral medicine assessment is to assess the presenting symptoms from a behavioral perspective. Keefe and Blu-menthal, in their excellent book, *Assessment Strategies in Behavioral Medicine,* (1982) state that the basic principle of assessment in behavioral medicine is to redefine the symptoms in "observable and measureable terms" (p. 13). If, for example, the patient presents with headache symp-toms, the objective of the behavioral medicine assessment is to analyze the symptoms as a series of observable, reportable events, such as muscle tension and the patterns of regional blood flow, or the pain experience, and then develop objective means for measuring them, such as EMG activity, skin temperature, or quantifiable pain reports.

The next step of the behavioral medicine assessment is to learn how the symptoms are experienced and function in the life of the individual. Self-monitoring is the basic tool for this phase of the evaluation. The patient keeps a daily symptom diary for a minimum of 2 weeks. Together, the patient and therapist learn to track the daily fluctuations in symptoms in the context of the patient's current life and to discover those factors which aggravate or alleviate the symptoms. As a therapist learns to identify patterns, he begins to develop hypotheses about factors that might have originally caused, and now maintain, the symptoms. The assessment of causative and maintenance factors is complex. It can only be tentative and, at various points in the treatment, will need to be reviewed and reformulated. The therapist also assesses the range of available coping resources and their adequacy.

Treatment Planning

Next, the clinician designs a comprehensive treatment plan. He must first decide whether the behavioral medicine intervention or some other therapeutic intervention is indicated. A heterogenous population of patients comes to a behavioral medicine clinic; and even the reasons for a particular symptom, for example, headaches, vary. For some patients medical treatment may be appropriate, but not behavioral medicine, because the cause of the symptom is purely somatic (for example, headaches associated with a tumor). For other headache patients, behavioral medicine may be inappropriate but dynamic psychotherapy or pharmacotherapy may not be, because the headaches mask some other psychopathology (for example, unconscious conflicts associated with neurotic conversion symptoms, posttraumatic stress, or depression).

Still other patients are less amenable to treatment by means of behavioral medicine and more to family systems therapy, because their headache maintains equilibrium within the family system or even in the health provider–patient system. A fourth group of patients is amenable to behavioral medicine interventions per se, relatively short-term behavioral medicine interventions being indicated without complications, untoward reactions, and with a high probability of favorable response to treatment.

Other patients may need a combined treatment approach, in which behavioral medicine interventions are utilized concurrent with another treatment, such as dynamic psychotherapy, family systems therapy or pharmacotherapy. An agoraphobic, for example, may be given antianxiety medication along with a behavior modification program emphasizing systematic exposure to unfamiliar environments. A headache patient who is also depressed about a recent loss may begin psychotherapy for the depression concurrent with a biofeedback program for the headache. An alcoholic patient with chronic headaches may need a behavioral medicine program for the headache, Alcoholics Anonymous for the alcoholism, and family therapy for the impact of the drinking and headaches on the family unit.

One reason for combining various approaches is that many factors usually contribute to an illness and interact in complex ways. For example, a chronic pain patient may also have a narcissistic personality disorder. Psychotherapy for the self-esteem issues—even a type of psychotherapy well matched to this kind of issue, like Kohut's (1971) self psychology, may fail because it is not likely to address the chronic pain directly by providing pain-coping strategies. Similarly, treatment in a very good multimodal chronic pain program, where the patient learns pain-coping strategies to alleviate the pain, may also fail. Why do psychotherapy and pain treatments alone fail? Because the patient presents with an interaction between dynamic-characterological issues and pain experiences: The patient's distancing and aloofness or vulnerability to severe depression undermine his self-esteem and prevent him from practicing the pain-coping strategies long enough to get a positive treatment effect; the persistence of the pain experience undermines the treatment alliance in the psychotherapy with the individual therapist. The patient's disappointment and rage at the therapist for not curing the patient's pain may result in a negative therapeutic reaction. Only a combined concurrent treatment, which appreciates this interaction, has a likelihood of success.

We advocate broad-spectrum, multimodal treatment plans. A multimodal treatment plan includes a number of specific interventions, each designed to address a different factor among the number of causative and maintenance factors that contribute to the overall variance of the illness. The task of careful assessment is to identify as many of these factors as possible, or at least the most influential ones producing and sustaining the symptoms; and the task of treatment planning is to develop treatment interventions to alleviate them. In the case of psychophysiological disorders, the multimodal treatment package is designed to address various levels of disregulation: (a) causative factors, including perceived stressors specific to the individual; (b) autonomic disregulation; (c) disregulation of specific organ systems; (d) disregulation at the local level mediated by the activity of various humoral agents; (e) maintenance factors, for example, conditioning of symptoms, anticipatory anxiety, and the like. The multimodal treatment plan includes one or more interventions at each of these levels. A treatment plan that operates at every level in the process of symptom formation and maintenance, increases the likelihood of a positive treatment outcome. For habit disorders such as smoking and weight problems, we also advocate a broad-spectrum treatment approach that includes interventions to alter motivation, behavior modification, cognitive therapy, social supports, and relapse prevention. Figure 1.2 summarizes each of the areas that must be addressed to increase the probability of a favorable treatment outcome in treating populations of patients with very complex behavioral problems such as smoking and weight. In the subsequent chapters we will illustrate this multimodal treatment approach to a variety of psychophysiological disorders (chronic pain, headaches, hypertension, etc.) and to a variety of habit and behavioral disorders (smoking, weight, etc.).

We also advocate individualizing the treatment plan. Each patient is unique. The specific components of the multimodal treatment plan will vary from one patient to another, as will the framing and communicating of interventions. It is a good idea to utilize in the treatment the patient's own imagery, fantasies, beliefs and concepts about the symptoms. For example, a 35-year-old woman presented with hypertension (blood pres-

I. ASSESSMENT
  A. Intake
    1. SYMPTOM HISTORY
    2. COPING HISTORY
    3. ASSOCIATED HEALTH AND PSYCHIATRIC SYMPTOMS
    4. IMPACT ON LIFESTYLE
  B. Motivation
    1. CONSCIOUS MOTIVATION
    2. UNCONSCIOUS MOTIVATION
    3. MOTIVATING THE UNMOTIVATED PATIENT
  C. Hypnotizability

II. BEHAVIORAL CONTROL
  A. Self Monitoring
    1. HIGH RISK TIMES
    2. HIGH RISK SITUATIONS
    3. REACTIVITY
  B. Self Regulation
    1. STIMULUS CONTROL
    2. BEHAVIORAL REGULATION
      a. Regulation of:
        1) quantity
        2) quality
        3) frequency
      b. Problem solving
      c. The behavioral act
        1) sensory enhancement
        2) rate
        3) substitute activity
      d. Visceral perception
      e. Function
      f. Goal setting/deadline date

III. COGNITIVE CONTROL
  A. Attitude
    1. AVERSION
    2. HEALTH BENEFITS
  B. Self-efficacy/ego strengthening
  C. Negative internal monologue
  D. Dynamic Meaning
    1. INTRAPSYCHIC CONFLICT
    2. BODY IMAGE
    3. SELF CONCEPT

IV. SOCIAL INFLUENCE
  A. Group Involvement
  B. Systems Interactions
    1. WORK RELATIONSHIPS
    2. FAMILY/COUPLES RELATIONSHIPS

V. RELAPSE PREVENTION
  A. Withdrawal
    1. PHYSIOLOGICAL EFFECTS
    2. PSYCHOLOGICAL CRAVING
  B. Relapse Situations
    1. ANALYSIS OF INITIAL SLIPS
    2. REHEARSAL OF COPING SKILLS
    3. THOUGHT MANAGEMENT
    4. LIFESTYLE MANAGEMENT
      a. Associated health risk factors
      b. Exercise; stress management

FIG. 1.2. Multimodal Approach to Habit Disorders

sure of 180/90 over a 1-month baseline). Based on the clinical material, the therapist suspected that there had been a repressed incest experience. The behavioral medicine treatment, therefore, was conducted concurrent with ongoing individual psychotherapy. The patient was highly anxious and unable to respond to progressive muscle relaxation either while the therapist was with her or when she was with a tape. She had an untoward reaction to hypnosis; she became very anxious, opened her eyes, and refused hypnosis. She exerted so much effort during EMG biofeedback training that she could only increase muscle tension. She was, however, able to produce waking imagery with open eyes. She was asked to imagine herself in a safe and protected place, which, to her, was an igloo in the arctic region. After many failed attempts to train her in thermal biofeedback by having her imagine warming her hands in various ways, she found a high idiosyncratic way to warm her hands. She imagined herself warming her hands in the fur of the huskies she imagined around the igloo. Each time she did this, she was consistently able to raise finger temperature and, later, limb temperature by several degrees. She developed a ritual by which she imagined herself in this way during stressful days. Over the next 15 weeks, she was able to lower her blood pressure to within normal limits (weekly mean of 140/90). The greater the congruence between the components of the treatment plan, the causative and maintenance factors specific to the patient, and the patient's idiosyncratic imagery and beliefs, the more effective the treatment.

TRENDS IN BEHAVIORAL MEDICINE

Clinical research in behavioral medicine has evolved through a number of phases: clinical efficacy, comparative efficacy of treatments, multimodal treatment, and individualization of treatment. The initial outcome studies in the field were designed to demonstrate the clinical efficacy of specific treatment strategies and answer such questions as: Does progressive muscle relaxation really alleviate pain, headaches, or irritable bowel syndrome? Is biofeedback an effective treatment for headaches, blood pressure, or Raynaud's Syndrome? Does contingency management help a person to stop smoking? The research questions were simple, and so were the research designs. Above all, these early studies were characterized by unidimensional treatment plans. These studies, though often controversial at first, began to accumulate. The evidence began to lead to more confident conclusions that progressive muscle relaxation, contingency management, and so forth worked for a significant number of patients.

As the field of behavioral medicine evolved, the number of treatment procedures available to the clinician multiplied. New studies began to emerge in the literature in which one or more treatment procedures were compared. The second phase of studies attempted to demonstrate the comparative efficacy of the various behavioral medicine procedures. Numerous experiments were designed to assess whether one procedure worked better than another, whether relaxation, for example, was better than hypnosis in the treatment of headaches or whether EMG biofeedback or thermal biofeedback were better than any of these other procedures. Over the last decade, thousands of clinical efficacy studies have appeared. The conclusions from most of these studies are similar. Whether one compares specific treatment modalities like progressive muscle relaxation, contingency management, biofeedback, hypnosis, or self-monitoring of chronic pain (Turk et al., 1983); headaches, (Jessup et al., 1979); or hypertension (Surwitt et al., 1982), to mention those areas where the most work has been done, the clinical efficacy of each of these procedures is about the same regardless of the procedure.

Most research in the area of behavioral medicine consists of clinical efficacy studies. Two new trends are emerging, and we believe them to be on the cutting edge of the field. One is characterized by a shift toward broad-spectrum or multimodal treatment. Multimodal treatment approaches originated in research on habit disorders: weight: (Ferster et al., 1962; Stuart, 1967) and smoking (Glad et al., 1976; Pomerleau & Pomerleau, 1977). Multimodal treatment packages or protocols have become the standard fare of the behavioral clinician. They are now available for the treatment of many psychophysiological disorders (e.g., Bakal, 1982). From the standpoint of clinical research, multi-modal treatments have distinct disadvantages. Complex multifactorial designs are required to ascertain the relative contribution of each treatment procedure to the overall treatment effect. These designs are often impractical to implement in all but very large clinics, where many patients are available. Nonetheless, multimodal treatment has a distinct clinical advantage over uni-dimensional treatments because outcome is improved for a greater number of patients in the overall population. Initial results indicate that multimodal treatment is even more effective than unimodal treatment. In the treatment of hypertension, for example, unimodal treatments yield only modest decreases in systolic and/or distolic blood pressure (Surwitt et al., 1982), whereas multimodal treatments yield far more dramatic decreases, which are maintained during reasonable follow up (Fahrion, 1980; Patel & North, 1975). Multimodal approaches are also now appearing for the treatment of headaches (Fahrion, 1980; Paulley & Haskell, 1975) and chronic pain (Gottlieb et al., 1977; Turk et al., 1983).

An even newer trend in behavioral medicine is characterized by a shift away from uniform treatment packages to greater individualization of the treatment packages. If, say, a multimodal treatment protocol for headache treatment consists of self monitoring, stress desensitization, progressive muscle relaxation, EMG biofeedback, cognitive therapy and relapse prevention, it is possible to place greater emphasis on some of these components than on others, depending on the response of each patient to the respective components in question. Especially when using self-control strategies, some patients may respond better to muscle relaxation, some to hypnosis, some to biofeedback, some to meditation. With hypnosis, some may respond to one type of hypnotic suggestion better than to another. The good clinician carefully thinks about how to tailor the treatment to the needs of the individual patient. The skilled clinical researcher also can ascertain the efficacy of an individualized treatment protocol by using single case designs.

This book is about the use of multimodal and individualized approaches to the treatment of psychophysiological disorders and habit disorders, because we believe that these approaches represent the state of the art and provide the greatest likelihood of treatment gain to the largest number of individuals. We emphasize the diversity of available treatments and their combinations in order to address the great diversity of patients and their individual needs encountered in the clinic. We hope to illustrate both the complexity of treating psychophysiological and habit disorders as well as the type of decisions which can lead to effective treatment.

2 Hypnosis and Hypnobehavioral Therapy

WHAT IS HYPNOSIS?

Hypnosis is a special state of consciousness in which certain normal human capabilities are heightened while others fade more or less into the background. Roughly 90% of the population has the talent to go into a hypnotic state—some more talented than other. Hypnosis can be combined with any type of therapy: behavior modification, supportive types of therapy, dynamic therapy. Combined with dynamic types of therapy, it is called dynamic hypnotherapy, or hypnoanalysis; combined with behavioral therapy, it is call hypnobehavioral therapy. Hypnosis itself is not a therapy, although the relaxation that accompanies it can be beneficial. We shall not discuss the history of hypnosis or hypnotherapy in this book. The reader can become informed about it elsewhere (Fromm & Shor, 1979, pp. 15–43; Hull, 1933; Weitzenhoffer, 1957).

Hypnosis as an Altered State of Consciousness

That hypnosis is an altered state of consciousness is now generally accepted. Ludwig (1966) coined the term "altered state of consciousness" (ASC), defining an altered state according to subjective experience and altered psychological functioning. Altered states can be produced by changes in sensory input, physiology, or motor activity, which result in altered alertness (Ludwig, 1966). In an altered state, one's perception of and interaction with the external environment are different than in the waking state, and one is more deeply absorbed in internal experience. In his classic works on altered states of consciousness, Tart (1969, 1975) essentially adopted Ludwig's definitions for ASC but more carefully defined the relationship between attention and changes in psychological functioning characteristic of ASCs. According to Tart (1975), an altered state of consciousness is defined as a "unique, dynamic pattern or configuration in psychological structures" (p. 5). Each altered state of con-

---

Portions of this chapter have been covered in greater detail in *Hypnotherapy* and *Hypnoanalysis* (Brown & Fromm, 1986) and are included here for those not familiar with that book and to refresh the memories of those who are.

sciousness is a stable pattern. It takes a certain energy and, especially important, attention to disrupt this stable pattern and to produce the new quasistable state, that is an altered state of consciousness.

Hypnosis meets the criteria for an altered state of consciousness as set forth by Ludwig and Tart. The altered state of hypnosis—the trance state—has been described both theoretically and experientially (Ås, 1962a, 1967; Ås & Ostvold, 1968; Field & Palmer, 1969; Fromm, 1977; Fromm et al., 1981; Gill & Brenman, 1959; E. R. Hilgard, 1977; J. R. Hilgard, 1970; Orne, 1959; Shor, 1959) along the dimension of absorption in an unusual experience, the fading of awareness of one's surroundings, and alterations in perception and in cognition.

Hypnotic Depth

The degree to which people become hypnotized is commonly referred to as hypnotic depth. Hypnotic depth may be viewed objectively as the behavioral response to hypnotic induction and hypnotic suggestions, for example, arm levitation, moving hands together, and the like. It may also be viewed subjectively as the sense of how deep into the *experience* of hypnosis the person feels he goes at any given time. Some confusion exists in the literature about the use of the word "depth." Sometimes depth refers to behavioral response; sometimes to experiential feeling; sometimes to both. Unfortunately, observable, objective behavior indicative of depth and subjectively felt depth do not always coincide. It is possible for a hypnotized person to feel deeply hypnotized and intensely absorbed in the hypnotic experience while failing to respond behaviorally to simple ideomotor suggestions. Whereas for some hypnotized persons depth may manifest itself in a more behavioral, for others in a more experiential, way, hypnotic responsiveness presumably involves a strong behavioral as well as experiential response, at least for highly hypnotizable individuals.

When hypnotic responsiveness or depth is defined *behaviorally*—as observable response to hypnotic suggestions, for example, arm levitation—it is the *degree of hypnotizabiltiy* or *susceptibility* that is measured objectively. When hypnotic responsiveness, or depth, is defined by subjective reports—as the subjective sense of being absorbed in the experience or being in an altered state of consciousness—one asks experiential questions and measures depth by the subjective experience. The position we take, like that of Hilgard (1965), is that assessment of depth involves both behavioral and experiential viewpoints. Hilgard defines hypnotic ability as "the ability to become hypnotized, to have the experiences characteristic of the hypnotized person, and to exhibit the kinds of behavior associated with it" (hypnosis) (p. 67). The sensitive clinician observes how the patient responds *and* encourages the patient to verbalize the experience of hypnosis. This is important for all patients, especially for those for whom there is a discrepancy between their observable behavior and their subjective experience.

Initial responsiveness to hypnosis is much less due to the skills of the hypnotist than to the ability or lack of ability of the person being hypnotized. Although the skill of the hypnotist is certainly important and becomes even more important as the hypnotic relationship develops over time, the depth reached in the initial encounters between the naive patient and a hypnotherapist reflects the patient's hypnotic ability more than the capabilities of the hypnotist.

Innumerable research studies, especially those with the Stanford Hypnotic Susceptibility Scales (Weitzenhoffer & Hilgard, 1959, 1962) and the Stanford Profile Scales of Hypnotic Susceptibility (Weitzenhoffer & Hilgard, 1963), have made it very clear that there are vast individual differences in behavioral response to hypnosis. Hypnotizability can be viewed as a quasistable trait, which some people have more of than do other people. Like any personality trait, hypnotizability is a relatively enduring characteristic that presumably exists independently of whether one has been hypnotized before. However, as with many traits, the degree to which this enduring characteristic is manifest varies with the situation. Expectation, motivation, attitude, anxiety, mood, and rapport with the hypnotist—all influence the degree of manifestation of this trait.

With regard to experiential depth, there are ways by which a person subjectively knows he is in trance. These do not always manifest themselves in observable behavior. The depth experienced by the hypnotic subject, how deep a person feels he is in hypnosis, can be described only by the person. Being in a deep trance is felt as qualitatively different from ordinary waking consciousness. The patient may report that he no longer was aware of his physical surroundings and that involuntarily and without conscious deliberation he allowed things to happen by themselves. He may report having experienced transference feelings with regard to the hypnotist. He may have felt relaxed, been aware of more vivid imagery (both quantitatively and qualitatively) than he ordinarily was in the waking state. He may also have been engrossed in the moment-to-moment experience and become aware of fanciful primary process ideation and of forgotten, emotionally charged memories (Shor, 1979). For good hypnotic subjects, trance is an altered state of consciousness with its own unique configuration of attentional, cognitive, perceptual, and emotional functioning.

Only moderate susceptibility is needed for most clinical situations. About 60% of all people are initially responsive enough to hypnosis to warrant considering hypnotherapy based on susceptibility alone. For those with less hypnotic talent, special parameters usually need to be introduced to maximize expectation of gain and motivation, to develop a helpful transference relationship, or to improve susceptibility through learning, so,that therapeutic change can occur. Eight percent of the total population are highly responsive to hypnosis, and most of the quick improvements through hypnotherapy are achieved with these highly susceptible individuals. With them, one can argue, the gain perhaps can be attributed to hypnotizability and not necessarily to other factors such as the hypnotic relationship.

In the great majority of all hypnotherapy cases, however, the therapeutic gain is due more to the meaning the hypnotic situation has for the patient (i.e., the expectations and the interpersonal relationship with the hypnotherapist) than to the effects of the hypnotic state.

Hypnosis and Attention

The central role of attention in hypnosis has only recently been appreciated, and there have been surprisingly few studies on attention in hypnosis. Yet, for the clinician, it must be emphasized that attention plays a critical role in the induction, deepening, and utilization of hypnosis. Hypnosis may be defined as careful attention deployment that results in an altered state of consciousness. The task of the clinician is to capitalize on the natural ability of some patients to attend selectively to certain stimuli; or by means of hypnotic instruction and posthypnotic suggestion to teach patients who are poor attenders better selective attention. For either good or poor attenders, the clinician must attempt to enhance attentional skill.

According to J. R. Hilgard (1970) and to Tellegen and Atkinson (1974), hypnosis involves the capacity for absorption. Absorption is "total attention, involving full commitment of available perceptual, motoric, imaginative, and ideational resources to a unified representation of the attentional object" (Tellegen & Atkinson, 1974, p. 274). Since attention during the ordinary waking state is largely unfocused, such "total attention" enhances the salience of whatever is being attended to at the suggestion of the hypnotist. One implication is that such a careful focus may have unusual perceptual effects (Orne, 1977). Although in general responsiveness to cues coming from the environment decreases (Shor, 1959), there is some reason to believe that careful focus may improve the efficiency of whatever perceptual information is *attended* to.

Related to the careful focus of attention is the ability to resist distraction by internal and external stimuli. Obliviousness to distracting stimuli is commonly reported by hypnotic subjects (Field & Palmer, 1969), More readily hypnotizable subjects seem to have an easier time shutting out distractions from both internal and external stimuli, but they generally are not aware of how they do this (Ås, 1962b). Hypnotizable subjects may become so absorbed in their experience that they don't even think about the need to shut out distractions, even though they are doing it.

Skill in focusing attention carefully and the related ability to resist distraction are essential for the induction of hypnosis. Another attention skill, expansive attention, may be important to the quality of the hypnotic experience after induction. Expansive attention means being aware of a wide range of contents floating by in the stream of consciousness. Increased expansiveness of attention is usually associated with effortless receptivity to the contents of the stream of consciousness. During hypnosis, attention may become diffuse (Hilgard, 1965) or expansive (Fromm & Hurt, 1980). Depending on the nature of the instructions, the clinician can enhance either selectively focused or expansive-receptive attention, or both alternately. Expansive-receptive attention widens access to feelings and memories that are usually out of awareness. Selective attention is more useful in the cognitive strategies needed for solving problems and altering symptoms and behaviors during hypnosis. Since both are important dimensions of hypnotherapy, hypnotic instructions should include both aspects of attention.

Hypnosis and Relaxation

Hypnosis is usually associated with relaxation. Most hypnotic inductions contain simple, direct suggestions for relaxation: for example, "You are becoming more and more relaxed." Some hypnotic inductions utilize elaborate and detailed protocols to produce a profound state of deep relaxation. The most common of these contain suggestions for alternately tensing and relaxing the major muscle groups in the body (Jacobson, 1938). Another induction or deepening technique includes suggestions for imagining waves of relaxation rolling through the body, carrying relaxation to each area, and pushing out tension. Relaxation of the body pertains to the subjective sense of the overall musculature becoming less tense. During the induction, the person may report some shift in bodily awareness as if the body were settling into itself.

Suggestions for maintaining an unstrained sense of tranquility often accompany the suggestions for deep bodily relaxation. The stream of consciousness no longer, then, manifests itself as a confusing, constantly changing process (James, 1961) but unfolds in an orderly way wherein distinct contents—thoughts, images, body sensations, memories and feelings—can be clearly recognized. The content may also seem to unfold at a slower rate than in the waking state. The relaxed person might feel a deep inner calm. His attitude may be unconcerned, yet interested, as the contents of the stream of consciousness unfold.

The subjective sense of deep relaxation does not necessarily mean physiological relaxation (Shor, 1979), the physiological effect Benson (1975) has called the "relaxation response." Physiological relaxation involves a decrease in muscle tonus, a slowing of the respiration rate, an increase in skin resistance, increased brain wave synchrony and co-herence, and various cardiovascular and metabolic changes. Careful con-struction of the induction in a particular way can certainly produce both the subjective sense of deep relaxation and a physiological state of relaxa-tion. Whether or not such a physiological state occurs depends on a number of variables, not the least of which are the individual charac-teristics of the hypnotized subject and the wording of the suggestions by the hypnotist. There have been a number of studies on the physiology of hypnosis. The results often are contradictory, and thus inconclusive (Sar-bin & Slagle, 1979). No reliable physiological concomitants of trance have so far been found. Slight changes in the wording of hypnotic suggestions can influence physiological variables. The use of each of the words or phrases, "relaxed," "drowsy," "focus on the breath," "focus your atten-tion," and the like may have unique physiological concomitants. Combin-ing such wordings in a single induction may result in considerable confounding of variables and confuse the physiological picture. Thus, while there is no single physiological state produced by hypnotic induc-tion, physiological relaxation can certainly be produced if the induction is done in a particular way (Edmondston, 1977).

Hypnosis also is commonly associated with some sort of change in arousal relative to the waking state. Throughout history, hypnosis has been viewed as a state related to sleep. Many hypnotists suggest sleepiness or drowsiness in their inductions. Hypnotized people often (but not always) spontaneously report feeling drowsy following a hypnotic induction. How-ever, it is possible to induce an active-alert (Banyai & Hilgard, 1976) or even a hyperalert state of trance (Gibbons, 1979) by carefully wording suggestions. It seems that the human organism is capable of both hypo-and hyperaroused states (Fischer, 1971). Hypnosis, then, can enhance either relaxation or arousal, depending on the wording of the hypnotic induction and the expectations of the subject.

Altered Perception During Trance

In the normal waking state we actively maintain an orientation to the reality around us. However, at times our reality orientation is a pre-conscious, not a fully conscious, one. For example, a driver driving a car on a two-lane highway at times may be aware of the solid or broken line dividing the two lanes; at other times he may be totally unaware of it or even of the road. Why does he not go off the road then—because he has a stable frame of reference to orient himself to the road, even when he does not minutely and carefully attend to external cues. This framework is called the "generalized reality orientation (GRO)" (Shor, 1959). The GRO is a cognitive schema in the background of awareness, which, in the waking state, allows us to attend to reality and maintain our orientation to it.

However, the GRO is not maintained in sleep and during hypnosis, when good hypnotic subjects are able to relinquish their GRO. During trance, one's perception of reality is altered. Hypnotized people usually report less awareness of, or responsiveness to, the immediate surroundings. They may register external sounds but find them less distracting, or they may fail consciously to 'hear' sounds that otherwise would be distracting, like a jet plane flying over their building or an ashtray crashing to the floor. If their eyes are open, they may see nothing but a small object placed right in front of them, or they may report being detached from the surroundings or being less concerned with the changing events around them than they would have been in the waking state. They are likely to be less attentive to peripheral details of external visual and auditory stimuli (Graham, 1970; Smyth & Lowy, 1983). In deep states of trance, most subjects are oblivious to their surroundings. They are, instead, preoccupied with or absorbed in their own imagery and in the content of the suggestions.

In the deeper states of trance, an inhibition of higher cognitive interpretations of sensory processes can occur, with or without suggestion, in the form of sensory changes: visual, auditory, olfactory, and gustatory hallucinations; or analgesia. Although suggested hallucinations occur only in deeply hypnotized subjects, they illustrate some of the perceptual alterations possible during trance. Some subjects are capable of positive hallucinations in which they construct percepts for which there are no external stimuli; for example, with open eyes, they may hallucinate a book lying on a chair across the room—the chair really stands there, but the book is a product of their imagination. Expectation effects may play some role in these subjects' hypnotic hallucinations, but these hallucinations cannot be reduced to expectation effects. Genuinely hallucinating hypnotic subjects are consistent in their description of the hallucinated phenomena, whereas nonhypnotizable people, asked to simulate trance and positive hallucinations, alter their description according to the context. For example, genuinely hallucinating subjects see the seat of the chair *through* a book placed on its seat. Genuinely hallucinating subjects also behave differently from simulators; they shy away from sitting on the chair when asked to; simulators do not. They just sit down (Bowers & Gilmore, 1969; Orne, 1959.

Hypnotically produced visual hallucinations such as the book are experienced by hypnotic subjects convincingly and as real and vivid as actual percepts seen in the waking state (Orne, 1959; Sheehan & McConkey, 1982). It is clear that hallucinating individuals do not objectively 'see' anything in terms of new external stimuli, yet they interpret available information as if 'seeing' additional stimuli. Individuals in the normal waking state possess a reality-monitor by which they distinguish external sensory percepts (i.e., "real" percepts) from internal imagery. During trance, this reality-monitor becomes inhibited for hallucinating individuals, so that imagined phenomena like the book are interpreted as external percepts (Kunzendorf, 1980).

The mechanisms by which negative hallucinations operate also involve inhibition. For example, an hypnotized subject may be told that a person previously present in the room would "no longer be seen in the room." The subject is then instructed to open his eyes and report what he sees. He fails to 'see' the person, even though the person is in reality still in the room. Hypnotically produced negative hallucinations seem to involve an inhibition of the *conscious experience* of seeing the person, while preconsciously or unconsciously the sensory information is still registered.

Hypnotically produced analgesia is related to negative hallucinations. Certain hypnotized people can be made to feel no pain, or to feel only numbness, in the presence of stimuli that in the waking state would be painful. Subjects still register the sensory component of the pain and respond to it physiologically, yet they do not consciously experience these sensations as pain. In a review of the many experimental studies of pain and hypnosis, E. R. Hilgard (1969) interprets the findings as an inhibition of the cognitive interpretation of the sensations as pain.

A consistent picture emerges from many studies, a picture that discloses an apparent underlying mechanism common to all perceptual alterations accompanying hypnosis—positive hallucinations, negative hallucinations, and analgesia. The trance state is characterized by a general inhibition of reality-oriented thinking, by which sensory data are interpreted in the waking state. This results in unusual perceptual effects—internal imagery can be experienced as real percepts (positive hallucinations), and external, objective, real percepts may not be consciously registered (negative hallucinations). Whereas visual hallucinations are seldom useful in clinical situations, other perceptual alterations definitely are, notably, the fading of the generalized reality orientation and analgesia. Even though few individuals manifest hypnotic hallucinations, what they do is experientially genuine. Therefore, such distortions in perception characterize something of the "essence" of hypnosis (Orne, 1959).

The Organization of Experience in the Trance State: Time Distortion and Timelessness

In trance, information is processed differently than in the waking state. The amount of information processed per unit of time is much smaller than that processed in ordinary waking consciousness. Hypnotized subjects take in less from the external surroundings due to the fading of the GRO. Their awareness is limited to the voice of the hypnotist and to what he suggests they should pay attention to. Suggestions are often worded in a repetitive manner. Therefore, the information a hypnotized person processes is both reduced and redundant (Bowers & Brenneman, 1979).

One consequence of the reduction in the amount of information processed is a greater efficiency in what is processed. Objectively, hypnotized subjects are able to process this reduced information load with greater accuracy and greater attentional skill. Subjectively, what is attended to is the focus of intense interest, so that phenomena are experienced in a new way.

The subjective sense of time is related to the amount of information processed per unit of time (Ornstein, 1970). Since the amount of information processed is considerably altered in hypnosis, it is not surprising that the ordinary sense of time is easily altered in trance. Subjects may either underestimate or overestimate the duration of the trance state (Schwartz, 1978), though the greater tendency is to underestimate it by as much as 40% (Bowers & Brenneman, 1979). Because hypnotized subjects lack their ordinary sense of temporal duration, they are more likely to anchor their time sense to external sources for such as the suggestions of the hypnotist. They readily respond to a hypnotist's suggestions for time distortion, to slow down time or to speed it up. For example, a patient who is in great pain may be given the suggestion in trance that he can experience several hours of clock time as if they were only a few minutes, or vice versa (Cooper & Erickson, 1959; Kraus, *et al.,* 1974).

Dissociation

Another dimension of the trance state is dissociation, in which an aspect of the experience is kept out of conscious awareness. According to Janet (1925), dissociation occurs when certain pathological contents of consciousness are split off from the conscious personality and operate independently. They become available only in trance. In Hilgard's (1974, 1977) reformulation of the concept of dissociation, dissociation is seen as an extension of normal cognitive functioning. During ordinary consciousness, information is processed on a number of levels by a hierarchy of cognitive operations and controls. Ordinarily these operations are integrated. During hypnosis, the integration decreases, and certain aspects of experience are no longer available to consciousness. Dissociation is part of many hypnotic experiences. For example, a person may experience automatic writing: his hand appears to be writing, but he has no conscious recognition of the content of the writing.

Hilgard (1977) has used an experiment involving hypnotic analgesia and automatic writing to show, however, that subjects are still capable of gaining access to those aspects which are dissociated from awareness during hypnosis. Waking subjects report a linear increase in the subjective experience of intensity of pain while immersing their hand in ice water. During hypnotic analgesia subjects do not report any increase in pain intensity; consciously they are experiencing no pain, but they still register the sensations physiologically. Subjects can be aware of the increasingly intense sensory input by means of a "hidden observer." While in trance, they can gain access to the physiological registration of pain usually dissociated from experience if the hypnotic situation is set in a certain way. Subjects can be told that their hand will represent the part that may still be aware of the pain on some level. The hypnotized subjects verbally report no conscious experience of pain, but automatically write down in numbers a linear increase in pain intensity. While the pain is dissociated and the patient does not experience pain, this hidden observer can be used to demonstrate that somewhere there is awareness of painful physical sensations. The same can be done with otherwise unavailable painful emotions.

Perceived Involuntarism

Another dimension of hypnosis is known as involuntarism, which we are renaming here "perceived involuntarism." Hypnotized subjects often seem to respond passively, involuntarily. This is known as the "classic suggestion effect" (Weitzenhoffer, 1974). During hypnosis, normal, purposeful behavior becomes inhibited, at the same time that a new condition of perceived involuntarism is established. Nevertheless, hypnotic behavior is goal directed (White, 1941) and, we feel, actively and voluntarily directed by the subject (though the subject is not consciously aware of his decision making and voluntarism). This paradoxical combination of subjectively sensed involuntarism and goal-directed enactment constitutes what is known as involuntarism in hypnosis.

In arm levitation, for example, hypnotized people typically experience the arm as lifting by itself (according to the hypnotist's suggestions), yet it is their own capacity for focused attention and imaginative involvement that causes the arm to rise. Involuntarism contributes to "effortless involvement" (Bowers, 1982) or "non-analytic attending" (Spanos et al., 1980) during hypnosis, which is similar to passive volition required during biofeedback training (Green et al., 1970). Nevertheless, hypnotic behavior is goal directed, hypnotized people preconsciously utilize various cognitive strategies, as well as imaginative involvement, to realize the hypnotic suggestions (Spanos, 1982; Spanos et al., 1977). But such strategies usually operate outside the subject's awareness. To the subject, the arms lift involuntarily or the hypnotist is making it lift. Thus, hypnotized people often feel compliant toward the hypnotist and go along with the hypnotist's suggestions, while failing to realize their own (voluntary), preconscious contribution to making the suggestions work.

Clinically, perceived involuntarism is a mixed blessing. Facilitating involuntarism is a way of deepening the trance experience. However, if the subjective sense of involuntarism is too strong, the patient cannot develop the confidence to cope with his problems. The clinician frequently must remind the patient that all hypnotic experiences are produced by the patient's own capacities of absorption and imagination. Perceived self-efficacy is a crucial ingredient in any form of therapeutic change (Bandura, 1977).

The Content of the Stream of Consciousness During Trance

The hypnotic state is associated with certain categories of content in the stream of consciousness: imagery, thoughts, memories, emotions, and bodily sensations. Extensive clinical observations of patients during trance (Gill & Brenman, 1959) and the detailed reports of subjects in experiments on self-hypnosis (Fromm et al., 1981) have elucidated the ways in which the content of the stream of consciousness typically manifests itself in trance. Changes in thinking from reality-oriented, sequential, logical thinking (secondary process thinking), which employs mainly the mode of inner language, to preverbal, pictorial, fantasy-full thinking (primary process thinking) are characteristic of the trance state. Reasoning and critical thinking are to a great extent suspended in hypnosis, and in their place appears dreamlike fantasy.

Here are some examples of the content of the stream of consciousness in trance:

Imagery: "I was swinging high on a swing in a dress that swirled around. I would fly out of the swing and twirl into the cloud. The cloud turned out to be a rain cloud, and I fell into the sea. A shark came by, and I held onto its fin. It brought me deep into the sea. At the bottom of the sea, an old, old turtle took me on its back. We swam through the sea. He brought me to a beautiful island. There I and the turtle lay in the sand in the sun. I decided to stay for a while. Then I became a turtle. . . ."

Memory: "(Such vivid memories. . . . I haven't thought of these things in years.) I remembered as a child going down the wooden steps to the beach, to avoid the poison ivy, running on the sand, picking sea shells smeared with clay . . . then jumping in the water. I could see the wave ripples in the sand . . . clumps of water grass and brownish-speckled fish. I had such a good feeling. Then I was sitting with the family under a maple tree in front of Uncle Abe's little house. Later I climbed up into my 'branch' in the tree, eating something and looking down at the grownups sitting on Grandpa's home-made log furniture, eating cookies, drinking tea, and talking a kind of Russian Yiddish with a little German and English thrown in."

Change of Body Image: "I decided to fly and centered on becoming a condor. My nose became my beak; I preened my feathers and quivered my arms as wings. Soon I was sailing above some mountains, tense winged, and flapping every once in a while."

Compared with some other altered states, notably meditation, in which there is little thinking (Brown et al., 1982/83), hypnosis is a highly cognitive process. In self-hypnosis, subjects use primary process cognition to create the hypnotic experience and secondary process thinking to plan self-suggestions and develop plans and strategies to help themselves go into trance or into deeper stages of trance. With heterohypnosis, of course, subjects also use a good deal of their own imaginative thinking, imagery that has not been suggested by the hypnotist or that amplifies the hypnotist given images. And subjects develop strategies and plans to respond to the hypnotist's suggestions (Spanos, 1982; Sheehan & McConkey, 1982); that is, they also use secondary process thought. The subject actively engages in thought processes throughout most of the hypnotic experience. However, he thinks quite differently from the way in which he thinks in waking consciousness namely, with much more primary than secondary process (Fromm, 78/79). Trance is characterized by a considerable increase in the quantity and quality of imagery. Spontaneous imagery readily occurs. Hypnotic imagery is usually experienced in greater detail and with greater vividness than is imagery in the waking state (Fromm et al., 1981; Lombard, Kahn, & Fromm, in press).

Memory changes also are characteristic of trance. During trance, a person is able to gain access to memories not readily available in the waking state, particularly emotionally relevant forgotten or repressed personal memories (Fromm, 1970). Age regression, either spontaneous or suggested, is also characteristic of hypnosis, it does not occur in other altered states (Brown et al., 1982/83). Emotions, too, are more available. A variety of specific emotions, some unavailable to normal waking consciousness, are likely to emerge in hypnosis, and there is a greater range of affect in trance than in the waking state. These emotions are often experienced with great intensity. The hypnotized person may also experience a variety of bodily sensations in trance: numbness, tingling, muscle twitches, pounding of the heart. Distortion of the body image, for example, changes in its size and shape, changes in attitudes about one's body, are also typically reported (Schneck, 1966).

These various changes in the ordinary content of the stream of consciousness have important clinical implications. Because patients under hypnosis have greater access to bodily sensations, emotions, memories, and fantasies usually beyond the grasp of waking consciousness, and also tend to think about these experiences in new ways, hypnosis is efficacious as an uncovering and an integrative method in therapy.

THE SPECIAL HYPNOTIC RELATIONSHIP

Another dimension of hypnosis is the interpersonal relationship. A number of special qualities of this relationship are not fully apparent in initial experiences with hypnosis, especially when the subject is hypnotized in the laboratory for experimental research only. If subjects have hypnotic experiences in the laboratory with a variety of experimenters, rather than one experimenter, the interpersonal relationship in general and certainly the hypnotic transference are minimized. Repeated hypnotic experience with the same hypnotist, however, particularly in a clinical situation, soon leads to a state in which several aspects of a special relationship emerge such as hypnotic transference and the working alliance between client and hypnotist.

The Effects of Hypnosis Per Se

Hypnotic Role.   Hypnosis is a relationship in which people take on special roles (Sarbin & Coe, 1972; Shor, 1962). Based on cultural stereotypes, most patients have a general view of how a hypnotized person would or "should" act. During hypnosis, particularly during early sessions, patients take on their conception of this role and try to act hypnotized. The role of the hypnotized person is further modified by the patient's perception of the hypnotist's tacit cues and explicit suggestions during the induction. For example, if the patient thinks that the hypnotic role involves passive compliance, he may try to be compliant during hypnosis, much as an actor tries to develop a role when acting. A well enacted hypnotic role is more convincing to both the subject and the hypnotist than a poorly enacted role just as a well-developed role in acting is more convincing to the actor and to the audience.

Some actors are more talented than others in developing a role. Similarly, some hypnotic subjects are more able to develop the hypnotic role during trance than others. Sarbin and Coe (1972) have conducted a detailed study of the factors that contribute to better role development in hypnosis. Good role development depends on the ability to read the hypnotist's cues to how the role is to be plyaed. Attention and imaginative involvement are important in developing the hypnotic role and carrying it out smoothly. In addition, the patient's role, is easier to adopt when it is congruent with some aspect of his self-image. For those who lack these elements of role development, the experience of hypnosis is less convincing to themselves and to an observer, and they carry out suggestions in an erratic, ambivalent, or idiosyncratic manner, not smoothly as defined by the hypnotic situation. For example, in carrying out an arm levitation, patients with poor hypnotic role development may lift the wrong arm, do it in their own way contrary to the suggestions, or struggle with it in some other way.

Hypnosis requires not ony the development of a particular role as a hypnotized person, but also a certain depth of participation in this role. Hypnotic role taking is not simply compliant, "as if" behavior. The deeply hypnotized person has integrated the role of a hypnotized person at a level involving participation of the total organism, both psychologically and physiologically (Sarbin & Coe, 1972); responds to the role at a non-conscious level (Shor, 1962, 1979); and believes in the role with some degree of conviction.

Communicative Influence.   One feature of the special hypnotic relationship pertains to the type of communication that becomes possible. Whether or not one subscribes to Sarbin and Coe's (1972) theory of hypnosis or not, hypnosis is certainly a form of communication between people in which therapeutic change can be maximized. Erickson and his students are perhaps best known for their studies of hypnosis as a form of communicative influence. (Erickson & Rossi, 1979) Erickson was especially interested in naturalistic observation and indirect forms of suggestion. Through his observations he articulated the subtle ways in which social influence is at work in most ongoing communication. Erickson insisted that the hypnotist train himself to become aware of these communicative influences so that he can utilize them in the service of therapeutic change. Much of Erickson's contribution focused on indirect forms of communication, especially the manipulation of ordinary and paradoxical forms of speech. Hypnotherapy is an interaction in which these subtle communicative influences are accentuated for the purpose of altering symptomatic behavior.

The Hypnotherapy Relationship.   Idiosyncratic and often deeply personal fantasies, memories, and emotions color the interactions between the patient in trance and the hypnotist. The patient in trance may be surprised or become afraid of the very personal nature of the experiences that arise with such spontaneity; the beginning hypnotist may feel similarly. The relationship may be very intense, and both the person in trance and the hypnotist must learn to become comfortable with this emotional intensity and depth of intimacy.

The Therapeutic Alliance in Hypnosis.   In hypnotherapy, repeated experience with trance fosters a strong therapeutic alliance. If the hypnotist is skillful in inducing hypnosis and offers a series of successful experiences without challenge, so that the patient will gain greater confidence in his own abilities, then trust builds in the relationship. Trust increases if the hypnotherapist fosters an atmosphere in which a great part of the experience emerges from the patient's own inner resources (Eisen & Fromm, 1983) rather than from a preconceived idea imposed by the hypnotist. The hypnotist should be sensitive to the needs of the person in trance and respect for the patient's inner resources.

Emotions spontaneously emerge, and the patient may share them with the hypnotist at a time when the patient is less defended than in the waking state and before the level of trust has been established through ongoing work. Such sharing brings forth a certain depth of intimacy in the hypnotherapeutic relationship. The increasing trust and intimacy that develop are two of the ingredients which contribute to a strong therapeutic alliance, but only when the hypnotic interaction is handled with care.

The Hypnotic Transference.   The most important aspect of the special hypnotic relationship for the clinician is the special hypnotic transference. During repeated hypnosis experiences with the same hypnotist in the clinical setting, a transference develops. The patient reexperiences patterns of relationships and feelings he had toward important figures in his childhood. The hypnotherapist might be seen as warm and nurturant, perhaps as the mother was, as hostile and domineering as the patient may have felt his father was, or as competitive, as brother or sister were felt to be. Greater access to fantasies, memories, and emotions creates a special transference relationship in which the personal qualities of both the patient and the hypnotist and their respective unconscious fantasies, clearly influence the manifest interaction. Most often the fantasies that emerge in hypnosis pertain to passive, infantile wishes that the hypnotist would take charge of and care for the patient, and to wishes to participate in the magical power of the hypnotist. These are the most common themes, but not the only ones. The clinically sensitive hypnotherapist will try to identify the individual patterns of transference for each patient. The style with which the hypnotist approaches the induction may further stir up a particular form of transference, especially if the hypnotist is exceedingly domineering or nurturant in his approach. As Ferenczi (1965) wrote:

The hypnotist with an imposing exterior, who works by frightening and startling, has certainly a great similarity to the picture impressed on the child of the stern, all-powerful father, to believe in, to obey, to imitate whom, is the highest ambition of every child. And the gentle stroking hand, the pleasant monotonous words that talk him/her to sleep: are they not a reimpression of scenes that may have been enacted many hundred times at the child's bed by a tender mother singing lullabies or telling fairy tales? (p. 177)

The hypnotic induction itself may be a "parameter of the therapy" (Eissler, 1958) which steers the transference in a particular direction. Nevertheless, the transference is likely to unfold according to the salient and repetitive patterns of the patient's object relations unless the hypnotherapist's style is so skewed toward being domineering, nurturant, or the like as to interfere with the natural unfolding of the transference.

The transference manifestations during hypnotherapy, while no different in content from those observed in nonhypnotic psychoanalysis and psychoanalytic psychotherapy, are different in the way they occur. In psychoanalysis it often takes many months for the transference to unfold with full intensity and with clear manifestations. The same intensity and clarity of transference manifestations can occur in hypnosis in the initial sessions. Full-blown transference manifestations occur very rapidly, often immediately upon induction. The sudden onset of intense and clear transference manifestations seems to be related to the state of trance, in which intense feelings and memories, in the context of the hypnotherapeutic relationship, lead to greater transference manifestations. These manifestations fluctuate rapidly during a single hypnotic session and over many sessions (Gill & Brenman, 1959).

The Realistic Perception of the Therapist as a Person.   Not all that transpires in hypnotherapy is due to transference. Not every emotion the patient feels for (or against) the therapist is unrealistic and reflects transference. Some hypnotherapists *are* warm and giving people; some *are* hostile. The patient also, to some degree, has a here-and-now relationship to the hypnotist. Besides transferring to the hypnotist the conflictual feelings that the patient has had towards important figures in his childhood, he also sees his therapist as the person he really is: as one who cares for him (or does not care for him), as one who genuinely wants to help him (or one who is more interested in money than in his patients). Thus, the patient also has reality-based emotional reactions to the hypnotherapist.

This means that the hypnotherapist must expect that the patient at times will give him a very honest and sharp evaluation of his own personality or motives. Sometimes he will hear favorable things that are true about him, and sometimes unfavorable ones that are equally true.

To have a warm, caring, but nonseductive person available with whom the adult patient, *here-and-now,* can form a mature, real relationship is of great importance in a patient's therapy. It helps the patient to feel that the therapist truly empathizes with his suffering and wants him to become better so he can fulfill his potential and live a happier life.

Because intense emotions often emerge quickly in hypnosis, in contrast to their slower unfolding in nonhypnotic psychotherapy, the therapist must be able to make the hypnotherapy a container for intense affective experience. He must be able to do this without the advantage of the preparatory understanding of such affective states gained through watching the material unfold slowly, as in nonhypnotic psychotherapy. While this may be a mixed blessing, the very intensity can quicken the pace of the therapy. The suggestive nature of hypnotherapy allows the hypnotherapist to structure the experience. Because of the greater access to symbolic material in trance, the hypnotherapist can also ask for the meaning of intense affective states directly, through dreams and imagery or through free association, and thereby offset the lack of preparatory understanding of these highly affect-laden states.

A clear understanding of all the dimensions of the hypnotic relationship is vital for the clinician who wishes to learn hypnosis. Yet, many experienced clinicians are overly fascinated with the parameters of the hypnotic state, the trance. In their attempts to understand its unusual features like the perceptual changes, dissociation, paradoxical voluntarism, and nonsequentiality, they unfortunately suspend their clinical experience. It is very important to remember that hypnotherapy is well within the confines of the traditional doctor–patient relationship. The same ground rules—respect for the patient, professional neutrality, consistency of approach, and a real desire to help the suffering patient to grow and learn to cope—are required in hypnotherapy as in any other form of psychotherapy.

EXPECTATION AND SUGGESTIBILITY

It is well known that expectation effects, which are manifest in the openness of the patient to the experience and the anticipation of a favorable outcome, are very important in successful clinical outcomes. Hypnosis is certainly no exception. Studies on the placebo effect have also contributed to an understanding of how patients anticipate whether or not a treatment like hypnotherapy will be successful. There are various kinds of expectation effects, which pertain to attitude, motivation, and efficacy beliefs (Barber & Calverley, 1962, 1963). Closely related to these expectations, either of the hypnotic experience in particular or of the overall therapeutic context in general, is the issue of suggestibility. Whereas expectation effects pertain to the receptivity of the person to hypnotherapy, suggestibility pertains to the responsiveness to the actual interventions made by the hypnotherapist. The clinician must always keep in mind how expectation and suggestibility affect the overall effectiveness of the treatment. The sensitive clinician will attempt to establish just the right atmosphere to capitalize on expectation effects and suggestibility and thereby maximize receptivity to the healing process (Erickson & Rossi 1979).

Expectation Effects

The patient's initial motivation and attitude toward hypnosis is extremely important. The patient who anticipates disliking hypnosis out of fear or lack of interest will not be as receptive as the patient who expects the experience to be interesting and enjoyable. Even more important than motivation, are the patient's efficacy expectations regarding the experience. The social behaviorist Bandura (1977) has defined efficacy expectations as "the conviction that one can successfully execute the behavior required to produce the outcome" (p. 193). He believes efficacy expectations are central to all forms of therapeutic change. These various expectation effects have an impact on the overall hypnotic effect (Barber & Calverley, 1962). One's belief in being capable of hypnotic experience is an important determinant of the outcome. In the clinical situation, patients who believe, or who through successful initial experiences with hypnosis are led to believe, in their ability to be hypnotized and to use hypnosis to alter their symptoms are more likely to have a favorable outcome. With pessimistic patients, one task of the clinician is to alter the patient's beliefs about hypnosis and the ability to change in therapy. With regard to waking state therapies, Frank (1962) has shown that altering both beliefs and assumptions about the symptoms, as well as one's ability to effect change in these symptoms (Bandura, 1977), can influence the therapy in a positive way. The same holds for hypnotherapy.

Suggestibility

Just how important suggestibility is to hypnosis has been a matter of long controversy. Suggestibility is the responsiveness of one person to the communications of another. Many have viewed hypnosis as a condition of "heightened suggestibility" (Weitzenhoffer, 1957), whereas others have questioned how different suggestibility during hypnosis is from suggestibility in the waking state (Evans, 1967). Certainly, hypnotized people are suggestible; so are many people while they are awake. People who are very suggestible in their everyday waking life are also likely to be suggestible when they are hypnotized (Graham & Greene, 1981). Conversely, people who are not very suggestible in waking life may not improve their suggestibility during hypnosis (Miller, 1980). Nevertheless, hypnosis cannot be reduced merely to waking suggestibility.

Whereas expectation effects and suggestibility contribute substantially to the total effect of hypnotic responsiveness, it is clear that hypnosis involves something more.

CLINICAL IMPLICATIONS

Figure 2.1 summarizes our current knowledge of the domain of hypnosis. Hypnosis involves an altered state, a special relationship, and expectation effects. It is difficult to assess just what portion of the domain of hypnosis is attributable to the state, the relationship, or expectation. The clinician should remember that the contribution of each to the total effect of hypnosis probably varies with each patient. The skilled clinician will take all these effects into consideration in his approach to and induction of hypnosis in the patient. For those patients highly responsive to hypnosis, the clinician can directly capitalize on the special features of the hypnotic state, the trance, with less need to adopt special parameters designed to alter expectations and cultivate the special hypnotic relationship. For patients moderately responsive to hypnosis, a negative attitude, low motivation, or doubt about their ability to be hypnotized may interfere with the manifestation of hypnotic potential. Even though we assume that hypnotic ability is a quasi-stable trait, manifestation of this trait may be less than optimal when expectation is poor. In such instances, special attempts to alter expectation may have to be made along with continuous utilization of the special hypnotic relationship in a permissive manner as a means to gain access to the unique characteristics of the hypnotic state. For those patients least responsive to hypnosis, hypnosis simply may not be indicated. If for certain reasons hypnosis is deemed desirable for poorly hypnotizable patients, the clinician needs to maximize the therapeutic effects of expectation and waking suggestibility and to adopt special parameters to facilitate the special hypnotic relationship, while not expecting much contribution from the special characteristics of the hypnotic state.

HYPNOBEHAVIORAL THERAPY

Hypnosis itself is not a therapy. The meaning of hypnosis to the patient, the hypnotic state, and the hypnotic relationship all can enhance the efficacy of therapy when hypnosis is used as an adjunct to some form of psychotherapy. The specific treatment effects are contingent on the therapeutic approach with which hypnosis is integrated. Hypnosis can serve as an adjunct to many therapeutic approaches—psychodynamic therapy, supportive therapy, developmental therapy, and behavioral

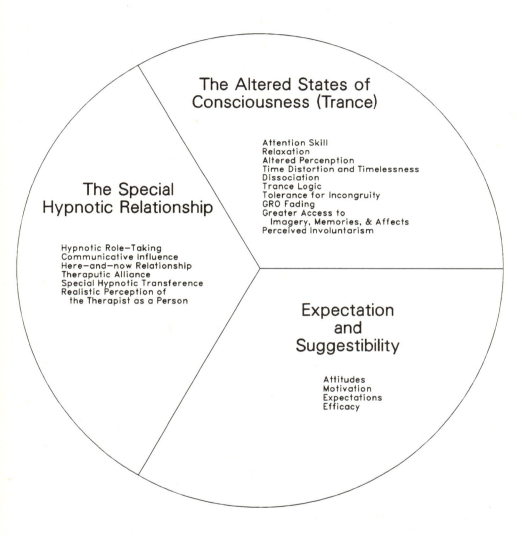

The Altered States of Consciousness (Trance)

Attention Skill
Relaxation
Altered Percenption
Time Distortion and Timelessness
Dissociation
Trance Logic
Tolerance for Incongruity
GRO Fading
Greater Access to
 Imagery, Memories, & Affects
Perceived Involuntarism

The Special Hypnotic Relationship

Hypnotic Role–Taking
Communicative Influence
Here–and–now Relationship
Theraputic Alliance
Special Hypnotic Transference
Realistic Perception of
 the Therapist as a Person

Expectation and Suggestibility

Attitudes
Motivation
Expectations
Efficacy

FIG. 2.1.   The Domain of Hypnosis

therapy—depending on the treatment goals in question. The three former types of hypnotherapy are described in some depth elsewhere (Brown & Fromm, 1986). When hypnosis is integrated with the last type, behavioral therapy, it is referred to as hypnobehavioral therapy.

There are very different types of behavioral therapies loosely woven around learning theory (Kanfer & Phillips, 1970). Hypnosis can be combined with virtually every type of behavioral therapy. Hypnosis has been combined with progressive muscle relaxation (Jacobson, 1938) to quicken and enhance the relaxation response (Astor, 1973). Hypnosis has also served as an adjunct to deconditioning therapies. Maladaptive behaviors and habits such as smoking and alcoholism, have been extinquished through hypnotic aversive conditioning (Dengrove, 1973, 1976; Feamster & Brown, 1963; Miller, 1959, 1965, 1974) or through covert sensitization enhanced by hypnosis (Cautela, 1975). In essence, the patient extinquishes the maladaptive behavior by producing an aversive state like nausea and vomiting in trance and then learning through posthypnotic suggestions to associate the nausea and vomiting with the targeted maladaptive behavior. Usually hypnosis is combined with systematic desensitization. The patient is hypnotized, relaxed, and asked to imagine scenes derived from a hierarchy of feared stimuli (Astor, 1973; Clarke & Jackson, 1983; Dengrove, 1973; Kroger & Fezler, 1976). The most detailed work on hypnotic desensitization is Kroger and Fezler's (1976) *Hypnosis and Behavior Modification; Imagery Conditioning.*

Other behaviorists have emphasized the role of posthypnotic suggestion in shaping behavior. According to Barrios (1973), posthypnotic suggestion is a type of "higher-order conditioning" (p. 32), functioning as positive or negative reinforcement to increase or decrease the probability of desired or undesired behaviors, respectively. Clarke and Jackson (1983) have utilized posthypnotic suggestion extensively to enhance the treatment effects of in vivo exposure to anxiety-eliciting situations, for example, in the treatment of agoraphobia.

Still other behavioral therapists have attempted to integrate hypnosis with the cognitive therapies. Hypnosis has been used to modify irrational beliefs (Greene, 1973) and negative self-statements (Clarke & Jackson, 1983) by presenting hypnotized patients with modified self-statements (Clarke & Jackson, 1983), affirmations (Kroger, 1980) or health-affirming beliefs (Spiegel & Spiegel, 1978). The positive efficacy expectations often attributed to being hypnotized can be utilized in the service of enhancing treatment effects (Lazarus, 1973).

Although the possible combinations of hypnosis with the behavioral therapies are as diverse as the types of behavioral therapies themselves, there have been few attempts to integrate hypnosis and the behavioral therapies in any systematic or comprehensive way. The earliest books on hypnobehavioral treatment are either loose collections of hypno-behavioral methods (Dengrove, 1976) or detailed accounts of a single hypnobehavioral approach (Kroger & Fezler, 1976). A more recent exception is a comprehensive text on the hypnobehavioral treatment of anxiety (Clarke & Jackson, 1983). A systematic exposition of hypnobehavioral therapies and their applications remains to be written. The attempt in this book is to present a broad spectrum of current hypnobehavioral approaches to the treatment of psychophysiological and habit disorders.

THE EFFICACY OF HYPNOSIS

Hypnosis both enhances the effectiveness of behaviorally oriented therapies and reduces the duration of treatment. The repetition characteristic of the hypnotic induction improves learning in hypnosis and heightens suggestibility (Weitzenhoffer, 1957). Hypnosis also facilitates the learning of deep relaxation (Edmondston, 1977). The condition of being in an hypnotic trance increases access to vivid imagery, which can enhance the process of in vivo desensitization (Dengrove, 1973); increases awareness of bodily sensations, which can enhance visceral perception as well as the visceral learning associated with biofeedback; and makes cognitive alteration possible, which can improve the efficacy of cognitive therapy. It is also possible to use hypnotic imagery to explore possible coping resources not consciously available to the patient. Posthypnotic suggestions can also directly influence the patient's behavior outside of the therapy hour. Posthypnotic suggestions can enhance stimulus-control procedures and serve as a means of reinforcement as an adjunct to behavioral self-regulation. For example, posthypnotic suggestions can be given to a smoker to smoke only in certain locations (stimulus control) and to eliminate the least needed cigarettes of the day (behavioral self-regulation). Posthypnotic suggestions can serve as cues to generate relaxation in an anxiety-provoking situation.

TREATMENT PLANNING WITH HYPNOSIS

Different types of patients respond to different approaches to hypnosis: short-term, behaviorally oriented, symptomatic hypnotherapy; supportive, ego-strengthening hypnotherapy; dynamic hypnotherapy and hypnoanalysis; and long-term hypnotherapy of developmental deficits (Brown & Fromm, 1986). Clinicians use very different styles of hypnosis: directive, permissive, and Ericksonian hypnosis (Brown & Fromm, 1986). The clinician must design a treatment plan matching the treatment and the style of hypnosis to the particular patient. Some patients, particularly highly hypnotizable patients with positive expectations about hypnosis, respond sometimes dramatically to simple, direct suggestions for symptom relief. The majority of patients respond to a systematic short-term protocol of hypnobehavioral methods. Symptomatic hypnotherapy is indicated for the majority of patients, as is a permissive style of hypnosis. Nevertheless, some patients fail to respond consistently to straightforward hypnobehavioral methods. For those patients who reach a treatment plateau with hypnobehavioral methods, another approach may be indicated, such as dynamic hypnotherapy or hypnoanalysis, where the goal is to uncover unconscious conflicts associated with the symptoms. Sometimes, nonhypnotic adjunctive family systems therapy is indicated, where the goal is to identify systems conflicts that maintain the symptoms in the identified patient. When patients continue to be unresponsive to even these interventions. Ericksonian indirect or paradoxical hypnotherapy may be indicated. The goal of Ericksonian hypnotherapy is to alter habitual frames of reference, beliefs, and illness behaviors, which also maintain the symptoms. A more complete discussion of the clinical decisions regarding the choice of approach to hypnotherapy and the style of hypnosis indicated for a particular patient can be found in *Hypnotherapy and Hypnoanalysis* (Brown & Fromm, 1986). Since the great majority of cases seen in the behavioral medicine clinic can be treated with a short-term symptomatic approach to hypnotherapy and a permissive style of hypnosis, the major emphasis of this book will be about this approach and hypnotic style.

Since it is not easy to know in advance which hypnotic procedure is best indicated for a particular patient, we recommend a very simple decision tree. First, the clinician should in the initial sessions routinely give direct suggestions and posthypnotic suggestions for symptom relief. A distinct subgroup of hypnotizable patients (no more than 20%) will respond favorably to such suggestions and will not need further intervention. Second, the therapist should proceed with a systematic protocol of hypnobehavioral treatment. The bulk of each successive chapter will include a description of these hypnobehavioral protocols. Third, if the patient fails to respond by roughly the fifth treatment session, or later reaches a treatment plateau, the therapist should switch to an exploration of the factors that may be operating to maintain the symptoms, particularly intrapsychic or systemic conflicts, and should adopt a dynamically based uncovering approach to hypnotherapy. Should the patient still fail to respond, the therapist can utilize Ericksonian methods, which are designed for patients resistant to more conventional therapeutic interventions. The reader who wishes to learn more about the use of dynamic hypnotherapy for the treatment of symptoms should refer elsewhere (Brown & Fromm, 1986).

THE PROBLEM OF EVALUATING TREATMENT OUTCOME: DOES HYPNOSIS OFFER AN ADVANTAGE?

The position set forth in this book, that hypnosis offers an advantage to certain patients in behavioral medicine treatment, is not heavily supported by clinical research. There is a paucity of outcome studies on hypnotherapy. Most are poorly designed, and many fail to demonstrate the efficacy of hypnosis. In an important review of the clinical research on hypnotherapy, Wadden and Anderton (1982) conclude that hypnosis has proven effective in only a few clinical areas—pain, asthma, and warts—and has been shown to be ineffective in most other areas, such as smoking, weight reduction, and alcoholism. When hypnotherapy is compared with nonhypnotic behavioral interventions, the results seldom differ—both are equally effective, for example, in the treatment of hypertension (Deabler et al., 1973; Friedman & Taub, 1977, 1978). Even where the clinical outcome is favorable, the outcome often does not correlate with hypnotizability (Mott, 1979).

Does this imply no advantage to using hypnosis in behavioral medicine? We believe that the problem lies less with hypnosis than with the way outcome studies on clinical hypnosis have been conducted. Researchers have asked the wrong questions. It is not appropriate to ask Does hypnosis work? in treating certain symptoms. The question is too simple. Its answer depends on the style of hypnosis used, the approach to hypnotherapy, the specific nature of the hypnotic suggestions given, and the way the suggestions are worded. The answer also depends on who conducts the treatment, the characteristics of the therapist, the experience of the therapist, and the quality of the therapeutic relationship as well as on who is being treated, the characteristics of the patient, and the type of presenting problem. It also depends upon the conditions under which the treatment is being conducted. Moreover, it is unlikely that researchers will ever significantly demonstrate a positive treatment outcome when directive or ego-strengthening suggestions are used as the main treatment interventions. Positive outcomes are more likely to occur for a significant portion of the population only when multimodal, individualized treatment plans are implemented.

We strongly advocate that the clinician carefully match the hypnotic style, the approach to hypnotherapy, the wording of suggestions, and the overall sequence of steps in the treatment protocol to the type of presenting problem the characteristics specific to the individual, and the nature of the treatment context. In the subsequent chapters, we have attempted to outline those treatment protocols we have found most useful in treating the majority of patients who seek hypnobehavioral treatment for psychophysiological and habit disorders. We hope that clinicians will find these protocols useful and that clinical researchers will take these treatment protocols as an occasion to frame more sophisticated research questions regarding the efficacy of certain types of hypnotic interventions administered by certain therapists to certain patients under certain conditions.

3

The Hypnobehavioral Treatment of Psychophysiological Disorders

A MULTIMODAL APPROACH TO THE HYPNOTIC TREATMENT OF PAIN

Establishing Rapport and Pain Assessment

Rapport Building. Establishing rapport with chronic-pain patients can pose difficulties, for these patients typically have a long history of treatment attempts and failures. They view their condition with deep despair and don't believe that *any* treatment will alleviate their suffering. They respond with a kind of learned helplessness to their pain (Seligman, 1975). Pain patients usually expect that doctors do not want to hear their pain complaints: all too often physicians do view pain patients as difficult, thwarting treatment. Too often they see them as demanding or hypochondriacal. The therapist's attitude toward the pain patient is critical to establishing good rapport. If he views the patient empathically, not as defensive or resistant, he reduces the likelihood of a negative therapeutic reaction. Studies on the association of pain and personality support an empathic view of treatment. Contrary to the stereotype that the premorbid personality of the chronic-pain patient is characterized by negative traits, Sternbach (1974) has shown that these so-called negative traits are consequent, not antecedent, to pain onset. In other words, living in continuous pain over months and years can make anyone more demanding, regardless of premorbid makeup. A therapist who takes this perspective is less likely to be judgmental and may find a way to enter the world of the chronic pain patient to understand how he experiences that world (LeShan, 1964).

Such extra sensitivity often comes as a surprise to the chronic-pain patient. The surprise is therapeutically useful as an initial step in reconceptualizing the pain experience (Erikson & Rossi, 1979). Pain patients are especially preoccupied with themselves (LeShan, 1964). They expect, and often find, the therapist to view pain as being "all in the mind." When the patient perceives the therapist in this way, the opportunity for successful treatment is curtailed. Therefore, the therapist must avoid stereotypes about chronic pain. The therapist should also devote sufficient time and attention to inquire about the *quality* of the pain experience. The patient should be asked to relax, to imagine a time when the pain is worst and describe what it is like. Or the patient can imagine a time when the pain sensations were first noticed (Turk, Meichenbaum, & Genest, 1983). Dermatome maps, pain magnitude ratings, and pain descriptions such as the McGill Pain Questionnaire (Melzack, 1975) are concrete ways to engage the patient around current pain experience.

Assessing Pain Experience.   The initial assessment of pain experience includes: an estimate of the magnitude of pain distress and pain intensity (Hilgard, 1975); a map of the pain location (Melzack, 1975); assessment of whether the pain is episodic or continuous; assessment of the quality of the pain (Melzack, 1975); and assessment of secondary postural pain phenomena and the pain-tension relationship (Draspa, 1959).

Assessing the Chronic Pain Syndrome.   The assessment also includes reconstruction of the stages in the development of the chronic-pain syndrome. Chronic pain is a progressive experience. During the acute phase, the patient tries to cope actively with the pain through reduction in physical activity, seeking professional help, and taking medication. During the prechronic phase, pain of variable intensity persists, and the patient begins to recognize that the pain cannot be controlled by the means used in the acute phase. During the chronic phase, the patient becomes convinced that the pain is uncontrollable and adopts a passive coping style toward a pain that varies little in intensity. Secondary postural pain phenomena and other psychophysiological disorders appear. Affective symptoms, such as anxiety and depression, also appear. The patient may become addicted to one or several pain medications. A pattern of unsuccessful doctor-shopping begins (Keefe, Block, & Williams, 1980). Chronic pain encroaches more and more on daily activities: work and household chores, physical activity, especially sports, and social interactions, especially sex. Pain behaviors develop as a mode of communication (Fordyce, 1976). Chronic pain patients may also undergo a personality change in the direction of greater irritability, demandingness, and the like (Sternbach, 1974). The therapist must try to locate the patient's presenting pain somewhere along the continuum of the acute–chronic pain cycle.

Assessing Pain Coping Resources.   The assessment also includes a history of the patient's pain-coping strategies. These include behavioral strategies, such as restriction of activity, visits to the physician for medication, nerve blocks, surgery, transcutaneous nerve stimulation, and behavioral medicine interventions. It is especially important to learn why previous treatments failed. Cognitive coping strategies for pain control should also be assessed by means of the Pain Coping Questionnaire (Brown, 1984).

Self-Monitoring of Pain Experience

An important component of the initial assessment is self-monitoring of pain experience (Bakal, 1982; Turk et al., 1983). The patient keeps a daily record of pain experiences, noting date, time of day, stress rating, rating of pain distress and pain intensity, situation (thoughts, feelings, activity), and pain coping attempts (restriction of activity, relaxation, medication). To improve compliance, the therapist reviews, reinforces, and offers encouragement about the pain diary at the beginning of each session. A baseline is kept for 2 weeks. Some patients discover that becoming aware of the pain by keeping such records itself alters pain experience. The therapist and the patient collaboratively review the records to discover patterns. Typical discoveries include: noticing the vicissitudes of daily pain experience, identifying high-risk times for increased pain experience, recognizing a relationship between particular stressful events (occupational, familial) or patterns of activity or inactivity and pain experience. This information is used to convey to the patient a new conceptualization of pain experience: pain is not a constant experience but an ever changing one that varies with life events and activities.

Assessment of Hypnotic Susceptibility and Initial Hypnotic Experience

A primary goal of the initial hypnotic assessment with chronic pain patients is to foster a sense of self-efficacy (Bandura, 1977). Many patients have unrealistic expectations about hypnosis. They are skeptical, fearful, or expect magical results. A positive yet realistic initial experience with hypnosis can correct attitudes about hypnosis and its potential use in pain treatment. Frankel (1976) has shown that a successful initial experience with hypnosis independent of treatment may generalize to treatment. It is, therefore, especially important to conduct the hypnotic induction with care and to arrange the sequence of initial hypnotic suggestions in a hierarchy from easy to difficult. For example, one may begin with eye closure and follow with waves of relaxation, magnets, arm drop, nonstructured imagery, and a daydream or dream. Then a simple posthypnotic suggestion can be given. The advantage of a graded difficulty, yet comparatively easy, sequence is that the patient gains confidence about being hypnotized. The disadvantage is that the aforementioned sequence is not a standardized test of hypnotic susceptibility. The Stanford Hypnotic

Clinical Scale for Adults (Hilgard & Hilgard, 1979) or the Harvard Group
Scale of Hypnotic Susceptibility (Shor & Orne, 1962) are alternatives.
However, since it contains more difficult items, it is less likely to foster the
degree of self-efficacy than an easier graded difficulty scale.

Waking Assessment of Coping Strategies for Pain Control

Because many patients enter treatment predisposed toward certain ways
of coping with their pain (Barber & Cooper, 1972; Chaves & Brown, 1978;
Keefe & Rosenstiel, 1980), each patient's own array of pain coping strategies must be assessed and treatment individualized accordingly. Pain-
coping strategies can be determined in the waking state following the
pinching method of pain induction (Spiegel & Spiegel, 1978). The acute
pain produced is more neutral than the chronic target pain, so that pain-
coping strategies can be assessed independently of the complicating
symptoms and behaviors associated with the chronic pain syndrome. In
each successive trial, the webbing of one hand between thumb and index
finger is pinched by the fingernails of the thumb and index finger of the
other hand to produce an acute, distinct pain. The patient first pinches to
establish a baseline for the pain. The magnitude of pain experience can be
rated on a 0–5 scale: 0 = no pain, 1 = mild, 2 = discomforting, 3 =
distressing; 4 = horrible, 5 = excruciating pain (Melzack, 1975). A new
pain-coping strategy is introduced in each successive trial of pinching.
Following each trial the patient is asked to compare, by means of the
rating scale, the baseline pain experience with the pain experienced after
the introduction of a pain-coping strategy.

A great variety of pain-coping strategies can be introduced to the patient
during successive trials. Figure 3.1 summarizes the pain-coping strategies
typically used in the treatment of pain. These pain-coping strategies have
been gleaned from a number of sources (Blitz & Dinnerstein, 1971; Chaves
& Barber, 1974; Crasilneck & Hall, 1973; Erickson, 1967; Hilgard &
Hilgard, 1975; Sacerdote, 1970; Sachs, Feuerstein, & Vitale, 1977; Scott &
Barber, 1977; Spanos et al., 1979; Turk et al., 1983). Though no empirical
factor-analytic studies of pain-coping strategies have been reported to
date, several investigators have attempted conceptually to sort the various
pain-coping strategies into a small number of discrete categories (Hilgard
& Hilgard, 1975; Scott & Barber, 1977; Turk, 1975; Turk et al., 1983). A
recent modification of these categories includes (Brown, 1984):

1. *Avoidance* or distraction
   a. Internal distraction, for example, mental arithmetic or pleasurable
      fantasy

Alleviation With Suggestions
- Direct Suggestion
- Symptom Substitution
- Numbness
- Imagined Analgesia

Alteration of Pain Experience
- Cognitive Change
  - Amnesia
  - Altered Meaning
- Perceptual Change; Reinterpretation
  - Altered Anticipation
- Dissociation

Avoiding; Distracting
- Fantasied Enjoyment
- Time Distortion
- Displacement
- Internal Distraction e.g. mental work
- External Distraction

Awareness of Pain Experience
- Sensory Information
- Sensory Awareness
- Reactivity to Pain Sensations

FIG. 3.1.   Pain Coping Strategies

b. External distraction, that is, shifting the focus of attention to a variety of environmental objects enumerated by the hypnotist
c. Displacement of the pain to some other location in the body
d. Time distortion, such as making the duration of the pain seem to be shorter than it actually is
e. Age regression to a pleasant time prior to the pain experience

2. *Alleviation*
   a. Direct or indirect suggestions for alleviation of the pain
   b. Symptom substitution
   c. Suggested numbness
   d. Application of an imagined analgesic substance
3. *Alteration* of the pain experience
   a. Cognitive alteration, for example, temporary amnesia; altering the meaning (imagining that the pain is experienced during an important and enjoyed life event, such as a sports competition or the caring for children)
   b. Perceptual reinterpretation of the pain, such as imagining the pain as some sensation other than pain, such as tingling, pressure, or itch
   c. Dissociation, separating oneself from the pain as if it is not happening to oneself
4. *Awareness* of the pain, for example, providing the patient with sensory information about the pain beforehand so as to establish an accurate mental set or applying full awareness to the pain experience to gain insight into the nature of pain perception (Meares, 1968) and also into reactivity to pain.

The patient is asked to rate the magnitude of the pain experience for each of the coping strategies and then to compare the ratings across all coping strategies. The goal of the comparative assessment is to establish an individualized hierarchy of pain-coping strategies from the most to the lest effective in coping with the pain induced by pinching. Agreement is reached between the patient and the therapist about which pain-coping strategies seem to be most effective. There may be differences in the utilization of pain-coping strategies for acute and chronic pain. The patient also may change his evaluation of a given pain-coping strategy as treatment progresses. The initial choice of coping strategies is dictated more by an interest in enhancing the sense of self-efficacy than by the intention to identify which pain-coping strategies will ultimately prove to be clinically most effective. Inasmuch as the strategies originally chosen by a given patient are presumably the most convincing to the patient, they are chosen for the initial phase of treatment of the chronic pain. In discussing the comparative assessment with the patient, the clinician introduces the idea that there are many ways to approach pain and that some may hold promise even to the patient. The hypnotherapist has thus begun to undermine the despair so characteristic of chronic pain patients.

The therapist can use the comparative assessment to educate the patient to the variety of ways his own mind can affect pain experience. For example, after having the patient imagine the pinched area to be numb, the therapist may say, "Perhaps you didn't now that your own imagination is able to affect the pain." Or, after giving instructions for distraction, the therapist may say, "Perhaps you didn't know that there is less pain when you turn your mind away from it." After awareness instructions, the therapist may say, "Perhaps you didn't know that placing awareness fully on the pain contributes to its seeming to change moment by moment." Most chronic-pain patients are genuinely surprised to discover that their own attention/awareness and thinking or imagery can significantly affect the magnitude of the pain experience. The patient's discovery of control over pain often leads to a reduction in anxiety and sometimes even in pain experience (Bowers, 1968). The patient who first learns the mind's potential effect on acute induced pain more easily learn to apply the discovery to his chronic pain.

Initial Hypnotic Treatment of Secondary Pain and the Development of Self-Efficacy

When the hypnotherapist has established the pain coping strategies that are most likely to be initially effective and has helped the patient to increase his hopefulness about treatment, the criteria are met for the initial hypnotic pain work. Because the chronic pain patient's despair about *any* treatment is deep seated, it is not advisable to start treatment with the primary or target pain. It is better initially to focus on building the patient's sense of self-efficacy through exposure to a hierarcy of pain experiences that are progressively difficult to master: induced acute, nonclinical pain; acute clinical pain (if experienced); secondary chronic postural pain(s); and target chronic pain. The sessions may begin with acute, nonclinical pain introduced during hypnosis. The pain pinching (Spiegel & Spiegel, 1978), cold pressor (Hilgard & Hilgard, 1975) and ischemic tourniquet methods (Sternbach, 1974) may be used. In trance the patient is given suggestions to effect that induced pain (lowest on the hierarchy), utilizing the previously chosen coping strategies. The immediate goal for the patient is to have a positive experience in reducing (nonclinical) pain distress and, if possible, the intensity of the pain sensations—but, most important—in increasing self-efficacy. If the patient is relatively successful, suggestions are then given to use the same strategies for coping with pain higher on the hierarchy.

A glove analgesia on one hand is next suggested. The patient is told he will experience no pain in the anesthetized hand, although he may still experience some sensation, such as pressure. The hypnotist then presses a pointed instrument (stylus, letter opener) into both of the patient's hands, deep enough to make an indentation, but not to pierce the skin. The patient is asked to compare the pain experience in the two hands and to notice the difference. Even if patients do not discern much difference, the exercise may still be useful. Since most patients experience some difference, even a very small one, suggestions can be given that the numbnesss will increase with practice. Once again, the emphasis is on the development of self-efficacy. The aim is for the patient draw his own conclusions about his own abilities to affect pain experiences.

Once the patient concludes he can use hypnosis to cope with non-clinical pain, the treatment proceeds to clinical pain. As a rule, one should first work with secondary or peripheral pain and with target pain only after the patient has gained confidence in his ability to cope with the secondary pain being experienced. Chronic-pain patients seldom mainfest a single pain location. Although the target pain may have first arisen at its primary site, secondary pain, usually less intense and distressful, later emerges at other sites. These are often due to postural modifications utilized in attempts to compensate for the target pain. Some patients do not clearly experience secondary pain. Even these patients are likely to report specific areas of muscle tension and discomfort that may suffice as treatment foci. Acute clinical pain, for example, dental pain, headaches, burns, and pain associated with injury, can also be used if reported by the patient.

The patient is hypnotized and asked to identify any salient secondary pain. If several areas of pain experience are reported, the least intense pain experience is selected first. The hypnotist gives suggestions to affect the pain, using one or several of the aforementioned pain-coping strategies. It is advisable at first to use these strategies to affect pain distress, not pain intensity; research has shown it is easier for people to affect pain distress than pain intensity (Hilgard & Hilgard, 1975; Mills & Farrow, 1981). The patient needs a successful experience in reducing pain distress in trance with *any* coping strategy. Once the patient has achieved this success, suggestions are given for reducing pain intensity.

Treatment continues in this manner often over a number of sessions as the patient gains confidence in using pain-coping strategies in hypnosis to affect the secondary pain phenomena. Suggestions can be given to experiment with a number of different pain-coping strategies to discover which are most effective in affecting the pain. After initial success with one of the preselected pain-coping strategies, it is not surprising for the patient to report strategies other than the preselected ones to be effective, sometimes even more effective than the preselected strategies. Self-efficacy ratings (Turk et al., 1983) and hypnotic dreams about pain experience can be used to assess the conscious and unconscious shifts in attitude about the pain work. Increased self-efficacy ratings and hopeful dreams about pain relief signify the onset of the next stage of treatment.

Direct Hypnotic Treatment of the Target Pain

The increasingly confident patient is now ready to use hypnosis in the treatment of the target pain. The hypnotized patient is asked to focus

careful attention on the area of target pain and to give a detailed description of the immediate pain experience (Sachs et al., 1977). (Some patients
report that the pain recedes as they try to focus on it, a good prognostic
sign.) Suggestions are structured so that the patient rates the magnitude of
the pain (0–5), describes the pain location, the size of the pain area, the
depth of the pain from the inside to the surface of the body, and the quality
of the pain (throbbing, stabbing, etc.) (See Melzack, 1975.) Each of these
descriptions can be utilized in the treatment.

The patient is instructed to use ideomotor signals to communicate
which of the pain-coping strategies he expects to be most effective in
working with target pain experience at this stage of the treatment—
distraction, dissociation, numbness, awareness, and so on. Suggestions
are given for each strategy in turn until some reduction in the magnitude of
pain is achieved. Additional suggestions can be given to displace the
location of the pain, reduce the area of felt pain, move the pain from depth
to surface, make the pain area more diffuse, or alter the quality of the pain,
for example, by making it into a dull ache instead of a sharp, stabbing
sensation. The immediate goal is to foster self-efficacy through the
achievement of some sort of positive experience alleviating the chronic
target pain.

If the patient fails to report any effect, additional practice with peripheral pain phenomena may be indicated. If he reports slight effects,
alternative pain-coping strategies may be indicated. The hypnotist and the
patient may need to experiment to find together which pain coping strategies are best suited for the target pain. The instructions are repeated
during the same session and across a number of sessions until there is a
clear reduction in the pain experience, in pain distress, pain intensity, or
both.

Skill Development

Those patients reasonably responsive to hypnotic suggestions for relief of
the target pain become hopeful and often become noticeably enthusiastic
about the treatment. The hypnotist capitalizes on the increased motivation
to provide further training designed to decrease the likelihood of relapse
and increase the generalizability of the effects. Within the hypnotic sessions, the hypnotist increases the time the patient spends actively practicing the pain-coping strategies. Extending the *duration* of directly paying
attention to the pain undercuts habitual pain-avoidance strategies used to
escape the constant pain and also undercuts the perception of the pain as
an unchanging experience. The patient is now actively encouraged to
explore a full range of pain-coping strategies. After success with the target
pain, some patients find new pain coping strategies to be especially useful
(sometimes those initially ranked high on the hierarchy). For example, at

this stage of the treatment, patients tend to shift away from strategies that direct them from the pain toward strategies that alter pain perception or turn awareness to the full pain experience. Avoidance and alleviation give way to alteration and awareness of pain.

The patient is also instructed to practice the pain-coping strategies while in an active trance state (Gibbons, 1974), that is, while standing, sitting, walking, and talking in an open-eyed trace. Graded posthypnotic suggestions are given that the distress and the intensity of the pain will decrease each day.

Patients are encouraged to do at least one half hour of daily self-hypnotic practice outside the hypnotic sessions. The transition to self-hypnosis is often disorienting to the patient. Even patients who are very successful in affecting their target pain claim they do not do as well by themselves as they do when the pain-coping strategies are suggested by the hypnotist. They may become discouraged and wish to discontinue self-hypnotic practice. A stepwise approach may improve the efficacy of the self-hypnosis. The steps include:

1. The initial self-hypnosis sessions are conducted in the office; the patient hypnotizes himself in the presence of the hypnotist.

2. When the patient practices self-hypnosis at home for the first few times, he should report the experience in a prearranged phone call to the hypnotist.

3. The patient is encouraged to practice self-hypnosis regularly and experience a wide range of self-hypnotic phenomena before practicing self-hypnosis with pain-coping strategies.

4. The patient practices with the pain-coping strategies, directly applying them to the vicissitudes of daily pain experience.

If these steps are not entirely effective, the hypnotist can audiotape the hypnotic sessions and give the tape to the patient to use at home as an aid to self-hypnosis. If the graded steps still do not yield the desired result, switching to a conflict model of treatment is indicated.

As the patient becomes increasingly skillful in pain reduction, both during the treatment hours and in self-hypnosis at home, the focus of the treatment shifts from the duration of attention to the pain to the *immediacy* of the pain reduction. During the hypnotic sessions, patients learn to refine their detection and discrimination of pain signals. Suggestions are given to detect "just noticeable" pain signals (Leventhal & Everhart, 1979) and to remove them as quickly as possible with the desired pain-coping strategy. The goal is to enhance the speed of both pain detection and application of the pain-coping strategies, so that the patient learns to reduce the pain without having to carry out an extended or ritualized procedure. Patients are also given the posthypnotic suggestion that as soon as they notice any pain, it will automatically occur to them to utilize the desired pain-coping strategies. The goal of these instructions is to replace formal hypnotic or self-hypnotic inductions and the carrying out of elaborate hypnotic pain-coping strategies by pain-coping strategies that operate automatically. Thus, the patient learns to diminish pain signals before they build up and reach the magnitude of his chronic pain experience. The aim is prevention.

Pain Challenge

Hypnotic pain-challenge suggestions are very effective in demonstrating to the patient his mastery over pain experience and increased capacity for pain tolerance. Hypnotic suggestions are given to increase the magnitude of pain. The hypnotist suggests the pain will increase in intensity with each number as he counts up from one to five. Additional suggestions are given that the patient quickly and automatically apply the desired pain-coping strategies to alleviate the pain as it increases. Patients discover they can cope with great increases in hypnotically suggested pain magnitude. This experience of mastery increases their confidence in their ability to relieve pain, although some remain skeptical because the increase in the magnitude of pain is artificially created. To make the discovery more convincingly "real," experimentally induced acute pain (e.g., cold pressor or tourniquet-induced acute pain) can be introduced. Instructions for quick and automatic pain reduction are again given until the patient is satisfied with the pain relief.

Pain challenge can then be generalized. This begins with hypnotic rehearsal in fantasy of the pain reduction in a variety of situations. Stressful situations that heighten the pain experience were previously identified through pattern analysis of the patient's self-monitoring records of daily pain experience. The hypnotist suggests that the patient imagine himself in these various stressful situations and imagine experiencing an increase in pain in each instance. Next, the patient imagines himself successfully coping with the pain as he previously learned to do. Life situations likely to contribute to an increase in pain can be arranged in a hierarchy, and hypnotic rehearsal in fantasy can proceed in a stepwise fashion (Turk et al., 1983). Patients can also be given posthypnotic suggestions for gradual exposure to similar real-life stressful situations and specifically instructed to reduce the pain. The goal of these forms of pain challenge is the prevention of relapse. Self-efficacy expectations improve and become congruent with actual performance in the face of pain-fostering situations.

Symptomatic Versus Dynamic-Systemic Interventions

In many instances, symptomatic treatment can proceed without complications. Patients will show a clear progression in the relief of pain over the course of the sessions (1–10 sessions). Some patients (approximately one-third) fail to respond to symptomatic treatment beyond a certain point. These patients reach a response plateau that may manifest itself in several ways: positive response to hypnotic interventions for peripheral pain, but not for target pain; initial partial positive response for target pain, which fails to improve; and repeated positive response to target pain during hypnosis sessions, but not outside these sessions. It is likely that a conflict exists in these patients which interferes with their response to a purely symptomatic treatment approach (Cheek, 1965). The conflict may be intrapsychic, within the family system, or both. In such cases, the treatment approach should be modified. Depending on the nature of the conflict, hypnotherapy and/or psychotherapy from either a dynamic (uncovering) or a family systems perspective must now be tried. Hypnoprojective methods, such as hypnotic dreams and the Theatre Technique, can be used to identify the nature of the conflicts. Treatment must be structured to work through the conflicts to relieve the pain. Once these conflicts are resolved, the patient is able to resume the effective use of pain-coping strategies.

Unfortunately, we have not yet advanced to the point of being able to identify, before starting therapy, which patients are likely to benefit from a symptomatic model and which from a conflict model of treatment. Intake history is not a good predictor of treatment response. Many patients initially presenting with obvious conflicts proceed through the stages of symptomatic treatment without complication. Long-term therapy for them would be unnecessary, though it is tempting to refer these patients for hypnoanalysis or psychotherapy. A better alternative is to start routinely with a symptomatic approach and to use the response plateau, if it does develop (usually by the fifth hour), as a criterion for referral to dynamic hypnotherapy or hypnoanalysis.

Rehabilitation Activity

As the chronic-pain patient begins to gain relief from the pain, he becomes impatient to assume normal life activities previously restricted by the pain. Those areas of life affected usually include: physical activity, work, daily chores, recreational activities, and social relations. The treatment emphasis now shifts from pain control to daily functioning in real life.

Hypnosis can be used in physical rehabilitation. Chronic pain greatly affects one's general activity level, and chronic-pain patients try to avoid pain through postural modifications. As a result, certain muscle groups go into chronic spasm; others atrophy from disuse. Pain patients tend to avoid certain patterns of movement; they often avoid even simple exercise altogether. Nevertheless, most hypnotizable patients are capable of some response to suggestions for motor activity and can learn greater awareness and control of their motor system.

Posthypnotic suggestions can be designed to reduce pain behavior. Chronic-pain patients who have been bedridden for long periods may increase the amount of time out of bed; those who have not been able to sit may begin to sit (Fordyce, 1976). Patients can also be assigned a routine of exercises, often performed with the assistance of a physical therapist. The exercises may include longer and longer walks, yoga, stretching and movement exercises, swimming, and the use of a stationary bicycle. Practice can be reinforced by posthypnotic suggestions.

The resumption of physical activity can prevent relapse into the chronic pain syndrome. Early in the development of the chronic pain syndrome the natural tendency to inhibit movement can disregulate the normal pain sensing mechanisms (Melzack, 1973). The return of normal movement patterns upon recovery reactivates the large sensory nerves, and the sensory feedback from the increased movement helps restore normal functioning of the pain sensing mechanisms and thereby prevents the return of pain.

Suggestions can also be given to imagine a series of daily activities—work, chores, recreation—the patient may wish to engage in, but which have been curtailed by the pain. These can be arranged in a hierarchy. In hypnotic fantasy the patient can rehearse engaging in these activities: household chores (e.g., repairs, cooking), recreation (playing a musical instrument, gardening, painting, engaging in sports), and work (sitting or standing for longer periods as the job requires). Hypnotic fantasies may also involve social relationships (imagining meaningful times with a spouse or close friend or playing with a child). Family therapy and group therapy (Sternbach, 1974) are often useful adjuncts to hypnotic fantasy work, especially when the patient is at high risk for relapse because he is part of a "pain-engendering environment" (Turk et al., 1983, p. 333). Posthypnotic suggestions can be given that the patient gradually engage in some activities on the outside. Care must be taken not to suggest too early that the patient resume physical activity, which will be too painful because of the muscle atrophy. Treatment involves a combination of hypnotic rehearsal in fantasy followed by enactment in daily life. Specific homework assignments can be formulated for the patient to complete. Assignments can be arranged in a guided sequence from simple to complex (Turk et al., 1983). As part of the overall plan of realistic relapse prevention, expectations can be set low at first, that is, that some setbacks can be expected to occur.

Withdrawal of Medication

Many chronic-pain patients become addicted to one or several pain medications, either prescribed or self-administered. Fordyce (1976) has estimated that over half of all chronic-pain patients manifest addictions. Hypnosis can be used as an adjunct to detoxification. Different substances produce specific physiological effects as well as specific alterations in consciousness. The specific pharmacological action of a given drug interacts with the psychological state of the recipient to produce an individualized reaction pattern (Khantzian, 1975).

Chronic-pain patients most likely to become addicted are those who, in addition to seeking pain relief, use the substances to regulate affects they are unable to tolerate—depression, anxiety, irritability (Krystal & Raskin, 1970). For these reasons it is very important to interview the patient carefully for individual reaction patterns. The therapist may ask, "What does [name substance] do for you, and how does it compare to [name other substance] in its effects?" The therapist records verbatim phenomenological descriptions of the patient's experience for each substance. For example, "It makes me mellow . . . numbs me out . . . makes me feel high." During trance he asks the patient to imagine ingesting the substance of choice and suggests the exact experiential effects of the substance, using the subjective descriptions previously provided by the patient. The imaginary drug experience is repeated in subsequent sessions and in self-hypnotic practice concurrent with systematic decreases in substance use.

Withdrawal, in addition to its effects on many organ systems, is a state of stress characterized by autonomic nervous system overactivity (Krystal, 1962). Hypnosis can be used to induce a deep state of physiological relaxation incompatible with the withdrawal stress response and thus to alleviate the symptoms typically accompanying withdrawal (Bourne, 1975). The combination of hypnotic relaxation and an imaginary drug experience enables the patient gradually to taper off drug intake while maintaining the same physiological and psychological effects formerly produced by the substance. In addition, treatment that also emphasizes enhanced self-efficacy will counteract the patient's usual resistance to reducing medication and finally relinquishing it. For patients who fail to respond to this symptomatic approach, psychotherapy (Wurmser, 1978) or dynamic hypnotherapy (Crasilneck & Hall, 1975) may be used to explore underlying conflicts associated with addiction.

Self-Image and Life Style Modification

No longer preoccupied with pain and able to some extent to resume life activities, the patient is likely to turn attention away from pain toward other life concerns. The sense of mastery gained from pain control generalizes to other life areas. Many patients experience a "ripple effect"— successful treatment of one problem is associated with spontaneous resolution of other problems sometimes unrelated to the treatment program (Spiegel & Linn, 1969). For example, patients may report they stopped smoking, lost unwanted weight, and experienced spontaneous remission of anxiety and phobias or changes in destructive relationships. Spontaneous generalization happens not infrequently in a treatment program emphasizing self-efficacy.

The therapist now changes the focus of treatment to persistent symptoms associated with the pain. These typically include affective symptoms, such as anxiety, depression, or irritability, and vegetative ones like insomnia. Hypnotic and posthypnotic suggestions for relaxation and enjoyment of pleasurable fantasies can be used in the treatment of such pain sequelae.

The patient learns new attitudes about self-care in the pain treatment program, which have implications beyond pain control. These self-care attitudes have an impact on daily life style. The therapist should help the patient make the transition from a "pain-dominated life style" (Turk et al., 1983) to a wellness-dominated life style. Individualized health-risk assessment and evaluation of daily stresses, such as stressful life events, psychological conflict, and time pressure, help the patient become aware of those specific factors which repeatedly have put him at risk. Hypnotic dreams and other hypnoprojective methods can be used to help the patient discover pleasurable activities not previously explored, for example, music, painting, gardening, or sports. Age regression and posthypnotic suggestions can be used to rediscover and reinforce pleasurable activities available to the patient prior to the development of the chronic pain syndrome. Diet and exercise counseling may also be indicated. Patients are encouraged to incorporate some form of relaxation—muscle relaxation, meditation, or self-hypnosis—into their daily life. The danger of relapse decreases when the patient improves the overall quality of his life style in a number of areas.

Patients are unlikely to undergo a drastic transformation from a pain-dominated to a wellness life style without some modification of their self-image. As Szasz (1968) has pointed out, one dimension of the chronic pain syndrome is the adoption of the identity of a person in pain; related to that is the increased use of pain as a mode of communication to others. During trance, therefore, patients can be asked to imagine a series of self-images, in particular, contrasting pictures of themselves—one in which they are in excruciating pain and one in which they go about their lives free from pain. Posthypnotic suggestions can reinforce the transition to a pain-free self-image as the patient engages in real-life situations. The patient may also form an ideal image of someone he wishes to emulate. Graded posthypnotic suggestions can be given that the patient will over time become more and more like that person as he goes about his life with less and less pain.

Termination

The goals of termination are to transfer the responsibility for treatment to the patient and leave the patient with the skills for preventing relapse. If each stage of the treatment was designed to enhance self-efficacy, termination should pose no problems for most patients, except those with unresolved conflicts specifically associated with separation. Such conflicts may need to be worked through in hypnotherapy.

Most patients, however, make the transition to total self-care smoothly. Increasing the interval between treatment sessions prior to the final session, encouraging greater reliance on self-hypnosis, and using ego-strenghtening suggestions (Hartland, 1965) facilitate a smooth termination. The final session is devoted to a review of the treatment stages; a discussion of specific risk situations that may contribute to episodic return of the pain, as well as ways to cope with the pain during episodes; and termination of the patient–therapist relationship. It is advisable to leave the patient with a tape recording of a previous session when the patient successfully utilized a number of pain coping strategies. Patients are encouraged to use the tape if the pain returns.

Clinical Outcome

Pain control is one of the few areas where the efficacy of hypnosis has been well documented. In their extensive studies on experimentally induced pain the Hilgards (Hilgard & Hilgard, 1975; Hilgard, 1975) have convincingly shown the analgesic effects of hypnotic suggestions. Reviews of the extensive case material on the clinical use of hypnosis for pain control have shown that pain control is one of the few areas where hypnosis has been especially effective (Wadden & Anderton, 1982). Nevertheless, there is still a paucity of carefully controlled outcome studies.

Several investigators have developed hypotheses on the mechanisms of hypnotic pain relief. The Hilgards understand analgesia in terms of dissociative mechanisms that result in amnesia for pain experience. Crasilneck and Hall (1973) view the action of hypnosis as a kind of "cortical inhibition." Spanos et al. (1979) emphasize the role of cognitive strategies for pain coping. Barber (1959) believes that all such explanations are reduceable to the various means by which attention is directed away from the pain.

The question remains as to the role of hypnotic susceptibility in hypnotic analgesia. Several studies have demonstrated a definite correlation between hypnotizability and pain relief (Hilgard, 1975; McGlashen et al., 1969). However, other studies have shown that waking pain coping suggestions are as effective as those given in trance for hypnotizable people (Barber & Hahn, 1962; Scott & Barber, 1977; Spanos et al., 1979). While hypnotizability is important, a formal hypnotic induction is not always necessary for pain control (Wadden & Anderton, 1982).

In their review of the clinical uses of hypnosis for pain control, Hilgard and Hilgard (1975) estimate that about 50% of pain cases show substantial improvement following hypnotic treatment. Using a single pain-coping strategy, namely, hypnotically suggested numbness, Crasilneck (1979) claimed that 83% of his chronic low back pain patients reported at least a 70% decrease in pain and a 60% reduction in the use of pain medication following hypnotic treatment. In an experimental investigation of non-clinical pain Scott and Barber (1977) found that combining a number of pain-coping strategies was more effective than utilizing a single pain-coping strategy like numbing alone. When hypnotic suggestions for pain coping are combined with additional interventions like relaxation and biofeedback the outcome is improved (Melzack & Perry, 1975). Multi-modal treatment plans for pain patients—wherein pain coping strategies are embedded in a broad-spectrum treatment plan that includes cognitive therapy, biofeedback, physical therapy and other interventions—yield the most favorable results both in the nonhypnotic behavioral treatment of pain (Gottlieb et al., 1977; Turk et al., 1983) and the hypnobehavioral treatment of pain (Sachs et al., 1977). The multimodal treatment approach presented in this chapter is summarized in Fig. 3.2

I. **Assessment**
   A. Establishing rapport
   B. Self-monitoring of pain experience
   C. Assessing hypnotizability
   D. Assessing pain-coping strategies

II. **Hypnotic Treatment of Pain Experience**
   A. Initial hypnotic treatment of secondary pain
   B. Direct hypnotic treatment of target pain
   C. Skill development
   D. Pain challenge
   E. Dynamic/systemic intervention

III. **Rehabilitation**
   A. Rehabilitation
   B. Withdrawal from medication
   C. Self-Image & life style modification
   D. Termination

FIG. 3.2.   Multimodal Treatment of Pain

HEADACHE

The Psychobiology of Headaches

Because headache pain may arise from a variety of different sources, it is important to identify the type of headache accurately. The Ad Hoc Committee on the Classification of Headache reported in 1962 no fewer than 15 types of headache. More recently these 15 types were reduced to three categories: (a) traction/inflammatory headache, (b) muscle-contraction headache, and (c) vascular headache (the classic migraine, common migraine, and cluster headache) (Diamond & Dalessio, 1978). Traction and inflammatory headaches have identifiable causes: a brain tumor or a subdural hematoma in the case of traction headaches, and bacterial infection, poisoning, or substance/alcohol withdrawal in the case of inflammatory headaches. Although these types of headache are not especially amenable to hypnotic intervention, muscle-contraction and vascular headaches are. Muscle-contraction and vascular headaches are common types of psychophysiological headaches, with muscle-tension headaches accounting for 85% to 90% of all headaches (Diamond & Diamond-Falk, 1982).

Numerous factors contribute to psychophysiological headaches: (a) eating foods that contain vasoactive substances, including nitrates, tyramine, monosodium glutamate, and histamines (Diamond & Diamond-Falk, 1982); (b) withdrawal from substances such as caffeine and alcohol (Diamond & Diamond-Falk, 1982); (d) dieting that lowers blood sugar (Dexter, Roberts, & Byer, 1978); (e) undergoing hormonal changes associated with menstruation or pregnancy (Dalton, 1973); (f) exercising (Diamond & Diamond-Falk, 1982); (g) oversleeping or inhaling fumes or vapors, which elevates blood carbon dioxide levels and causes a rebound dilation of the cranial arteries (Dalessio, 1980); (h) being hypersensitive to environmental stimuli, for example, temperature changes, glaring light, motion, changes in weather or altitude (Adams, Feuerstein, & Fowler, 1980); (i) suppressing emotions, especially anger (Fromm-Reichmann, 1937; Harrison, 1975); (j) abuse of medication, especially overuse of ergotamine and caffeine (Bakal, 1982). In short, headaches are associated with any stimulus that affects vasomotor or myospastic response (Adams et al., 1980). Headache-prone people are oversensitive to stress (Henryk-Gutt & Rees, 1973). Which specific stimuli trigger headaches for a given individual depends on the individual's characteristic cognitive and emotional response pattern by which certain stimuli are found to be stressful and others are not (Mitchell & White, 1977). It is likely that headache-prone people react idiosyncratically to triggering situations. The therapist should attempt to identify as many trigger situations as possible.

Psychophysiological headaches are mediated by the autonomic nervous system. Headache-prone individuals have a hyperactive autonomic nervous system (Bruyn, 1980; Friedman, 1968; Graham, 1975; Kentsmith, Strider, Copenhaver & Jacques, 1976; Lance, 1973; Sargent Walters, & Green, 1973; Selby & Lance, 1960). For a given person, the autonomic nervous system may be too sensitized to certain classes of stimuli and becomes readily activated. Moreover, headache patients react to certain stimuli with less variation than do normal individuals (Price & Clarke, 1979; Rickes, Cohen, & McArthur 1977). The autonomic nervous system mediates both vasomotor response and muscle contraction. A headache may be caused by vascular changes, contraction of the head muslces, or a combination of both. The headache may be a vascular, tension, or a mixed headache, depending on the relative degree of vasomotor or muscular response.

Headache-prone patients show increased activity of certain head muscles. While myospasm of any of the muscles in the head and neck may contribute to a headache, overreactivity of the frontalis muscle (and sometimes the temporalis) is characteristic of most headache patients. In fact, the frontalis muscle appears to be especially reactive to stressful stimuli, even more than other physiological indices, such as heart rate, skin response, or respiratory rate (Philips, 1977; Vaughn, Pall, & Haynes, 1977). Not only is the frontalis muscle more likely to contract readily in response to stressors, but the contraction may be sustained. Chronically high levels of muscle activity, for example, sustained muscle contraction, are characteristic of headache patients both during and between headaches (Bakal & Kaganov, 1977; Budzynski, Stoyva, & Adler, 1973; Haynes, Griffin, Mooney, & Parise, 1975; Peck & Kraft, 1977; Philips, 1977; Pozniak & Patewicz, 1976; Vaughn et al., 1977). When the muscles remain contracted, certain areas within the muscle ("trigger areas," Travell, 1976) manifest increased intramuscular temperature and pressure, the water content of the tissue increases, and mucopolysaccharides accumulate in the tissue (Brendstrup, Jesperson, & Asboe-Hanson, 1957).

Headache-prone patients with a vascular component to the headache also show increased vasomotor responsiveness. Vascular headaches are biphasic (Graham & Wolff, 1938). In the preheadache phase the individual undergoes vasoconstriction of the extracranial and sometimes the intracranial arteries. The extent of the cranial vasoconstriction varies across individuals. Although constriction of the extracranial arteries characteristically occurs in all migraine patients, intracranial vasoconstriction does not. Intracranial vasoconstriction directly interferes with blood flow to the brain, which contributes to such sysmptoms as visual effects, numbness, disturbance of balance, and nausea (Dukes & Vieth, 1964). Whether or not patients manifest prodromal symptoms depends on the extent of constriction in both the intracranial and the extracranial arteries. In all headaches, regional blood flow is considerably reduced, especially in the smaller blood vessels (O'Brien, 1971; Skinhoj & Paulson, 1969). For many migraine patients, the vasoconstrictive response tends to persist even during headache-free intervals (Appenzeller, 1978).

The vascular headache itself is caused by subsequent vasodilation of the cranial arteries, especially the extracranial and sometimes the intracranial arteries. Normal in headache-free intervals, cerebral blood flow increases during the headache attack (Henry, Vernhiet, Orgogozo, & Caille, 1978; Matthew, Hrastnik, & Meyer, 1976) and has a highly irregular pattern (Marshall, 1978). The dilation of the arteries stretches the nerve fibres around the artery. This stretching contributes to the characteristic throbbing pain of the migraine (Dalessio, 1980, p. 52).

The vasomotor changes are mediated by a number of vasoactive substances. During the preheadache phase, the platelets agglutinate concomitant with an increase in plasma serotonin (Dalessio, 1980). The platelets then disintegrate, and, along with mast cells and basophils, they release a variety of vasoactive substances, (histamine, prostaglandins, kinins, and acetylcholine). These humoral substances mediate a number of local changes: vasodilation of the blood vessels, increased vascular permeability, increased edema of the tissue, lowering of the pain threshold, decreased endorphin production, and release of substances associated with immune activity, for example, complement (Anselmi et al., 1976; Chapman, Ramos, Goodell, & Wolff, 1960; Dalessio, 1980; Sicuteri, Fanciullaci, & Michelacci, 1978). The outcome of this cascade of humoral changes is a "sterile inflammatory reaction" (Dalessio, 1974) of the arterial wall and surrounding tissue, along with painful sensitivity of this tissue.

Headache-prone persons have a "similar psychobiological predisposition" regardless of whether the headache symtoms are muscle-tension-predominant or vascular-predominant (Bakal, 1982). Both tension and vascular patients show high levels of head muscle activity. In fact, patients with vascular headaches exhibit even greater levels of head muscle activity than patients with muscle-tension headaches (Bakal & Kaganov, 1977). Both exhibit cranial vascular variability, especially a "pervasive vasoconstrictive state" (Bakal, 1982), and idiosyncratic and stereotyped vascular changes in response to certain normal stimuli (Rickes et al., 1977) during the headache-free intervals. Bakal (1982) speaks of the "dual susceptibility" of both the vascular and the musculoskeletal systems to such changes.

The vascular and muscular changes also interact in complex ways. Muscle contraction can trigger vascular changes, and vice versa. In headache patients for whom muscle tension originally predominated, sustained contraction of the muscles compresses the smaller blood vessels and leads to tissue ischemia. In response to this vasoconstriction, a rebound vasodilation sometimes occurs. The muscle tension headache then becomes compounded by a vascular headache. Patients for whom vascular constriction originally predominated also anticipate the intense headache pain with "excessive (muscular) bracing" (Whatmore & Kohli, 1974), by which the muscles remain in a state of *partial* contraction as a defense against the pain.

Headaches tend to become progressively worse over time. Because of the interaction of the vascular and muscular systems, patients who begin having primarily muscle tension headaches and those who begin with primarily vascular headaches manifest mixed headaches over time. In the muscular tension headache group there is also some tendency to shift symptom dominance (Bakal, 1982): whereas the great majority of patients experience tension headaches at first, they tend to experience a greater vascular component to their headaches over the years. Since vascular headaches are usually accompanied by more severe pain, headaches tend to progress to greater severity (Bakal, 1982; Waters, 1974).

In addition, the psychobiological response takes on a life of its own. The sequence of biological changes resulting in the headache begins to occur with only mild provocation, even in the absence of any stimulation (Henryk-Gutt & Rees, 1973). The relationship between the stressful situation and headache onset becomes less clear cut over time. Once the progressive headache syndrome has become established, it is no longer possible to identify discrete stressors for the majority of the patient's headaches (Dalsgaard-Nielsen, 1965). Excessive use and abuse of vasoactive medications such as ergotamine and caffeine contribute to the persistence of vascular dysfunction (Bakal, 1982). Conditioning may also contribute to the psychobiological hypersensitivity. Those factors which originally caused the headache may be quite different from those which maintain it.

It is useful to view the causative events of the headache on a number of levels as illustrated in Fig. 3.3: (a) stressors or triggering situations; (b) autonomic hyperactivity; (c) peripheral and cranial vasomotor and muscular hyperactivity; (d) local biochemical changes related to the sterile inflammatory response; (e) secondary maintenance factors (persistent vasomotor and musculoskeletal dysfunction, conditioning, and anticipatory bracing). Many of these levels were arrived at through pharmacological investigation. Drugs are available to intervene at any level in the headache response pathway. Anxiolytic substances (e.g., Librium, Valium) decrease reactivity to triggering situations by acting at the level of the central nervous system. Alpha and beta blockers (e.g., Clonidine and Propranolol) decrease the excitation of the receptors of the sympathetic nervous system. Ergotamine, caffeine, and Methylsergide facilitate direct vasoconstriction of the cranial arteries. Anti-inflammatory substances act at the local level. For example, aspirin is an antagonist to platelet ag-

I. Primary Causative Factors

	BEHAVIORAL	MEDICAL

STRESS   Life Events
         Exercise
         Temp. Changes

Self—monitoring   CNS Barbiturlate

AUTONOMIC
INSTABILITY   Relaxation Training   Beta Blockers
(Biological   (eg. Inderol)
Vulnerability)

PHYSIOLOGICAL   Thermal   Vasoconstrictors
CHANGES   Biofeedback   (eg. Ergot; Caffir

Muscle   Blood Flow
Tension   Changes
            (peripheralvasoconstriction;
            CRANIAL VASODILATION)

LOCAL HUMORAL   Breathing   Amyl Nitrate
CHANGES   Exercises   Aspirin
    Neurokinins; Histamines
    Catecholamine Release

II. Secondary Maintenance Factors
Conditioning
Anticipatory Panic

FIG. 3.3.   The Causative Pathway of Headache and the Stages of Behavioral and Medical
Treatment

glutination. Sandomigraine has an antihistamine and antiserotonin effect. Pharmacological interventions, however, pose difficulties. Each substance has side-effects: some are quite addictive; others, if misused, make the cranial vasculature even more unstable and reactive in the long run. Interactive effects make drug combinations problematic, so that it is impossible to create a drug combination that works at each level in the headache causative pathway. Hypnotherapy is a workable alternative.

Hypnotic Treatment of Headaches

Direct Suggestions.   It is not always necessary to design an elaborate hypnotic treatment protocol for the headache patient. A subgroup of headache patients respond to direct hypnotic suggestions for headache relief. For acute headache symptoms, the patient may be given a direct suggestion that the headache will go away when he comes out of trance (Harding, 1961; Horan, 1953; Levendula, 1962). For long-term prevention, the patient may be given a graded posthypnotic suggestion that the headaches will occur with less frequency over time, or that they will be less painful and debilitating (Crasilneck & Hall, 1975). Direct hypnotic suggestions for headache relief sometimes yield dramatic results. However, their effectiveness is limited to the subgroup of more hypnotizable headache patients, probably comprising less than 20% of all headache patients. For the remainder of headache patients, it is possible to design a combination of hypnobehavioral interventions, one for each specific level of the headache-causing system.

Hypnobehavioral Treatment.   Hypnobehavioral treatment begins with a detailed anamnesis of the headache symptoms: age at onset; duration of headache symptoms; family history of symptoms; presence or absence of early warning signs; course of headaches; frequency and duration of the headaches; diurnal variation of headache symptoms; assessment of headache pain (severity, quality of pain, degree of fluctuation, location, unilaterality versus bilaterality, mode of onset (e.g., sudden or slow); associated symptoms (depression, anxiety, irritation, or sleep disturbance); usual headache coping strategies (e.g. medication); and effects of the headache on life style.

The treatment begins by teaching the patient to self-monitor the headache symptoms. The patient is asked to keep a diary (Bakal, 1982; Boudewyns, 1976; Budzynski et al., 1973;) in which he records the date, time of day, rating of headache pain intensity, situation (thoughts, feelings, and activity at the time of the headache), and coping strategies (medication, restriction of activity, etc.) The Bakal headache chart (1982) has a convenient drawing of each side of the face so that the patient can also record the exact location of the headache. The patient should keep the headache diary daily for 2 or 3 weeks prior to the start of treatment in order to obtain a good baseline. The importance of accurately keeping the headache diary must be stressed. About half the patients show some degree of noncompliance with self-monitoring. Instead of recording pain for each headache immediately as it occurs and for as long as it continues, these patients neglect the ongoing record and fill out the pages of the diary all at once by recollection of past headaches.

The patient and therapist work together to identify high-risk times and high-risk situations. Some patients report a greater likelihood of getting a headache at certain times of the day; (on awakening, or as the work day proceeds, or after the day is finished). Each patient has one or a number of high-risk situations specific to him. The patient may report that he usually gets a headache after a fight with a family member or his boss, after rushing to get things done, after eating certain foods, or after encountering harsh light. The purpose of self-monitoring is to increase the patient's awareness of the triggering situations so he can avoid them. For a few patients, self-monitoring alone can decrease headache symptoms.

Having identified discrete trigger situations typical for the patient, the therapist uses either stimulus-control, hypnotic desensitization, or both to reduce the patient's conditioned vasomotor or myospastic reactivity to the offending stimuli. Nonhypnotic control of environmental stimuli is sometimes indicated—softer lighting, dietary restriction, or improved time management (Boudewyns, 1982). Nonhypnotic behavioral desensitization has also been used effectively to "raise the stress threshold" and to reduce internal reactivity to such stimuli (Mitchell & White, 1977, cited in Bakal, 1982, p. 110). For hypnotizable patients, desensitization to triggering stimuli can be conducted effectively in hypnosis (Dengrove, 1968). After deep hypnotic relaxation is induced, the patient imagines the trigger situation while attempting to sustain the deeply relaxed state. Posthypnotic suggestions are given to induce relaxation in real-life trigger situations.

Relaxation training itself is useful in its own right as a treatment intervention. Nonhypnotic deep muscle relaxation (Andreychuk & Skriver, 1975; Lutker, 1971; Paulley & Haskell, 1975; Tasto & Hinkle, 1973; Warner & Lance, 1975) and hypnotic relaxation (Blumenthal, 1963; Horan, 1953; Levendula, 1962; Stambaugh & House, 1977) are effective in the treatment of headaches. The patient is hypnotized and instructed to relax systematically each of the main muscle groups in the body and to imagine the entire body becoming relaxed by means of waves of relaxation, or to relax to the beat of an imaginary metronome. The goal of relaxation training is to decrease hyperactivity of the autonomic nervous system (Adams et al., 1980; Dalessio, 1980; Sargent et al., 1973). Effective relaxation training results in decreased levels of humoral substances that mediate autonomic response (Kentsmith, Strider, Copenhaver, & Jacques, 1976). Because relaxation training directly affects autonomic activity, its significance for the overall treatment protocol cannot be underestimated. Blanchard, Theobald, Williamson, Silver, and Brown (1978), consider the development of relaxation training to be "the final common pathway" of all the levels of treatment for headaches.

A further goal of treatment being to reduce vasomotor and muscular hyperactivity in the head region associated with the headache symtoms, various methods for producing voluntary control over the vasomotor response have been shown to alleviate headache symptoms effectively. These methods include temporal or cranial pulse amplitude biofeedback (Elmore & Tursky, 1981; Friar & Beatty, 1976) and temperature training or hand warming (Mitch, McGrady and Lannone, 1976; Sargent, Green, & Walters, 1972; Sargent et al. 1973; Wickramasekera, 1973a).

Hand warming is the simplest procedure and is quite effective. Raising the temperature of the fingers or hands is made possible through peripheral vasodilation. By warming the hands via imagery, the patient learns to gain voluntary control over the blood flow. Hypnotic suggestions are given to imagine the blood vessels in the head growing smaller and smaller (Anderson, Basker, & Dalton, 1975; Basker, 1970; Harding, 1961) or to imagine the hands becoming warmer and warmer (Daniels, 1976, 1977; Graham, 1975). The warming effect (the vasodilatory effect) is enhanced when sensory imagery is used in hypnosis (Kroger & Fezler, 1976). It is not clear how hand warming works. According to a hemodynamic hypothesis, warming the hands should produce peripheral vasodilation and cranial vasoconstriction, the opposite of both phases of the vascular headache response. But hand warming does not necessarily produce reductions in cranial blood flow (Bakal, 1982; Dalessio, 1980; Sovak, Kunzel, Sternbach, & Dalessio, 1978). Handwarming is more likely to work by stabilizing the vasomotor response pattern in general rather than by altering regional blood flow in specific areas. The overall effect of handwarming is to reduce the likelihood of getting a headache in the first place, rather than directly reversing cranial vasodilation during the headache. From this point of view, it is absolutely essential to practice hand warming on a regular basis in order to train voluntary control over the vulnerable vasomotor system. We recommend 3 to 5 minutes of temprature training six times a day, with or without self-hypnosis, to be reinforced by posthypnotic suggestions over a 20-week period. Temperature changes in the hand should be measured by the patient by means of a finger thermometer, and the patient should attempt to increase the temperature in the hand by one to two degrees in each training session (Fahrion, 1980). Because retraining of the vasomotor system is the goal, daily consistency in effecting even small temperature changes is more important than the magnitude of change in any single session.

Hyperactivity of the head muscles must also be addressed in the treatment. Physical therapy, especially neck rotations, is a useful adjunct to the treatment (Epstein, Hersen, & Hemphill, 1974). Frontailis EMG biofeedback has been shown to be quite effective in reducing headache symptoms (Budzynski et al., 1970; Budzynski, Stoyva, Adler, & Mullaney, 1973; Kondo & Canter, 1977; Philips, 1977; Wickramaskera, 1973b). Similar effects can be accomplished with hypnosis by having the patient carefully focus on specific head muscles, visualizing the frontalis or any other head muscle as if it were composed of many strands made out of rubber bands. Then the patient imagines loosening strand after strand until the muscle is loose and limp.

The vasodilatative, endorphin-antagonistic and inflammatory substances released into the tissue during the headache response may be quickly metabolized following hypnotic breathing exercises. The patient is hypnotized and taught slow, rhythmic diaphragmatic breathing. The patient is then encouraged to practice diaphragmatic breathing daily for 20 minutes as part of self-hypnotic practices. A minimum of 20 minutes of continuous diaphragmatic breathing is necessary to produce the physiological effects—breathing causes an uptake of catecholamines (Stone & DeLeo, 1976). It is also advisable to introduce hypnotic analgesia suggestions; such suggestions raise the pain threshold and increase pain tolerance in headache patients (Stacher, Schuster, Bauer, Lahoda, & Schulze, 1975). It remains to be demonstrated whether or not such suggestions operate at the level of indigenous analgesic (endorphin) production. More research is needed on the effects of hypnotic suggestions on the biochemical substances implicated in the headache response.

Once the patient has learned each of the hypnotic exercises, they are incorporated as a unit into his daily practice of self-hypnosis. The patient begins self-hypnosis with general relaxation followed by relaxation of specific head muscles implicated in the headache. Next, the patient practices hand warming and diaphragmatic breathing. The overall effect of the set of practices over time is stabilization of the autonomic nervous system and the associated vasomotor and muscular activities.

Whereas the first phase of treatment pertains to long-term physiological stabilization, the next phase has to do with control of the acute headache symptoms. The goal of this phase of treatment is to avert the headache at its onset. The therapist first conducts a detailed inquiry into the preheadache symptomatology. Because preheadache symptoms are extremely variable from patient to patient (Dalessio, 1980), it is especially important to ascertain the specific early warning signs characteristic for the individual patient: "What do you notice that tells you a headache is coming on?" The patient is encouraged to compile a list of early warning signs, however subtle or obvious these may be. From this list of early warning signs the patient and therapist construct a chain of events: the very first sign; the manifest symptoms; the point of no return (where the headache inevitably follows); a brief symptom-free period; the onset of the headache itself. Every effort is made to detect the very first sign of the preheadache phase—the first change the patient is able to recognize before the attack. As the patient attempts to discriminate the sequence of events over time, he learns to recognize more subtle earlier warning signs heretofore undetected and becomes skillful in tracking the sequence of events characteristic of his particular headache pattern.

The patient then is asked at what point he takes steps to cope with the oncoming headache. Many patients report the employment of coping strategies (e.g., taking medication, lying down) only after the point of no return and are advised to initiate coping strategies at the earliest warning sign. Posthypnotic suggestions are given to reinforce the use of coping strategies early in the preheadache phase: "Whenever you notice [name earliest warning sign], it will automatically occur to you to breathe deeply . . . you will feel relaxation spreading throughout your body, and your hands will become warmer and warmer." The patient who has learned to exercise voluntary control over the desired psychophysiological changes can now frequently abort the headache attack during the preheadache phase.

For those headache attacks the patient fails to prevent, he is taught additional coping methods. Sometimes the patient is given direct hypnotic suggestions for pain alleviation (Andreychuk & Skriver, 1975; Harding, 1961; Levendula, 1962). An alternative method is to suggest glove anesthesia and then have the patient transfer the numbness to the painful area (Kroger, 1963; Stambaugh & House, 1977). Although such direct suggestions work for a distinct subgroup of pain patients, we recomend a more generally applicable approach. A waking assessment of the patient's individual pain coping strategies is conducted using the pain-pinching method described earlier. The therapist then individualizes the pain-coping suggestions according to whether the patient is more skilled at avoidance, alleviation, alteration, or awareness strategies for pain control. Avoidance and attention-diverting suggestions are more generally applicable than other pain coping strategies and are therefore popular in headache clinics (Bakal, 1982, p. 117). Each patient, however, should be offered the full range of pain-coping strategies to determine which work best for him.

Another dimension of working with the headache is the cognitive and affective reactions that exacerbate the headache response. When the early warning signs are noticed, a pattern of negative thoughts usually begins. Chronic headache patients tend to catastrophize the headache symptoms

(Meichenbaum, 1978, in Bakal, 1982, p. 116) through a series of negative thoughts such as "Here comes another headache, I won't be able to do anything to stop it . . .", "I know this is going to be a real bad one." The headache-related negative cognitions and the associated anticipatory anxiety make the headache worse by generating additional stress. A vicious cycle sets in: fear of the recurrence of a headache exacerbates—or even causes—the headache response (Van Pelt, 1954).

The typical anticipatory cognitions must be addressed as part of the overall treatment. The hypnotherapist points out to the patient the pattern of negative thoughts that is characteristic of that patient (Holroyd & Andrasik, 1978; Reeves, 1976). In addition, the patient is given posthypnotic suggestions to notice and recall whatever thoughts and feelings occur at the onset of a headache, especially thoughts associated with worrying about the headache. The patient keeps a record of negative thoughts associated with each headache over a period of time until the characteristic pattern of negative thoughts becomes evident. The therapist helps the patient see how these thoughts aggravate the headache and interfere with the utilization of available coping strategies. The hypnotherapist also helps the patient construct a list of positive self-statements to counteract habitual negative thoughts: "I am able to use the skills I have learned to help with the headache," "I have some control over the course of the headache." The habitual negative self-statements are taken as cues to remind oneself of positive self-statements. The therapist gives a posthypnotic suggestion: "At the onset of a headache, when you find yourself thinking (name negative thoughts(s)), it will occur to you to start thinking [name positive self-statements(s)]." General ego-strengthening suggestions are also helpful with headaches (Anderson et al., 1975; Basker, 1970): "Using the skills you are learning here, you will find yourself becoming increasingly confident of your ability to contol the headache."

The patient is strongly advised to practice self-hypnosis regularly and to increase the duration of each self-hypnotic session, especially the psychophysiological interventions—relaxation training, hand warming, and diaphragmatic breathing—because treatment outcome is directly related to the amount as well as the consistency of practice (e.g., Kroger, 1963). Self-hypnosis is best done as part of a daily routine, incorporated into one's life style.

As the patient becomes increasingly skillful in the voluntary control of psychophysiological processes, he should be able to produce immediate physiological changes just by intending the desired effect. The treatment focus then shifts from increasing the duration of the practice in the office to effecting immediate changes as needed in daily life. Posthypnotic suggestions are given to link the beneficial effects previously produced only in the office with the recognition of the early warning signs of the headache:

"As soon as you notice [specify symptom], it will automatically occur to you to become relaxed, breathe, the way you have learned . . . your hands will become warmer and warmer . . . this will happen quicker and quicker . . . and the discomfort you were just beginning to notice goes away quickly . . . there will be no more headache . . . and you find yourself becoming increasingly confident in your ability to prevent and control headaches using your new skill." The purpose of the posthypnotic suggestion is to increase the likelihood that the treatment effects will generalize. Such suggestions are particularly indicated in the treatment of headache patients for whom other interventions, such as EMG biofeedback, have failed to generalize (Epstein et al., 1974).

An effective way to demonstrate to the patient that he has mastered the headache response is to induce a headache hypnotically and then suggest that the patient alleviate it using the learned methods for psychophysiological control and pain coping. Having alleviated the headache through relaxation, breathing, hand warming, and the application of specific pain coping strategies, the patient gains confidence in his ability to control the headaches.

The patient then rehearses coping with a headache in fantasy, imagining a situation in his everyday life where an intense headache occurs. As the headache begins, the patient imagines taking the necessary steps to abort the headache response and reduce the discomfort. Posthypnotic suggestions are given to apply the coping strategies whenever the patient encounters real-life situations comparable to those rehearsed in fantasy.

Next, the patient in trance imagines a series of activities (work, chores, recreation) he may wish to engage in, activities that have been curtailed by the headaches. They can be arranged in a hierarchy. In hypnotic fantasy, the patient rehearses engaging in each of these activities. Graded posthypnotic suggestions are given for the patient to engage in these activities when he is ready to do so. Treatment entails a combination of hypnotic rehearsal in fantasy followed by enactment in daily life. One goal of the rehabilitative phase of the treatment is to facilitate the patient's return to normal life activities. A related goal is to reduce the "illness behavior" (Demjen & Bakal, 1981), for example, and the psychopathological symptoms associated with the headache response (Sternbach, 1974; Swanson, Swenson, Maruta, & McPhee, 1976). For those headache patients for whom suppression of emotions contributes to the headache response, adjunctive assertiveness training may also be useful (Dengrove, 1968).

Dynamic Hypnotherapy and Systemic Intervention.   If the patient fails to respond to the hypnobehavioral treatment after the number of sessions in which psychophysiological response typically can be expected (10–20 sessions), it is likely that there is emotional resistance to change because of underlying conflict. The therapist then switches to a hypnodynamic approach and uses dynamic hypnotherapy techniques to uncover and work through the intrapsychic conflicts associated with the headache symptoms (Anderson et al., 1975; Blumenthal, 1963; Cedercreutz, 1972; Van Pelt, 1954). In certain cases, the headache symptoms are associated with conflicts within the family system. Here, adjunctive family therapy is conducted concurrent with the hypnobehavioral treatment.

Clinical Outcome

The success of nonhypnotic behavioral treatment of headaches is very impressive. Depending on the type of treatment protocol, relaxation training and biofeedback are effective in reducing tension headache frequency by 40–80%; migraines, by 40–90% (Jessup et al., 1979). Studies using false biofeedback have demonstrated that the positive treatment outcome in many instances cannot be attributable to placebo effects (Budzynski, et al., 1973; Kondo & Canter, 1977; Fahrion, 1978). Studies comparing hypnotherapy to these other modalities have yielded comparable positive outcome data with no significant differences between hypnotherapy and the other treatment modalities (e.g., Andreychuk et al., 1975). However, outcome data for hypnotherapy are at the lower end of the continuum (36% in Andreychuk et al., 1975; 44% in Anderson et al., 1975; 65% in Kroger, 1963) because most hypnotic treatment has been unidimensional.

Multimodal treatment protocols (e.g., Adler & Adler, 1976; Stambaugh & House, 1977) generally improve the outcome (Hutchings & Reinking, 1976) and are strongly recommended. Since headache patients constitute a heterogeneous population, it is advisable to offer a comprehensive array of treatment interventions designed to meet the needs of a wide range of patients. It is also advisable to individualize the treatment to the needs of the given headache patient, as described here. Further research with this individualized method of hypnotherapy needs to be done.

HYPERTENSION

The Psychobiology of High Blood Pressure

Normal blood pressure maintains the flow of the blood to the tissues throughout the body against the peripheral resistance inherent in the vascular beds. Blood pressure also counteracts the effects of gravity. Life cannot be supported without maintaining a minimal blood pressure. Chronically elevated blood pressure causes damage to the arterial walls and is associated with a variety of cardiovascular diseases; stroke, left ventricle hypertrophy, retinal hemorrhage, and arteriolar nephrosclerosis. Maintaining blood pressure within an optimal range reduces the risk of cardiovascular disease.

Blood pressure is the product of cardiac output and peripheral resistance: blood pressure = cardiac output × peripheral resistance. Cardiac output, in turn, is a product of heart rate and stroke volume. Heart rate is mediated by the autonomic nervous system. Cardiac sympathetic nerves control increases in heart rate, while the parasympathetic vagus nerve controls decreases. Stroke volume is determined by the rate of return of the venous blood. Peripheral resistance is determined by the extensiveness of the vascular beds, the size of the vessels, and the viscosity of the blood.

Ninety-five percent of hypertension is of unknown origin. However, it is clear that hypertension evolves over the course of the life cycle. For instance, blood pressure reactive to stress in adolescents correlates significantly with the development of sustained hypertension later in life (Falkner, Onesti, & Hamstra, 1981). Some (e.g., Reisel, 1969) have attempted to classify the stages in the development of hypertension. The earlier forms of hypertension, notably labile and borderline hypertension, are characterized by cardiac hyperactivity in response to stressful stimuli ("hyperkinetic heart"), a chronic pattern of sustained cardiac output, great variability in blood pressure, but normal peripheral resistance (Julius & Esler, 1975). The later forms, sustained and malignant hypertension, are characterized by increased peripheral resistance with normal cardiac output. The increase in peripheral resistance often results from atherosclerotic thickening of the arterial walls, obesity, autoregulatory responses to the high cardiac output, and changes in kidney functioning.

Normal regulation of blood pressure is exceedingly complex. Because blood pressure is such a vital process, the body has many hierarchically organized mechanisms that regulate blood pressure. Only some of them have been fully identified and are clearly understood. Each is designed to control blood pressure within a certain range of pressure under certain conditions and for a certain duration (Guyton, 1980). The interrelationship between these mechanisms is controlled by feedback loops. Each feedback regulatory system is part of an integrated system within the overall network of regulatory mechanisms. This complex integrative system enables the organism to regulate blood pressure across a wide range of situations: from major adjustments, in the case of medical emergencies on one end of the continuum, to finely tuned adjustments during the shifting demands of ongoing behavior, on the other. But once self-regulation has failed, the complexity of the system makes it difficult to know exactly where in the system treatment should be directed.

It is encouraging, however, that a number of discrete regulatory systems have been identified: the volumetric, the biochemical, the hemodynamic, and the neurogenic systems. Failure in any one of these systems can disregulate blood pressure (Fahrion, 1980). The volumetric system, the kidneys, controls fluid volume and sodium retention. It functions in the long-term maintenance of blood pressure. Antidiuretic hormones (e.g., vasopressin) increase fluid retention. This, in turn, increases the amount of venous blood returning to the heart, which, in turn, increases cardiac output. An "autoregulatory" response follows wherein the ensuing generalized vasoconstriction maintains a constant flow of blood at the expense of an increase in peripheral resistance and an increase in blood pressure (Guyton, 1980). In sustained hypertension, the relationship between blood pressure and fluid volume is altered so that the body acts as if fluid were retained (Fahrion, 1980).

The biochemical system steps up its functioning when blood volume is lost, as in the case of hemorrhage, or when sodium intake is low. The renin-angiotension-aldosterone system is designed to regulate blood pressure and sodium content specifically for the kidney. When sodium is lost (e.g., by sweating), aldosterone serves to retain sodium. The sodium loss also activates renin and in turn angiotension, which produces a vasoconstrictive response. The vasoconstrictive effects resulting from these biochemical changes can contribute to hypertension by increasing peripheral resistance.

The hemodynamic system regulates long-term blood pressure by directly controlling the diameter of the blood vessels. When tissue perfusion is excessive, an autoregulatory response follows in which peripheral blood vessels are constricted (Guyton, Coleman, Bower & Granger, 1970). In the case of hypertension, vascular hyperreactivity evolves into sustained peripheral vasoconstriction and an increase in peripheral resistance associated with the elevated blood pressure (Julius & Esler, 1975).

The neurogenic system is the most complex and the most relevant to most hypertension of unknown origin. The baroreceptor reflex is associated with changes in heart rate. When heart rate increases, the baroreceptor cells are activated, an effect which, in turn, activates the vagus nerve, mediated by the brain stem. Heart rate is reduced through the increased parasympathetic activity. The baroreceptor reflex normally regulates heart rate. In hypertension the baroreceptors are reset so that parasympathetic inhibition of cardiac output is reduced (Compagno, Leite, & Krieger, 1977; Fahrion, 1980,) and elevated cardiac output is maintained.

The autonomic nervous system is critical to an understanding of how stress affects blood pressure. Whereas the parasympathetic-cholinergic system has an inhibitory effect, on, for example, cardiac output, the sympathetic-adrenergic system is associated with cardiovascular activation. Sympathetic response determines "the level of 'engagement involvement' with one's current surroundings" (Surwitt, Williams, & Shapiro, 1982, p. 39). Two specific patterns of cardiovascular response have been identified. The first is the well-known fight-or-flight reaction (Cannon, 1932). Beta adrenergic neurons affect an increase in cardiac output and vasodilation of the blood vessels in the muscles. The organism prepares itself for vigorous action. Alpha adrenergic neurons affect vasoconstriction of the skin and viscera. Whereas the classic fight-or-flight reaction is associated with the emergency defense in both animals and humans, more recent studies have shown that the same cardiovascular response pattern is manifest in a number of ordinary situations pertaining to engagement with the environment: motor activity, mental activity, and emotional expression (Surwitt et al., 1982). The second cardiovascular pattern is associated with sensory intake (Williams, 1981). Alpha adrenergic neurons affect a generalized vasoconstriction, especially in the blood vessels of the muscles, but also in the blood vessels of the skin and viscera. The pervasive vasoconstrictive effect results in increased peripheral resistance. Heart rate deceleration often accompanies sustained attention to sensory events. This cardiovascular pattern also is observed when the organism manifests "immobile anticipation" of danger in emergency situations and effortful attention in ordinary situations (Surwitt et al., 1982).

In hypertension, the autonomically mediated cardiovascular response patterns, which normally operate in most ongoing situations, manifest an abnormal response. Since cardiovascular response can be conditioned in both animals and humans (Surwitt et al., 1982), there is reason to believe that disregulation of the autonomically mediated cardiovascular responses is learned and is the consequence of long-term habitual perceptions of and responses to stress. Hypertension may be a result of altered adrenergic function or of increased adrenergic receptor sensitivity (Frohlich, 1977). Autonomic hyperactivity is characteristic of at least an important subgroup of hypertensive patients (Esler, Zweifler, Randall, Julius, & DeQuattro, 1977; Julius & Esler, 1975).

The early stages of hypertension are characterized by an alteration of the normal fight-flight cardiovascular response pattern: high cardiac output and vasoconstriction of the blood vessels of the skin and viscera. The difference is that with prolonged stress, the beta adrenergically mediated vasodilation of the blood vessels in the muscles becomes habituated. The additional increase in peripheral resistance resulting from habituation of muscle vasodilatation, on the one hand, and the sustained vasoconstriction of the skin and viscera, on the other, contributes to an overall increase in peripheral resistance (Fahrion, 1980,). The combination of increased peripheral resistance and high cardiac output is characteristic of early hypertension (Julius & Esler, 1975).

Prolonged stress also elicits compensatory responses to block the sustained cardiovascular response patterns. According to Guyton (1980), an "autoregulatory response" is activated to counter the sustained high cardiac output. The organism attempts to reduce the high cardiac output by means of the alpha adrenergically mediated vasoconstrictive response. Furthermore, prolonged stress tends to activate the baroreceptor reflex, a reflex that lowers the heart rate. The effect of these autoregulatory operations is an increase in the total peripheral resistance and a decrease in cardiac output. The combination of increased peripheral resistance and normal cardiac output is indicative of sustained hypertension.

Acute stress induces catecholamine release (Keegan, 1973; Raab, 1966). Prolonged stress may cause the autonomic nervous system to become sensitized. Hypertensives excrete excessive amounts of catecholamines in response to stress (Julius & Esler, 1975; Nestel, 1969). One result is vascular hyperactivity (Fahrion, 1980,). In sustained hypertension, reversible structural changes occur, namely, hypertrophy of the arterial wall. More pathogenic, reversible changes also occur. For example, excessive release of humoral agents can change the endothelial lining of the arterial wall and alter receptor sites, so that free fatty acids bind more easily to the cell wall. This speeds up the atherosclerotic process (McKinney, Hofschiro, Buell, & Eliot, 1984).

Once high blood pressure is established, a complex array of regulatory mechanisms maintains it. The normal regulatory mechanisms are reset. Over time, blood pressure is reset at higher and higher levels (Frolich, 1977; Surwitt et al., 1982).

The Pharmacological Treatment of Hypertension: Stepped Care

The current pharmacological treatment of hypertension is based on the Stepped Care approach (Freis, 1978). The first step is to approach high blood pressure from the perspective of fluid volume. Diuretics are used to deplete blood volume through the excretion of water and sodium, which reduces cardiac output. Diuretics are effective for about 50 percent of hypertensive patients. The next step is to alter the fight-or-flight cardiovascular response pattern by means of adrenergic blocking agents. Beta blockers directly block cardiac output. Alpha blocking agents block the vasoconstriction of the skin and viscera, and alpha antagonists block renin release. The third step is to use vasodilative substances to decrease peripheral resistance. The fourth step, if all else fails, is to use a peripheral sympathetic depletor to affect vasodilation. The advantage of pharmacological intervention is that the drugs often have a synergistic effect, the combination of several drugs potentiating the effect of each. The disadvantages are the potential side-effects, such as hypokalemia and postural hypotension. The pharmacological approach, however, offers a model for the steps in any treatment, including hypnobehavioral treatment: identification of stress and dietary factors; altering the autonomic response; altering the vasomotor response; and modifying the local biochemical response. The stages in the causation and maintenance of high blood pressure as well as the approaches to treatment are summarized in Fig. 3.4.

Hypnobehavioral Treatment of Hypertension

Hypnobehavioral treatment of hypertension begins with a detailed evaluation of the hypertension: history of the hypertension (age of onset, course, family history, fluctuations in blood pressure associated with life events); risk factors (e.g., smoking, weight, diet, Type A behavior); associated medical complications; history of treatment and coping strategies, including type of medication, exercise, and relaxation. It is especially important to rule out known medical causes of hypertension (renal failure, hyperaldosteronism, use of birth control pills, alcohol consumption).

Next, the patient is taught to self-monitor his blood pressure. The patient is given a daily blood pressure recording sheet (Fig. 3.5) in which to record the date and time of day when blood pressure is taken. He also records his systolic and diastolic blood pressure and heart rate. He rates his tension level and describes his thoughts, feelings, and activity at the time of the recording. He also lists his coping strategies (e.g., taking medication) and other factors that might affect blood pressure (e.g., salt intake, exercise, caffeine intake, alcohol consumption). The patient is encouraged to buy a blood pressure recording device. The automated digital blood pressure recording devices are the easiest to use. The patient brings the recording device to the office and is taught how to read his own blood pressure. He is instructed to measure the blood pressure in exactly the same way each time, that is, on the same arm and while sitting. The patient is told to inflate the cuff rapidly to avoid filling the arm with venous blood and to deflate the cuff at a rate of 2–3 mm/sec.

The patient must practice measuring his blood pressure a number of times until it is established that he measures and records both systolic and diastolic blood pressure with consistent accuracy. The patient must learn to detect accurately the exact moment when the Korotkoff sounds (K-sounds) are heard in a regular series and when they disappear. The patient is also taught to avoid common errors in recording the blood pressure: artifactual elevations in diastolic blood pressure resulting from confusing an auscultatory gap or a muffled beat with the genuine disappearance of the K-sounds; artifactual elevations in systolic blood pressure resulting from watching the bounce of the dial instead of listening for the series of

	Behavioral Treatment	Pharmacological Stepped Care

I. Causative Factors in Blood Pressure Elevation

  A. Volumetric Disregulation
     (fluid volume / sodium retention)   Dietary Control   Diuretics

  B. Neurogenic Disregulation
     Stress   Self–Monitoring
     Autonomic Hyperactivity   Relaxation Training   Alpha & Beta Blockers

     | Elevated Cardiac Output | Heart Rate Biofeedback

  C. Hemodynamic Disregulation
     Vasoconstriction of Skin   Blood Flow Regulation   Vasodilators
        and Viscera   (Head / Limb Warming)
     Generalized Vasoconstriction

     | Increased Peripheral Resistance |

  D. Biochemical (Humoral) Disregulation

     Catecholamine Release
                                                 Breathing Exercises   Peripheral Sympathetic Depletors
     Renin–Angiotension–
        Aldosterone Disregulation

II. Maintenance Factors in Blood Pressure Elevation
    Autoregulatory Resetting of Blood Pressure

FIG. 3.4 Factors in the Causation, Maintenance, and Treatment of High Blood pressure

Name _____ Weight _____ Week Of _____ Average BP _____ Average Tension _____

Tension Level

0	25	50	75	100
Not at all Tense	Slightly Tense	Moderately Tense	Very Tense	Extremely Tense

Date	Time	Tension Level (0–100)	Blood Pressure Systolic/ Diastolic	Finger Temperature Before	After	Situation	Thoughts/ Feelings	Diet, Exercise, Medication

FIG. 3.5. Daily Blood Pressure Recording Sheet

K-sounds. Even when it is established that the patient consistently records his blood pressure correctly, it is advisable periodically to calibrate the patient's blood pressure recording device against the clinic device. A dual stethoscope serves the purpose. The therapist should also periodically review the manner in which the patient reads his blood pressure to ensure he is doing it correctly.

To establish a baseline, the patient is encouraged to record his blood pressure once a day at the same time each day over a 3-week period. An alternative approach is to have the patient record his blood pressure several times each day in many situations over the 3-week interval. The patient calculates the mean blood pressure for each of the weeks, then the mean for the 3 weeks, and uses the 3-week mean as a baseline.

The patient will more readily comply with self-monitoring if he is shown the Metropolitan Life Insurance chart on the reduction in life expectancy associated with elevated blood pressure (Goodfriend, 1983, p. 102). Most patients will consistently record their blood pressure if they are enlisted as active participants in the treatment process. For sustained interest, the patient must come to see the value of daily home blood pressure recording. At first, most patients complain that individual blood pressure recordings are highly variable, but these patients are often surprised to discover that weekly mean blood pressures are relatively stable over time. Patients sustain their enthusiasm for blood pressure recording if they can track their progress by plotting the weekly mean blood pressures on a graph. In some patients, self-monitoring alone is sufficient to reduce blood pressure.

A related goal is to facilitate the patient's discovery of an association between blood pressure and life events. The patient and therapist must work together to identify high-risk times and high-risk situations. Some patients learn that blood pressure tends to increase or decrease at certain, well-defined periods of the day. Each patient discovers one or a number of high-risk situations specific to him. The patient may, for example, find that blood pressure increases after he rushes to get things done or after he experiences a certain emotional state. Many patients also manifest an "office visit artifact," in which blood pressure recordings in the therapist's office are higher than at home as a result of performance anxiety.

A number of other factors are also typically associated with elevations in blood pressure. Dietary factors, notably salt intake, are important for a subgroup of patients. Certain medications (amphetamines and anti-histamines) elevate blood pressure. Caffeine and alcohol increase blood pressure, as does being overweight. The increased vasculature of each pound of fatty tissue requires higher blood pressure to maintain the flow of blood to the tissues. Patterns of exercise also affect blood pressure, especially isometric exercises, vigorous workouts, and sexual activities. Postural changes, even getting up from a chair, can also alter blood pressure in some patients. A number of environmental factors have been associated with increased blood pressure: urban overcrowding, noise pollution, exposure to cold temperatures, and pain-producing stimuli. Exposure to traumatic situations, such as natural disasters, accidents, and combat, contributes to posttraumatic elevations in blood pressure. Emotionally disturbing stimuli (a stressful interview, daily tensions) also raise blood pressure (McKegney & Williams, 1967; Wolff & Wolf, 1951). Whereas, for most people, acute elevations in blood pressure are associated with free emotional expression, chronic elevations in blood pressure for a subgroup of patients are related to a style of suppressing emotional expression, especially anger. Although there may be no genuine "hypertensive personality" (Alexander, 1939), patients who have a style of suppressing anger (Esler et al., 1977; Harburg et al., 1973; Shapiro, 1978) or an inhibited power motive (McClelland, 1979) often evidence greater sympathetic activation, higher cardiac output, increased catecholamine levels, and higher blood pressure than normal individuals. The time pressure associated with Type A behavior also contributes to chronic elevations in blood pressure. The therapist and the patient together must identify and refine the awareness of high-risk factors over the weeks of the treatment. What often emerges is a clearcut pattern of risk factors specific to the individual.

A combination of stimulus control and hypnotic desensitization is used to reduce the patient's reaction to those factors which normally increase blood pressure. When it is indicated, the patient learns to control salt intake. Adjunctive programs should be recommended to help the patient stop smoking, reduce caffeine or alcohol intake, or lose weight. A regular exercise program should be encouraged. The patient also learns to avoid stressful stimuli and events that typically elevate his blood pressure; for example, a noise or physical cold can usually be avoided. Hypnotic relaxation may be introduced to the patient, following which the patient rehearses in fantasy encountering the stressful situation. The goal is to desensitize the patient to those factors which were previously associated with elevations in blood pressure.

As the patient continues to identify risk factors, the therapist teaches the patient relaxation. Both nonhypnotic deep muscle relaxation (Jacobson, 1939; Shoemaker & Tasto, 1975; Taylor, Farquhar, Nelson, & Agras, 1977) and associated practice such as metronome-conditioned relaxation (Brady, Luborsky, & Kron, 1974), meditation (Benson, Rosner, Marzetta, & Klemchuk, 1974; Benson & Wallace, 1972; Stone & DeLeo, 1976; Wallace, 1970) and EMG biofeedback (Moeller & Love, 1974), as well as hypnotic relaxation (Deabler, Fidel, Dillenkoffer, & Elder, 1973; Friedman & Taub, 1977; 1978) have been effective in lowering systolic and diastolic blood pressure in normal and hypertensive patients. In the Deabler study, patients were given hypnotic suggestions for relaxation, heaviness of the limbs, and drowsiness. They were also given suggestions to relax the internal organs, especially the heart and blood vessels. With hypnotic relaxation, blood pressure reductions were a little more than 20% below baseline. The goal of relaxation training is to help stabilize the autonomic nervous system by teaching the patient voluntary control over sympathetic activity (Surwitt et al., 1982). Relaxation training also disrupts the feedback mechanism associated with maintaining the elevated blood pressure (Abboud, 1976).

A related goal of the treatment is to reduce cardiac output. People are able to lower their heart rate using heart rate biofeedback (Bell & Schwartz, 1975; Blanchard, Young, Scott, & Haynes, 1974; Colgan, 1977; Lang, Troyer, Twentyman, & Gatchell, 1975; Sirota, Schwartz, & Shapiro, 1974, 1976; Stephens, Harris, Brady, & Shaffer, 1975; Wells, 1973). Some people can produce the same effect voluntarily without the feedback (Bergman & Johnson, 1971). Direct suggestions to lower pulse rate can be effective for certain patients (Collison, 1970; Van Pelt, 1958c), but for others they are ineffective (Jana, 1967). We recommend a combination of hypnotic suggestion and heart rate biofeedback. The patient is hypnotized while heart rate is continuously monitored. The patient is given either direct suggestions to slow the heart rate or suggestions to relax until the heart rate lowers. Feedback is given to the patient when heart rate is successfully lowered. Posthypnotic suggestions and self-hypnosis are used to sustain the lowered heart rate in everyday life.

Another treatment goal is that the patient gain voluntary control over peripheral vasomotor activity as a means of decreasing total peripheral resistance. Both nonhypnotic thermal biofeedback (Green, Green, & Norris, 1980; Fahrion, 1980; Keefe & Gardner, 1979) and hypnotic finger and hand warming (Barabasz & McGeorge, 1978; Maslach, Marshall, & Zimbardo, 1972), as well as the combination of thermal biofeedback and hypnosis (Roberts, Kewman, & MacDonald, 1973), are effective for reducing blood pressure. The ability to affect temperature and regional blood flow, however, does not appear to be related to hypnotizability (Engstrom, 1976; Frischholz & Tryon, 1980; Roberts, Schuler, Bacon, Zimmerman, & Patterson, 1975), although certain types of hypnotic suggestions may improve blood flow, at least for some people. We recommend a combination of hypnotic hand warming and biofeedback.

The patient first obtains a baseline recording of digital temperature with a thermister (a finger thermometer). Then he is told to relax and imagine the fingers or the hand becoming warm. Open-ended suggestions allow the patient to discover his own ways of increasing finger temperature; for instance, "soon you will discover some way to make your fingers feel warmer." Finally, the patient opens his eyes, reads the thermister, and notes the magnitude of change. Skin temperature is linearly related to peripheral vasodilation up to about 94°F, after which the relationship becomes complex. At that temperature, a ceiling effect occurs beyond which pervasive peripheral vasomotor changes occur with little or no further increases in skin temperature. For the most part, because warming the fingers and hands produces peripheral vasodilation, hand warming is a means of reducing peripheral resistance.

The patient is also taught slow, rhythmical diaphragmatic breathing (Datey, Deshmukh, Dalvi, & Vinekar, 1969; Fahrion, 1980; Patel, 1973, 1975; Stone & DeLeo, 1976). The patient should practice the breathing for at least 20 minutes. Regular practice of breathing exercises affects blood pressure regulation at a humoral level by reducing levels of catecholamines and renin (Fahrion, 1980; Stone & DeLeo, 1976).

The combination of heart rate reduction and hand warming reduces both aspects of the fight-or-flight reaction implicated in elevated blood pressure, namely, increased cardiac output and peripheral vasoconstriction associated with increased peripheral resistance. The combination of interventions is especially important because of the multilevel regulatory mechanisms operating to control blood pressure. The positive treatment effects of developing voluntary control over either heart rate or peripheral resistance may very well be offset by autoregulatory changes. Numerous studies using direct blood pressure biofeedback have found consistent, but small, decreases in blood pressure (Benson et al., 1971; Blanchard et al., 1979; Deabler et al., 1973; Elder et al., 1973; Miller, 1975; Seer, 1979; Shapiro et al., 1977; Surwitt et al., 1982, p. 70; Weiner, 1970), presumably because more significant biofeedback-mediated reductions are canceled out by autoregulatory increases in cardiac output. Williams (1975) believes that, therefore, the only effective way to circumvent these autoregulatory reactions is to offer biofeedback for reduction in both cardiac output and peripheral resistance. Others believe that facilitating general autonomic nervous system stability by means of progressive muscle relaxation is more important than either biofeedback strategy. Multimodal interventions have the advantage of addressing multiple levels of blood pressure regulation: (a) generalized autonomic nervous system activity, (b) cardiac output, (c) peripheral resistance, and (d) release and uptake of catecholamines, renin, and aldosterone-angiotensin.

It is especially important to encourage the patient to practice regularly at home (Green & Green, 1979). Compliance with home training is associated with a positive treatment outcome (Kristt & Engel, 1975). Training in voluntary control over some of the psychophysiological mechanisms involved in blood pressure regulation requires diligent, regular practice. As with learning any physical skill, for example, playing tennis, "visceral learning" (Miller, Di Cara, Solomon, Weiss, & Dworkin, 1970), or the development of a "psychophysiological self-regulatory skill" (Fahrion, 1980), requires consistent training toward specified training goals. One goal of practice is to produce quickly a generalized relaxation-response (Benson, 1975). Another goal is to become proficient in altering the peripheral vasomotor response. Fahrion (1980) uses a criterion of greater than or equal to 95°F as the goal of regular hand-warming practice. He also emphasizes that patients should attempt progressively to warm larger and larger surface areas of the body, starting, for example, with the fingers and moving on to the hand, the lower arm, the entire arm, the toes, the feet, and finally the entire legs. Patients who can warm large surface areas quickly and consistently are most likely to benefit from the treatment.

Once the patient has learned this self-regulatory skill, we recommend practice in high-risk situations. Labile hypertensives show elevations in blood pressure in particular situations (Surwitt et al., 1982). Self-monitoring is the means of identifying the high-risk situations specific to the individual. The patient is encouraged to anticipate those situations that are associated with elevated blood pressure and to practice just prior to entering the given situation. Skilled patients are able to produce the generalized relaxation response and the vasodilatory response within a very few minutes, sometimes in seconds, just by thinking about them. Posthypnotic suggestions are used to reinforce the production of the psychophysiological response just prior to and during a high-risk situation. Sometimes it is necessary to desensitize the patient to trigger situations, that is, those to which blood pressure is especially reactive (Surwitt et al., 1982). Nonhypnotic (Suinn, 1974) and hypnotic (Yanovski, 1962) desensitization can be used to disrupt the dissociations between certain classes of stimuli and cardiovascular reactivity. A hierarchy of situations associated with greater and greater elevations in blood pressure is constructed. Instructions for hypnotic relaxation and hand warming are given. The patient then tries to maintain the relaxation and vasodilation while imagining a series of stressful situations along the stimulus-hierarchy.

Fahrion (1980) recommends a course of behavioral training that takes about 10 to 20 weeks to produce a stable effect on blood pressure. Our own hypnotic treatment follows this protocol. The goal of the treatment is to lower blood pressure to 120/80 (or 140/80 or 150/80 for patients over 65 years of age) (Goodfriend, 1983). We recommend lowering both diastolic blood pressure and systolic blood pressure. Traditionally, diastolic blood pressure is the target of behavioral interventions and has been associated with morbidity and mortality (Kannel & Dawber, 1973), but systolic blood pressure is more closely associated with morbidity and mortality in men over 45 years of age. A related goal is to enable the patient to maintain the lowered blood pressure while reducing the use of medication (Fahrion, 1980). About one third of all patients are able to attain normotensive levels without the use of medication. These patients are likely to produce a postural hypotensive response at some point in the course of treatment because of the synergistic effect of the pharmacological and behavioral treatment. There need be no guess work about when to reduce medication. A graph is made of the weekly mean blood pressure. When the diastolic blood pressure reaches a mean of 80 or below and is maintained for 4 weeks at that level, medication is reduced by 20%. If the normotensive blood pressure is maintained, about 20% reduction is made and kept until the blood pressure elevates. If it does not, more 20% cuts are made until the medication has been discontinued. By using the graph, the patient and his physician can see the progress and know exactly when to decrease or increase medication according to the established criterion.

There is a tendency for blood pressure to drift up over time, even when treatment has been successful (Miller, 1975). This phenomenon appears to be the result of an autoregulatory mechanism that resets blood pressure (Fahrion, 1980). To prevent relapse, the patient must have at his disposal a set of tools for maintaining the positive treatment effects (Patel & North, 1975; Taylor et al., 1977); otherwise, the hypertension returns. Frumkin, Nathan, Prout, & Cohen (1978), Miller (1975), and Surwitt et al. (1982), recommend periodic booster sessions or multiple courses of treatment to offset the displacement of the baseline upward over time.

Cognitive therapy, especially regarding thoughts associated with poor time management, and life style counseling also are useful in the service of relapse prevention. Weight reduction and smoking cessation programs are a "must" where appropriate. A regular exercise program is recommended, although patients must learn to avoid isometric exercise because it elevates blood pressure.

Some patients fail to benefit from the hypnobehavioral treatment of blood pressure. The reasons for the failure are often unclear. Some of these patients fail because of underlying emotional conflicts associated with maintaining elevated blood pressure. Although it is not always easy to identify these patients, an exploratory hypnodynamic therapy may uncover conflicts associated with causing or maintaining the elevated blood pressure, or with noncompliance with the hypnobehavioral treatment regimen. Psychotherapy (Moses, Daniels, & Nickerson, 1951; Reiser, Brust, & Ferris, 1951; and hypnoanalysis (Bryan, 1960) are sometimes useful for reducing blood pressure in such cases.

Clinical Outcome

Outcome studies of the hypnotic control of blood pressure are rare. Although Deabler et al. (1973), and Friedman & Taub (1977; 1978) report modest decreases in blood pressure resulting from a combination of progressive muscle relaxation and hypnosis, these studies fail to consider the training effect emphasized in the Fahrion (1980) nonhypnotic behavioral treatment protocol. Deabler's training lasted only four days; Friedman and Taub's, only 3 weeks. Our own impressions are consistent with those of Fahrion: a minimum of 10 to 20 weeks of *consistent* daily practice both at home and in high-risk situations is necessary to effect significant and lasting reductions in blood pressure. We hope that this outline of the treatment protocol will stimulate further outcome studies on multimodal hypnobehavioral interventions of relatively longer duration than those reported in the current literature.

ASTHMA

The Psychobiology of Asthma

Asthma is a psychopsysiological disorder that may be defined as abnormally increased responsiveness of the airways to various stimuli. The airways become significantly narrowed. There is an interference with air exchange, primarily with expiration (Dawson & Simon, 1984; Purcell & Weiss, 1970). Asthma represents an intermittent, variable, and reversible form of obstruction of the airways (Chai, 1975; Chai, Purcell, Brady & Falliers, 1968). Frequence of occurrence is irregular, and manifestations vary from mild to severe. Spontaneous remissions are not infrequent. The obstruction of the airways is due to several factors. The smooth muscles constituting the airways involuntarily contract. In most asthmatics, this condition, the bronchospasm, is the primary cause of obstruction of the airways. Inflammation of the tissues and excessive mucus production also contribute to the narrowing of the bronchial passage in many asthmatics. Because the normal flow of air through the airways is disrupted, the asthmatic is unable to breathe properly. Inhaled air remains trapped in the small airways. Expiration is forced, difficult, and slow. The wheezing sounds commonly accompanying asthmatic breathing are caused by air flowing through a spasmed region of the larger airways.

Wheezing is often taken by the patient to signify increased obstruction of the lung passages, although it does not invariably accompany such obstruction (Purcell & Weiss, 1970). Wheezing itself is a poor indicator of the degree of bronchospasm (Dawson & Simon, 1984). Though a history of repeated episodes of wheezing alternating with symptom-free periods is suggestive of a diagnosis of asthma, valid diagnosis often depends on spirometric measures of pulmonary function. Because asthma is an intermittent disorder, pulmonary function may be normal between episodes.

And because asthma is defined by the bronchospastic response of the airways to various stimuli, a confirmed diagnosis sometimes depends on direct tests of bronchial hyperactivity. If the patient's ordinary pulmonary function decreases by more than 20% when challenged by exercise, aeroallergens, or bronchospastic drugs such as Methacholine, the patient is very likely to have hyperactive airways.

There are various causes of hyperactivity of the airways: allergens; infections; irritants; medications; and stress. One or several of these precipitants may increase the obstruction of airways in a given person. Allergic persons show increased sensitivity of the airways when exposed to aeroallergens, such as pollens, spores, and animal hair. If the asthmatic episodes are seasonal, pollen and spores are suspected. When the episodes are perennial, dust spores and other allergens in the home may cause the asthma. If the episodes occur sporadically contact with an allergen such as a cat or dog is suspected. In each instance, exposure to the allergen results in the production of immunoglobulin E antibodies. Histamine and other substances are then released into the bronchial tissues. Inflammation of the tissues and bronchospasm through stimulation of the airways' receptor sites develops (Dawson & Simon, 1984). Allergens are an important class of precipitants, but their role in asthma may have been overemphasized. About 50% to 70% of all asthmatics manifest an immune-mediated hypersensitivity, but no more than 5% of asthmatic episodes (Dawson & Simon, 1984).

Infections—upper respiratory infections, acute bronchitis, and the common cold—are the most frequent precipitants of asthmatic episodes in both children and adults (Creer, 1979). The airways may also be highly sensitive to a variety of air pollutants, especially sulfur dioxide. Among the list of irritants, tobacco smoke poses the greatest danger (Dawson & Simon, 1984). Certain drugs have been implicated in asthma attacks. About 8% of all asthmatics are sensitive to aspirin (Dawson & Simon, 1984; Stevenson, Simon, & Mathison, 1980). Sulfites commonly used as food preservatives can also contribute to bronchospasm. Even the drugs used to control asthma, if abused, may exacerbate the condition. Overuse of bronchodilator inhalants may increase the reactivity of the bronchial muscles to slight variations in stimuli and thereby contribute to bronchial hyperactivity. Exposure to low temperature is a powerful stressor. Cold air directly stimulates the airway receptors, resulting in bronchospasm. Stress induced by continuous exercise (more than 5 minutes) also can cause bronchoconstriction of the large airways (Ghory, 1975). Bronchospasm is not caused by the exercise, but rather by the cold air. During strenuous exercise, individuals tend to breathe through the mouth. Cold air is taken directly into the airways without being warmed and humidified by the nasal passages (Strauss, McFadden, Ingram, & Jaeger, 1977). Nasal breathing attenuates the degree of bronchospasm (Shturman, Zeballos, & Buckley, 1978).

Emotional stress may also precipitate asthmatic episodes. Discussion of unpleasant memories and situations can increase bronchospasm and wheezing (Faulkner, 1941; Stevenson & Ripley, 1952). Dekker and Groen (1956) selected stressful emotional stimuli from the personal history of each of their patients and used those stimuli to induce attacks. The contribution of affective states as a precipitant of asthma is complex. When certain emotions become associated with asthmatic episodes, distinguishing cause from effect can be difficult: Does the emotion cause the episode, or is the emotion a consequence of the episode? More often than not, anxiety, depression, frustration, and anger are the result of having an asthmatic attack rather than its cause (Purcell & Weiss, 1970). On the other hand, emotions are a powerful class of triggers, at least for some people. In them, the experience of certain emotions—fear, anger, excitement—may directly activate the autonomic nervous system, which, in turn, may trigger the bronchospasm and mucous secretion characteristic of the asthmatic episode (Purcell & Weiss, 1970). Or the expressions accompanying certain emotions may indirectly stimulate the vagus nerve, which, in turn, triggers the attack because the expression of certain emotions is accompanied by radical changes in air flow, for example, holding one's breath, crying, laughing, gasping (Gold, Kessler & Yu, 1972).

Underlying the multiple causes of asthmatic episodes is a common underlying mechanism: whatever triggers the condition that narrows the bronchial passages (bronchospasm, mucous plugging, or inflammation) contributes to asthma. This obstruction of the airways can occur through direct stimulation of the airway receptors as mediated by the vagus nerve (emotional expression), the autonomic nervous system, the immune system (allergic response), or a combination of these. Inasmuch as most of these triggers contribute to bronchial hyperactivity, and only some contribute to mucous plugging and inflammation, bronchial activity is the main defining feature of the disorder. A number of factors singly or in combination may provoke an episode for a given patient.

"Autonomic hyperactivity" (Magonet, 1960) is an important dimension along the continuum of events resulting in asthma, at least for those people for whom stress, especially emotional stress, is significant as a provoking factor, and perhaps also where other triggers are implicated. Whether autonomic sensitivity is a characteristic of all types of asthmatics remains to be demonstrated. Evidence suggests dysfunction of the beta adrenergic receptors, (Szentivanyi, 1968; Dolovich, Hargreave, & Kerigan, 1973; Mathe & Knapp, 1971), so that sympathetic activation through stressful stimulation induces bronchospasm.

Bronchial hyperactivity in response to a variety of stimuli is the most important dimension along the continuum of events in asthma. For asthmatics, the small airways usually manifest some degree of chronic bronchospasm, although the degree of spasm varies with the stimulus conditions. The existence, and sometimes the severity of chronic spasm, of the small airways often goes unnoticed by the patient. When an acute brochospasm forms in the large airways along with the chronic spasm of the small airways, the patient experiences an asthma attack.

In addition to the bronchospasm, the mucosal cells thicken. Irritation may contribute to excessive discharge of mucus. Water may be lost, so that the mucus becomes increasingly viscous. Mucus plugs may narrow the bronchial lumen beyond the decreased size already produced by the bronchospasm. An inflammatory response may also accompany the bronchospasm. Histamine and other mediating factors are released into the tissue. Eosinophils and desquamated epithelial cells infiltrate the bronchial muscle layers.

For some asthmatics, hyperactivity of the airways is not always the direct result of triggering stimuli. Numerous studies have shown that genuine asthma attacks can be conditioned in animals and humans (Franks & Leigh, 1959; Turnbull, 1962).

Ottenberg, Stein, Lewis and Hamilton (1958) were able in classical conditioning experiments to produce asthma in a guinea pig, a result that has been replicated. Justesen, Braun, Garrison, and Pendleton (1970) and Deeker, Pelser and Groen (1957) were able to condition asthma in two patients with allergic and emotional stimuli. The patients were conditioned to produce asthma attacks in response to a neutral solvent, but the result could not be replicated. Recent studies have forced some qualifications of the notion of learned asthma. Only certain asthmatics manifest a conditioning effect, probably those who have hyperactive airways, are reactive to emotional stimuli (Horton, Suda, Kinsman, Souhrada, & Spector, 1977), and are exposed to the right kind of learning situations (Creer, 1979). In such patients, the hyperactivity of the airways takes on a life of its own, partially dissociated from the original provoking stimuli. The bronchial hyperactivity is maintained even in the absence of such stimuli.

Figure 3.6 summarizes the different stages in the causative pathway of asthma: (a) primary causative factors (trigger stimuli); (b) autonomic hyperactivity; (c) chronic bronchial hyperactivity of the small airways with an acute overlay of large airway hyperactivity corresponding to the asthma attack; (d) local changes (e.g., mucus buildup and inflammation); (e) secondary maintenance factors (conditioning effects and anticipatory panic).

Many of the stages of this model were derived from pharmacological investigations. Certain substances are available to intervene at any level in

I. Causative Factors

	BEHAVIORAL	MEDICAL

A. Stress / Environmental Factors
Self—Monitoring
Stimulus—Control
Desensitization
Hyposensitization
Cromolyn

B. Autonomic Instability
Relaxation Training

C. Bronchospasm

1. Chronic Bronchospasm of the Small airways
Peak Flow
Biofeedback
Breathing Exercises
Bronchodilators

2. Acute Bronchospasm of the Large Airways
Discrimination of Stages of Onset of Asthma Attack and Use of Coping Strategies

D. Local Changes

1. Mucus Plugging
2. Inflammation
Visualization of Humidified Breathing
Steroids
Mucolytic Agents

II. Maintenance Factors

A. Conditioning of the Airways
B. Anticipatory Panic
Systematic Desensitization

FIG. 3.6. Factors in the Causation, Maintenance, and Treatment of Asthma

the causative pathway. For example, drugs can be used to manage provoking stimuli. Cromolyn sodium controls asthma by inhibition of the mast cell activation in immunoglobulin E-mediated asthma. Antimicrobial agents control bronchial infection and thereby reduce the possibility of bronchospasm secondary to the infection. Certain sympathomimetic agents correct the dysfunction of the autonomic adrenergic receptors. Methylated xanthine bronchodilators directly reverse the bronchospasm by relaxing the bronchial smooth muscle. Other substances work on the local level. Mucolytic agents stimulate the bronchial glands, and thereby decrease the viscosity of the mucus so it can be expectorated easily. Anti-inflammatory agents, notably the corticosteroids, exert a powerful effect on the inflammatory component. Each substance has potential side-effects. The corticosteroids are the most harmful. Because of the side-effects and drug interactions, it has so far been impossible to produce a combination drug that acts at each level along the causative continuum.

Hypnobehavioral Treatment of Asthma

One advantage of behavioral and hypnotic intervention is that it is possible to design a multidimensional treatment protocol to include specific interventions at each level of the causative pathway. Multidimensional treatment offers a clinical advantage: the outcome of multidimensional treatment interventions is considerably better than that of unidimensional treatment. Although most of the behavioral and hypnotic literature discusses unidimensional treatment, we advocate a multidimensional approach, as follows.

Hypnotic treatment of asthma begins with a careful assessment in the following areas: (a) identification of the classes of trigger agents by means of the patient's history; (b) current pulmonary functioning by means of spirometric measures; (c) the extent of bronchial hyperactivity by means of challenge tests; (d) hypnotizability; (e) subjective symptoms during the asthma attack; (f) usual coping strategies during the attack; (g) current use and abuse of medication; (h) emotional and behavioral sequelae to attacks; (i) reaction of significant others to the asthma; (j) impact of asthma on behavior, life style, and self-concept.

The asthmatic patient is taught to keep a daily record of the fluctuations in pulmonary functioning and of the context in which these fluctuations occur. Self-monitoring of pulmonary functioning must include both subjective and objective measures. The patient is told to rate, three or four times a day, the degree of wheezing on a 5–point Likert scale. The patient can objectively monitor pulmonary functioning with the aid of a mini-Wright Peak Flow Meter. The peak flow device is an inexpensive portable plastic tube into which the patient can blow. As the expired air is expelled, it moves an indicator calibrated in liters per minute. The reading is a valid indicator of the flow through the large airways. A low reading signifies airway obstruction; a high reading, normal air passage. The measure of peak expiratory flow rate (PEFR) correlates very highly ($r = .86$) with forced expiratory volume (FEV_1) obtained in the laboratory with the more expensive spirometer (Creer, 1979). In other words, the device has the distinct advantage that the patient can take it home and check his pulmonary functioning (at least, that of the large airways) objectively.

Both subjective and objective measurements are taken because asthmatics are notoriously inaccurate in their awareness of pulmonary functioning. Changes in subjective reports seldom reflect similar changes in objective physiological measurements in pulmonary functioning (Chai et al., 1968). The patient may report a marked increase in wheezing with no apparent change in bronchial activity, or he may report no wheezing during an episode of major bronchospasm sufficient to precipitate an asthma attack. Fifteen percent of patients are unable to detect the presence of airways obstruction large enough to cause a full asthma attack (Rubinfeld & Pain, 1976). One advantage of having patients keep both subjective and objective records is to impress on them the initial inaccuracy of their subjective judgment of their pulmonary functioning and to teach them a valid way to learn to detect fluctuations in bronchial activity, so they can learn to prevent or master them.

The patient should assess pulmonary functioning at frequent intervals. The frequency of self-monitoring may be the most important factor in training patients to detect airways activity (Chai et al., 1968; Creer, 1979). Calculating the daily and weekly mean of peak flow, rather than utilizing single measurements, also corrects for factors that bias individual readings, such as effort and motivation (Harm, Marion, Kotses, & Creer, 1984).

The patient must carefully record peak flow and the degree of wheezing at various intervals throughout the day. Each time a reading is taken, the patient should carefully note the context—record where he is, the nature of the environment, what he is doing, and what he is feeling at the time. It is also important to record exactly when medication is taken during the day, because antiasthmatic medication clearly confounds the interaction between bronchial activity and the provoking situation.

The patient and the therapist inspect the self-monitoring records regularly. After correcting for the medication effect, they search for underlying patterns to identify which situations consistently are associated with decreases in peak flow measurements and which are associated with increases in peak flow. Through careful study of the records, it is usually possible to identify high-risk situations and high-risk times associated with bronchial hyperactivity. If the patient keeps careful records of the context in which his attacks occur, it is often possible to identify specific provoking stimuli. Sometimes the patient confirms what he already knows. He sees, for example, that a particular aeroallergen has a direct effect on his bronchial activity. Sometimes the patient is surprised to discover new stimuli associated with bronchospasm, agents he had not expected to cause him any trouble. The objective self-monitoring of peak flow, unlike the estimations of wheezing, take the guesswork out of assessing bronchial activity. More important, the patient takes an interest in and responsibility for his own pulmonary functioning.

According to Simon (1984), "The best method of treating asthma, where it is applicable, is to identify and avoid the provoking factors" (p. 133). Through self-monitoring, the patient learns to identify trigger stimuli. He is counseled to avoid or alleviate them. For example, the allergic patient may need to reduce contact with dust by remaining outside while the house rugs are brushed, or he may have to refrain from eating even small amounts of foods to which he is allergic. Motivation to alleviate or avoid trigger stimuli can be reinforced with posthypnotic suggestions.

Once the likely trigger stimuli have been identified, a specific intervention can be designed. Two types of interventions are recommended: (a) stimulus-change and (b) desensitization. Many asthmatics make a remarkably quick recovery when removed from their natural environment and hospitalized (Purcell & Weiss, 1970). Presumably the asthmatic is removed from the environmental agents (aeroallergens, irritants) that cause the bronchospastic reaction. However, asthmatics sometimes show improvement in the hospital, even when their room is sprayed with the dust of their own homes. The improvement is due partly to an alteration in their expectation of an attack and partly to the lack of family reinforcement of maladaptive responses to the anticipation of an attack. Stimulus-control must include attempts not only to avoid trigger stimuli but also to ascertain the psychological meaning of the particular stimuli to the patient.

It is more practical to desensitize patients to trigger stimuli than to attempt stimulus-control, especially when it is impossible to avoid certain stimuli. For allergic asthmatics, immunotherapeutic hyposensitization is done by exposing them systematically to increasing amounts of the allergen. If bronchospasm occurs (as measured by peak flow readings), it is controlled by medication (e.g., isoprenaline). The patient gradually develops a tolerance for greater and greater amounts of the allergen (Herxheimer & Prior, 1952).

For asthmatics in whom stress and emotions trigger attacks, systematic desensitization or hypnobehavioral desensitization is indicated. Nonhypnotic behavioral desensitization has been successfully used to increase the asthmatic's tolerance for stressful stimuli (Cooper, 1964; Creer, 1974;

Creer, Renne, & Christian, 1976; Moore, 1965; Walton, 1960). The patient and the therapist first construct a hierarchy of stressful stimuli usually associated with the asthma attack. The patient is then taught progressive relaxation. While in a relaxed state, the patient imagines a series of scenes in which he encounters the stressful stimuli from the least to the most stressful. The patient continues to practice relaxation over a number of sessions until he can remain deeply relaxed while imagining contact with those stimuli that previously were most likely to produce an asthmatic episode. The outcome of such behavioral desensitization is very impressive. Creer claims 100% improvement in a sample of 30 asthmatic patients (Creer, 1974). Success was achieved when objective measures of pulmonary functioning (peak flow) were used to evaluate desensitization (Moore, 1965).

Hypnotic desensitization is indicated for hypnotizable patients. The few clinical papers on hypnotic desensitization of asthma deal with a limited range of stimuli to which the desensitization method was applied. Hypnotic desensitization has been used to desensitize the patient against anticipatory anxiety and panic regarding the onset of an asthmatic episode. Trance was induced by suggesting waves of relaxation (Kennedy, 1957; Moorefield, 1971). We recommend hypnotic desensitization to the full range of stimuli that have been determined to be noxious to the individual patient. Hypnosis has the advantages of allowing the therapist in a single session to present the patient with a number of situations from the stimulus hierarchy and reinforcing generalization of the results to everyday contact with the provoking stimuli by means of posthypnotic suggestion. The trance also is a tool for discovering strategies for coping with provoking stimuli, strategies that might otherwise not be accessible to consciousness.

Another level towards which the clinician addresses interventions is the autonomic hyperactivity characteristic of at least an important subgroup of, if not of all, asthmatics (Magonet, 1960). Self-hypnotic relaxation of asthmatics (Fry, 1957; Maher-Loughnan, 1970; Maher-Loughnan, MacDonald, Mason, & Fry, 1962), self-hypnosis combined with relaxing imagery (Maher-Loughnan, 1975), and self-hypnosis combined with ego-strengthening suggestions (Collison, 1968; Diamond, 1959) have all been shown to produce significant reductions in the subjective reports of wheezing. Unfortunately, none of the hypnotic relaxation studies have utilized objective measures of pulmonary functioning. However, studies utilizing nonhypnotic progressive relaxation with asthmatics (Alexander, Miklich, & Hershkoff 1972; Davis, Saunders, Creer, & Chai, 1973) have demonstrated a significant improvement in peak flow (PEFR) as compared to normal control subjects.

The patient who learns the skill of relaxation and incorporates it into his everyday life style diminishes the sensitivity of the autonomic nervous system. Relaxation has been shown to increase parasympathetic activity while decreasing sympathetic activity (Moorefield, 1971) and stabilizing the activation of the autonomic nervous system in response to stimuli (Germana, 1969). Therefore, the hypnotized patient is given suggestions for deep relaxation and is encouraged to practice self-hypnotic relaxation daily.

Still another level to which the clinician addresses interventions is the bronchial hyperactivity itself, both the chronic bronchospasm of the small airways and the acute bronchospasm of the large airways (the asthma attack). The immediate goal of the intervention is to expand the bronchial passages (bronchodilation) so that air exchange is not obstructed; the ultimate goal is to stabilize bronchial activity, i.e., to reduce the vulnerability to bronchospasm. There are various ways to achieve these goals: (a) direct hypnotic suggestion for relaxed breathing; (b) systematic breathing training; (c) biofeedback of pulmonary function with or without hypnosis.

Direct suggestions can be given to the patient to "relax and breathe easier" (Citron, 1968; Moorefield, 1971; Stewart, 1957; White, 1961). Such suggestions typically make the patient feel better, and he reports that breathing is, indeed, easier. The patient may also become convinced that the degree of bronchospasm has been reduced. However, direct hypnotic suggestions such as these seldom lead to any improvement in pulmonary functioning. In fact, peak flow may decrease, even though the patient genuinely believes his condition has improved (White, 1961). If direct suggestions are at all useful in affecting bronchospasm, their effect is limited to a small subgroup of asthmatics. Although no systematic investigations have been undertaken, we suspect that direct suggestions are useful only for highly hypnotizable asthmatics.

A more reliable way to influence bronchospasm is through hypnotic systematic training in physiological breathing (Marchesi, 1949). Because asthmatics have difficulty with forced expiration, Marchesi had his patients breathe in a way that emphasized exhaling. After being instructed in diaphragmatic breathing, patients were told to "breathe in such a manner that the expiration is longer [in duration] than the inspiration" (p. 16). We recommend a slight modification of this procedure inasmuch as the issue is one of the ability to expire, not the duration of the expiration. The patient is first taught diaphragmatic breathing. It is our belief that unlike breathing exercises used elsewhere, proper diaphragmatic breathing is not "belly breathing," which confounds the use of the abdominal muscles with diaphragmatic action. To ensure proper diaphragmatic action, we teach our patients *bellows* breathing. The patient places his hands on his waist above his hips, with the fingers extending slightly over the sides of the stomach and the thumb slightly over the side of the back. He is told to focus his attention carefully on how his hands are moved when he breathes and, specifically, to detect the degree of outward movement (like the bellows expanding sideways). In proper diaphragmatic breathing, the main thrust of the hands is outwards to each side; if the diaphragmatic action is confounded by the movement of the abdominal muscles, the main thrust of the hands is forward. The patient can thus use the hands as a feedback device to train himself in diaphragmatic breathing.

Next, the patient is given instructions for expiratory breathing. He is asked to inspire normally but to put slight but persistent emphasis on the expiration as if slightly but gently pushing each breath. (Too much effort can increase the degree of bronchospasm.) Sometimes the patient can enhance the effect with imagery, for example, by imagining that he is sitting in a comfortable chamber with expandable or elastic walls. On each expiration, the patient imagines pushing the walls back with the force of the breath. The patient practices the combination of diaphragmatic and forced expiratory breathing each day in self-hypnosis. Daily peak flow readings are used to monitor the progress. These breathing exercises constitute a form of visceral learning, which enables the patient to dilate the bronchial passages, and, if the practice is incorporated into everyday living, to stabilize bronchial activity. As one patient, who imagined pushing out the walls of the room with each expiration, described them, the exercises were a way of increasing his "breathing room."

Sometimes self-efficacy with regard to the breathing exercises can be improved with biofeedback. Peak flow measurements can be conditioned. The patient is provided with feedback in the form of ongoing peak flow measurements and positively reinforced for high readings (bronchodilations) (Renne & Creer, 1976). Direct biofeedback of the degree of airways resistance has also been shown to improve pulmonary functioning (Feldman, 1976; Olton & Noonberg, 1980; Vachon & Rich, 1976). In other words, bronchial activity is to some extent subject to operant conditioning. When reinforced or given feedback, patients can learn to gain voluntary control over bronchial activity. Peak flow feedback ensures that the patient is conducting the breathing exercises properly. The patient should take his peak flow measurements prior to, immediately after, and 30 minutes after self-hypnotic breathing practice.

The final level to which the therapist addresses interventions is the local level, namely, the local tissues and the chemical changes that occur in them in the asthmatic condition. Hypnosis is known to affect physiological processes (Barber, 1961), and direct hypnotic suggestions are sometimes effective in reducing mucus plugging. Magonet (1960) suggested to his patients, ". . . whatever phlegm you have got is going to dry up and you are not going to make any more" (p. 124). Actually, such a suggestion is questionable, because the problem is not to dry up the mucus but to loosen it, for, in the asthmatic, the mucus has lost its water content and become dry and viscous (Dawson & Simon, 1984). It is better to give the patient suggestions that the mucus is becoming more liquid, is loosening up, and is being expectorated. Imagery suggestions enhance the effect. The patient imagines being in a pleasant climate and a place of his own choosing where there is warm but moist air. On each inhalation the patient imagines breathing in the warm, moist air so that the air taken into the lungs is properly humidified. Systematic training in imagining that one breathes in moist air helps clear mucus plugging. Whether or not such visualizations represent direct effects on inflammatory processes remains to be investigated.

The four levels of intervention—altering sensitivity to provoking stimuli, stabilizing the autonomic nervous system, reducing bronchospasm and stabilizing bronchial activity, and reversing local effects—taken as a unit constitute a comprehensive, multidimensional approach to asthma treatment through reversal of the chronic psychophysiological changes associated with asthma. After the patient has learned the treatment sufficiently well, the treatment emphasis is shifted to prevention of the acute episode, the asthma attack itself. The patient begins this phase of the treatment by learning to recognize early warning symptoms (Creer, 1979). In the waking state the patient is asked to identify whatever signs he is aware of that immediately precede an asthma attack, such as moodiness, excited feelings, watery eyes, or a "funny feeling" in his chest. Next the patient is given an extensive list of early warning signs typically reported by asthma patients. The list includes signs the patient frequently experiences but forgot to report. Then the patient rank-orders the list into a "behavioral chain" of events leading up to the attack itself (Creer, 1979). The patient prepares a similar list of typical coping strategies and identifies the typical steps taken to alleviate the anticipated attack. The object of the inquiry is to have the patient identify earlier and earlier warning signs to be able to put learned coping strategies rapidly into effect.

Hypnosis is used to discover early warning signs and coping strategies normally out of the patient's conscious awareness. For this, hypnoprojective techniques are employed. The hypnotherapist suggests that the patient imagine a scene or play or have a dream in which the very earliest sign of an asthma attack is somehow expressed in the imagery. Hypnoprojective methods are also used to uncover new coping strategies for the attack itself. The patient imagines a scene or has a hypnotic dream that discloses even more effective ways to prevent the attack from coming on.

It is also advisable to teach the patient to identify the acute changes in pulmonary functioning at the onset of the attack itself. Rubinfeld and Pain (1977a, 1977b) have devised a nonhypnotic method for the patient to learn to detect small changes in the bronchial activity of the large airways at the very onset of an attack. Patients are challenged with increasing doses of bronchospastic drugs (e.g., Methacholine) to recognize the point of just noticeable tightness. The procedure can be repeated until the patient clearly recognizes the signs of acute deterioration in pulmonary functioning association with the onset of an asthmatic episode. Once the patient learns accurately to recognize the beginning of a major bronchospasm of the large airways, he can practice the appropriate coping strategies before the attack has the opportunity to develop.

The patient can also scrutinize his self-monitoring records in order to learn to predict attacks (Taplin & Creer, 1978). If the patient has faithfully kept self-monitoring records over an extended period of time, it is possible to identify critical PEFR values associated with impending asthma episodes. Once he has discovered his own critical peak flow values, he can identify, even in the absence of early warnings signs, critical periods when he is at high risk for an attack.

Having identified the time and signs predictive of an asthma attack, the patient practices the previously learned coping strategies to minimize the possibility of bronchospasm and mucus plugging. Again, posthypnotic suggestions are especially useful: "At the very first moment you notice any of the signs of an asthma attack or otherwise suspect an attack could occur, it will automatically occur to you to become deeply relaxed, inhale the warm, moist air, and gently push out the air." Posthypnotic suggestions can be tailored to individual coping strategies: they increase the likelihood that the patient will put the coping strategies into practice exactly when they are most needed. The goal is to put them into effect quickly enough to induce bronchodilation and thereby cut off the impending attack before it develops.

There is some reason to believe that suggestions or post-hypnotic suggestions applied in this way have a direct effect on the activity of the large airways implicated in the asthma attack. Waking suggestions for either bronchoconstriction or bronchodilation have been shown to have a direct effect on the size of the large airways, at least for those who both have hyperactive airways, as defined by challenge tests, and also manifest autonomically mediated physiological changes in response to emotional stimuli (Horton et al., 1977; Spector, Luparello, Kopetzky, Souhrada, & Kinsman, 1976). That is, patients whose asthma attacks are stress induced are more likely to be responsive to direct suggestions for bronchodilation. Sinclair-Gieban (1960) reports the successful treatment of a patient with status asthmaticus by using the simple suggestion, "Now you will find the wheezing stops and your breathing becomes free and easy" (p. 1651). Of course, the effects for most patients are rarely that dramatic, yet there is some reason to believe that posthypnotic application of learned breathing exercises and other coping strategies at the onset of an asthma attack can have a direct effect on the large airways. The breathing can stimulate bronchodilation and thus prevent the attack.

The final dimension of working with the acute episode is to alleviate the anticipatory panic that accompanies the attack in a significant subgroup of patients. Such an intervention is especially recommended for patients whose "asthma comes by sudden onset and tends to worsen rapidly" (Creer, 1979, p. 177). Hypnotic desensitization (Moorefield, 1971) is used as previously described, but the desensitization hierarchy is constructed around the panic experience itself and not around the provoking stimuli. Ego-strengthening suggestions (Hartland, 1965) are also given to increase the patient's confidence in coping with the attack (Collison, 1968; Hanley, 1974; Rose, 1967). Where the panic is especially resistant to desensitizaton and ego-strengthening suggestions, dynamic hypnotherapy or hypno-analysis is used to uncover the meaning of the panic (Van Pelt, 1949, 1953).

The efficacy of the multidimensional treatment protocol for both the chronic and the acute components of the asthmatic obstruction of the airways is contingent on the patient's practicing. Skillful practice requires taking the peak flow readings and practicing the exercises (relaxation, breathing) regularly for a reasonable period. The frequency of practice is critical; practice three to four times daily is recommended. Consistency is also important; it is better to practice briefly each day than to practice irregularly but for longer times. Practice results in the ability to produce the desired effects immediately. Patients are encouraged to practice until they are able to relax on cue (Sirota & Mahoney, 1974) and can produce bronchodilation on cue. The patient should strive to create a conditioned reflex (Marchesi, 1949).

Symptom challenge can be utilized with highly skilled patients. Symptom challenge leads to genuine mastery and decreases the likelihood of relapse over time. Typically, Methacholine and exercise have been used to provoke bronchospasm. Because the large airways are subject to the effects of suggestion, it is advisable, at least for some asthma patients, to attempt symptom challenge through suggestion. Hypnotic suggestions have been used both to provoke and then to alleviate asthma attacks (Brown, 1965; Chong, 1966; Crasilneck & Hall, 1975; Hanley, 1974; Marchesi, 1949). When the patient has learned voluntary control over the bronchospasm, he is hypnotized and given the suggestion that an asthma attack will soon develop. He is also assured that he will be able to successfully stop the attack by utilizing the coping strategies he has already learned. The procedure is repeated until the patient can quickly stop the attack. Then the patient is given a posthypnotic suggestion to apply the same technique whenever an attack begins to occur in the future.

This detailed, multidimensional treatment protocol represents a hypno-behavioral approach to asthma, that is, an integration of hypnosis with the current trends in behavioral medicine as applied to the treatment of asthma. Direct hypnotic suggestions alone are seldom useful in treating asthma except for a limited subgroup of patients. On the other hand, patients may become resistant to the hypnobehavioral interventions and the therapist must change to a hypnodynamic model of therapy in order to explore underlying psychological factors related to either the cause or the maintenance of the asthma. For example, patients can be age-regressed to their first asthma attack (Diamond, 1959) to discover causal factors, or the origins of a panic that maintains an attack can be explored (Hanley, 1974; Van Pelt, 1949, 1953).

The final stage of treatment is designed not for the asthma itself but for the significant consequences it has had for the patient: restriction of activity (Creer, 1979), especially physical activity; impact on self-concept and body image; secondary symptoms, such as, sleep disturbances, substance abuse; depression; and family problems (Creer et al., 1976). A hierarchy of activities is constructed. The patient rehearses in fantasy activities that have previously been avoided, especially exercise, and gradually implements these in everyday life according to his ability to engage in them. Posthypnotic suggestions reinforce enactment of the behavior in everyday life (Marchesi, 1949). Hypnotic visualizations are used to explore and modify the patient's body image and self-concept. Dynamic hypnotherapy can be used to explore the meaning of the illness in the patient's life (Collison, 1968). Ego-strengthening suggestions can enhance the patient's self-image. Emphasis is placed on how much fuller the patient's life can become once the asthma is controlled (Rose, 1967). The goal of rehabilitation is to de-emphasize the central role of the asthma in the patient's life and to emphasize normal adjustment (Creer et al., 1976).

Clinical Outcome

According to Purcell and Weiss (1970), treatment of asthma should achieve three goals: (a) modification of physiological functioning (stabilization of the autonomic nervous system and bronchial activity); (b) narrowing of the range of trigger stimuli; (c) modification of the patient's attitude toward the disorder. Unfortunately, there are very few systematic outcome studies on hypnosis and asthma. Anecdotal studies have been consistently positive. Studies utilizing subjective measures of change, for example, wheezing, have also reported favorable outcomes (Maher-Loughnan, 1970). The discrepancy between subjective and objective measures of pulmonary functioning is well documented (Rubinfeld & Pain, 1976); hence, outcome studies based solely on subjective measures cannot be taken too seriously. Studies utilizing objective measures of pulmonary functioning, have consistently reported negative results (Edwards, 1960; Smith & Burns, 1960; White, 1961), including a deterioration in pulmonary functioning in hypnosis. The hypnotic interventions made in these studies were, however, ill-conceived. Most were limited to simple, direct suggestions to breathe more easily, suggestions likely to be effective for only a relatively small subgroup of asthmatics only, but which were used on unselected groups of asthmatics. So we do not know yet the extent to which more comprehensive hypnotic interventions designed to stabilize autonomic and bronchial activity are effective in controlling asthma.

Moreover, it is as yet unclear whether hypnotic interventions are useful for all asthmatics or only for certain subgroups. Some researchers have argued strongly for discrete subgroups of asthmatics: high allergic potential with low psychological conflict, and low allergic potential with high psychological conflict (Block, Jennings, Harvey, & Simpson, 1964); rapidly remitting asthmatics who do not need drugs versus steroid-dependent ones with slow improvement (Purcell, 1963). The underlying factor cutting across these various classificatory schemata appears to be psychologically induced versus biologically vulnerable asthmatics. Other researchers have challenged the existence of such subgroups (Creer, 1979; Jacobs et al., 1966). We favor the subgroup approach. Although the clinical hypnosis literature on asthma seldom reports details on patient characteristics, what little information is available suggests that hypnosis is most useful for patients meeting the following criteria: (a) mild asthma (Davis et al., 1973; Maher-Loughnan et al., 1962); (b) hyperactive airways, as measured by challenge tests (Horton et al., 1977); (c) asthma readily triggered by emotional stimuli (Diamond, 1959; Maher-Loughnan et al., 1962); and (d) high hypnotizability (Maher-Loughnan et al., 1962; Turner-Warwick, 1966).

THE HYPNOTIC TREATMENT OF GASTROINTESTINAL DISORDERS

Gastrointestinal disorders include: disorders of the upper GI tract (diffuse esophageal spasm, reflux esophagitis, achalasia, and peptic ulcer disease) and disorders of the lower GI tract (irritable bowel syndrome and inflammatory bowel disease). Treatment of GI disorders with hypnosis has not yet evolved substantially compared with, say, hypnotic treatment of pain or other psychophysiological disorders. Few detailed and proven treatment protocols are available. Nevertheless, some suggestions for an approach to treatment can be made.

Psychophysiological Disorders of the Esophagus

Psychophysiological disorders of the esophagus include: achalasia, reflux esophagitis, and diffuse esophageal spasm. Globus hystericus is technically not a psychophysiological disorder but a neurotic symptom, treatable by means of dynamic hypnotherapy or hypnoanalysis.

Achalasia is an organic condition in which the lower esophageal sphincter fails to relax owing to the loss of ganglion cells caused by a lesion in the parasympathetic nerves. As a result, the upper esophagus remains massively dilated, while the lower esophagus is constricted. Food accumulates in the upper esophagus. This condition is not amenable to hypnotic treatment. Functional achalasia, also called *diffuse esophageal spasm* or sometimes *cardiospasm,* whose symptoms are often confused with the organic condition, is amenable to behavioral treatment. Diffuse esophageal spasm is essentially a disorder of motility (Schuster, 1983) and manifests as a large, nonperistaltic contraction of the esophagus accompanied by pain in the substernal area. The spasm of the esophagus may be caused by blackflow of acid from the stomach into the esophagus or, more frequently, by emotional stress. It is well established that stress, especially emotional stress, may result in hypermotility in the esophagus (Rubin, Nagler, Spiro, & Pilot, 1962; Stacher, 1983). At least for some people, this motor reaction, which normally functions only as a defense against physical irritation, becomes the basis for a psychophysiological disorder (Wolff & Almy, 1949). Waking suggestions for relaxation (Wolf & Almy, 1949) and nonhypnotic progressive muscle relaxation have been used effectively to treat diffuse esophageal spasm (Jacobson, 1927). Relaxation training has a direct effect on the motility of the esophagus. The number and magnitude of spasms decrease as relaxation increases (Stacher, 1983). Hypnotic suggestions have also been effective for some patients (Faulkner, 1940). Hypnotic suggestions for generalized bodily relaxation usually suffice to decrease the esophageal spasm. Posthypnotic suggestions are given to reinforce induction of relaxation during stressful situations previously associated with esophageal spasms. Schneck (1958), however, reported a case in which the tendency to relapse was quite high. In that case, hypnosis was used to explore conflicts associated with the cardiospasm. Lasting success followed the working through of the conflicts.

Reflux esophagitis is a condition that results from the upper esophageal sphincter's not remaining tightly closed. As a result, acid flows back into the lower esophagus and causes "heartburn." To our knowledge, there have been no studies on hypnotic treatment of esophageal reflux. Direct biofeedback by means of catheter insertion of the lower esophageal sphincter has shown some promise. In a few hours of biofeedback training (Schuster et al., 1973), patients are able to learn voluntary control over the smooth muscles of which the esophageal sphincter is composed. It has been established that some people can gain voluntary control over the activity of this sphincter; it is possible, then, that hypnotizable individuals can effect such control through hypnotic relaxation.

Peptic Ulcer Disease

Peptic Ulcer Disease (PUD) is characterized by: increased gastric acid and pesin production at the sight, smell, sound, taste, and thought of food; inadequate mucus secretion; and gastric pain that occurs when the stomach is empty. The causes of PUD are unclear, but it is known that damage to the gastric mucosa caused by certain drugs (steroids, salicylates) contributes to the disease. In many cases, stress-related hyperactivity of the autonomic nervous system also contributes (Kroger & Fezler, 1976). Autonomically mediated stress responses may contribute to the disregulation of the mechanisms that normally control secretion (Brooks & Richardson, 1980; Walker, 1983). It is well established that a variety of stimuli can affect gastric motility as well as gastric secretion: eating, thinking about eating, or perceiving stimuli associated with eating; exercise; cognition, for example, mental arithmetic; and emotional stress, for example, anger, anxiety, or depression (see Walker, 1983, for review). In animals, intermittent stress in situations over which the animal has little control or cannot counteract not only affects gastric functioning but leads to tissue damage. It is possible to "induce" ulcers in rats and monkeys (Brady, 1958; Weiss et al., 1976). Whether ulcers in humans are the direct result of similarly stressful situations is unclear, but the research strongly suggests that emotional stress and maladaptive ways of coping with emotions may contribute to peptic ulcer disease, at least for certain people (Walker, 1983; Walker & Sandman, 1977). Compared with normal persons, patients with PUD give a variety of atypical physiological responses (heart rate, galvanic skin potential, electrogastrogram, and electromyogram) to stimuli (Walker & Sandman, 1977). This atypical response pattern suggests stress-related chronic disregulation of gastric activity.

Hypnobehavioral treatment of peptic ulcer disease begins with daily self-monitoring of the gastric pain associated with PUD. Patients keep a daily record of each episode of the gastric pain and rate its intensity. They also record the time of day they felt the pain (in relation to meals), the situation, and whatever they were thinking or feeling at the time. They also record when they took medications (Walker, 1983). The therapist and patient try to identify the patient's specific high-risk times and high-risk situations. Kroger and Fezler (1976) used hypnosis to revivify the specific situations, thoughts, or feelings associated with triggering the gastric symptoms.

Next, the patient is taught relaxation training. Nonhypnotic EMG biofeedback (frontalis muscle), combined with daily relaxation training (Aleo & Nicassio, 1978; Beaty, 1976), has been effective with ulcer patients, as is hypnotic relaxation. A hypnotic induction alone, even without specific suggestions to effect gastric secretion, alters gastric secretion. Although the results regarding the effects of hypnotic induction by itself may be inconsistent (Badgley, Spira, & Senay, 1969; Eichorn & Tracktir, 1955; Luckhardt & Johnston, 1924), they imply that hypnotic relaxation, especially sustained hypnotic relaxation (Moody, 1953), may be beneficial for stabilizing gastric activity, that is, normalizing the autoregulatory processes involved in gastric activity.

Specific hypnotic suggestions may be designed to effect the gastric activity directly. Nonhypnotic EGG (electrogastrogram) biofeedback and PH biofeedback have shown that people can learn voluntary control over gastric muscle activity (Walker, 1983; Walker, Lawton, & Sandman, 1978; Whitehead, Renault, & Goldiamond, 1975) and gastric secretion (Welgan, 1974), although the effects are not sustained after the biofeedback has been discontinued (Moore & Schenkenberg, 1974). Although systematic clinical hypnosis studies are lacking, it is conceivable that some hypnotizable patients can achieve voluntarily control over gastric activity and secretion through specific hypnotic suggestions. Ikemi et al. (1959), demonstrated the direct effects of hypnotic suggestion on gastric motility and gastric secretion in healthy subjects and in patients. Given suggestions, patients can, for example, decrease gastric acid secretion by imagining they are eating bland meals. Gastric secretion also decreases when patients direct their attention elsewhere for example, to pleasant fantasies. Similarly, patients are given suggestions and graded posthypnotic suggestions to increase mucus production.

Because gastric pain is a primary symptom in peptic ulcer, hypnotic suggestions are also directed to the pain. Sometimes directly suggesting that the patient will "no longer feel concerned with pain" is effective (Moody, 1953). Zane (1966) was able to effect increases and decreases in gastric pain in ulcer patients by hypnotically suggesting fantasies involving conflictual and pleasurable experiences, respectively. Graded posthypnotic suggestions that gastric pain will be less and less over time are also recommended.

Peptic ulcer disease may also be partly a conditioned response to certain classes of stressful stimuli, and Kroger and Fezler (1976) recommend hypnotic desensitization. Learned sensitivity to certain stimuli may serve to maintain the ulcer. When the patient and therapist have identified triggering events, the patient is taught hypnotic relaxation. While in a relaxed trance, the patient systematically imagines encountering each of the stressful situations from least to most stressful until reactivity to them is diminished. Chronic worry may also maintain the ulcer. Ego-strengthening suggestions designed to increase self-confidence, combined with rehearsal of pleasant, worry-free fantasies, are useful (Chappell, Steffano, Rogerson, & Pike, 1936). Adjunctive assertiveness training (Brooks & Richardson, 1980) and hypnotic rehearsal of assertion in fantasy are also recommended (Kroger & Fezler, 1976).

Dietary control is another dimension of the treatment of the ulcer patient. Posthypnotic suggestions are used to reinforce adherence to a bland diet as prescribed by the physician.

Irritable Bowel Syndrome

Irritable Bowel Syndrome (IBS) is a very common gastrointestinal disorder. Somewhere between 50% and 70% of all patients with gastrointestinal symptoms suffer from IBS (Kirsner & Palmer, 1958). IBS is characterized by abdominal pain and changes in bowel motility, both of which must be present for a positive diagnosis of IBS. IBS is distinguished from inflammatory bowel disease in that it does not involve inflammation or ulceration of bowel tissue (Latimer, 1983). Adult IBS bears some relationship to recurrent abdominal pain symptoms (RAP) in children, except that motility changes—diarrhea and constipation—are more characteristic of adult IBS. Some patients manifest pain-predominant IBS; others, diarrhea-predominant IBS (spastic colon) (Whitehead, Engel, & Schuster, 1980). In addition to these primary symptoms, IBS patients often report a wide variety of related symptoms: abdominal distension, rumbling and gurgling of the bowel, rectal bleeding, mucus in the stools, loose stools, digestive complaints, nausea, and headaches. The most common symptoms reported are abdominal distension, loose stools, greater frequency of movement, and pain relief following a bowel movement.

IBS patients as a group can be distinguished from most other groups of gastrointestinal patients by the high incidence of psychopathology. A very high proportion of IBS patients carry psychiatric diagnoses of neuroses (Latimer, 1983; Liss, Alpers, & Woodruff, 1973; Young, Alpers, Norland, & Woodruff, 1976). Anxieties, phobias, and depression are likely to be present. It is difficult to know whether psychological factors contribute to the causes of IBS or are a secondary consequence of having a chronic disease. But it is clear that, at least for a subgroup of IBS patients, psychological stress and emotions contribute to the development of IBS.

The events that trigger IBS vary from person to person. Lactose intolerance has been shown to produce symptoms very similar to IBS and is often confused with it (Latimer, 1983). Hypersensitivity to food intake is an important factor for a subgroup of IBS patients. Some patients complain that eating a normal meal results in pain or hyperactivity of the bowel after the meal (Connell, Jones, & Rowlands, 1965; Schuster, 1983; Snape, Matarazzo, & Cohen, 1978). Emotional stress is also an important cause of symptoms in a subgroup of IBS patients. About half report a stressful experience immediately preceding the onset of symptoms (Chaudhary & Truelove, 1962). In experimental studies, stress tends to alter the physiological responsiveness of the colon (Latimer, 1983) for some patients, a response probably mediated by the autonomic nervous system (ANS) (White & Jones, 1938). The high amounts of catecholamines found in the urine of IBS patients have been interpreted as an indicator of ANS hyperactivity (Wright & Das, 1969).

There are two kinds of normal bowel activity: (1) segmental contractions, which impede the passage of the colonic contents for the purposes of storage and dehydration; (2) propulsive contractions, whose function is evacuation of the contents. The bowel exhibits a form of "paradoxical motility" (Connell, 1962): the main type of motility of the colon keeps the colonic contents stationary. Constipation is a result of hyperactivity of the normal segmental movements; diarrhea, the result of hypoactivity. Each arises from some exaggeration of the normal colonic responsiveness.

Not all patients manifest abnormal colonic motility. IBS represents a "spectrum of disorders" (Latimer, 1983). Abnormal bowel motility has been reported in some studies (Bloom, LoPresti, & Farrar, 1968; Chaudhary & Truelove, 1962; Wangel & Deller, 1965) but not in others (Connell et al., 1965; Murrell & Deller, 1967). The most convincing evidence comes from colonic myoelectrical investigations. Within the 3 cpm range, IBS patients show greater slow wave contractions than normals (Snape, Carlson, & Cohen, 1976; Taylor, Darby, Hammond, & Basu, 1978). IBS patients also show changes in peripheral nerve receptors so that they are more sensitive to pain in specific localized areas (Whitehead & Schuster, 1985). The implication is that at least some IBS patients have a biological vulnerability for IBS symptoms. Other patients manifest normal colonic responses to stressful events (Almy & Tulin, 1947; Almy et al., 1949). Still other IBS patients manifest normal colonic activity which they misperceive. IBS patients are likely to report greater pain than normals in response to normal distension of the colon (Ritchie, 1973). Sometimes IBS patients report symptoms having no relationship to bowel activity. Physiological and cognitive activity in such cases has become desynchronized (Latimer, 1983). Patients may feel pain or report changes in bowel activity during normal bowel response, or they may fail to report symptoms during times of such activity. To some extent IBS symptoms represent learned maladaptive responses (Whitehead, Winget, Fedoravicius, Wooley, & Blackwell, 1982). For example, the patient who repeatedly allows a child with an alleged stomach ache to stay home from school may inadvertently train the child to misperceive normal gastrointestinal activity. More than most other patients with psychophysiological disorders, IBS patients have very little capacity to accurately perceive visceral changes. Patients learn to fear the onset of the symptoms in certain situations and also condition themselves to produce the symptoms (Latimer, 1983). Conditioning tends to maintain the IBS symptoms independent of triggering situations and somewhat independent of physiological activity. According to Whitehead and Schuster (1985), IBS arises from an interaction of a physiological predisposition, psychological triggering events, and learning.

Direct hypnotic suggestions are sometimes useful with IBS patients. Byrne (1973) demonstrated glove anesthesia to his patients in order to convince them that they could exert some degree of control over physiological processes. Then he gave his patients direct suggestions for control of bowel motility. Patients were given posthypnotic suggestions that bowel habits would return to normal. Similar suggestions can be given to alleviate pain (Kroger & Fezler, 1976).

For patients less responsive to direct suggestion, a hypnobehavioral approach is recommended. Treatment begins with self-monitoring of bowel activity (Mitchell, 1978). The patient keeps a daily diary of the time of each bowel movement, level of anxiety, intensity of pain, the situation and feelings at the time of the bowel movement, and medication taken. It is also advisable to teach patients to attend to the characteristics of the stool. Its consistency, weight, and volume often are indicators of physiological activity (Latimer, 1983). The therapist helps the patient to identify high-risk times, high-risk situations, and triggering events. The patient also is given a stethoscope and told to monitor bowel sounds before and after meals and during nonstressful and stressful situations. The patient pays special attention to bowel sounds following the high-risk times and high-risk situations identified through self-monitoring. Because of the degree of dysfunction between physiological events and cognitions for most IBS patients, many patients find the monitoring of bowel sounds especially uncanny at first. The purpose is to familiarize the patient with bowel sounds under a variety of circumstances and to reduce gross misperception of visceral events.

The patient is then hypnotized and taught relaxation. Nonhypnotic relaxation (Giles, 1978; Jacobson, 1927) and hypnotic relaxation (Dias, 1963) have been shown to alleviate IBS symptoms, presumably by stabilizing the autonomic nervous system. Next, the patient is given specific suggestions to alter bowel activity. Whorwell, Prior, & Faragher, (1984), begin with a general hypnotic relaxation, followed by an exercise to illustrate voluntary control over physiological processes. Patients are told to place a hand on the abdomen and to generate a sense of warmth. Having produced the warmth, the patient is told that he will be able to control bowel activity in the same way he was able to control the temperature of the gut. The patient visualizes the bowel and imagines controlling its activity. Ego-strengthening suggestions are also used.

For patients unable to control bowel activity through hypnotic visualization, biofeedback of bowel sounds may be used. An electronically amplified stethoscope can be used to feed bowel sounds back to the patient. The patient is then told to increase or decrease the bowel sounds. Patients at least learn greater awareness of bowel activity and some may directly alter bowel activity with the aid of feedback. Symptoms often diminish as the patient learns to control gut activity (Furman, 1973). Direct feedback of colonic motility with invasive procedures has been shown to stabilize the bowel motility (Bueno-Miranda, Cerulli, & Schuster, 1976; Whitehead, 1984) but is impractical in most clinical settings.

Because of the extent to which IBS symptoms represent learned behaviors, desensitization is also used (Cohen & Reed, 1968; Hedberg, 1973; Kroger & Fezler, 1976). A hierarchy of stressful situations and triggering events is constructed. The patient is hypnotized, relaxes, and imagines encountering the stressful situation while remaining in a relaxed state. IBS symptoms diminish concurrent with desensitization to triggering events. The patient also constructs a typical chain of events leading up to the IBS episode. Posthypnotic suggestions are given to practice relaxation and to control bowel activity at the earliest noticeable warning sign. Ego-strengthening suggestions are also used to undercut the patient's typical fear response.

Though there have been very few clinical studies on hypnosis and IBS, a very solid outcome study is available (Whorwell, *et al.,* 1984). Patients were randomly assigned to hypnosis, psychotherapy, and placebo treatments. Only the hypnotherapy patients showed dramatic improvement of all symptoms. Curiously, the efficacy of hypnosis did not appear to be related to hypnotizability.

Inflammatory Bowel Disease

Inflammatory bowel disease (IBD)—ulcerative colitis of the large intestine and Crohn's disease of the small intestine—manifests symptoms much like those of IBS, with the addition of a serious inflammation of the bowel and often ulceration of the bowel tissue. The common symptoms are abdominal pain, discharge of blood and mucus, and sometimes diarrhea and weight loss. Psychiatric symptoms typically associated with IBD include depression, irritability, obsessions (Gerbert, 1980) and possibly neuropsychological complications (Latimer, 1978). Because of ulceration of the tissue, IBD can be a serious, life-threatening illness. There is also a strong association between IBD and cancer of the colon.

There is some association between stress and IBD symptoms. There is some evidence that stress may play a role in the cause of the disease (Engel, 1973); stronger evidence exists that stress, especially emotional stress, at least exacerbates the condition (Gerbert, 1980; Zisook & De-Vaul, 1977). Colitis symptoms often occur following periods of emotional stress (Fava & Pavan, 1976/1977).

The treatment of IBD bears some resemblance to that of IBS. Both begin with self-monitoring of bowel activity and stool characteristics (Best, Becktel, Singleton, & Kern, 1976) for IBD, it is especially important to teach the patient to examine the nature of the discharge and to estimate the extent of inflammation and bleeding. Self-monitoring of bowel activity with a stethoscope is necessary only in cases involving excessive diarrhea. Because diarrhea causes irritation of the tissue, excessive diarrhea may increase the inflammatory process. Therefore, it is important to reduce diarrhea as a complicating factor. Treatment for diarrhea in IBD is similar to that for diarrhea in IBS (Weinstock, 1976).

Teaching the patient to induce deep relaxation is integral to the treatment. Improvement has been reported from extensive training in both nonhypnotic (DeGossely, Konincky & Lenfant, 1975) and hypnotic (Dias, 1963; Kroger & Fezler, 1976) relaxation. Because stress is so strongly associated with the illness, it is equally important to desensitize the patient to specific stressful situations. After the suggestion of pleasant, relaxing imagery, Kroger and Fezler (1976) have their hypnotized patients recall specific emotions associated with the onset of the symptoms.

Psychotherapy has been recommended as a useful treatment in IBD. Supportive psychotherapy alone (Groen & Bastiaans, 1951; Karush et al., 1977; Zisook & DeVaul, 1977) and combined with dietary control and antibiotic medication (Grace, Pinsky, & Wolff, 1954) protect the patient from the impact of life stressors, inspire confidence, and encourage the healthy discharge of aggression through assertive expression. Dynamic psychotherapy is usually contraindicated because the insights gained may in themselves be stressful and thereby aggravate the condition (Whitehead & Schuster, 1985). However, hypnodynamic therapy combined with hypnotic relaxation allows the patient to explore the meaning of stressors without exacerbating the condition. Initial results with hypnodynamic therapy have been very promising (Taub et al., cited in Whitehead & Schuster, 1985, p. 140). An ego-strengthening approach to hypnotic treatment is especially recommended. According to Kroger and Fezler (1976), "the major objective is to continually reinforce their [the patients'] confidence and outlook toward life" (p. 398). Hypnotically induced relaxation combined with ego-strengthening suggestions is the treatment of choice in most cases. Patients are asked to imagine a series of scenes wherein they feel increasingly confident in interpersonal and work situations (Kroger & Fezler, 1976).

IBD may also involve a dysfunction of the immune system (Kirsner & Shorter, 1982; Shorter, Huizenga & Spencer, 1972; Whitehead & Schuster, 1985). One approach to treatment is to attempt to stabilize immune activity through hypnotic relaxation and visualizations of immune activity. The patient tries to develop a series of images associated with healing of the inflamed tissue.

SKIN DISEASES

The Psychobiology of Skin Diseases

There is a large variety of skin diseases, most of which are characterized by: some form of cutaneous alteration (lesions, eruptions, blisters, scales, thickening, crusting, or fissuring); vasomotor changes (reddening, swelling, or weeping); sensory alterations (itching or pain). Skin diseases also can become complicated by secondary skin infections and by maladaptive habits such as excessive scratching or picking at the skin. Common skin diseases considered here include eczema, psoriasis, neurodermatitis, pruritis, acne, warts, and herpes.

The etiology of skin diseases is complex. Few experts believe that any skin disease has a single cause. A multitude of factors are likely to contribute to the formation of any skin condition (Scott, 1960). For certain skin diseases, some of the contributing factors are known; for many others, the causes are still unknown. It has been clearly established that psychodynamic factors are relevant to the etiology of most skin diseases, except in neurodermatitis. For this disease, the contribution of psychodynamic factors has been well documented (Scott, 1960), as has been the success of dynamically based psychotherapy and hypnotherapy (Scott, 1960). The contribution of emotions to the etiology of most skin diseases, however, is probably more indirect, namely, through the effects of maladaptive patterns of emotional expression on the functioning of the autonomic nervous system. Autonomic nervous hyperactivity clearly is a facor in certain skin conditions (Bethune & Kidd, 1961) Chronic autonomic instability can mediate regional vasomotor changes. One consequence may be the redness and swelling that accompany many skin diseases. Autonomic instability can also affect the activity of the sweat glands and the sebaceous glands (Scott, 1960). Excessive dryness of the skin, such as in neurodermatitis, may be the result of sweat gland disregulation. The oily quality of acne may likewise be the result of abnormal activity of the sebaceous glands (Behrman, Labow, Rozen, 1978). The vasomotor, sweat, and sebaceous changes contribute to an altered internal milieu. Certain bacteria and fungi that are part of the normal flora of the skin may become pathogenic under the altered conditions. Infectious and inflammatory responses may develop and contribute to the overall skin condition. The relative contribution of immune dysfunction to skin diseases is not yet clearly understood, but may be important.

Some skin diseases are mediated by slow viruses. For example, common warts are caused by the papilloma virus. The virus infects a person and under certain conditions produces a benign epidermal tumor (Mendelson & Kligman, 1961). Whether or not the virus remains active in the host depends largely on the nature of the local tissue environment; certain conditions must develop. Autonomically mediated alterations in the local chemical milieu either favor or disfavor the growth of the virus. The wart virus does not find the human body an especially favorable environment. Even slight changes in skin temperature and regional blood flow can activate or deactivate it (Ullman, 1959). One's relative state of stress or relaxation is therefore associated with the appearance or disapperance of the wart. Other viruses, notably the herpes viruses, are more robust and are therefore more resistant to fluctuations in the local tissue environment.

In addition to the variety of factors that go into to the formation of a skin condition, others contribute to its maintenance. The development of cutaneous alterations may affect the itching and pain thresholds of the skin. This can lead in turn to excessive scratching and rubbing (Scott, 1960). Over time, the appearance of the cutaneous alterations can also become conditioned to a variety of previously neutral stimuli. Maladaptive habits may develop, such as compulsive scratching and skin picking, behaviors that contribute to further irritation of the skin. A vicious cycle can ensue in which the very behaviors designed to bring temporary relief, like scratching, exacerbate and maintain the condition. Psychodynamic factors also contribute to the maintenance of some skin conditions. Excessive scratching can gratify masochistic and self-destructive impulses. Compulsive rubbing and scratching can be a form of autoerotic stimulation. The heightened sensitivity of certain body areas affected by the skin condition may represent hypercathexis of certain body areas associated with narcissistic preoccupation with the body or exhibitionistic impulses. Although the individual dynamics vary in each case, dynamic factors may increase the person's involvement with his skin condition and thereby worsen it. Skin disease also creates conflicts for the patient. As the skin disease becomes chronic, the patient's self-concept and body image are affected. Temporary, and sometimes permanent, disfigurement accompanies chronic skin disease. Over the course of time it becomes very difficult to determine whether dynamic conflicts contributed to the development of the skin diseases or are a consequence of it.

There are three approaches to the hypnotic treatment of skin disease: (a) direct suggestion; (b) systematic hypnobehavioral treatment; and (c) dynamic hypnotherapy. The patient may be hypnotized and given a direct suggestion that upon awakening his skin lesions will be gone and his skin will return to normal (e.g., Bennet 1955). A posthypnotic suggestion may be given that the area of irritation will become smaller and smaller over time or will become more and more localized in a certain area of the body (Scott, 1960). Imagery often enhances the response. The hypnotized patient imagines applying an hallucinated salve or soothing ointment believed to have the power of healing the tissue (Fernandez, 1955–56). For certain patients, direct hypnotic suggestions and imagery suggestions alone bring relief. We recommend that these suggestions be tried first.

If they are not effective, systematic hypnobehavioral treatment is indicated. The patient is taught to keep daily self-monitoring records of subjective estimates of stress levels, the fluctuations in skin irritation, the situation he is in the time of the itching, compulsive scratching or picking, and the use of medication. The patient and therapist try to identify those environmental, dietary, and emotional factors which exacerbate the condition. Then the patient is taught hypnotic and self-hypnotic relaxation. Next, the hypnotized patient learns to produce a variety of local sensory changes, especially voluntary control over regional vasomotor response through hypnotic visualization (Kline, 1954). Hypnotic desensitization is used for that aspect of the skin disease which has become conditioned (Kroger & Fezler, 1976). Posthypnotic suggestions are used to counteract the compulsion to scratch or to pick at the skin (Fernandez, 1955–56; Hollander, 1959; Sacerdote, 1965). The long term effects of the skin disease on the patient's body image and self-image may be explored using the unconscious hallucinated body image method (Freytag, 1965) or the Ideal Self Technique. Ego-strengthening suggestions also can be very helpful (Fernandez, 1955–56). In cases where the patient fails to respond to the short-term hypnobehavioral approach, dynamic hypnotherapy is indicated. The therapist uses hypnoprojective methods to uncover and work through the conflicts associated with the cause and maintenance of the skin disease (Scott, 1960).

Acne

Acne is a condition caused in part by an autonomically mediated disregulation of the sebaceous glands. As a result, the follicular orifices become plugged by fatty acids, and lesions form (blackheads). The activity of bacteria on the skin contributes to a secondary inflammation. Also aggravating the condition are maladaptive behaviors such as not keeping the skin adequately clean and compulsive picking. Acne is a progressive disease often characterized by pustules, cysts, and self-induced excoriations and scarring.

There have been only a few clinical reports on the hypnotic treatment of acne. Direct posthypnotic suggestions have been used to reduce skin-picking behavior. Patients were told to remember the word "scar" whenever they felt the urge to pick at their faces (Hollander, 1959). We recommend a multimodal hypnobehavioral approach in which the patient is systematically ,taught: to self-monitor stress and fluctuations in the appearance of acne and picking behaviors; self-hypnotic relaxation; hypnotic visualization of normally functioning sebaceous glands; hypnotic exploration of coping strategies to deal with picking behaviors; cognitive therapy regarding the negative statements associated with the maintenance of acne; hypnotic reconstruction of the body image; and ego-strengthening suggestions. Sometimes it is advisable to explore unconscious conflicts associated with acne. Scott (1960) used age regression to explore the conditions under which acne first appeared in his patients.

Pruritis

Pruritis is a skin condition characterized by excessive itching. Many factors contribute to the development of pruritis: extreme temperature and humidity changes, excessive bathing with alkaline soaps, and aging. Habitual scratching is a hallmark of the condition. As a result of compulsive scratching, the skin becomes red and thickened. Scratch marks are usually present. In chronic pruritis, the skin becomes lichenified like an elephant's hide (Behrman et al., 1978). For certain patients, direct hypnotic suggestions that the skin irritation will go away and the skin will return to normal are effective (Bennett 1955). Twerski and Naar (1974) describe a case in which they introduced a brief symptomatic intervention. The patient imagined bathing in the cool and gentle water of the ocean. She could feel the soothing effect of the hallucinated water on her skin and was able to gain relief from the itching in this way. The patient was able to discontinue the use of corticosteroid medication without a worsening of the skin condition. After recurrence of the condition, she was taught to practice the sea bathing fantasy in self-hypnosis and the condition cleared up.

Psoriasis

Psoriasis is a skin disease characterized by reddish plaques covered with thick, whitish scales. They usually occur on the elbows, knees, and scalp.

Sometimes large areas of the body may be involved. The etiology of psoriasis is unknown, but genetic alteration of the metabolism of the epidermal tissue is suspected in which the epidermal tissue is produced at an unusual rate. Stress also seems to aggravate the condition (Behrman et al., 1978). In Kline's (1954) "hypnotic sensory imagery technique" for the treatment of psoriasis, the patient is hypnotized and told to experience a variety of sensations throughout her body—lightness, heaviness, warmth, coldness, constriction, and expansion. After the patient successfully generates the suggested sensory experiences, she is told to feel these same sensory experiences only in areas where she has the psoriasis. The patient becomes increasingly skillful at producing sensory alterations in her body through regular practice of self-hypnosis. Frankel and Misch (1973) describe a similar approach in which the particular sensory imagery is individualized. The patient reported that sunbathing improved his condition. Therefore, it was suggested in hypnosis that the patient imagine basking in the sun. The patient visualized the sunlight touching those areas of his body afflicted with the psoriasis. The patient was told to practice the exercise for a few minutes about six times each day. The adjunctive hypnotic treatment was conducted as part of long-term psychotherapy, which focused on, among other things, dynamic issues associated with the skin disease. In both reported cases improvement occurred.

Eczema

Eczema is a nonspecific term for a variety of skin diseases, all characterized by redness and swelling and sometimes by weeping, fissuring, and scaling. Irritation to the skin caused by soaps and clothing, temperature changes, and emotional stress contributes to the skin condition. Direct suggestions sometimes bring about symptomatic improvement (Gordon, 1955). Goodman (1962) hypnotized a patient and suggested that her fingers would tingle and become numb. Then the patient learned to transfer the soothing numbness to the afflicted skin areas. Posthypnotic suggestions were given to reinforce daily self-hypnotic practice of this technique. The patient was able to sustain a general remission of her eczema except for a few recalcitrant areas she continued to treat with medication. Hypnotized patients also may hallucinate a soothing, healing salve, which they imagine themselves applying to the afflicted areas. They imagine experiencing relief from itching and the skin gradually returning to its healthy condition. Direct posthypnotic suggestions are given to decrease the habit of scratching (Fernandez, 1955–56). Posthypnotic suggestions can also be used to reinforce habits that promote healing of the tissue, such as keeping the skin dry, avoiding irritation to the skin, judicious cleansing, and so forth. Hypnotic relaxation training also reduces the stress associated with eczema. As with psoriasis, in cases where the short-term symptomatic treatment fails to give relief, dynamic hypnotherapy is used to uncover conflicts associated with the eczema (Mittleman, 1947; Scott, 1960).

Neurodermatitis

Neurodermatitis is a chronic skin disease characterized by bilateral lesions, thickening of the skin, and crusting; sweat retention and dry. skin; pruritis with intense itching; changes in skin pigmentation, and sometimes secondary infections. Compulsive itching and picking result in excoriation of the skin. The condition may be either generalized or localized. Allergic sensitivity may contribute to the development of this condition in at least a subgroup of patients. The progress of the condition is most likely mediated by autonomic hyperactivity and associated disregulation of sweat gland functioning, regional peripheral vasomotor response, and immune functioning. In at least some patients, psychodynamic factors are important to the development of neurodermatitis. In fact, dynamic factors are more clearly involved in neurodermatitis than in other skin diseases. Specifically, inhibiting the expression of hostility plays an important role in some cases. Conflicts over gratification of dependency needs constitute the central dynamics of neurodermatitis. Miller (1948) stated that the patient, unable to get dependency needs gratified, handles the dependency wish by stroking and scratching the skin. Miller feels that the regression to skin eroticism is accompanied by an increase in aggression toward the object for failing to gratify the patient's need for contact. The aggression then is masochistically turned toward the self. According to French (personal communication, 1962), shame, not hostility, is the reactive motive in the dynamics of neurodermatitis. These patients have a great need to be touched, held, and stroked but consider this need to be infantile and are ashamed of it. So they defend themselves against this wish by (stroking) scratching their skin so hard that it becomes raw and bloody and no one else would *want* to touch it. The symptom expresses both the wish and the defense against it.

Hypnosis has been used fairly extensively in the treatment of neurodermatitis. Direct hypnotic suggestions are sometimes useful. Horan (1950) reported improvement in two cases in which patients were told that the sensations such as itchiness, pain, or tenderness would be gone sometime after awakening from hypnosis. Scott (1960) used direct suggestions to transfer generalized itching to more and more localized areas of the body. Kline (1953) used the previously described sensory imagery technique with a woman who was resistant to seeing any emotional base to her neurodermatitis. The patient was able to achieve complete remission of her condition in 6 weeks and become more open to exploring problems in ongoing therapy. Because of the dynamics of neurodermatitis, hypno-behavioral treatment of neurodermatitis has seldom been attempted. However, because dysfunction of the autonomic nervous system (the sweat glands, the vasomotor system, and the immune system) plays a role in neurodermatitis, a regimen of daily self-hypnotic relaxation is indicated in most cases. Furthermore, because compulsive scratching typically worsens the condition, teaching the patient to self-monitor scratching behavior is a useful starting point for a variety of behavioral and dynamic interventions regarding scratching. Posthypnotic suggestions also are quite useful to reduce scratching behaviors (Sacerdote, 1965).

The typical treatment of neurodermatitis, however, is usually psycho-dynamically based. Schoenberg and Carr (1963) have developed a nonhyp-notic approach to the therapy of the neurodermatitis patient. Patients are encouraged to learn about the expression of aggressive impulses and to develop healthy channels for it. Positive treatment outcome is associated with the degree to which the patient develops means to express hostility. Successful hypnodynamic treatments have taken a similar approach. Lehman (1978) used age regression to explore conflicts associated with the development of neurodermatitis in a patient. The central conflict around aggression, being "irritated," was expressed through the skin irritation. The patient gained insight into the connection between her symptoms and the inhibition of aggression. She learned through hypnosis to develop healthier ways of becoming more assertive.

Virus-Mediated Skin Diseases: Warts and Herpes Lesions

Virus-mediated skin diseases (warts, herpes simplex lesions) are produced by the activity of the virus. Warts are benign tumors caused by the in-coporation of the virus into the structure of the epidermal cells. Herpes simplex lesions and blisters and herpes zoster (shingles) lesions are also caused by the incorporation of the virus into the cell structure and a subsequent change in cellular metabolism. Whether or not the virus is activated and causes the lesion is in part a function of the local tissue milieu. Alterations in temperature, pH, blood flow, as well as the presence of humoral factors, contribute to the activation or deactivation of the virus. Therefore, successful hypnotic treatment of virus-mediated skin diseases depends on voluntary control over local physiological responses. Although hypnosis cannot remove the virus from the host, it can under certain conditions help make the climate unfavorable to its growth.

Helig and Hoff (1925) and Ullman (1947) were able to induce herpes blisters in patients by means of direct hypnotic suggestions. It was not clearly demonstrated, however, that such blisters were the result of reac-tivation of the slow virus, even though the patients in the earlier study were known to be virus carriers. Nor has it been demonstrated that hypnosis was the necessary agent of this effect (Johnson & Barber, 1978). Nevertheless, these reports are suggestive that the appearance and disappearance of symptoms associated with virus-mediated skin diseases can at least in part be influenced by suggestion.

Herpes simplex lesions are characterized by clusters of tiny, fluid-filled vesicles or blisters, which usually crust within 2 days after their appearance and disappear within a week or two. The lesions are often accompanied by an uncomfortable itching or painful sensation. A number of situations may trigger the appearance of the lesions; sunlight, mechanical irritation, intercourse, fevers, emotional stress. Direct hypnotic suggestion has seldom been effective with patients with manifest herpes simplex lesions (Bennet, 1955), presumably because the virus is fairly robust in human tissue. Sensory imagery shows promise in certain cases. The hypnotized patient learns to produce a variety of sensory changes, such as warmth and cold, in the afflicted area, and practices generating these effects a number of times a day. The patient may also imagine applying a hypnotically hallucinated salve to the lesion and visualize the soothing ointment drying up the lesion. Regular self-hypnotic relaxation training may help reduce stress associated with an exacerbation in the symptoms. Scott (1960) recommends hypnotherapeutic exploration of the dynamics associated with the symptoms. Hypnotized patients are asked to recall the situations in which the lesions typically occur and to recall the situation when the lesion first occurred. Sometimes the emergence of lesions follows a clear pattern associated with particular conflicts.

Herpes zoster (shingles) is characterized by lesions that cluster around a nerve in linear distribution. A frequent consequence is post-herpetic neuralgia. Extreme and persistent pain often follows the virus attack. The lesions of herpes zoster may be treated similarly to those of herpes simplex with modest success in certain cases. The pain may be treated by the pain coping strategies discussed earlier in this chapter.

The hypnotic treatment of warts has an impressive success rate, presumably because the papilloma virus is less robust that the herpes virus in human tissue. Attesting to the instability of the virus in the body, warts are known to remit spontaneously if the delicate balance between susceptibility and immunity is even slightly altered (Allington, 1952). There is a long history of the use of magic, waking suggestions (Ulman, 1959), and psychotherapy (Allington, 1952) in the treatment of warts. Direct hypnotic suggestion (Tasini & Hackett, 1977) and sometimes hypnotic relaxation (Ullman & Dudek, 1960) are often quite successful. The typical approach to warts is to give hypnotic suggestions to generate tingling sensatiions at the site of the warts. After the patient produces a distinct tingling sensation, he is given a posthypnotic suggestion that the tingling will continue and the warts will disappear sometime later (McDowell, 1949; 1959; Scott; 1960; Surman, Gottlieb, & Hackett, 1972; Surman, Gottlieb, Hackett, & Silverberg, 1973; Ullman & Dudek, 1960). This method is usually effective because hypnotic suggestions for tingling effect local vasomotor changes, which make the local environment unfavorable to the growth of the virus (Surman et al., 1972). However, such suggestions are not always effective (Stankler, 1967; Tenzel & Taylor, 1968). Clark (1965) has criticized the apparent success of hypnosis in the removal of warts on the grounds that it may be due to spontaneous remission of the warts. The most impressive argument against this position is a study by Sinclair-Gieben and Chalmers (1959) in which patients with multiple warts were given a posthypnotic suggestion that the warts would disappear only on one side of the body. They did. It is hard to imagine that warts would have spontaneously disappeared on only one side of the body were it not for that posthypnotic suggestion.

Clinical Outcome

Despite general agreement that hypnosis is effective in the treatment of skin diseases, there have been surprisingly few controlled outcome studies. Scott (1960) reported a 60% improvement or cure in a population of mixed cases of skin diseases treated with hypnosis. Zhukov (1961) reported that 58% of his patients showed marked improvement or complete recovery. More systematic outcome studies are needed. It is also unclear to what extent hypnosis itself contributes to the overall treatment effect. Direct suggestions are effective with certain subgroups of patients; hypnobehavioral methods, with others; and hypnodynamic interventions, with still others.

HYPNOSIS AND IMMUNE-RELATED DISEASES

Immune Disregulation

The immune system protects the body from foreign agents—both external, infectious agents and internal, aberrant cell formations. The immune system has been described as a "complex recognition system" (Besedovsky & Sorkin, 1981, p. 546). It comprises multiple regulatory processes, several categories of cells, and a complex differentiation of labor between these cell-types. Historically the immune system has been conceived of as having two main branches or lineages of cells, B- and T-lymphocytes. The humoral, or B-cell, system is composed of cells from the bone marrow. These cells manufacture and secrete a variety of proteins or immunoglobulins. These highly specific immunoglobulins constitute the circulating antibodies that protect the body from infectious agents or antigens, such as bacteria and viruses. The cell-mediated, or T-cell, system is thymus dependent. The T-cells do not manufacture circulating antibodies. T-cells have a cytotoxic effect on tumorous cells and sometimes on bacteria and viruses (Burnet, 1971). T-cells also serve an important regulatory function. The B- and T-cell systems interact in a complex way. Some T-cells serve as "helpers" to B-cells; others act as "suppressors," preventing B-cells from becoming activated by antigens. A highly specialized group of T-cells, called natural killers (NK) is designed to search out and destroy tumor cells when they first appear in the body (Herberman & Holden, 1979). Another system of larger cells, the monocyte-macrophage system, is also very important in controlling tumors by consuming tumor cells. All these systems function in the service of "immunological surveillance" to protect the organism from invasion by bacteria and viruses, and from spontaneous mutations during reproduction of the body's own cells (Burnet, 1971).

Proper protection depends on careful regulation, "auto-regulation," within the immune system itself and outside the immune system through the hypothalamic-pituitary axis of the nervous system (Besedovsky & Sorkin, 1981). However, the overall balance between the functions of each of the branches of the immune system can be disturbed. One or another of these brances may become dysfunctional (Solomon, Amkraut, & Kasper, 1974). A number of disorders can produce an immunological imbalance or dysfunction: autoimmune diseases, bacterial and viral infections, allergies, and cancer. Autoimmune diseases and allergies represent hyperactivity of the B-cell system. In the case of allergies, the B-cells incorrectly manufacture antibodies against heretofore neutral stimuli. In the case of autoimmune diseases, the B-cells incorrectly manufacture antibodies against normal body cells. Because of the interactions between the B- and T-cell systems, allergic and autoimmune diseases can also be seen as a failure of the suppressor T-cells to inhibit B-cell activity. (Reinherz et al., 1979). The latter, infections and cancer, represent hypoactivity of these systems. Infections occur when the B-cells fail to manufacture and secrete antibodies against the invading bacteria or viruses. Resistance diminishes, and the infection is able to develop. Cancer occurs when the T-cell, natural killer, and macrophage systems fail to recognize and destroy certain types of aberrant cell formations which are allowed to multiply uncontrollably. Figure 3.7 summarizes these classes of diseases associated with disregulation of immune function.

Cancer

Immunodysfunction and Cancer Risk

Numerous studies have shown that animals in which tumors had been induced (by means of chemicals, transplantations, or radiation) and were

antigen	hyperactive immune functioning	hypoactive immune functioning
endogenous	autoimmunity	cancer
exogenous	allergy	infection

FIG. 3.7. Classification of Diseases Associated with Disregulation of Immune-Functioning Adapted from Theodore Melnechuk, 1986, personal communication.

then exposed to acute stressors (electrical shock, bright lights, extreme temperatures, rapid rotation, immobilization, isolation, overcrowding, confrontation with other—feared—animals) suffered from immunosuppression. Rapid tumor growth was facilitated in the stressed animals. The accumulated data for humans, although not so extensively documented, are similar and suggest that acute stressors result in immunosuppression or tumor facilitation in humans (Cooper, 1984; Sklår & Anisman, 1981). For example, examination stress is associated with immunosuppression (Kiecolt-Glazer et al., 1984), and stressful life events frequently precede the appearance of cancer (Bahnson & Bahnson, 1966).

Chronic stress affects immunocompetence in a variety of ways. In animals, chronic physical stress, such as daily immobilization, punishment, or exposure to cold temperature, typically results in immunosuppression followed by immunoenhancement (Monjan, 1981; Riley, Fitzmaurice, & Spackman, 1981). The pattern of immunosuppression tends to persist when the animal is unable to avoid stress. Immunoenhancement follows when the animal can use muscular activity to alleviate stress (Corson, 1966). Chronic social stress caused, for example, by isolation, overcrowding, or predator-threat is also associated with immunosuppression, but not with immunoenchancement (Sklår & Anisman, 1981). Sklår and Anisman (1981) summarized the effects of stress on immunocompetence and tumor growth as follows: (a) acute stress typically suppresses immune functioning; (b) chronic physical stress does not suppress immune functioning and may actually enhance it as one learns ways to adapt to the stressful situation over time; (c) chronic social stress contributes to sustained immunosuppression, and adaptation to social stress in terms of immune functioning does not seem to occur; (d) the extent to which stress disregulates immune functioning depends more on one's ability to cope with the stressful situation and less on the stressful situation itself; (e) previous encounters with extremely stressful or traumatic situations may sensitize some people at the biological level so that they are more prone to immune disregulation in the face of subsequent stress. Some people have an altered immunologic responsivity on account of early traumatic stress (Solomon et al., 1974). Ader and Cohen (1975) have also demonstrated that immunosuppression can be conditioned in animals. Although yet to be demonstrated, there is no reason to believe that humans are less vulnerable to conditioned immunosuppression. Life contingencies and learned behavioral patterns may sustain a pattern of chronic immunosuppression and increased vulnerability to immune-related illnesses. The importance of patterns of behavior and one's relationship to the social environment, as well as one's repertoire of coping strategies, cannot be underestimated in the etiology and treatment of immune-related diseases.

The links between psychological factors and immune functioning are the central nervous system (especially the hypothalamic-pituitary axis and its humoral products, corticosteroids, and catecholamines) and the autonomic nervous system. Stressful stimuli affect hypothalamic activity (Stein, Schleifer, & Keller, 1981). Stress is associated with increased secretion of adrenal-corticosteroids, especially cortisol. Within several minutes after the stressful event is perceived, plasma cortisol levels become elevated. Corticosteroids are known to interfere with protein synthesis and hence with lymphocyte metabolism. Within the few hours after the stressful event, a consequence of corticosteroid secretion is evident: suppression of lymphocyte (T- and B-cell) and macrophage activity, in other words, generalized immunosuppression (Riley, Fitzmaurice & Spackman, 1981). Acute stress also affects the release of catecholamines and contributes to catecholamine depletion. Catecholamine depletion increases tumor growth (Sklår & Anisman, 1981) and contributes to suppression of T-cell activity (Holden, 1978). In addition, stress may alter neuroendocrine balance. For example, stress-induced alterations in estrogen levels increase the risk of breast cancer in women (MacMahon, Cole, & Brown, 1973), presumably because such hormones also cause immunosuppression. These biochemical changes are strongly implicated in disregulation of immune functioning. The immune system is unable to accurately recognize and destroy foreign agents, and the person becomes vulnerable to infection, cancer, allergies, and autoimmune diseases, depending on the specific nature of the dysfunction.

Cancer results when abnormal cells within the body proliferate uncontrollably, invade normal tissue, and metastasize to distant sites. Most experts agree that cancer progresses through a number of discrete stages (Fox, 1981; Sklår & Anisman, 1981): (a) the genesis of cancer cells and tumor formation; (b) the progressive growth of the tumor cells; (c) and the metastasis of these cells to other locations within the body and the development of secondary cancer sites. Cancer begins with a spontaneous cell mutation. A variety of mutagenic agents contribute to accidents in cell division: radiation and sunlight, oncogenic viruses, air pollutants, toxic chemicals, tobacco smoke, food additives, drugs, and the like (Reif, 1981). Each of these causes damage to the cells' DNA. Though the normal cell is equipped with enzymes to repair the damage, the repair process is vulnerable to error (Fox, 1981). Most mutant cells are not cancerous. Some mutant cells manifest a "high proliferative advantage" (Burnet, 1971). These particular mutations, to which some people genetically are more susceptible (Knudson, 1977), may represent vestiges of a regenerative trait lost through evolution. The reproductive mechanisms of the cell are uncontrollably released in the mutant cell, and the cell has the potential to grow in epidemic proportioins, crowding out and destroying healthy cells (Rosch, 1979).

Since the cancerous mutation, like any other mutation, begins as a single cell (Burnet, 1971), it can easily be destroyed by a healthy immune system before it has the opportunity to divide and proliferate. With the billions of cells that make up the human body, there is a high statistical likelihood that some cancerous cells are present at all times in the human body but that they seldom amount to any consequence. The likelihood of cancer as a disease increases with heightened exposure to mutagenic agents (in the modern world we have managed to saturate our environment with potential mutagenic agents) or when the immune system fails to restrain the growth of the cancer cells.

Burnet (1971) is credited with the immunological surveillance theory. According to this now accepted theory, certain classes of cells in the immune system specialize in detecting and destroying all kinds of tumor cells, including cancer cells. The natural killer cells are highly mobile cells that have very powerful cytotoxic effects on tumor cells. They are, however, effective only with small numbers of cells. Natural-killer activity is suppressed by the presence of large tumors. Natural killer cells are specialized to destroy cancer cells shortly after their appearance through mutation. They represent the first line of defense (Herberman & Holden, 1979). T-cells are designed as a second line of defense protecting the organism against progressive tumor growth. If the cancer cells evade killer cell surveillance and proliferate, they begin to manufacture and secrete antigens. If the cancer cells grow to the point of producing significant amounts of antigens, they are detected by the T-cells. The T-cells detect cancer cells by recognizing their antigens and thereby destroying the cancer cells. Macrophages also deter tumor growth by ingesting the cancer cells. Tumor growth is also held in check by the balance of hormones regulating cell division.

Cancer growth progresses when normal immunosurveillance fails (Barofsky, 1981; Burnet, 1971). Stress-induced suppression of natural killer and T-cell activity or macrophage activity increases the likelihood that the cancer cells will grow. Stress may also alter hormone balance so that tumor growth is stimulated (Sklår & Anisman, 1981). As cancer cells grow, they may release certain types of antigens into the blood, which in themselves cause immunosuppression (Carter, 1976). Cancer cells also release products that stimulate the vascularization of the tumorous tissue (Sklår & Anisman, 1981). Once the immune system is rendered inoperative and the tumor secures its own fresh blood supply, it is capable of rapid and unrestrained growth. It then becomes detectable as a mass. As the cancer cells continue to generate, they eventually metastasize to other sites. When cancer cells first enter the bloodstream, however, they are highly vulnerable to detection by the immune system. The patient's realization that he has cancer, with its concommitant death anxiety and traumatic medical procedures, may further render the immune system dysfunctional and contribute to the metastatic process.

It is clear that stress-induced elevations in corticosteroids and catecholamines are capable of suppressing immune functioning and most likely are an important factor in the etiology of cancer. It is less clear exactly what types of psychological factors contribute to the development of cancer. For many years researchers have tried to discover the so-called cancer-prone personality, and although their results show many inconsistencies, several themes have emerged. In early work (LeShan & Worthington 1955, 1956) identified a basic pattern in the life of the cancer-prone person: the person avoids relationships because relationships are perceived to be dangerous. Eventually the person enters into a relationship and makes it the center of his life. Following the loss of that relationship, the person is unable to find a substitute and retreats into withdrawal and depression. From such formulations a number of related concepts arose regarding the cancer-prone person. Cancer was associated with loss in the lives of persons prior to the development of cancer. Cancer was also associated with inhibition of emotional expression, expecially the expression of anger (Bahnson & Bahnson, 1966; Greer & Morris, 1975; Kissen, 1966; Peterson, Popkin, & Hall, 1981).

More recent work has shifted the emphasis from stressful life events—important losses or lack of social support systems to the coping resources available to the person to deal with the stressful event. Recent reviews (e.g., Temoshok & Heller, 1984) and experimental studies (Bieliauskas & Garron, 1982) have shown that the two most important psychological factors in cancer risk are: (a) inhibition of emotional expression; and (b) a subjective sense of helplessness or perceived lack of control. In other words, cancer is a problem of coping style (Sklår & Anisman,1981) as well as of a chronic deficiency in coping ability (Bieliauskas & Garron, 1982;

Holden, 1978). Persistent failures in psychological coping are believed to repeatedly elevate corticosteroid levels and contribute to long-term reduction in immunological competence associated with increased cancer risk.

The Role of Hypnosis in the Treatment of Cancer

A primary goal of cancer treatment is to arrest the progressive growth of the cancer cells and, it is hoped, to eradicate cancer cells (in a relative sense). Carter (1976) suggests a multidimensional treatment approach, with the primary goal of reducing the tumor load by means of surgery, radiotherapy, or chemotherapy and a secondary goal of rehabilitating immune functioning so that the immune system can restrain any subsequent growth of the cancer cells. It is, however, unlikely that the immune system can handle cancer once it is visibly detectable. Even a small cancerous growth contains billions of cells, a number far in excess of what even the healthiest immune system could handle. The earlier the cancer is detected, the greater the likelihood of destroying its cell mass. Surgery, radiotherapy, and chemotherapy necessarily constitute the first line of treatment; psychological interventions aimed at stress reduction may also play an important role. Any psychological intervention that contributes to "non-specific immuno-enhancement" can be beneficial as an adjunctive treatment (Carter, 1976). There are three ways to accomplish this: stress reduction, wellness enhancement, and direct immunotherapy.

Stress Reduction. Both hypnotherapy and nonhypnotic therapy are useful in alleviating the stress in a cancer patient's life. The therapist first must identify stressful situations. Stressful life events, chronic difficult problems, and lack of social support contribute to cancer (Paykel & Rao, 1984), as does an inhibited style of emotional expression (Bieliauskas & Garron, 1982). Psychotherapy and hypnotherapy can desensitize the patient to stressful situations (Simonton, Matthews-Simonton, & Sparks, 1980), teach the patient ways to communicate appropriately, and help the patient discover more effective coping strategies (Newton, 1983). Since the death anxiety and depression accompanying the discovery that one has cancer constitute considerable stress, psychotherapy (Simonton et al., 1980) and hypnotherapy (Grosz, 1979; Olness, 1981) can be used to work through the feelings. Grosz, for example, has the cancer patient rehearse death in hypnotic fantasy. The hypnotized patient is encouraged to view death as a "journey and temporary separation."

Teaching the patient the skill of relaxation is also helpful. Progressive muscle relaxation accompanied by breathing exercises (Simonton, Matthews-Simonton, & Creighton, 1978; Simonton et al., 1980), intensive meditation (Meares, 1979, 1983), hypnotically assisted profound relaxation (Newton, 1983) and self-hypnotic restful fantasies (LeBaw, Holton, Tewell,

& Eccles, 1975) have all been useful in improving the quality of survival and sometimes in prolonging survival. To produce the physiological effect, namely, the reduction in plasma corticosteroid levels, the patient must regularly achieve a very deep state of relaxation. Hypnosis is clearly a means to this end. Sachar and his colleagues (Sachar, Fishman, & Mason, 1965; Sachar, Cobb, & Shor, 1966) have shown that 1 to 2 hours of hypnotic relaxation is associated with a profound drop in plasma cortisol levels for at least 90 minutes in selected hypnotic subjects. The reduction in cortisol levels produced by hypnotic relaxation is not a function of hypnotizability, but of the hypnotic relationship. In other words, both the quality and the intensity of the involvement between the patient and therapist, as well as the consistency of the hypnotic relaxation training, are necessary to bring about the physiological effect (Hall, 1983).

Wellness Enhancement.   Any intervention that enhances the patient's well-being and mental health may also stimulate immune activity. The Simontons (Simonton et al., 1980) advocate taking advantage of the patient's expectations of treatment. Their now very popular cancer program is "designed to help make the positive expectancy more explicit" (p. 232). What the patient believes the treatment will do for him seems to be more important than what the treatment actually is. A prerequisite to cancer remission seems to be the patient's strong faith that the treatment program he has chosen will work for him, regardless of the objective value of the treatment (Ikemi, 1978; Oliver, 1983; Rosch, 1984). The clinician's task is to help the patient develop a strong belief system with regard to the treatment in question (Newton, 1983).

The therapist should first explore the patient's attitude toward his disease and his conscious and unconscious expectancies in its progression. Achterberg and Lawlis (1978) asked their patients to visualize and draw the activity of the immune cells attempting to control the cancerous growth. This projective method is useful in exploring defeatist attitudes, which can then be worked through in psychotherapy or hypnotherapy. Similarly, Gardner and Lubman (1983) asked their patients to produce images of the future. The patient imagines what his life will be like each successive year after the diagnosis of cancer. Negative expectations about the future as expressed in the images, for example, the expectation or wish to die (Newton, 1983), and resistances to treatment are worked through, and the patient is encouraged to devise positive, future-oriented imagery (Gardner & Lubman, 1983).

Patients should be encouraged to develop an aggressive and positive stance in combating their illness (Rosch, 1984), and to express freely any concerns about the treatment and its progress. In addition, patients should learn to experience positive emotional states regularly. We know that hypnosis can generate a variety of affective states, including the intensity of felt positive emotional states (Hodge & Wagner, 1964). Emotional stimulation through movies depicting humor (Cousins, 1979) and loving compassion (McClelland, Alexander, & Marks, 1982) have been shown to enhance immunoactivity (Dillon, Minchoff, & Baker, 1985–86). Hypnotic suggestions for intensely positive affects, followed by self-hypnotic generation of such emotional states, may stimulate immune functioning. Margolis (1983) used hypnotically suggested mystical religious experiences to generate a strong sense of well-being in her cancer patients. She also recommends helping the patient to develop happy memories and imagery he particularly enjoys. Hypnotic ego-strengthening also contributes to the well-being of children suffering from cancer by engendering a sense of mastery (Olness, 1981). Finkelstein and Howard (1983) have demonstrated that a simple 10–minute tape of hypnotic relaxation and ego-strengthening suggestions improves coping skills.

Above all, the focus of the treatment is to help the patient improve the overall quality of life (Dempster, Balson, & Whalen, 1976; Grosz, 1979; LeBaw, Holton, Tewell, & Eccles, 1975). In addition to helping the patient cope with the illness and the prospect of dying, the therapist directly addresses the patient's lifestyle. One goal is to help the patient develop better habits of daily living: reduction of unhealthful habits, such as smoking and problematic eating and cultivation of healthful routines of relaxation, meditation, and exercise. Another goal is to help the patient develop latent interests, hobbies, and talents. The patient is encouraged to explore what he most wants to do with his life in the uncertain amount of time remaining.

A strong emphasis is on improving the quality of relationships in the patient's current life. Patients are encouraged to complete unfinished business with friends and to spend quality time with intimates (Grosz, 1979). The Ideal-Self Technique and pseudotime orientation are useful hypnotic tools to these ends. The hypnotized patient visualizes his ego-ideal and merging into it, that is, becoming progressively more like the person he would want to be—healthy, competent, and strong. He also imagines himself at various future times effectively living the kind of life he would most like to live. Posthypnotic suggestions are used for reinforcement. Such hypnotic work can best be carried out when there is an intimate relationship between the patient and the therapist (Margolis, 1983), and the focus is on enjoyable imagery (Olness, 1981).

Direct Immunotherapy.   The third approach to stimulating immune activity is by direct immunotherapeutic imagery. The Simontons (1978), who pioneered this approach, teach nonhypnotic relaxation combined with somatic imagery. The patient is taught to visualize the healing forces within his body—his own immune cells attacking and destroying the cancer cells. The Simontons reported that repeated practice with such imagery is associated with increased suvival time and sometimes with remission in a highly select group of cancer patients (Simonton et al., 1980). Subsequent clinical studies suggest that routine application of such visualizations is not in itself sufficient. The clinician must pay careful attention to the quality of the imagery. Patricia Norris (personal personal communication 1981) has her patients generate and experiment with a variety of images. She claims that certain spontaneous images (not always of immune functioning) have an experientially distinct "sense" about them and are highly specific, bodily felt images of one's natural healing forces. Their appearance increases the likelihood of a positive treatment response. Newton (1983), Margolis (1983), and Shapiro (1983) have combined hypnosis with visualizations of effective immune functioning. The patient is hypnotized and encouraged to visualize the immune cells attacking the cancer cells and joining forces with the medical treatment, such as chemotherapy. The patient is asked to practice these visualizations a number of times each day (Shapiro, 1983). The efficacy of these visualizations, however, may be limited to highly hypnotizable patients (Bowers & Kelly, 1979).

Hypnosis and Autoimmune Diseases

Autoimmune diseases represent a class of illnesses in which the immune system mistakenly manufactures autoantibodies against the normal cell constituents of the body and destroys certain types of healthy tissue. The specific symptoms of the disease depend on the type of body tissue mistakenly attacked by the immune system. Autoimmune diseases include: systemic lupus erythematosis, rheumatoid arthritis, spondyloarthritis, polymyositosis, scleroderma, and multiple sclerosis. Systemic lupus erythematois is an attack in part directed against indigenous cellular DNA, which results in a nonspecific chronic inflammation, typically characterized by fatigue, fever, erythematosis (rashes), and sometimes by alopecia, arthritis, and skin photosensitivity. It is sometimes accompanied by renal complications and neuropathy. Rheumatoid arthritis represents an attack specifically directed against the synovial cells of the small and sometimes large peripheral joints. It is accompanied by variable symptoms of fatigue, diffuse muscle stiffness, paresthesia, vasomotor instability, and typically joint pain and swelling, muscle stiffness, and a high degree of muscle atrophy. Ankylosing spondylitis is specific to the cartilaginous joints of the axial skeleton. It is accompanied by episodic low back pain of variable intensity, significant morning stiffness, a progression of symptoms along the spinal column, and eventual loss of spinal mobility. Polymyositosis, an autoimmune disease of the striate muscle tissue, results in progressive muscle weakness and extensive inflammation of the muscle tissue. Schleroderma is a progressive autoimmune disease of the connective tissue; fibrotic tissue replaces the epidermal tissue of the skin and internal organs. Exposure to coal dust, gold, silica, and polyvinyl chloride contributes to the disease. Multiple schlerosis is an illness whose course is variable but progressive and in which the myelin sheath of nerve tissues is attacked by autoantibodies and destroyed.

All the autoimmune diseases share common etiological features: each represents "defective immuno-regulation" (Fauci, 1981). Though, autoimmune diseases are not well understood, the current theory is that all are a consequence of impaired B- and T-cell interactions. The suppressor T-cells are thought not to function properly. In people with advanced autoimmune diseases, the total number of suppressor T-cells is significantly lower than in normal persons (Kohler & Vaughan, 1982). The balance between helper and suppressor T-cells may also be impaired (Fauci, 1981). Since the T-cell system acts as a regulator of B-cell activity (Ader, 1981), T-cell, disregulation contributes to hyperactivity of the B-cells (Solomon, 1981). The B-cells are allowed to manufacture antibodies in an unrestrained manner. For reasons not yet understood, the B-cells produce antibodies against endogenous antigens, that is, against normal cell constituents. These antibodies are produced in significant quantities and released into the blood and lymphatic systems. Some have been identified, such as an antinuclear antibody associated with systemic lupus and a rheumatoid factor associated with rheumatoid arthritis. Circulating autoantibodies mistakenly attack certain types of cells, for example, the cells of the synovial joints, the striate musculature, the connective tissue, the cartilage, the myelin sheath, or certain cellular components such as DNA (Solomon, et al., 1974). It is still unclear why only certain types of tissues are selected for attack. Genetic predisposition may be associated with changes in the cell surface structure, which makes certain types of tissue vulnerable to mistaken recognition (Fauci, 1981). Autoantibody-antigen complexes activate proteolytic enzymes capable of eroding and denaturing normal body tissues and replacing them with scar tissue. These complexes also stimulate the release of histamines and other humoral agents from mast cells, which produce the inflammatoy response (Solomon & Moos, 1964). In the case of rheumatoid arthritis, macrophages also mistakenly attack the cartilage, and tissue degeneration occurs. The antigen complexes stimulate the production of the synovial cells so they proliferate at an unusual rate and crowd the joint space.

Stress contributes to the variability of the symptoms and possibly to the etiology of autoimmune diseases. Failure to cope adequately with psychological stress may also contribute to the development of rheumatoid arthritis (Solomon & Moos, 1964; Solomon, 1981). It is doubtful that a rheumatoid personality exists, but a person is more likely to manifest the disease when coping resources are inadequate and when strategies against stressors persistently fail. (These are exactly the conditions that contribute to immune disregulation in the case of neoplastic disease.) Patients with rheumatoid arthritis are notoriously poor at fantasizing and verbalizing feelings (alexithymia) (Achterberg & Lawlis, 1980); they think operationally. These findings suggest that a coping style of inhibited emotional expression may contribute to the disease. The frequent intensification and remission characteristic of autoimmune diseases are likely to be stress related (Achterberg & Lawlis, 1980). Moreover, contracting the disease itself becomes a major source of psychological stress, which further impairs immunocompetence and moves the illness in the direction of progressive impairment.

Unfortunately, the treatment of autoimmune diseases by psychological means is largely undeveloped. A treatment protocol similar to that used for cancer is being developed. The clinician begins by teaching the patient to self-monitor the vicissitudes of the autoimmune symptoms. The patient keeps daily records of the symptoms, noting daily activities and subjectively rating the level of tension. The therapist helps the patient uncover the relationship between stressful situations and the exacerbation of symptoms.

Next, the patient is taught some means of stress reduction. Nonhypnotic relaxation (Achterberg & Lawlis, 1980) and hypnotic relaxation (Millikin, 1964) have been used. In the case of rheumatoid arthritis, in which the outbreak of symptoms is often preceded by increased muscle tension, (Gottschalk, Serota, & Shapiro, 1950) relaxation training may have a prophylactic effect (Achterberg, McGraw, & Lawlis, 1981). Desensitization to the stressful events that typically occur in the patient's life and the development of coping skills through hypnosis are also useful. Emotional conflicts associated with the illness can be worked through in hypnotherapy (Cheek & LeCron, 1968). Patients with autoimmune diseases must live with a high degree of uncertainty about the ebb and flow of symptoms. Educational and support groups for autoimmune patients enable the patient to learn more about the illness and its impact on his life (Achterberg & Lawlis, 1980). A variety of hypnotherapeutic procedures can be used to enhance the patient's well-being, positive emotional state, self-efficacy, and quality of life in the face of the illness. To our knowledge, no systematic studies are available on direct hypnotic immunotherapy with autoimmune patients. It remains to be demonstrated whether or not hypnotic visualization of effective immunofunctioning is beneficial to autoimmune patients. Nevertheless, any method or combination of methods that improves health acts in the service of immunoenhancement and contributes to healing (Bowers & Kelly, 1979).

Clinicians have explored methods designed to rehabilitate the degenerative tissue. Since muscle atrophy is reduced when rheumatoid arthritic patients exercise, some have used nonhypnotic joint-EMG biofeedback to improve joint muscle functioning (Achterberg & Lawlis, 1980; Gottschalk, Serota, & Shapiro, 1950). Hypnotic and self-hypnotic suggestions have been used to increase joint mobility and to encourage exercise (Millikin, 1964). Not only do these methods maintain tissue health, they help to improve the patient's overall functional status. With rheumatoid patients, thermal biofeedback (Achterberg & Lawlis, 1980) and hypnotic visualizations can be used for voluntary control over vasomotor response in the affected areas. An important consequence of these psychophysiological manipulations may be a decrease in intra-articular temperature. An increase in intra-articular temperature is associated with progression of the disease process. Achterberg, McGraw, & Lawlis, (1981), have shown that such psychological interventions produce a fall in sedimentation rate. Inasmuch as sedimentation rate correlates positively with the intensity of the symptoms, one can hypothesize that such psychological interventions can affect the disease at a biological level. Comparable studies using hypnotic intervention as yet do not exist, but we hope our comments will stimulate interest in these areas.

The pain and discomfort accompanying these diseases can more often than not be treated with hypnosis with good results (Crasilneck & Hall, 1975; Kroger & Fezler, 1976; Millikin, 1964; Smith & Balaban, 1983; Van Pelt, 1961). We recommend individualized assessment of the application of pain coping strategies discussed earlier in this chapter.

The Hypnotic Treatment of Allergies

Allergies are also a consequence of disregulation of immune functioning. As with autoimmune diseases, the interaction between B- and T-cells is altered. The suppressor T-cells, which ordinarily control the levels of immunoglobulin produced by the B-cells, fail to regulate B-cell activity adequately (Katz, 1978). In allergic persons, the B-cells are believed to be hyperactive (Hall, 1983). B-cells produce a variety of proteins, or immunoglobulins, one of which IgE, has been implicated in allergic responses (Hamburger, 1976). Patients showing allergic sensitivity have elevated levels of serum IgE. The normal person manifests allergic responses under certain conditions, for example, when serum from an allergic person is injected into his skin. This allergic response, called passive transfer, is mediated by the production and release of IgE from the B-cells. It is not so much the elevated IgE levels but their persistence that characterizes the allergic individual (Hamburger, 1976). This abnormal IgE response is probably the consequence of B-cell hyperactivity and the failure of the suppressor T-cells to hold production in check. The unusual response is in part genetically determined. Genetic factors may also be involved in the altered ability to recognize antigens. The allergic person mistakenly recognizes otherwise neutral external stimuli as antigenic agents and produces an inflammatory response. The IgE molecule has highly specific binding sites by which it is able to attack the mast cells and basophils. The mast cells contain the chemicals that mediate the inflammatory response (e.g., histamine). Once IgE attaches to the mast cell, these substances are released into the tissue. The result is typically a localized inflammatory response, and sometimes a generalized and serious systemic inflammatory response or anaphylaxis.

There is a range of symptoms that constitute the localized resonse, from a slight irritation to a visible weal (urticaria) and flair (erythema) in the case of skin sensitivity; rhinitis and sneezing in the case of nose and sinus sensitivity; and bronchospasm in the case of asthma. The allergic reaction is often immediate but is sometimes delayed.

The events that trigger allergic responses are highly variable. A wide variety of otherwise neutral environmental stimuli can trigger attacks: dust, molds, pollens, animal dander, and the like. Foods can also trigger allergic responses. The evidence for an "allergic personality" is inconclusive, but the evidence that psychological and emotional stress trigger allergic response in at least a subgroup of allergic patients is strong (Freeman, Feingold, Schlesinger, & Gorman, 1964). Most allergic patients show sensitivity to a wide range of stimuli over time, so that it would be difficult to find an allergic patient in whom psychological stress or a single allergen was the only trigger (Clarkson, 1937). There is also reasonable evidence that allergic responses may be conditioned (Clarkson, 1937; Freeman et al., 1964). As allergic sensitivity progresses, some patients manifest full-blown allergic responses even in the absence of provoking stimuli. The traditional medical treatment is hyposensitization. The patient is systematically presented with lower to higher doses of the allergens, until the allergic response is alleviated.

With a few notable exceptions, the clinical use of hypnosis with allergies remains a largely undeveloped area. Most of the studies are anecdotal case reports with one or several subjects. Moreover, the typical hypnotic approach to the allergic patient has been the utilization of direct suggestion. Clarkson (1937) treated an 18-year-old girl with an egg allergy by hypnotizing her and simply telling her that no allergic reaction would occur as a result of the injection of the antigen into the skin. Following hypnosis the patient did not produce the characteristic weal and flair. Using a similar approach, Zeller (1944) failed to alleviate the allergic response in asthmatic patients who were sensitive to ragweed and animal dander. Using direct and indirect suggestions, Erickson, Hershman, & Sector, (1961), successfully eliminated the weal response in several allergic patients. Bartlett (1970) treated a young woman for an allergy to local anesthetics. She was hypnotized and told she would give up the allergy. Following hypnosis, she was able to accept the local anesthetic without producing her characteristic rash or fainting spells. A subsequent session entailed a symptom challenge, in which suggestions were given for the patient to produce the itching rash to skin injections of the anesthetic. The patient produced the itching but not the visible inflammation.

Several clinicians have treated allergic persons by means of hypnotic rehearsal in fantasy. Kroger (1964) instructed a 12-year-old boy allergic to cat fur, ragweed, and chocolate to imagine, while he was in hypnosis, playing with a cat walking through a weedpatch, and eating chocolate. Posthypnotic suggestions reinforced encountering these triggering events in reality without producing the allergic response. Perloff and Spiegelman (1973) treated a ten-year-old girl with an allergy to dog dander in a similar manner. In trance she rehearsed playing with her favorite kind of dog, a German shepherd. Suggestions were given that her skin would feel perfectly comfortable and there would be no itching. Following a successful response, suggestions were repeated prior to her playing with a real dog. She was able to enjoy her pet without producing an allergic response.

The work of Stephen Black and his associates stands out as the most significant contribution to hypnosis and allergies. In a classic study, Mason and Black (1958) treated a 27-year-old woman with asthma and hay fever, who had previously attained only partial relief from traditional hyposensitization. Direct hypnotic suggestions were given that she would no longer have difficulty breathing nor would she react to skin tests. Following hypnosis, the woman exhibited no allergic symptoms nor any reaction to a skin test. Mason and Black were able to evoke positive skin response in a nonallergic person by means of a passive transfer—by injecting the serum of the allergic patient into the skin of a nonallergic individual. They concluded that the allergic patient's blood still contained a serological basis of the allergic hypersensitivity, but that direct hypnotic suggestions caused an inhibition of the visible allergic symptoms.

In subsequent studies Black (1963a, 1963b) was able to replicate the original inhibition of the immediate allergic skin hypersensitivity in a highly select group of trained hypnotic subjects. Black used simple but emphatic direct hypnotic suggestions that no reaction to the allergen would occur when it was injected into the skin. In another study, Black, Humphrey, and Niven (1963) produced inhibition of the positive allergic response to injection of tuberculin protein into the skin (Mantoux test) in four subjects who were previously known to be Mantoux positive. Black also tried to ascertain the mechanisms by which hypnosis alleviates the allergic symptoms. In his study of the Mantoux skin test, it was found: (a) macroscopically, the visible weal and flair characteristic of the positive response to the skin test did not occur; (b) microscopically, the cellular infiltration characteristic of the inflammatory response did occur, although it was not visible. Hypnosis inhibited a particular part of the allergic reaction but not all of it.

Because the inflammatory response is mediated by the immune system, Black and Friedman (1965) conducted another study in which cortico-steroid levels were measured. While stress-inducing direct hypnotic sug-gestions to experience intense fear did effect a rise in cortisol levels as predicted, direct hypnotic suggestions to alleviate allergic response to a skin test were not associated with any change in cortisol levels, even though the allergic response was visibly inhibited.

Taken together, these experiments show that direct hypnotic sugges-tions can inhibit vascular components of the allergic response (weal and flair) but not the immunological components (B-cell production of IgE and cellular infiltration). It appears that hypnosis allows the patient to exercise voluntary control over both the vasomotor response (reduce the flair) and the degree of tissue permeability (reduce the weal). It is unclear from these studies whether hypnotizability is associated with the outcome. Mason (1963) correctly criticizes the failure to use adequate control subjects. Thus, it remains uncertain whether the inhibition of the allergic response is due to hypnotizability, task motivation, or both.

It is also unclear whether a more elaborate protocol of hypnotic inter-ventions, rather than simple, direct suggestion, would have had a more pervasive effect on the allergic response, that is, on not only its gross manifestations (weal and flair; itching, sneezing, etc.) but its immu-nological basis. Is it possible to devise a hypnobehavioral protocol that corrects for the disregulation of the immune system that is implicated in the etiology of allergic sensitivity—can one help to restore normal sup-pressor T-cell regulation and to reduce B-cell hyperactivity? Although no systematic work has been done in this area, a few suggestions can be made.

The hypnobehavioral treatment of allergy should begin with a careful assessment of situations that trigger the allergic response. The patient should learn to keep daily self-monitoring records of allergic reactions, the situation in which the reaction occurred, and the level of subjectively felt stress. A battery of skin tests is also recommended. Patient and therapist together should compile a list of triggering stimuli and attempt to ascertain the extent to which specific stressors contribute to the allergic response. Hypnotic desensitization then can be used to reduce sensitivity to trigger stimuli.

In a relaxed trance state the patient is systematically presented in fantasy with each of the stimuli known to trigger the allergic response along a continuum of least to most allergic (Ikemi, 1967). If the stressors are emotional, hypnotherapy can be used to uncover and work through the conflicts associated with the origins of the allergic response or its maintenance (Aston, 1959; Raginsky, 1962; Schowalter, 1959). The patient should also be encouraged to practice self-hypnotic relaxation regularly and to develop it as a skill. A variety of hypnotic methods can be used to foster a sense of well-being in the patient: ego-strengthening suggestions, evocation of intense, positive emotional states, and strategies to improve the overall quality of life. It is unclear whether direct hypnotic immunotherapy is useful to the allergic patient. To our knowledge, no one has attempted to have the allergic patient visualize the cells of his immune system functioning in a healthy and effective way. It is our belief that any intervention that reduces stress and contributes to lowering plasma corticosteroid levels is likely to have a beneficial effect on immune functioning and is worthy of further investigation. We hope that the future will bring more sophisticated treatment of allergies in which the patient systematically learns skills to desensitize himself to allergy-producing stimuli and learns voluntary control over the vascular and immunological changes that mediate the allergic response.

4

The Hypnobehavioral Treatment of Habit and Behavioral Disorders

SMOKING CESSATION

Assessment

The Smoking History. Assessment of the smoker begins with a detailed smoking history, which includes: the number of years he has been smoking, the circumstances under which smoking commenced, a history of changes in smoking habits, and previous attempts to quit. Assessment of current smoking behavior includes the number of cigarettes smoked per day, the situations in which smoking is most likely to occur, the psychological uses of the cigarette, the extent to which the smoke is inhaled, and the brand of cigarettes smoked. Knowing the brand enables the clinician to ascertain whether the intake of nicotine and tar is relatively low or high so he can estimate how problematic nicotine withdrawal is likely to be.

The Psychiatric History. It is also important to evaluate present and past smoking behavior in the total context of the patient's life history. Medical and psychiatric symptoms should be noted, especially where they may affect the persistence of smoking cessation. For example, because depressive and borderline patients use smoking as a self-soothing behavior, it may be particularly difficult for them to quit smoking. When the patient is at the same time trying to prevent relapse of other addictions, such as alcoholism or caffeinism, difficulties may be increased. The clinician also assesses stress factors, such as stressful life events, daily hassles, and health risk factors (overweight, type A behavior, or lack of physical exercise) as these may relate to smoking behavior. In addition, the patient's social support system must be assessed, especially whether those closest to the patient are or are not smokers.

Motivation. The single most important factor to evaluate is the patient's motivation to quit smoking. The patient's answers to the question, "Why do you want to stop smoking?" typically reflect various fears of harmful consequences to health or the social and personal benefits of quitting. The answer is a strong predictor of treatment outcome. Patients who are concerned with specific existing health problems (Matarazzo &

151

Saslow, 1960; Straits, 1966) and have a high degree of personal responsibility for quitting (Bernstein, 1969; Clark, 1974; Glad, Tyre, & Adesso, 1976) are most likely to alter smoking behavior.

Conversely, those whose reasons to quit are vague and who externalize responsibility are poor candidates. They need interventions specifically designed to clarify or increase their motivation. With them, the clinician can take advantage of the group process in which group members brainstorm and generate as many reasons as they can to stop smoking. The reasons are discussed in the group, and group members often learn from one another good reasons to quit. Following the discussion, each member writes down a list of his own reasons to stop (Sanders, 1977). If the group as a whole is unconvinced about the deleterious effects of smoking, the group leader may present a brief lecture on smoking as a health risk or ask members to imagine and discuss each person's future health deterioration as a result of smoking (Moses, 1964). To increase motivation, patients need to see the consequences of smoking as imminent and must maintain an orientation to the future. If a patient externalizes the responsibility for quitting ("I want to quit because my doctor (or spouse) tells me I have to" [Clark, 1974]), the focus of the group discussion must place responsibility firmly on the patient (Glad et al., 1976). Sensitive group confrontation of the patient's refusal to take responsibility can often increase the patient's motivation.

Sometimes the patient's answers to the question, "Why do you want to stop smoking?" do not sufficiently tap motivation but instead reflect conscious motivation. Unconscious motivation can work for or against the conscious commitment to stop smoking. Where poor motivation persists, the clinician must address the issue of unconscious motivation. Underlying conflicts and resistances that interfere with the commitment to stop smoking can be worked through in psychotherapy (Povorinsky, 1961) or hypnotherapy (Kroger & Libott, 1967; Nuland & Field, 1970). Hypnoprojective methods are especially useful in such cases. Cues that speak to the patient's unconscious wish to get better can also be utilized in the hypnotic suggestions (Erickson, 1964).

Where patients remain poorly motivated after assessment of conscious and unconscious motivation, a payback contract with a refundable deposit can be used (Elliot & Tighe, 1968; Keutzer, Lichtenstein, & Mees, 1968). At the onset of treatment, patients are asked to deposit a fixed amount of money, a sum separate from treatment fees. They receive a portion back for attendance, for following the steps of treatment, and for fully giving up smoking on the prearranged quit date. Patients who remain poorly motivated and are noncompliant with treatment forfeit the money. If the deposit sum is sufficiently large, motivation and acceptance of responsibility are heightened. A related approach is to have the hypnotized patient visualize spending the money saved from quitting smoking on something pleasurable (Watkins, 1976).

Coping Resources. The hypnotherapist also assesses the range of coping strategies the patient employs to resist the temptation to smoke. The clinician asks, "If you have attempted to stop smoking in the past, how did you go about it?" Patients who on occasion have quit but then relapsed often describe coping strategies such as self-rewards, substitutes, breathing, relaxation, talking themselves out of smoking, and the like. Often these same coping strategies can be strengthened through hypnotic interventions, which also can be used to bring to light and develop new idiosyncratic coping strategies. Patients can reflect in trance on possible ways to stop (Nuland & Field, 1970). Or an indirect approach can be used: patients visualize in trance someone who is trying to stop smoking and then imagine how that person goes about the task of stopping (Hershman, 1956). Through such explorations, coping strategies can be tailored to each patient, whose ideas can later be fed back in the form of specific hypnotic suggestions (Nuland & Field, 1970).

Hypnotizability. The patient's hypnotizability should be tested either by standardized scales or by clinical assessment procedures. Assessment by standardized scales allows the research-oriented clinician to collect data on the contribution of hypnotizability to smoking cessation and its maintenance (Berkowitz, Ross-Townsend, and Kohberger, 1979; Wadden & Anderton, 1982); individual clinical assessment procedures allow the therapist to incorporate hypnoprojective methods directly into the assessment of hypnotizability to become familiar with the patient's individual motivations and coping strategies.

Nonhypnotic and Hypnotic Self-Regulation of Smoking Behavior

Self-monitoring. An important component of the initial assessment is self-monitoring of smoking behavior (Abrams & Wilson, 1979; Glad et al., 1976; Pomerleau & Pomerleau, 1977; Pyke, McK.Agnew,& Kopperud, 1966). To alter an overlearned habit such as smoking, self-monitoring is the "single most important variable" in directing the patient to automatic behavior previously out of awareness (Hunt & Matarazzo, 1970). Patients keep an accurate record of each cigarette smoked daily over 2 to 3 weeks before making any attempt to alter the smoking habit. They frequently use a "wrap sheet," (Fig. 4.1) a record sheet on which they record each cigarette smoked (*before* they light up) and then wrap the sheet around the

Date: _____
Day: _____

Number	Time	Activity or Situation	Need for Cigarette
1			
2			
3			
4			
5			
6			
7			
8			
9			
10			
11			
12			
13			
14			
15			
16			
17			
18			
19			
20			

Need for cigarette: 1 = Most Important; 5 = Least Important.

Other Comments or Observations:

FIG. 4.1.   Cigarette Wrap Sheet. From Brown, R. A., & Lichtenstein, E. (1979). The Oregon Smoking Control Program, The University of Oregon and from *Quitter's guide: 7 day plan to help you stop smoking cigarettes* (1978). American Cancer Society. Adapted by permission.

cigarette pack. In addition to recording the number of cigarettes, the patient may record the time of day each cigarette is smoked, the situation in which each is smoked, and the need for each on a 5–point scale (5 = no need; 4 = slight need; 3 = moderate need; 2 = fairly strong need; 1 = intense need. A "butt bottle," into which the butts of all cigarettes smoked in one day are placed, can be used as an alternate cue. The number of cigarettes per day can be tallied from the number of butts in the bottle. This is also an olfactory and visual counterstimulus to smoking.

The therapist and the patient each review the self-monitoring records to determine the patient's specific pattern of daily smoking. High-risk times can be identified for each smoker by looking at when cigarette use is heaviest during the day. Some smokers are more at risk upon awakening, taking a break at work, or seeing others smoke. A variety of stressful situations may contribute to individual smoking patterns—time pressure, daily hassles, or significant changes in life events. The daily quota of cigarettes (the fewest needed before treatment) can also be determined by calculating the lowest number of cigarettes for which there is at least a slight need on a given day over the 2 to 3 weeks of baseline self-monitoring.

The Functions of Smoking

It is especially important to study the patient's ratings of need for a cigarette. It helps teach the patient that cigarettes are used throughout the day for different purposes and that some are more easily given up than others. Researchers (Ikard, Green, & Horn, 1969; Tomkins, 1966; Waingrow, Horn, & Ikard, 1968) have identified the varous functions of smoking and have classified smokers accordingly. These functions, listed in terms of percentage of people who smoke for each, include: sedative smoking (to manage negative affects); addictive smoking (to prevent buildup of tension and withdrawal symptoms); relaxant smoking (after a meal, to feel more confident in social situations); stimulant smoking (to begin the day or to get a lift); sensorimotor smoking (to have something to do, e.g., handling the cigarette, manipulating the breath, or watching the smoke); habitual smoking (automatic smoking without realizing it). Smoking may fulfill various needs for any given patient. Patients also fall into various categories: some patients smoke for sedation, others because of addiction, and so forth. After the patient has ascertained the various uses of smoking throughout the day, a priority list is developed (Pomerleau & Pomerleau, 1977), in which each patient ranks on a scale of one to five which cigarettes, for whatever reasons, will be the easiest and which the most difficult to give up. On completion of the review, the patient and the therapist both should have a reasonable idea of the specific ways smoking behavior is manifest in the patient's daily life. They can then begin to devise better strategies for altering smoking behavior. It is not unusual, however, for patients to cut down cigarette intake as a result of self-monitoring alone as they learn to become more aware of the characteristics of their own smoking behavior.

Stimulus-Control.   Hypnotic treatment can now be undertaken in conjunction with stimulus-control (Bernstein & McAlister, 1976). Over time, smoking becomes associated with and reinforced by numerous environmental cues and situations (Bernstein & McAlister, 1976). Cue control is a necessary component of the hypnotic treatment (Dengrove, 1970). The patient must agree to limit smoking to those situations identified through self-monitoring as high-need situations. Smoking may also be limited to certain rooms or areas (Nolan, 1968). Smoking paraphernalia is made less available by having the patient remove from sight and reach cigarettes, matches, ashtrays, and the like or buy only one pack of cigarettes at a time (Dengrove, 1970; Von Dedenroth, 1964). Switching to a less enjoyable brand also helps (Von Dedenroth, 1964). These strategies can be rehearsed in hypnosis and reinforced by posthypnotic suggestions designed to modify cue-controlled smoking behavior.

Self-Regulation and Contingency Management. The next step in treatment is to help the patient reduce cigarette intake toward a defined goal (Hershman, 1956; Pyke et al., 1966). Whether the goal of treatment is total abstinence or reduction (Flaxman, 1978; Mausner, 1966) depends on the needs of the individual patient. Total abstinence, the best goal, is not always possible. While a small number of patients respond to direct suggestions to abstain immediately from smoking (Hall & Crasilneck, 1970; Moses, 1964), for example, by making a commitment to health (Spiegel, 1970; Spiegel & Spiegel, 1978), the majority of smokers need more extensive interventions designed to alter the habit of smoking gradually but significantly.

Cutting down cigarette intake may be accomplished by several means, in a stimulus-hierarchy, for example, (Pomerleau & Pomerleau, 1977). While in a relaxed trance state, the patient rehearses in fantasy going through a typical day without a cigarette rated as #5 ("no need"). Then the patient is given a graded posthypnotic suggestion that it will be easier and easier to go without the "no-need" cigarettes as each day passes. Once the patient is able to reduce the "no-need" cigarettes over time, the procedure of hypnotic rehearsal and posthypnotic reinforcement is repeated over successive sessions for the "slight need" (#4), the "moderate need," and so on, cigarettes. The pace of progression through the hierarchy varies according to the patient. When the treatment is conducted in a group format, social pressure quickens the pace for the slower patients.

An alternative approach is the quota method (Pomerleau & Pomerleau, 1977). The hypnotist specifies a fixed number of cigarettes for each week or each day and suggests that the patient will be satisfied with the specified number of cigarettes (Johnston & Donaghue, 1971). The quota of cigarettes for any given time period can be decided through group discussion. Each patient's quota is stated publicly to the group. The quota can also be developed in hypnosis by asking each patient in trance to spontaneously generate a number for the fewest daily cigarettes he thinks he can be comfortable with until the next session.

A third approach is the timer method (Pomerleau & Pomerleau, 1977), in which delays are imposed on the patient before he lights up a cigarette.

The goal of this method is to introduce through posthypnotic suggestion longer and longer periods of abstinence to break up the smoking routine (Dengrove, 1970; Hershman, 1956). Specific periods of abstinence may also be introduced through posthypnotic suggestions—after eating, before going to bed, and the like (Von Dedenroth, 1964).

While each of these methods may be best suited for different types of patients, each serves the same end, namely, to reduce significantly the cigarette intake by modifying habitual smoking behavior. It is wise to have the patient set a quit date, on which he will cease to smoke *any* cigarettes, including those rated as "intense need" on the priority list (Von Dedenroth, 1968). Potential quit dates can be explored through hypnoprojective methods, or they can be arrived at by consensus. The hypnotized patient then imagines how good he will feel, having stopped on the quit day (Watkins, 1976).

The Act of Smoking.   Another dimension of smoking that needs to be addressed is the act of smoking itself. Smoking entails complex visual, auditory, tactile, gustatory, and olfactory stimulation (Mausner, 1966): handling the cigarette, watching the smoke, manipulating the breath, moving the tongue and lips, inhaling the smoke so as to feel the irritation and warmth, hearing the sound of inhaling and puffing, and sensing the pleasurable taste and smell of the smoke. To break up the automatic motor habit, hypnotic suggestions can be given that the patient switch hands or hold the cigaretete between fingers different from those he usually uses (Kroger, 1963). Suggestions can be given for various motor substitutes, such as fiddling with worry beads. The oral stimulation provided by smoking can be modified by a number of oral substitutes (Glad et al., 1976): eating Lifesavers (Kroger, 1963) or lozenges (Gould, 1953), using a refreshing mouth wash (Von Dedenroth, 1964), drinking tea, chewing gum, eating vegetable sticks. Low-calorie substitutes should be specified because of the relationship between smoking cessation and weight gain.

Hypnosis is very effective for developing awareness of the beathing process and enhancing the sensations associated with normal breathing. Most patients are surprised to discover that intentional breathing is a very pleasurable activity. At least part of the pleasure of smoking is derived not from the smoke inhaled but from the manipulation of the breath in the process of inhaling the smoke. Patients in trance are told to imagine themselves in a place where there is fresh, clean air—in the mountains or by the ocean. Suggestions are given for slowly inhaling deep breaths of that fresh, clean air. They are told to feel the air as it goes into the nostrils or the mouth and to note the sensations as they imagine the air moving through the air passages from the nose to the lungs. They are told to relax and let out any tension as they inhale (Stein, 1964). Suggestions are given to magnify the pleasurable quality of the sensations or heighten the pleasure in intentionally manipulating the breath. Thus, the patient engages in breathing activity comparable to that involved in inhaling smoke and learns to get as much pleasure from nonsmoke breathing as from smoke breathing, or even more. Once the patient learns to use the breathing for pleasure and relaxation, posthypnotic suggestions can reinforce the reduction of cigarette intake: Whenever the patient reaches for a cigarette, he will take a slow, deep breath of fresh, clean air and find himself relaxing, so there is less and less need to smoke that cigarette (Nuland & Field, 1970).

The Cognitive Control of Smoking

Emotional conflict and a variety of cognitive processes support smoking behavior. Attitudes about smoking, beliefs about what smoking does for the person, one's self-image as a smoker, negative efficacy expectations, and psychological conflicts all contribute to a continuation of smoking or to relapse after quitting. A comprehensive approach to smoking must include interventions designed to alter these factors.

Altering Attitudes Toward Smoking.   Most smokers explicitly or implicitly harbor positive attitudes toward smoking, even when they are aware of the potential health hazards. Therefore, attitude change must be a primary focus of intervention. There are two approaches to attitude change: helping the patient develop a dislike for or a strong aversion to smoking; and helping the patient cultivate a liking for nonsmoking with its potential benefits.

Aversive treatment has a long history in behavioral psychology in general and in hypnotic approaches to smoking in particular. For example, the patient may be told in trance to associate the pleasurable sensations of smoking—the smell and taste (Kroger, 1963) or the touch of the cigarette to the lips (Miller, 1965)—with nausea. Or the hypnotherapist may use covert sensitizaton (Cautela, 1975) to have the patient visualize himself smoking and become nauseated. Hershman (1956) used the Theatre Technique to have the patient visualize a distressing scene associated with smoking and a peaceful scene associated with nonsmoking. Although aversive conditioning may be effective for certain patients, it has not proved especially effective as a primary intervention for large numbers of patients (Bernstein, 1969). One of the reasons for its lack of success may be that telling patients that smoking tastes and smells bad is contrary to the experience of most smokers (Von Dedenroth, 1964). Therapists who wish to use aversive methods are advised to consider the rapid-smoking method (Lichenstein, Harris, Birchler, Wahl, & Schmahl, 1973) in conjunction with hypnosis.

More effective for attitude change is cultivating a positive attitude toward nonsmoking by suggesting its benefits (Orleans, & Shipley, 1982) and fostering a commitment to health. In fact, some effective hypnosis smoking programs are structured entirely around the health plea (Spiegel, 1970; Spiegel & Spiegel, 1978). The Spiegels use hypnotic suggestions to enable the patient to make a commitment to health. During trance, patients reflect on three points: (a) for the body, smoking is a poison; (b) you need the body to live; (c) you commit yourself to a healthy body by stopping smoking. These points are reinforced by posthypnotic suggestions and self-hypnotic practice. Patients may be reminded in trance of the harmful aspects of smoking (Moses, 1964) or, out of trance, through group discussion or films (Pyke et al., 1966). Health pleas have been shown to be more effective when the patient manifests, and is concerned with, specific health problems associated with smoking (Straits, 1966; Swinehart & Kirscht, 1966). In trance, the patient can be reminded of his cough, for example, and its connection to smoking (Hershman, 1956). The patient can also be reminded of the improved health that is likely to follow from stopping smoking (Cruickshank, 1963; Nuland & Field, 1970).

Efficacy Expectations and Self-Statements. Another area for intervention is the patient's efficacy expectations (Bandura, 1977). Many patients hold irrational beliefs about themselves and their ability to stop smoking. Some despair of stopping, believing that they are too weak, lack will power, or lack the requisite coping skills. Others try to stop but harbor a defeatist attitude. They expect failure and so sabotage every attempt to stop with self-doubts and self-criticism. Others worry excessively about the side effects of stopping smoking and undermine their own efforts to stop. The therapist helps the patient to identify such negative beliefs about themselves by asking in the waking state, "What do you say to yourself when you think about stopping smoking?" In hypnosis, the therapist asks, "Notice what comes to mind about stopping smoking."

An antidote for such cognitive distortions and negative self-statements is the cultivation of positive self-statements and self-efficacy. One goal of treatment is to build an expectation of success about quitting (Koenig & Masters, 1965) or "a sense of victory" over smoking (Watkins, 1976). Self-efficacy relates not only to quitting but to continued cessation (Condiotte & Lichtenstein, 1981; DiClemente, 1981). Various ego-strengthening methods can be used (Stanton, 1978). Patients can be given hypnotic suggestions that they will be confident and strong (Hartland, 1965) as they attempt to resist smoking. They can rehearse in fantasy situations in which they effectively resist smoking and develop a feeling of pride in each accomplishment (Hershman, 1956). They can also rehearse in fantasy situations in which they are not smoking and the sense of accomplishment in not smoking exceeds the previous pleasures of smoking (Edwards, 1964). Positively reinforcing suggestions can be given each time the patient successfully cuts back or succeeds in quitting on the quit date (Von Dedenroth, 1964, 1968).

Beliefs about the Functions of Smoking. Still another area for intervention is the patient's beliefs about the function of smoking (Glad et al., 1976), that is, whether it is involving in a sensorimotor way, sedating, addictive, relaxing, stimulating, or habitual (Tomkins, 1966). After determining the patient's beliefs (as part of the initial assessment), the therapist uses hypnosis to develop alternative ways of achieving the purpose the smoking serves for the patient (Watkins, 1976). For example, if smoking is seen as sedating, posthypnotic suggestions are given that "whenever you notice feeling tense when you reach for a cigarette, it will automatically occur to you to relax as you now are doing instead of reaching for the cigarette." If the cigarette has a sensorimotor function, the posthypnotic suggestion might be worded, "As you find yourself just beginning to reach for a cigarette, the hand will find something else to do instead."

Self-Image as a Smoker. A most important area for intervention is the patient's self-image as a smoker. For the veteran smoker, cigarettes have become an integral part of the self-concept (Mausner, 1966). Advertising reinforces a variety of self-images related to smoking. Smokers are depicted as attractive, successful, and strong. They have good taste. They enjoy the outdoors and athletics. They have romantic relationships. It is especially hard to relinquish smoking when it is associated with desirable aspects of one's identity.

Effective treatment of smoking must directly attempt to alter the patient's established and reinforced self-concept as a smoker. Sanders (1977) has her patients produce hypnotic dreams about being nonsmokers. She also uses the technique of Time Progression. The patient is told, "Now, picture yourself sometime in the future, the way you want to be, a nonsmoker . . . Some scenes will come to mind in which you imagine yourself as a nonsmoker, feeling differently about yourself because you are a nonsmoker. Take a few minutes to experience what it is like to be a nonsmoker, your new identity." The patient rehearses in fantasy a number of activities as a nonsmoker. These visualizations are reinforced with posthypnotic suggestions. The hypnotist continues, "As time passes, you will more and more be able to identify yourself as a non-smoker."

The Social Control of Smoking

One of the major obstacles to stopping smoking is the strong social pressure to smoke. The patient who tries to stop smoking is surrounded by people who smoke; friends or spouses may directly or indirectly exert pressure to continue to smoke. People tend to smoke because they see others smoke (Glad & Adesso, 1976). Adults smoke more in public, especially in small groups and at parties (Foss, 1973). Adolescents smoke for the first time because of peer pressure. To smoke is to be "in." Smoking becomes a symbol of maturity (Salber, Welsh, & Taylor, 1963) and of status.

How do patients resist these pressures? Research has shown that, indeed, people do not resist them well (Marlatt & Gordon, 1980). The best preventive measures are strong counterinfluences. This is where groups become so important. They are a milieu for the dissemination of accurate information about the health hazards associated with smoking to offset the myths created by advertising (Lawton, 1967). Free discussion groups foster a sense of cohesion around the shared goal of quitting smoking (Mausner, 1966). Patients learn to support one another in quitting. When patients report their weekly self-monitoring records to the group, each member becomes aware of his progress relative to the group. Social pressure builds to have noncompliant or slowly progressing members catch up with the group.

Not only are nonhypnotic free discussion groups effective (Pyke et al., 1966), but also groups using hypnosis hold promise (Kline, 1970; Sanders, 1977). The best results are achieved with groups that offer members close contact with the hypnotist/leader (Graff et al., 1966) and in which the leader is a persuasive communicator (Koenig & Masters, 1965). For these reasons it is difficult to justify individual treatment of smoking in most cases.

The Prevention of Relapse

Relapse Rates. The main problem in the modification of smoking behavior is not that the patient stop smoking, but that he stop smoking permanently. Any responsible treatment program must directly address this issue (Bernstein, 1969)—the relapse rate for addictive behaviors is quite high. The relapse rate for smoking is comparable to that for other addictions, notably alcohol and substance addiction (Hunt, Barnett, & Branch, 1971). In a comprehensive review of 122 studies of smoking (89 with follow-up data), Hunt and Bespalec (1974) found that more than ⅔ of patients who quit smoking relapsed within 3 months. The risk is greatest in the first 3 weeks after quitting (Marlatt & Gordon, 1980), primarily because of the occurrence of withdrawal symptoms. Relapse gradually levels off beyond that point. In these studies, 20%–30% remained abstinent after 12 months.

These relapse rates depend somewhat on the type of treatment. Hunt and Bespalec's classic study (1974) on relapse was conducted prior to the refinement of behavioral treatments for smoking. With improved behavioral interventions, relapse rate declines: About one half of those who quit relapse over the first three months. When various treatments are compared for their efficacy in sustaining nonsmoking over time, hypnosis is the most effective, followed by group therapy, behavioral regulation, aversive therapy, and drug therapy (Hunt & Bespalec, 1974). Nevertheless, even with hypnosis, the likelihood of relapse remains high, and treatment should include a means to reduce relapse.

The Nicotine Withdrawal Syndrome.   The physiological and psychological effects of nicotine have been established. The nicotine in the cigarette is mildly addictive (Knapp, Michael, & Wells, 1963). Smokers who inhale and use high-nicotine cigarettes develop a tolerance for nicotine; they also regulate smoking behavior to keep the amount of nicotine fairly constant (Dunn, 1973). Psychologically, nicotine reduces responsiveness to stressful situations (Nisbett, 1973; Russell, 1974). No single characteristic withdrawal syndrome inevitably follows abstinence (Bernstein, 1969), although the range of withdrawal symptoms is wide. Indeed, some patients experience none at all. Nevertheless, it is fair to say that some version of a "cigarette abstinence syndrome" (Gritz & Jarvik, 1973) exists for a significant number of patients, especially those whose nicotine intake is high. The withdrawal symptoms occur during the 1st and 3rd weeks after quitting, being especially prevalent in the first week, less so in the second, and prevalent again in the third. They usually disappear altogether after the 3rd week (Shiffman & Jarvik, 1976). These symptoms are one of the main determinants of the high relapse risk during the first weeks after quitting.

Of the many withdrawal symptoms, certain ones are quite common. Even though the patient experiences smoking as relaxing, nicotine addiction results in a state of chronic sympathetic arousal, a condition known as "paradoxical arousal" (Nisbett, 1973). The patient abstaining from smoking is likely to experience discomforting physiological changes, such as cardiovascular changes (deceleration of the heart rate and a drop in blood pressure) (Knapp et al., 1963) and the release of catecholamines into the bloodstream (Glad et al., 1976). Nicotine also suppresses gastric activity and fat storage metabolism, so that abstinence is accompanied by an increase in gastric activity and fat storage. Patients complain of feeling hungry and empty, but if they increase food intake, they are likely to gain some weight.

Psychological Withdrawal.   The psychological symptoms accompanying nicotine withdrawal are more varied than the physiological symptoms.

They include: irritability, restlessness, disturbed appetite and sleep; lethargy; disturbances in memory and concentration; shifts in mood; and somatic withdrawal complaints. The craving to smoke can be quite intense. Patients who have difficulties with other addictions (alcohol, drugs, caffeine, food) are at high risk for relapsing in those areas: Quitting smoking may be accompanied by increased caffeine intake or a loss of sobriety in the recovered alcoholic (Nuland & Field, 1970).

Relapse rates can be reduced if the clinician directly addresses the issue of withdrawal. Patients should be forewarned and educated about the possibility of withdrawal symptoms in the first 3 weeks after quitting. The patient should be told *prior to quitting* to abstain for 1 day and attend to the sensations resulting from abstinence (Povorinsky, 1961). Having accurate information about the symptoms in advance reduces the anxiety when such symptoms occur. The patient acknowledges the weeks after quitting as a critical period and marks off the days. Regular telephone contact with the therapist during the high-risk weeks also reduces relapse (Hall & Crasilneck, 1970; Nuland & Field, 1970).

Hypnosis can alleviate the withdrawal symptoms themselves. Direct suggestions have been used to reduce craving (Crasilneck & Hall, 1968). Hypnotically induced relaxation cuts the edge off of the physiological symptoms (Nuland & Field, 1970). The patient is told to practice self-hypnotic relaxation whenever signs of discomfort arise. Engaging in physical exercise is also beneficial (Hall & Crasilneck, 1970). Kline (1970) developed a method to extinguish the intense craving for cigarettes that occurs during the withdrawal period. Patients attend a 12-hour group hypnotherapy session. The treatment approach entails both desensitization and symptom challenge. Hypnosis is used to induce periods of relaxation as well as to intensify the urges and sensations accompanying smoking deprivation. By alternating relaxation and induced deprivation and practicing ways to handle the deprivation over the 12-hour period, patients learn to control the urges, cravings, dysphoria, and physiological symptoms typically associated with abstinence. This approach is also very effective for individuals who resume smoking after having quit (Powell, 1980).

These hypnotic procedures, generally effective for the majority of patients, are less effective for patients who are not very hypnotizable and who have a long history of nicotine intake. For them, it is a good idea to use supplemental nicotine fading (Foxx & Brown, 1979), with the patients using self-monitoring to follow the daily intake of nicotine and tar. Each week, the patients change brands to one containing progressively less nicotine and tar. By the quite date, the effects of the nicotine have been sufficiently reduced so that the likelihood of experiencing withdrawal symptoms after quitting is also reduced.

Relapse Situations.   Another determinant of relapse over the first few months, in addition to withdrawal symptoms in the first three weeks, is high-risk situations. Marlatt and Gordon (1980) and Shiffman, Read, Maltese, Rapkin, & Javrik, (1985) conducted studies of relapse episodes in order to find out what sorts of situations lead to a resumption of smoking. Only 6% of patients relapse because of a craving for cigarettes. Another 51% relapse because of difficulty in coping with emotional stress. Eighteen percent relapse because of difficulties coping with interpersonal conflicts (12%) or a wish to enhance positive feelings towards others (6%). The remaining 25% relapse because of direct or indirect social pressures to resume smoking, usually from others who smoked. In other words, beyond the first few weeks, when withdrawal puts the patient at risk, the situations that put the patient at risk as time passes are coping with emotions and social pressure. Relapse is most likely to occur when the patient feels low self-efficacy (Marlatt & Gordon, 1980) or when the patient does not expect to be able to handle the situation other than by reaching for a cigarette (Mausner, 1973). Furthermore, cigarettes carry with them the nearly magical expectation that they can solve all problems. After the patient has quit, there is little opportunity to reality-test this belief.

The clinician's first task is to identify high-risk situations with the individual patient: "If you were to start smoking again, under what circumstances would it be?" (Marlatt & Gordon, 1980). Similar questions can be asked in trance by means of hypnoprojective techniques. Suggestions may be given, for example, that scenes will spontaneously come to mind about situations in which the patients starts smoking again. A hierarchy of risk situations is constructed. Then, additional hypnoprojective methods are used to help the patient discover ways of effectively coping with each of these situations: "Now, imagine yourself in the situation again. This time something will occur to you that will help you cope with the situation, and you will imagine yourself taking steps so you won't need to reach for the cigarette." Open-ended suggestions reveal in trance the patient's own inner resources for coping. Hypnoprojective methods are used to identify coping strategies the patient may use for each risk situation on the hierarchy. The patient rehearses in fantasy both encountering each risk situation and effectively coping with it. Posthypnotic suggestions are given that the respective coping strategies will automatically occur to and be used by the patient whenever he finds himself in the given risk situation. The patient also reinforces the strengthening of coping strategies with daily self-hypnotic practice. The purpose of these exercises is to develop skill training and self-efficacy. Each time the patient effectively resists reaching for the cigarette, confidence is increased.

Relapse itself must be addressed as part of the treatment. Of course, a slip is different from a relapse—reaching for one cigarette is not the same as relapsing to the original cigarette intake of one to two packs a day. Many people slip. Most have a strong negative emotional reaction to slipping—what Marlatt and Gordon (1980) call the "abstinence violation effect." Slipping is a violation of one's developing self-image as a non-smoker. Patients often attribute the occasional slip to internal weakness or personal limitations, rather than to situational stresses, and become frustrated or feel guilty. They may feel they are failures and give up on utilizing coping strategies. The slip then progresses to full relapse.

One way to handle slips is to educate patients that slips are not the same as relapses. Patients are taught to anticipate the likelihood of slips in certain high-risk situations and to learn from the slips. Sometimes it is advisable to instruct them actually to slip so they can gain insight into their reactions to slipping (Shiffman et al., 1985). The therapist then helps the patient to learn how to manage the negative self-statements and feelings associated with slipping (Marlatt & Gordon, 1980). Since there is a relationship between the reactions to the first slip and subsequent cigarette use, interventions designed to increase coping with slips help prevent the progression from slip to full relapse. We estimate that when such systematic preventive measures are taken, about 70% of the smoking cessation patients are able to quit smoking and stay nonsmokers. To attain a good success rate requires a multimodal hypnobehavioral treatment program that addresses each dimension of this complex, overlearned habit.

Dynamic Hypnotherapy for Smoking

When the patient reaches a plateau in the progressive reduction of cigarette intake prior to the quit date, or if he successfully quits but resumes smoking even after adequate steps have been taken toward relapse prevention, it is likely that some intrapsychic or systemic conflict underlies the need to smoke. The clinician then switches the treatment approach from a hypnobehavioral to a hypnodynamic treatment. Such hypnoprojective methods as the Theatre Technique can be used to explore underlying conflicts (Hershman, 1956), and the therapist interprets the underlying wish to maintain smoking or the resistance to quitting (Kroger & Libott, 1967). Hypnotherapy is needed for certain subgroups of smokers, although it is difficult to predict for which smokers hypnotherapy is indicated. At lease one subgroup for which hypnobehavioral treatments may not be effective are patients in whom the smoking is clearly associated with neurotic conflicts, for example, rebellion against parents or patients for whom smoking is an expression of self-destructive impulses. Another subgroup for which hypnobehavioral methods are consistently not effective are patients with deficits in the capacity to tolerate affects, notably personality-disordered and borderline patients. These patients use smoking for sedation when threatened with overwhelming affect, or they use cigarettes as transitional objects to ward off the terror of aloneness. For neurotic patients, an uncovering approach to hypnotherapy is used; for more disturbed patients, a developmental approach. To quit smoking becomes a focus only after the underlying conflicts have been resolved or the developmental deficits corrected.

Clinical Outcome

Hunt and his associates (1971; 1974) reviewed 89 studies on smoking cessation where treatment was conducted with a variety of methods including aversive therapy, pharmacotherapy, group therapy, behavioral modification and hypnosis. The results indicated that regardless of the initial high success rates (75%) with different treatments there was a high rate of relapse across treatment modalities. Regardless of treatment only about 20–25% of the patients maintained abstinence by 1 year posttreatment. These data have necessitated a shift in emphasis in treatment strategies. Most clinicians now focus as much on maintenance as on the problem of quitting smoking itself (Bernstein, 1969).

Clinical studies on smoking cessation have been plagued by poor research design and serious methodological limitations, which make it hard to draw accurate conclusions (Bernstein, 1969; Keutzer, Lichtenstein & Mees, 1968). These reviews caution us about drawing any conclusions about the efficacy of behavior modification over more traditional treatments, for example, drug therapy. In general, abstinence rates for behavioral modification and group therapy are consistent with the Hunt & Bespalec (1974) data, when long-term abstinence is considered (more than 6–12 months); initially high abstinence rates (e.g. 75–84%, in Koenig & Masters, 1965) tend to drop off over time to a baseline of 20% ($\pm$5%). The one clear exception to these recidivism rates are the multimodal treatment programs, in which abstinence is maintained longer (e.g. 76% at 6 months posttreatment, in Lando, 1977).

The reviews of outcome studies using clinical hypnosis show them to be notoriously poorly controlled and of offering little research worthy of evaluation (Johnson & Donaghue, 1971). In their review of the few carefully controlled clinical outcome studies, Wadden and Anderton (1982) conclude that "hypnosis does not offer a unique strategy for smoking cessation" (p. 226). The reported success rates are highly variable, from 4% to 88% (Holroyd, 1980). Despite their overall conclusion, there is some reason to be optimistic, especially when these clinical hypnosis studies are separated into distinct groups. In one group, abstinence rates are modest. They range from 10% to 40%, with either short-term aversive procedures (Moses, 1964; Miller, 1965) or single-session methods designed to change attitudes about smoking (Barkley et al., 1977; Berkowitz et al., 1979; Francisco, 1973; Perry & Mullen, 1975; Shewchuk et al., 1977; Spiegel, 1970). Perry, Gelfand, and Marcovitch (1979) found that a single session of hypnosis was significantly less effective than a single session of aversive rapid smoking, which itself is not very effective. Another group reports higher abstinence rates (60%–95%), which are alleged to be maintained for 6 months to a year after treatment. Crasilneck and Hall (1968) report 68% success in quitting smoking, maintained 12 months posttreatment. They used direct hypnotic suggestions. Some of the most effective approaches are those involving multimodal treatment protocols where there is a high amount of contact between patient and therapist (Graff et al., 1966, 88% maintained 3 months; Von Dedenroth, 1964, 1968, 94% maintained 18 months). Others claiming high success rates have emphasized individualized treatment (Nuland & Field, 1970, 60% over 6 months; Watkins, 1976, 67% over 6 months; Sanders, 1977, 68% over 10 months). Kline (1970), who specifically trained his smokers in relapse prevention methods, claimed an 88% success rate over 12 months.

While it is difficult to draw sound conclusions when the available data are not adequate by sound research standards, the trends in these data are nevertheless consistent with what we have seen in other areas. Direct suggestions are effective for at least some smokers. Multimodal, individualized approaches give consistently better results, especially if relapse prevention methods are used. Hypnotic susceptibility does not correlate with treatment outcome (Perry & Mullen, 1975; Mott, 1979; Perry et al., 1979). While hypnotizability does not seem to offer any advantage, except to a subgroup of smokers, the hypnotic situation does. Outcome may be low in well-controlled studies because of the many factors other than susceptibility that may contribute to a successful outcome: motivation (Wadden & Anderton, 1982; Francisco, 1973; Perry et al., 1979); intensity and duration of contact with the therapist (Graff et al., 1966; Holroyd, 1980); embedding hypnosis in the context of ongoing counseling or hypnotherapy (Pederson, et al., 1975, 1979); type of approach to hypnosis; individualization of treatment (Nuland & Field, 1970; Watkins, 1976); and follow-up contact (Holroyd, 1980). It is too simple to ask merely whether hypnosis is effective. Rather, researchers need to evaluate approaches to hypnosis, what type of suggestions are effective, with whom, over what period of treatment, for what type of person and under what treatment conditions. When such questions are framed we believe research will demonstrate more favorable outcomes.

WEIGHT CONTROL

Assessment

Percentage Overweight.   To choose the right approach for weight problems, it is necessary first to determine the patients' proportionate overweight, which can be calculated by finding on the Metropolitan Life
Insurance Tables (1960) the median weight of people of the patient's
gender, age, height, and bone structure and comparing that to the patient's
actual weight. Mildly overweight patients are less than 40% over their
ideal weight. Their weight problem is largely due to an increase in the size
of the fat cells, and they respond well to behavioral and hypnobehavioral
treatment. The weight problem of moderately overweight patients (40%–
100% over their estimated weight) stems from a combination of an increase in both number and size of fat cells. These patients do not respond
well to behavioral and hypnobehavioral treatment alone, unless the treatment is supplemented by fasting or drug treatment. Massively overweight
patients, greater than 100% of their estimated weight, also do not respond
well to behavioral or hypnobehavioral treatment alone. Surgery and supportive psychotherapy designed to foster self-efficacy are the suggested
treatments. Since 90% of all weight problems fall into the mildly overweight range, behavioral tratment is a useful intervention in most instances (Brownell, 1983).

The Weight History.   The assessment of weight problems should include a thorough weight history, including the age at which the weight first
became a problem. Obesity that begins in childhood differs from
adulthood obesity. In the former there is usually a greater number of fat
cells; in the latter, larger fat cells than those found in nonobese people.
Since it is impossible to decrease the *number* of fat cells, patients with
childhood-onset obesity may have a biological limit to their ability to lose
weight (Hirsch & Knittle, 1970). The therapist attempts to ascertain significant variations in weight over the course of the life cycle and looks for
changes in life events associated with these weight changes. Both current
weight and recent fluctuations in weight are noted.

The Diet History.   A detailed diet history is taken, including self-
initiated diets, enrollment in such self-help groups as Weight Watchers or
TOPS, and previous behavioral or hypnotic treatment. The therapist tries
to understand the particular reasons that led the patient to undertake the
weight control measures on each occasioin. It is especially important to
determine why the diet failed each time, so that the current treatment does
not repeat the same mistakes. Untoward responses to dieting (anxiety,
depression) and factors contributing to relapse are noted.

Activity Level. The patient's pattern of physical activity should be noted. Many overweight individuals have adopted a sedentary life style, with a concommitant decrease in energy expenditure. The therapist assesses whether the patient participates in a regular exercise program and estimates the amount of daily physical exercise gained through doing household chores, participating in occasional recreational sports, or walking.

The Psychological Consequences of Weight Gain. The therapist also evaluates the impact of weight problems on the patient's life style: medical complications, psychiatric symptoms (anxiety, depression, irritability), avoidance of social and sexual encounters, avoidance of exercise, and economic stress such as that entailed in the need to buy new clothes.

Hypnotizability. An assessment of hypnotizability is also indicated. Although obese persons have not been shown to differ from others in hypnotizability (Deyoub, 1978, 1979b), more highly motivated and hypnotizable patients are likely to benefit from hypnosis used as an adjunct to behavioral treatment of weight problems. (Thorne, Rasmus, & Fischer, 1976)

Motivation. The single most important factor to evaluate is the patient's motivation to lose weight: "Why do you want to lose weight?" or "How do you consider weight to be a problem for you?" The patient's answer is likely to reflect health concerns (e.g., increased cardiovascular risk), psychological benefits (improved body image and self-esteem), or social benefits (looking more attractive to others or improved social relations). Patients whose reasons for losing weight reflect unrealistic expectations or an externalization of responsibility are poor candidates for treatments. These patients need interventions designed to clarify or increase their motivation. Each overweight patient lists adverse consequences to overeating and the benefits of losing weight (Christensen, Jeffrey, & Pappas, 1977; Ferster, Nurnberger, & Levitt, 1962; Wollersheim, 1977). These lists can be discussed in a weight reduction group, where, as in the stop-smoking groups, group members learn from one another additional reasons for losing weight. Here again, the therapist may present data to the group on the increased health risks associated with being overweight. Each person's specific reasons for losing weight are incorporated into posthypnotic suggestions to strengthen the patient's desire for weight loss (Crasilneck & Hall, 1975; Winkelstein, 1959). Sometimes nonspecific direct suggestions, such as "You will want to lose weight," are effective for some patients (Crasilneck & Hall, 1975, p. 150). The patient's responses to this line of inquiry reflect only conscious motivation; unconscious motivation can work for or against the conscious commitment to lose weight. Hypnoprojective methods are useful for exploring unconscious motivation (Winkelstein, 1959). For example, the patient imagines a television program or a stage play: "The play will somehow be about the reasons you wish to lose weight at this time." Unconscious motivation is symbolically portrayed in the program or play. Once clarified, these reasons can be incorporated into highly individualized suggestions used to increase conscious motivation.

Where patients remain poorly motivated after assessment of conscious and unconscious motivation, behavioral contingency contracts may be used (Tighe & Elliot, 1968), in which the patient is required to deposit a fixed amount of money at the onset of treatment. The patient recovers portions of the money for attending, keeping a regular eating diary, and losing the prescribed amount of weight each week. Similarly, paying fees for weight reduction improves the chances for a good outcome of hypnotherapy (Stanton, 1976).

Coping Resources. The hypnotherapist also assesses the range of coping strategies available to the patient for losing weight. "If you have attempted to lose weight in the past, how did you go about it? What worked? What didn't work?" Patients who have successfully lost weight, but have relapsed, often report such strategies as dietary restriction, calorie counting, enlisting the support of friends, exercise, and positive thinking. Often these same coping strategies can be strengthened through hypnotic suggestion. Hypnosis is also a means to discover new coping strategies unique to each patient. The patient may be asked in trance to reflect on possible ways to lose weight or to imagine himself reaching for a high-calorie snack and then resisting the temptation by some means (Kroger & Fezler, 1976, p. 220). In this way, the patient himself discovers which coping strategies or sets of coping strategies help him to resist, and they can be incorporated into specific hypnotic suggestions.

Self-Regulation of Eating

Self-Monitoring. Also essential is the assessment of eating behavior (Hanley, 1967; Mahoney, 1974; Stuart, 1967, 1971). Patients keep an accurate daily diary of typical eating habits for a minimum of 2 weeks prior to any attempts to lose weight. The patient records the time of day any food is eaten, the type and amount of food consumed, the number of minutes spent eating, the situation in which eating occurs, the location of eating, the degree of hunger (on a 0–3 scale from slight to very hungry), thoughts and feelings at the time of eating, and the presence or absence of other people. The patient keeps records for snacks as well as regular meals. The

FIG. 4.2. Daily Eating Behavior Record

Time	Type/Amount of Food Eaten	Time Spent Eating	With Whom	Location	Degree of Hunger* (0-3)	Situation/Event Associated with Eating	Thoughts, Feelings

*Degree of Hunger
0 not at all hungry 2 somewhat hungry
1 slightly hungry 3 very hungry

patient also records those urges to eat which he was able to resist (Wollersheim, 1977). An example of a self-monitoring sheet is found in Fig. 4.2.

The therapist and patient together regularly review the self-monitoring records to identify high-risk times, problematic eating patterns, and the environmental, psychological, and social factors associated with problematic eating typical for the patient. Is the person more at risk for high-caloric intake at certain times of the day? Does the patient have trouble with particular types of food? Are there certain factors that increase the chance of eating—emotional upsets, boredom, self-consciousness, or availability of food cues? By self-monitoring, the patient is made aware of automatic eating behaviors, becomes sensitized to the specific antecedents to his problematic eating patterns, and is counseled on ways to modify them. Some patients find that they begin to lose weight by self-monitoring alone (Romanczyk, 1974). Romanczyk, Tracey, Wilson, & Thorpe, (1973) have shown that self-monitoring of caloric intake alone is as effective as behavioral regulation of weight control under certain conditions, especially when patients record *prior* to food intake, although the effectiveness is limited to short-term weight control.

In addition to recording daily eating habits, patients make a weekly graph of their average weight (Cheek & LeCron, 1968, p. 186; Wick, Sigman & Kline, 1971) and the range of fluctuations in weight (Stuart, 1967). Because of normal fluctuations in weight, daily weight recordings are not used.

Stimulus-Control.   Hypnotic treatment of weight problems is done in conjunction with stimulus-control (Aja, 1977; Ferster et al., 1962). Eating is an overdetermined behavior that becomes associated with numerous environmental cues and situations. The therapist encourages the patient to limit the situations in which eating occurs by separating eating from all other activities (watching television, going to bed, reading, etc.). The time of eating is also regulated. One approach requires the patient to eat only when hungry (Mahoney & Mahoney, 1976). Another approach attempts to make eating a predictable behavior; the patient is put on an eating schedule (Kroger & Fezler, 1976). Posthypnotic suggestions are used to reinforce *not* eating between scheduled meals (Cheek & LeCron, 1968, Glover, 1961; Kroger, 1970; Winkelstein, 1959). The patient learns to shop at predictable times and to plan meals (Ferguson, 1975). The location of food and eating is also regulated. Patients are told to eat only in appropriate eating places (at the kitchen table, not in the living room or bedroom), to sit at the table only to eat, and to leave the table when they finish the meal. Posthypnotic suggestions reinforce eating only at the proper time and in the proper location (Winkelstein, 1959). Patients are less likely to snack when food is made less visible and temptations are minimized. Therefore, food and food paraphernalia are removed from visible locations around the house except for specified storage areas. Fattening foods are not stored in the house.

Self-Regulation and Contingency Management.   The next step in treatment is behavioral management by regulation of both the quality and the quantity of food. Although direct suggestions to lose weight have been used (Hershman, 1955), the emphasis of the treatment is to help the patient develop normal eating habits, not merely to lose weight. "The culprits are patterns, not pounds" (Mahoney & Mahoney, 1976, p. 25).

Hypnotic suggestions may be given to alter the type of food eaten. Emphasis is on alteration of food intake and the development of appropriate eating behaviors (Brodie, 1964). In the waking state patients are advised on proper diet (Tullis, 1973). They are particularly advised to eliminate those high caloric foods that by themselves produce weight problems, a phenomenon known as "dietary obesity" (Sclafani, 1980). In hypnosis patients may be given suggestions to eat the right type of food (Hershman, 1955; Kroger, 1970; Winkelstein, 1959); eat foods with fewer calories (Glover, 1961); reach satiety with certain types of food (Glover, 1961); resist fattening and unnecessary foods (Aja, 1977; Mann, 1953); or enjoy eating healthful foods previously thought to be distasteful (Shibata, 1967). Hypnotic suggestions may also be given to reduce the amount of food. Patients may be given posthypnotic suggestions to fast periodically (Brodie, 1964; Glover, 1961; Stanton, 1975); to restrict caloric intake (Brodie, 1964; Kroger, 1970); to reduce their appetite (Crasilneck & Hall, 1975; Glover, 1961); or to eat smaller meals (Kroger, 1970; Stanton, 1975). Graded posthypnotic suggestions may be given to diminish food intake by a fraction each week (Wollman, 1962). The hypnotist may also specify a daily calorie quota, which is reinforced with posthypnotic suggestions. It is important that the hypnotist find which suggestions apply best to the given individual.

Most researchers have found that weight reduction of 1–2 lbs. a week is a realistic goal (Christensen et al., 1977; Ferster et al., 1962; Kroger, 1970; Stuart, 1967; Winkelstein, 1959). Patients who expect to lose large amounts (e.g., 5–10 lb./wk.) are likely to become discouraged. Even if they lose that much weight, it is primarily water loss, and the weight loss is unlikely to be maintained. Gradual weight reduction is achieved through progressive changes in energy output and energy expenditure. The therapist should help the patient set a realistic overall goal and to establish self rewards for changing eating habits (Mahoney, 1974). In trance, the patient visualizes himself weighing what he would like to weigh (Stanton, 1975; Wollman, 1962) or looking as he will look after losing the desired amount of weight (Glover, 1961). Once the desired goal has been determined, the hypnotist has the patient, while in trance, project a deadline date for reaching that weight (Kroger, 1970; Kroger & Fezler, 1976, p. 218). The deadline date should be realistic, based on a rate of change of 1–2 lbs. a week.

Problematic Eating Patterns.   As the patient approaches the goal, residual problematic eating patterns (emotional eating, patterns of snacking, night eating, holiday binging; Stunkard, 1976) become the focus of the treatment (Stuart, 1967). Direct hypnotic suggestions to reduce the desire to eat between meals are sometimes useful (Hanley, 1967). Hypnotic rehearsal in fantasy helps the patient cope with these problems. In trance, the patient imagines a television program in which he is tempted by a snack or binging at a social gathering. Then the patient switches to another channel (or series of channels) in which he sees himself effectively resisting the temptation. The patient is told, "As the program unfolds, it will somehow suggest ways you can resist the temptation to eat or snack." Once discovered, the coping strategies are incorporated into posthypnotic suggestions. Patients are told that it will occur to them to utilize the coping strategies when they encounter the snacking or binging situation in real life.

The therapist reviews the self-monitoring records with the patient to discover specific emotional needs met by eating. Eating can function as a form of relaxation: some people use sweets, milk, and the like to soothe themselves; others find that they eat more during work breaks. Eating can also be a way of managing negative affects: Some people eat when they are angry or depressed; others punish themselves by overeating. Eating can also be a stimulant. Certain foods, especially sweets, can be used as a pick-me-up when one is bored. Eating is also a form of sensorimotor and cognitive stimulation: food stimulates all the senses; cooking can be a creative activity. Sometimes eating does not serve a particular emotional need, but is purely habitual. Highly routinized eating behaviors take on a life of their own. The therapist and patient together must identify the specific types of problematic eating behaviors to which the patient is prone.

Hypnosis can uncover alternative means of meeting the same needs. For example, patients have used nonhynotic progressive muscle relaxation (Mahoney & Mahoney, 1976) or hypnotic waves of relaxation (Crasilneck & Hall, 1975) instead of reaching for food for relaxation or to manage negative emotional states. Suggestions for hypnotic states of arousal (Gibbons, 1979) can be used to relieve boredom. Posthypnotic reinforcement of activities that don't involve eating (working with tools or gardening) creates substitutes for eating. Direct hypnotic suggestions can eliminate those eating episodes which are purely habitual.

The Act of Eating.   Another dimension is the very act of eating. Many overweight people have eating habits different from those of normal people. They eat automatically, without full awareness, and they eat very quickly. It is especially important that these patients learn to eat slowly, either through direct suggestions (Brodie, 1964) or through hypnotically induced time distortion. For example, the patient can be told, after only 5 minutes have elapsed, that he has been eating leisurely for an hour (Erickson, 1960; Kroger & Fezler, 1976, p. 221). Patients who respond to the time distortion are likely to slow down their eating.

Treatment is also designed to modify the way the patient eats, specifically to make it more purposeful and to enhance the sensory quality of the eating experience. Brodie (1964) and others (Aja, 1977; Hanley, 1967; Mann, 1953) used hypnosis to facilitate a "vivid gustatory experience." In their treatment, the hypnotized patient imagines he is eating like a gourmet, enjoying a pleasant meal and being carefully aware of the arrangement of the food. He imagines pausing to enjoy the sight of the food and to take in its pleasant aromas. He imagines slowly taking a small mouthful, savoring the food in his mouth for some time before swallowing. He senses the texture of the food that touches his tongue and teeth as he chews it. He chews very slowly and intentionally, noting the range of tastes and other sensations he experiences while chewing the food. Then he imagines swallowing the food slowly and deliberately. Once the patient, through hypnotic imagery, has become familiar with the possibility of eating as a vivid sensory experience, he is given a posthypnotic suggestion to eat right meals in the same manner. Food might even be brought to the hypnotic session to enhance the hypnotized patient's sensory experience while he actually eats the food.

Visceral Perception and Hunger.   Overweight people may also need to be taught to become more careful discriminators of hunger cues. Some— still controversial—evidence seems to indicate that overweight people are poor discriminators of internal experiences. They do not easily differentiate between hunger and other internal, viscerally based experiences, such as anxiety, anger, boredom (Holland, Masling, & Copley, 1970; Mahoney & Mahoney, 1976). Eating depends on a variety of external cues: the sight (and sometimes the smell) of food, the time of day, and the thought of food (Rodin, 1980a; Schachter, 1967).

Kroger (1970) has used hypnosis for what he calls "interoceptive conditioning." The hypnotized patient first learns to produce simple physiological changes, notably temperature changes in the limbs. Then he learns to produce more complex sensory experiences, such as hunger, satiation, and aversion to specific types of foods. The goal is to teach patients to identify visceral experience more accurately. The patient might also imagine a variety of emotional states and attempt to discriminate the pattern of visceral sensations associated with each emotion. Patients can thus learn to discriminate between hunger and emotional states and to eat only when they are hungry.

The Cognitive Control of Eating

A variety of cognitions contribute to maintaining eating behavior. Attitudes about eating, beliefs about food, one's self- and body image as an overweight person, negative efficacy expectations, and psychological conflicts all contribute to a continuation of maladaptive eating habits or to relapse after weight loss. A comprehensive approach to weight problems must include interventions designed to alter all of these factors.

Attitudes Toward Eating.   A popular, albeit incomplete, approach to the control of weight aims at modifying the individual's attitudes toward eating. The hypnotic literature shows two approaches to attitude change: the development of a strong aversion for certain types of foods and the cultivation of a positive attitude toward the benefits of maintaining healthy weight.

The aversive approach combines hypnosis with covert sensitization (Cautela, 1970). The hynotized patient imagines becoming nauseated when encountering certain types of high-calorie or problematic foods (Kroger & Fezler, 1976; Miller, 1974; Tilker & Meyer, 1972) or learns to associate such foods with terrible tastes and smells (Aja, 1977). Alternatively, hypnoprojective means (e.g., the Theatre Technique) can generate imagery associated with emotional states. In trance the patient learns to associate pleasant experiences with adherence to diet and unpleasant experiences with breaking the diet (Hershman, 1955). Aversive hypnotic techniques can be useful in very specific situations for certain people, especially when problematic eating habits persist after otherwise successful behavioral regulation of eating behavior (Stuart, 1967); nevertheless, we do not recommend them as the primary intervention.

Developing a positive attitude toward the benefits of weight reduction is generally more effective than developing aversion toward certain foods (Oakley, 1960). Spiegel and Spiegel (1978) and Spiegel and Debetz (1978) use hypnosis and self-hypnosis to enable the patient to develop greater respect for his body. They say to him:

1. For your body, overeating is, in effect, poison. This is just like the situation with water; you need water to live but too much water will drown you. Similarly, you need food to live but too much of this very same food in effect becomes poison.
2. You cannot live without your body. Your body is the precious physical plant through which you experience life.

3. To the extent that you want to live life to its fullest, you owe your body this commitment to respect it and protect it. This is your way of acknowledging the fragile, precious nature of your body and at the same time it is your way of seeing yourself as your body's keeper. You are in truth your body's keeper. (Spiegel & Spiegel, 1978, pp. 221–222)

The hypnotic suggestions emphasize health benefits directly and eating behavior indirectly; they do not address weight loss in an obvious way.

Efficacy Expectations and Self-Statements.   Ego-strengthening suggestions (Hartland, 1971) are an integral component of the overall hypnotic treatment protocol. Hypnotized patients are told that they will find themselves becoming increasingly "self-assured" or "confident" (Glover, 1961, p. 250; Mann, 1953) or will find themselves "growing stronger and stronger, healthier and healthier" (Stanton, 1975, p. 36). Such suggestions are especially effective when patients are able to resist problematic foods: "Whenever you find yourself capable of resisting that sweet, a feeling of pride will swell up in you, and you will grow more confident." Many overweight patients have poor self-efficacy. Out of despair, they easily give up attempts to control eating. Ego-strengthening suggestions used at each stage of the treatment enhance the patient's sense of self-efficacy.

Overweight patients manifest a variety of cognitive distortions regarding the control of eating (Mahoney & Mahoney, 1976). They typically harbor unrealistic expectations regarding weight loss and exercise and react with extreme despair at the slightest setback. Some think in absolute terms—anything short of total abstinence from problematic foods is believed to be total failure. Most also carry on a negative private monologue that typically includes negative statements about their own character traits ("I'm a fat slob" or "I'm a failure") or coping strategies ("There's no way I can lose this weight."). Or unlikely imperatives ("I'll never snack again" or "I'll always be fat."). These thoughts, which often continue outside the patient's awareness, exert a powerful influence over eating behavior.

The therapist's task is to help the patient become aware of these cognitive distortions and learn to think in a more positive and healthy way about eating. Nonhypnotic cognitive therapy is an important component of behavioral weight control programs (Mahoney & Mahoney, 1976), as is hypnotic cognitive therapy for hypnotizable individuals. Kroger (1970) first examines the "rationalizations for overeating" (p. 167) in the waking state. Then he teaches the patient in trance a series of "affirmations," such as "Get the most mileage out of each morsel and each drop" or "Think thin" (p. 172). Though Kroger's suggestions are very general, highly specific, individualized affirmations can be designed, provided the therapist first works with the patient to identify the patient's specific patterns of cognitive distortions regarding eating. Hypnosis can help to bring these cognitions into awareness: "Notice what thoughts come to mind that contribute to the problem of losing weight, and then let them become clearer and clearer."

Self-Image and Body-Image as a Fat Person.   Being overweight often becomes incorporated into the person's self-concept and body image. Some chronically overweight patients view themselves and their bodies as grotesque and loathesome. Once a negative self-concept or distorted body image is established, it is hard to modify and weight reduction alone will not necessarily alter body image (Stunkard & Mendelson, 1967). Those who lose weight may even regain it in order to keep body weight congruent with the distorted self- or body image.

One of the most important areas for direct intervention is the patient's self- or body image as an overweight person. The nature of the body image is first assessed in hypnosis. The hypnotized patient visualizes himself naked in front of a mirror and describes how he sees himself (Miller, 1974). Self-image and body image distortions usually are evident in the patient's report. Using some variation on the Ideal Self Technique, the patient then imagines himself at the weight he would like to be or looking the way he would like to look (Hanley, 1967). He can imagine a "pleasing body image" (Brodie, 1964) or visualize himself in clothes he would like to wear and that make him attractive (Hanley, 1967; Wollman, 1962). Sometimes the patient is told actually to buy preferred and affordable clothes several sizes too small and to hang these clothes in a visible place as a reminder to continue with the efforts to lose weight. Hypnotized patients can also be encouraged to "think thin," to hold the ideal image throughout their daily life (Kroger & Fezler, 1976, p. 216).

The Social Control of Eating

One of the major difficulties in controlling weight is strong social pressure to overeat. Advertising bombards individuals with food stimuli and makes high-calorie junk foods seem desirable. Obese people who are sensitive to external cues are especially susceptible to the effects of advertising. Spouses and relatives may unwittingly contribute to the patient's maintaining maladaptive eating behaviors and undermine efforts to lose weight. Family members influence what the patient eats and how much and how often he eats (Mahoney & Mahoney, 1976, p. 75). Food rituals in the home do not change easily. The treatment protocol must include ways to counteract these strong influences if they are detrimental. The goal is to "reprogram the social environment" (Patterson, Hawkins, McNeal, & Phelps, 1967).

Because of the strong social dimension to weight problems, groups are the treatment of choice. As they do for smoking cessation, groups foster a sense of cohesion around the shared goals of modifying eating habits and losing weight (Wollersheim, 1970). Patients learn to support one another's efforts. Patients can report weekly self-monitoring results to the group and each member is made aware of his progress relative to the group. Social pressure builds so that noncompliant and slowly progressing members catch up with the group. Group hypnotic treatment of weight problems is well documented (Aja, 1977; Devine, 1978; Glover, 1961; Hanley, 1967; Kroger, 1970; LeCron, 1959; Wick, Sigman & Kline, 1971; Winkelstein, 1959; Wollman, 1962).

Treatment of the social dimension of weight problems begins with self-monitoring. The patient learns to identify differences between eating behaviors when he is alone and when he is with others. He tries to keep track of verbal exchanges with others about food to identify ways in which others are supportive of or disruptive to his weight control efforts (Stuart & Davis, 1972, p. 83). The patient may ask family members to become actively involved in his weight control efforts at home by modifying their reactions to the patient's eating habits and weight control efforts and by cooperating with the patient's attitudes to reduce exposure to food in the house. Because the family group exerts such a strong influence over the patient's eating behavior and weight reduction efforts, some treatments directly address that influence (Brownell, 1983; Mahoney & Mahoney, 1976).

The Prevention of Relapse

Relapse Rates. Many treatment programs that focus exclusively on losing weight fail to consider the problem of maintaining weight loss. Many persons who have lost weight, by whatever means, tend to gain it back after the first posttreatment year. Without specific interventions directed at relapse prevention, most people return to their pretreatment weight within 5 years after treatment, although they continue to experience marked fluctuations in body weight (Stunkard, 1977, p. 348).

One important reason for the reversal of the treatment effect is the body's biological tendency to defend its original weight. According to Set Point theory (Keesey, 1980; Nisbett, 1972), weight is biologically set at a certain defined point. If dieting or behavioral treatment results in weight loss, the rate of energy expenditure is adjusted accordingly so that the body can return to its original weight over time.

Exercise and the Maintenance of Weight loss. Exercise can counteract the biological tendency to regain weight, but patients should not be led to have unrealistic expectations for the role of exercise in weight reduction. Even very vigorous exercise is unlikely to result in the loss of more than a pound or two. Exercise does help to expend caloric energy, but the benefits of exercise lie more in the area of long-term maintenance of weight loss than in weight loss itself (Harris & Hallbauer, 1973; Miller & Sims, 1981; Stalonas, Johnson, & Christ, 1978). Exercise helps to maintain weight loss possibly by resetting the set point and increasing basal metabolic rate (Brownell, 1983). While dieting reduces the basal metabolic rate, exercise increases basal metabolic rate, thus canceling out the negative impact of metabolic rate on weight reduction. Exercise also prevents loss of lean body tissue. Many people who lose weight rapidly do so at the expense of lean body tissue and are highly likely to regain within the first year after the weight loss—but almost entirely in fat body tissue. In this sense the weight reduction attempt has been harmful. Exercise, however, prevents the loss of lean body tissue (Brownell & Stunkard, 1980) and for many people, it also suppresses appetite. For these reasons a routine of moderate exercise is a necessary component of any weight reduction program.

Adherence to exercise programs, however, is very poor (Taylor, Buskirk, & Remington, 1973). Because compliance with exercise routines—walking, stretching, running in place—is higher than compliance with scheduled programmed activities—aerobics classes, swimming, or jogging (Brownell & Stunkard, 1980), patients are encouraged to start slowly exercising as part of their normal daily routine. Patients are encouraged to plan exercise along a hierarchy. First, they increase the activities they do daily anyway, such as walking and using stairs (Mahoney & Mahoney, 1976) And, next, to add a realistic daily home routine (e.g., calisthenics). Then episodic (tennis) and finally regular programmed activities (e.g., aerobics classes) are encouraged. Patients may keep daily records of their exercise (Ginsburg & Baker, 1977) and, from available tables (Brownell & Stunkard, 1980, pp. 310–311; Ferguson, 1975, pp. 8, 15–16), calculate the total number of calories expended. Patients who participate in regularly scheduled exercise, especially aerobics, are most successful in maintaining long-term weight loss (Miller & Sims, 1981).

Hypnotherapy increases the likelihood of compliance with the exercise program (Kavanagh, Shephard & Doney, 1974; Kavanagh, Shephard, & Pandit, 1970). Patients systematically rehearse in fantasy a series of situations from their exercise hierarchy, for example, walking. Posthypnotic suggestions are used to reinforce actually engaging in the exercise in daily life.

The Consequences of Restrained Eating. A second reason for the reversal of the treatment effect is the patient's psychological failure to tolerate restrained eating (Herman & Polivy, 1980). People who diet systematically restrict themselves from eating in the usual ways they eat. They take considerable pains to suppress the urge to eat, but once they stop dieting, many eating inhibitions are removed. Dieters who have experienced self-imposed restrained eating undergo a period of "counter-regulation," when they are likely to eat to excess in reaction to the previous restriction. Treatment programs that encourage regular meals of moderate caloric intake and restrict only excesses are likely to avoid counterregulatory effects.

Untoward Reactions to Dieting.   A related reason for failure to maintain weight loss is the dieter's inability to tolerate the side effects of dieting. Weight loss through caloric restriction results in untoward effects in more than 50% of all dieters. These effects include nonspecific symptoms (anxiety, depression, irritability, fatigue and medical symptoms (e.g., abdominal cramps). These side effects are most common where weight loss is achieved through traditional medical outpatient treatment (pharmacotherapy, dietary control) and less common in behavioral outpatient treatment (Stunkard & Rush, 1974; Taylor, Ferguson, & Reading, 1978). Inpatients do not suffer these effects at all. Side effects specific to the individual sometimes occur, such as anxiety symptoms resulting from conflicts over increased independence or increased attractiveness as a consequence of weight loss. Specific side effects need to be a focus of hypnotherapy. The more gradual the weight loss and the greater the social support, the less likely the side effects.

States of Deprivation.   Still another reason for relapse is the difficulty of controlling feelings of deprivation (Stuart & Davis 1972, p. 86; Wick, Sigman & Kline, 1971). Overeaters have learned to use food as a solution for emotional hunger, fatigue, or boredom. Even the successful dieter is likely to experience spontaneous episodes of intense craving, although it may not be clear whether this craving is related to hunger, energy deprivation, emotional deprivation, or boredom. Some people have considerable difficulty controlling these urges. As part of the behavioral treatment, putting the patient on a schedule of regular meals significantly decreases the occurrence of states of deprivation (Stuart, 1972). If they do occur, individual and group hypnosis can help (Wick, Sigman & Kline, 1971). Sometimes direct suggestions to "tolerate this diet with minimal desire for food" or to "decrease hunger" (Winkelstein, 1959) decrease subsequent urges (Crasilneck & Hall, 1975, p. 150).
    Glove anesthesia can also control the urges. The patient is given a posthypnotic suggestion to reduce hunger urges by spontaneously inducing a glove anesthesia and transferring it to the pit of the stomach (Kroger,

1970). A symptom challenge gives the patient a greater sense of mastery over these urges. The hypnotized patient first imagines a relaxing situation and then a situation in which he experiences intense but tolerable hunger cravings. The patient switches back to the relaxed condition until the cravings subside. The sequence is repeated a number of times, and each time the suggestion is given that the craving to eat will be more intense. The patient learns to tolerate very intense cravings. Posthypnotic suggestions are given for the patient to induce the relaxed state automatically whenever he encounters such cravings in everyday life. Suggestions can also be given to link the craving to healthful foods the patient previously disliked (Shibata, 1967). If the patient still succumbs to the cravings (for example, when bored), hypnotherapeutic exploration of the meaning of the situation is indicated (Crasilneck & Hall, 1975, p. 150; Shibata, 1967).

Relapse Situations. A major cause of relapse is the patient's vulnerability to certain high-risk situations over which he has no sense of control. Sternberg (1985) and Rosenthal and Marx (1981) studied high-risk situations in order to find out just what sort of situations lead to a slip, that is, a temporary resumption of maladaptive eating behaviors. According to Sternberg, about 48% of patients slip because of difficulty in coping with negative emotions, such as anxiety, depression, and boredom. Another 32% slip because of a tendency to use food in social situations to enhance positive affect,—going to parties, socializing with friends, or traveling. About 10% slip because of direct or indirect social pressure, usually from within the family, to resume maladaptive eating patterns. Another 10% overeat after some interpersonal conflict. Relatively few patients report slipping because of uncontrollable hunger urges or inadequate will power. Psychological cravings for food contribute more to repetitive than to initial slips. According to the Sternberg study, situations in which the individual fails to cope with emotions constitute the main risk. Obese persons are more prone than nonobese persons to slip under stress (Glucksman, Rand, & Stunkard, 1978). Slips are likely to result when the person has little expectation of control, does not have the available coping skills, and expects some positive gain from eating in the old, maladaptive ways (Marlatt & Gordon, 1985). The goals of relapse prevention are to enhance the patient's self-efficacy, help him develop the necessary coping strategies, and reality-test what he can gain from eating less.

As with the smoker, the therapist begins by identifying the high-risk situations specific to the patient: "If you started to eat again in your old ways, under what circumstances would it be?" Similar questions can be asked in trance through hypnoprojective techniques. Suggestions may be given that scenes will spontaneously come to mind about situations in which the patient starts to eat in maladaptive ways again. A hierarchy of risk situations is constructed. Then, additional hypnoprojective methods are used to discover ways to cope effectively with each situation: "Now, imagine yourself in the situation again. This time something will occur to you that will help with the situation, and you will imagine yourself taking steps so you won't need to eat in your old ways again." It is better to use open-ended suggestions so as to discover in trance the patient's own inner resources for coping. Hypnoprojective methods are used to identify strategies the patient may use for each risk situation in the hierarchy. The patient rehearses in fantasy both encountering these risk situations and effectively coping with them. Posthypnotic suggestions are given that the respective coping strategies will automatically be used by the patient whenever the finds himself in the risk situation. Self-hypnosis reinforces the developing of coping strategies with practice.

A slip in a weight program is a failure to use any method of controlling eating behavior within a 24-hour period. A relapse is a series of slips resulting in a gain of more than 5 pounds over a 60-day period (Sternberg, 1982). Since *all* patients slip (Rosenthal & Marx, 1981), the expectation that the patient will slip should be built into the treatment. The problem is, how the patient deals with the slip. Many patients who slip believe they have failed and are destined to be fat. In despair, they give up all attempts to lose weight. Patients need to be taught to anticipate the likelihood of slips in certain high-risk situations. The therapist works with the patient to define situations most likely to produce a slip. Should a slip occur, the hypnotized patient tries to reconstruct what he was doing and thinking at the time of the slip. The therapist adopts a problem-solving approach (Kroger, 1970) and reframes the slip as an event from which to learn (Brodie, 1964; Hanley, 1967). A slip provides a useful experience to contrast with ongoing eating habits. Finally, the therapist hypnotizes the patient and asks him to imagine the situation in which he slipped and then to imagine an effective way to deal with it. In self-hypnosis the patient rehearses in fantasy ways of dealing with each type of slip. Next, the therapist examines the patient's negative reactions to the slip and helps the patient develop a series of positive statements about the ongoing attempts to control weight.

Dynamic Hypnotherapy for Weight Loss

Some patients fail to respond at all to the hypnobehavioral treatment of weight problems, either because they did not adhere to some aspects of the behavioral regimen, for example, self-monitoring, stimulus-control, or the behavioral regulation of eating habits. Other patients make initial progress and then reach a plateau—after a number of weeks they simply stop losing weight. Still others make substantial progress and then relapse.

When strong resistances arise, a change to an hypnodynamic approach to the treatment is recommended.

While nonhypnotic therapy has been used to explore resistances to dieting (Kaplan & Kaplan, 1957), hypnosis can be used as an uncovering therapy to identify conflicts associated with longstanding maladaptive eating behaviors. For example, through age regression problematic eating behaviors can be explored (Kroger, 1970; Shibata, 1967). The patient can be questioned about unconscious reasons for overeating by the use of ideomotor signalling (Cheek & LeCron, 1968). Hypnoprojective dreams can be used to explore excessive hunger drives (Winkelstein, 1959). Through hypnotherapy specific resistances can be explored as they emerge in the course of treatment. These are usually indicative of underlying conflicts, such as fear of abandonment (Crasilneck & Hall, 1975) or the wish for oral gratification (Mann, 1953). Conrad (1954) identified typical conflicts associated with weight problems: fear of loss of love, fear of sexual or aggressive impulses, or a wish to be pregnant. Family conflicts also contribute to resistance and can be explored in hypnotherapy (Flood, 1966). Hypnotherapy, likewise, can be used to explore the reasons for relapse (Hanley, 1967).

Some patients require long-term psychotherapy, psychoanalysis, or hypnoanalysis. Wick and her colleagues (1971) described two groups of overweight patients who manifest psychiatric symptoms: a larger group, with primary weight problems and psychiatric symptoms such as depression and anxiety secondary to their weight reduction attempts; and a smaller group with primary psychopathological manifestations and secondary weight problems. In the latter group, being overweight takes on a particular psychodynamic meaning. These patients do not respond well to hypnobehavioral treatment but do respond well to hypnoanalysis. Wick recommended two types of treatment: hypnobehavioral treatment for the former group of patients and hypnoanalytic treatment for the latter group. They described a case of hypnoanalysis with a patient with a primary emotional disturbance, for which being overweight was a symbolic representation of an underlying conflict. As is typical in such cases, a year or more of hypnoanalysis was required before any attempt at weight reduction was feasible. This finding is consistent with reports of nonhypnotic therapy for obesity. Rand and Stunkard (1977; 1978) report that many obese patients in psychoanalysis spontaneously lose significant amounts of weight by the termination of analysis, even though weight was never explicitly addressed. Presumably, the psychoanalysis resolved underlying conflicts associated with being overweight, so that there was no longer any need to maintain the weight. Likewise, intensive hypnoanalysis is indicated for some overweight patients with primary psychopathology. When hypnobehavioral and hypnoanalytic methods fail, sometimes paradoxical interventions are indicated. Erickson (1960), for example, reported success by paradoxically instructing a patient both to gain and to lose weight. A more detailed discussion of paradoxical interventions is found elsewhere (Erickson & Rossi, 1979).

Clinical Outcome

Is is unclear which patients respond best to behavioral and which to hypnobehavioral treatment. The best predictors of treatment outcome are the patient's percentage of overweight at pretreatment, the response to treatment in the first few weeks (Brownell, 1983; Jeffery, Wing, & Stunkard, 1978; Wilson, 1980). Mildly overweight patients who are able to reduce caloric intake and weight in the first few weeks of treatment are the most likely to succeed. Moderately overweight patients respond best to initial pharmacological treatment or low-calorie diets, which enable the patient to lose a quick 20 to 50 pounds, followed by behavioral treatment designed to maintain the weight loss (Craighead, Stunkard, & O'Brien, 1981). Massively overweight patients respond very poorly to behavioral treatment because of a biological limit to losing weight (excessive number of fat cells and a maladaptive habit of a sustained high-caloric diet). Surgery and sustained low-calorie diets are the only treatments to claim any success with such patients (Van Itallie & Kral, 1981). Except for anecdotal cases, there are no systematic studies yet of success with moderately or massively overweight people.

Unfortunately, there are few good outcome studies on the hypnobehavioral treatment of weight problems (Mott & Roberts, 1979; Wadden & Anderton, 1982). As far as one can tell from the sparse outcome data reported (Wadden & Anderton, 1982), the outcome of hypnotic weight control is comparable to that of behavioral weight control. The numerous, more carefully controlled nonhypnotic reviews of the multimodal behavioral treatment of weight problems consistently agree that behavioral methods allow patients to lose an average of 1 to 2 pounds per week, to a maximum of 10 to 15 pounds. The average weight loss is, however, highly variable across individuals. While the average is 10 to 15 pounds, some people may lose much less, some much more. The multimodal treatment protocols yield the best results (Abramson, 1977; Harris, 1969; Mahoney, 1978; Miller & Sims, 1981; Penick et al, 1971; Stuart, 1967; 1971; Stunkard, 1980). Sophisticated treatment protocols result in an average weight loss of nearly 25 pounds (Rodin, 1980b). Although the weight lost by behavioral treatment is modest, the studies show that the loss is maintained over the years, despite the body's efforts to regulate back to the baseline (Jeffry et al., 1978; Stunkard, 1972; 1978; Stunkard & Penick, 1979).

The outcome of the hypnotic control of weight is comparable, although the studies, largely uncontrolled, must be interpreted with some caution. Crasilneck and Hall (1975) reported an average weight loss of 10 pounds per month for good hypnotic subjects, but did not specify the total weight lost. According to their claims, 80% of the weight loss was maintained. Aja (1977) reported an average weight loss of 9.5 pounds maintained over a 6-month period. These studies are more in line with the typical behavioral studies. Two studies report better results: Stanton (1975) reported an average weight loss of 20 pounds maintained over 2 years; Winkelstein (1959) reported an average weight loss of 27 pounds over a 6-month period. Like the more complex, nonhypnotic studies (Rodin, 1980b), both of these hypnotic studies are multimodal.

Control studies comparing hypnosis with nonhypnotic treatment are largely negative. In their review of the studies, Wadden and Anderton (1982) claimed that a hypnotic induction did not add anything to the treatment effect and that treatment outcome did not correlate with hypnotizability (Cohen & Alpert, 1978; Deyoub, 1979; Deyoub & Wilkie, 1980). They concluded that "hypnosis does not appear to be of unique value for weight reduction" (p. 224) and that the positive treatment gains were due to expectation effects, not to the hypnotic condition. We believe, however, that the case is not settled. The studies that failed to show a difference between hypnotic and nonhypnotic treatment utilized simple, direct suggestions for weight loss (Wadden & Flaxman, 1981) or simple suggestions for changing eating habits and self-image (Miller, 1974). In other words, the hypnotic treatment protocol used in all these studies was ill-conceived and simplistic. Further controlled outcome studies are needed on the efficacy of broad-range or multimodal hypnotic treatment protocols for hypnotic weight reduction, as outlined in this chapter.

HYPNOTIC TREATMENT OF SUBSTANCE ABUSE AND ALCOHOLISM

General Approaches to Substance Abuse

Treatment of substance abuse follows a multimodal protocol similar to that used in the treatment of smoking and weight problems. Treatment begins with a detailed assessment of the pattern and course of drug abuse; the history of substance abuse (duration and course); the periods of abstinence and the life events and coping strategies which contributed to abstinence; the impact on lifestyle (especially antisocial behaviors, impaired self-care, and impaired self-esteem); associated medical, psychiatric, and neuropsychological problems; and current detoxification status. Drug screening is useful to identify substances not reported by the patient.

Conscious and unconscious motivation is also assessed, motivation having an association with treatment outcome (Baumann, 1970). Assessment of hypnotizability is complicated by the fact that hypnotic susceptibility increases in certain intoxicated states, for example, in narcotically induced states (Vogel, 1937), and hypnotizability measures may be different during drug and drug-free periods of the patient's life.

One approach to treating substance abuse is to use hypnosis to train the patient in "cognitive self control" (Katz, 1980). A variety of hypnocognitive approaches have been utilized. Hypnosis can be combined with covert sensitization to develop an aversive attitude toward drug use. The patient learns to associate feeling sick or undergoing withdrawal with contact with the drugs (Ludwig & Lyle, 1964). Hypnosis can also be used to generate positive attitudes regarding the benefits of ceasing drug use. Hypnoprojective methods can be used to explore individual coping strategies. Using a variation on the Ideal Self Technique, Ludwig, et al. (1964), have their patients imagine a television show in which the hero is trying to overcome a drug addiction. As the program unfolds, the patient describes the successful coping strategies used by the hero. Once discovered, these idiosyncratic strategies are incorporated into hypnotic suggestions and posthypnotic suggestions and are fed back to the patient.

Ego-strengthening suggestions designed to enhance the substance abuser's self-confidence are extremely important (Ludwig et al., 1964; Paterson, 1974). Many substance abusers suffer from chronic impairments in self-esteem, and repetitive exposure in hypnosis and self-hypnosis to ego-strengthening suggestions for increased well-being and pride in specific accomplishments helps improve self-esteem over time.

Another important dimension of treatment for the substance abuser is social influence. Since peer pressure is a strong factor in effecting control of antisocial behavior, groups, especially those involving role-playing of relapse situations or hypnodrama of such situations, are quite useful. Ludwig et al. (1964) recommend a multimodal group treatment with adjunctive hypnosis. Their treatment includes educational talks, group induction of hypnosis, suggestions for gaining insight into the reasons for using substances, suggestions for the development of coping strategies and alternatives to the use of substances, and group hypnodramatic rehearsal of situations in which the individual is at risk of relapse. Ludwig, et al., noted, however, that group interaction was poor in the educationally focused groups, except in the hypnodrama, where interaction was specifically encouraged.

Hypnosis is an extremely useful adjunct to detoxification. Krystal (1975) characterizes the "basic pattern" of withdrawal as a condition of "overreactivity of the autonomic nervous system" (p. 55). While drug withdrawal affects many organ systems, most of the withdrawal symptoms are autonomically mediated. According to Krystal, 91% of the symptoms are a result of parasympathetic activity (e.g., nausea and vomiting, belching, chills, sweating, and diarrhea); some of the remainder are due to sympathetic activity (e.g., increases in systolic blood pressure); and some stem from adrenocortical activity. Three symptoms typically accompanying drug withdrawal are a generalized feeling of malaise, a histamine-mediated stuffiness and running of the nose, and hypothalamically mediated arousal changes (drowsiness or yawning). The withdrawal pattern is predominantly somatic in nature but may be accompanied by anxiety and depression. Since the withdrawal symptoms are mediated largely by the autonomic nervous system, gaining voluntary control over autonomic activity is likely to reduce the severity of the withdrawal symptoms. Training the patient in deep hypnotic and self-hypnotic relaxation alter autonomic activity directly and thereby reduce withdrawal symptoms (Bourne, 1975; Ludwig et al., 1964; Paterson, 1974). Hypnotic relaxation training is done in conjunction with medical detoxification, and a good working relationship with the physician who will conduct the detoxification should be developed. Prior to detoxification, the patient is introduced to hypnosis and learns hypnotic relaxation. Once adequate relaxation can be achieved consistently in self-hypnosis, the medical detoxification begins. The amount of drugs taken is systematically controlled and progressively reduced over a period of time during which the patient attempts to alleviate withdrawal symptoms by practicing self-hypnotic relaxation.

To convince the patient that he has voluntary control over the severity of the withdrawal symptoms, a symptom challenge is introduced. Prior to detoxification, the patient is hypnotized and asked to imagine a situation in which he is at the peak of withdrawal. Hypnotic suggestions for the withdrawal state result in the full range of withdrawal symptoms: sweating, chills, drowsiness, increased restlessness, and so on. These physiological and subjective effects are similar, but not identical, to those of actual withdrawal, although usually not as severe. Hypnotic suggestions to terminate the imagined withdrawal state are also effective (Ludwig & Lyle, 1964). By inducing and then reversing the withdrawal state through hypnotic suggestion a number of times, the substance abuser develops some control over the withdrawal. Posthypnotic suggestions are used to associate relaxation with becoming aware of withdrawal symptoms (Ludwig et al., 1964) and mastering them.

Effective treatment must also address the psychological states produced by drugs. The early literature on substance abuse emphasizes the nonspecific psychological effects of a variety of substances (Rado, 1926, 1933). Rado's "theory of morbid craving" sets forth the view that the psychological craving for any drug stems from the motivation to reduce painful states and generate pleasurable states. Seeking the "high," or a state of well-being ("pharmacogenic elation"), was believed to be the goal of the addict. However, more recent studies show that many addicts are motivated more by the need to reduce painful states than by pleasure-seeking (Wieder & Kaplan, 1969). According to the craving theory, one drug is easily exchangeable for another. Craving for any drug, or "pharmacothymia" as Rado called it, arises from diffuse oral needs. It is unclear, however, just how many substance abusers report a generalized craving state when denied substances, although Ludwig's pioneering work with hypnosis and substance abuse represents this view. From this perspective, hypnotic evocation of the craving state, followed by hypnotic relaxation, is the preferred treatment (Ludwig & Lyle, 1964; Ludwig et al., 1964).

The Treatment of Specific Substance Problems

The more recent literature on substance abuse emphasizes the specificity of the psychological effects of the substances. Different people are likely to report different psychological states induced by specific drugs. These specific psychological states represent the interaction of the person's psychodynamic conflicts and coping style with the specific pharmacological effects of the drug (Milkman & Frosch, 1973; Wieder & Kaplan, 1969). That is, certain persons exhibit a predilection for certain drugs because the pharmacological effects of a particular drug(s) match their coping needs. Preferential drug abuse occurs when the person consistently uses the same substance to generate a particular ego state (Khantzian, 1975; Milkman & Frosch, 1973). The specificity theory addresses the specific psychological state sought by the substance abuser who repeatedly prefers the same substance or substances.

The therapist begins by asking the patient, "What does [name of substance] do for you? What effects does it have? How does it compare to the effects of [name other substance]?" The therapist is careful to note the patient's verbatim response so that it can be incorporated later into the hypnotic suggestions. Because denying the substance abuser the psychological state induced by the substance increases the likelihood of relapse, the therapist tries to induce the same psychological state with hypnosis but without the substance. The hypnotized patient imagines ingesting the specified substance. Next, time distortion suggestions enable the patient to imagine the drug beginning to take effect. The patient describes the state induced by the imagined substance, and hypnotic suggestions enhance the effect. Posthypnotic suggestions are given for the patient to generate the state whenever needed as an alternative to using the actual substance.

Opiates.   Opiates (e.g., opium, heroin, codeine) are preferred by people who need to reduce their responsiveness to the environment and to dampen the force of their drives, especially the aggressive drives. They are used by people whose main defenses are repression and withdrawal and who suffer from painful dysphoric states as a result the inadequacy of these defenses (Milkman & Frosch, 1973). Pharmacologically, the opiates act as analgesics, muting physiological and emotional pain.

The literature on the hypnotic treatment of opiate addiction emphasizes the nonspecific psychological effects of substances and fails to appreciate the psychological specificity of opiates per se. Baumann (1970) had his patients hypnotically hallucinate an injection to produce a "gastric orgasm." Ludwig and Lyle (1964) had their patients hypnotically hallucinate "one of the best shots ever," with further hypnotic suggestions given to intensify the high. Although we agree that hypnotically imagined drug states serve quite useful purposes, we believe this earlier work was guided by incorrect assumptions about allegedly pleasurable states induced by narcotics. Instead, we suggest the following modification: the hypnotized patient is asked to imagine giving himself the injection; time is speeded up with time-distortion suggestions; the patient is asked to describe the effects; relaxation is induced; suggestions are given to reduce responsiveness to given stimuli; pain reduction suggestions are given according to the patient's subjective report of drug effects; and graded posthypnotic suggestions are given to reinforce attaining the analgesic or relaxation effect with less and less reliance on the use of the drug as time passes.

Sedatives.   Sedatives and barbiturates (like alcohol) are "releasant drugs" (Khantzian, 1975). In moderate doses, these drugs remove inhibitions by acting at the level of the control of behavior and result in a "disinhibition euphoria" (Smith & Wesson, 1974) and a sense of relief from anxiety and distress associated with internal conflicts. According to Fenichel (1945), the superego is "that part of the mind that is soluble in alcohol" (p. 379). Khantzian (1975) argues that release from superego inhibitions is characteristic of most sedative and barbiturate drugs, not just alcohol. Hypnosis can be used to generate the releasing effects of these substances. Hypnotized patients are asked to imagine injecting the drug into themselves and to describe its effects. Hypnotic suggestions enhance the releasing effects. Hypnotic rehearsal and fantasy are also used. The patient imagines himself in a variety of social situations in which he feels more relaxed and at ease with himself, more expressive, and more self-confident in a way similar to that gained previously from the substance use. Similarly, Baumann (1970) had his adolescent sedative-abuse patients uncover in hypnosis things they wished to communicate to their parents, but which they believed would shock their parents. In fantasy, the patients rehearsed communicating these things directly to their parents.

Amphetamines.   Amphetamines (speed, cocaine) are preferred by persons who need to enhance their responsiveness to the environment and increase drive strength, whose main defenses are masochistic grandiosity and active confrontation and mastery (Milkman & Frosch, 1973). Pharmacologically, amphetamines are "energizers" (Khantzian, 1975), heightening physiological and emotional awareness. The hypnotized patient imagines ingesting an amphetamine, without resorting to the actual use of the substance (Baumann, 1970), and rehearses in hypnotic fantasy nondrug activities designed to generate an energized state. Paterson, for example, (1974) had his amphetamine abusers in hypnosis imagine themselves working steadily on some project. We also recommend the use of sensation-seeking imagery (e.g., racing cars, white water rafting) to generate the energized state, so that the patient learns to generate the state in self-hypnosis without the need for the actual substance.

Hallucinogens.   Major   hallucinogens   (LSD,   mescaline,   and psilocybin) are preferred by people who experience a sense of disconnection from their internal experience or from their relationship with others. Pharmacologically, hallucinogens "crack the autistic shell" (Wieder & Kaplan, 1969) so that the person is able to discover new worlds both within and outside himself. Ritualized group hallucinogenic drug use becomes a means to develop a sense of social cohesion (Galanter, 1976). With minor hallucinogens such as marijuana it is especially important to get an accurate description of the specific effects typically experienced by the individual patient. The psychological effects of marijuana are highly variable and greatly influenced by the patient's mental set or the setting he is in (Tart, 1971). Marijuana accentuates the acuity of external and internal perception (Wieder & Kaplan, 1969). Baumann (1970) used hypnosis to produce an experience even more pleasurable and interesting than the actual drug experience, so that his adolescent patients might come to realize that they have the capacity for such experiences within themselves. Hypnotic suggestions are given for both sensory enhancement and relaxation. The patient then learns self-hypnosis.

Baumann (1970) and Greenwald (1970) also used hypnotic suggestions to revivify previous good LSD experiences as an alternative to the actual use of LSD. Nonhypnotic desensitization (Matefy, 1973) and hypnotic desensitization can be used to treat LSD flashbacks. We have also used hypnotic guided imagery, with or without music, to uncover conflicts associated with flashbacks. The patient is hypnotized and imagines a scene and reports the continuation of the scene in a story-like manner as it unfolds. As the scene unfolds, conflictual themes emerge. Often the progression of themes reaches its own solution within several sessions, regardless of whether or not these conflictual themes are interpreted to the patient in the waking state.

Polydrug Use.   Polydrug users—those who do not preferentially use a particular drug—are a distinct subgroup of substance abusers. They do not respond favorably to the kinds of hypnotic interventions previously mentioned (Baumann, 1970) and perhaps better fit the nonspecific theory of psychological craving. Treatment approaches designed to reduce psychological craving have had some success with these patients. Copemann (1977) combined hypnosis with covert sensitization to treat the polydrug abuser. His treatment began with a detailed analysis of the sequence of events leading to each instance of substance abuse. The patient was then hypnotized and asked to rehearse in fantasy the entire chain of events leading to ingestion or injection. At that point, suggestions were given that the patient become nauseated, and the patient broke into a cold sweat. In subsequent sessions the hypnotic sensitization was repeated, using progressively smaller segments of the overall chain of events leading to substance abuse. Although nonhypnotic relaxation and aversion therapy have been used with polydrug abusers (O'Brien, *et al.,* 1972), Copemann (1977) claims that his patients were unable to produce clear imagery without hypnosis.

Relapse Prevention

Even when the substance abuser eventually learns to handle the psychological and physiological states associated with withdrawal, he is at risk of relapse. Relapse rates for substance abuse parallel those for other addictive behaviors. About 80% of drug abusers relapse by the first year after withdrawal (Hunt, Barnett, & Branch, 1971). Hence, effective treatment must incorporate methods of relapse prevention, including an analysis of situations in which initial slips occur, the patient's cognitive and affective reactions to slipping (Marlatt & Gordon, 1980), and teaching the patient hypnotic coping imagery (Wadden & Penrod, 1981) or hypnotic relaxation (Katz, 1980) to help him deal with the situations in which he is likely to slip.

Developmental Hypnotherapy of the Drug Addict

Savitt (1963) once said that there is a considerable difference between treating a drug addiction and treating a drug addict. Working with cognitive states and the physiological and psychological states accompanying drug withdrawal is an appropriate approach to drug addiction. It is often necessary, however, to address the ego deficits of the drug addict. Khantzian (1975), Krystal and Raskin (1970), and Savitt (1963) have emphasized the substance abuser's ego deficits in affect tolerance. According to Krystal and Raskin, substance abusers are prone to affect regression. They readily undergo a "resomatization" of affect: They experience states of intolerable bodily discomfort instead of specific tolerable affective states. Krystal and Raskin (1970) and Wurmser (1978) also emphasize the deficits in development and integration of self- and object representations in substance abusers, and the resultant impairment of their capacity for intimate relationships (Hendin, 1974). According to Krystal and Raskin, substance abusers have impoverished self- and object representations. The drug serves as a transitional object, a soothing companion to the patient in times of need. According to Savitt (1963), drug abuse is a "restrictive attempt" to reestablish a lost object representation. Wurmser (1978) describes the use of substances by narcissistically vulnerable individuals in terms of the resolution of narcissistic crises. In response to narcissistic injury, such patients regress to more primitive affect and experience diffuse rage reactions. Substances serve as "pharmacogenic defenses," correcting for the deficit in psychological structure by magically allowing the patient to regain a sense of power and the illusion of narcissistic control over reality.

A developmental approach to hypnoanalysis is useful in working with the drug addict's ego deficits. Hypnoanalytic methods enhance affect experience and the development of affect tolerance and foster the integration and stability of self- and object representations. (These methods have been described in detail in Chapter 7.) Exploration of specific conflicts associated with substance abuse is sometimes indicated, using an uncovering approach to hypnotherapy. In a significant number of drug abusers, the abuse is progressive. With prolonged use, some substance abusers are more prone to withdrawal from social relationships, antisocial life styles, and psychological regression (Glover, 1932; Zinberg et al., 1978). Hypnoanalysis is also a means to explore the vicissitudes in the course of drug-related behaviors.

Clinical Outcome

There are as yet no systematic outcome studies on the use of hypnosis with drug abuse. We recommend the multimodal treatment protocol outlined in this chapter and hope it will stimulate outcome research along the lines suggested here.

Hypnotic Treatment of Alcoholism

Hypnobehavioral Treatment. Except for a few notable qualifications, the treatment of alcoholism should follow the same multimodal protocol as the treatment of weight and smoking problems. First, whereas direct hypnotic suggestions or posthypnotic suggestions to reduce drinking have been used (Björkhem, 1956; Bryant, 1958; McCord, 1967; Von Dedenroth, 1965), these are seldom useful as a sole intervention (Smith-Moorhouse, 1969). Second, dynamic hypnotherapy with the goal of uncovering conflicts associated with problem drinking is not recommended. Historically, dynamic hypnotherapy (Hartman, 1976; Langen, 1967; Van Pelt, 1958a), or dynamic hypnotherapy done in conjunction with aversive behavioral hypnotherapy (Feamster & Brown, 1963; Kroger, 1942) has been the main approach to the hypnotic treatment of the alcoholic. We agree that both nonhypnotic psychotherapy (Vaillant, 1981) and uncovering hypnotherapy (Gabrynowitz, 1977) may be harmful to the alcoholic because they stir up negative affective states that the alcoholic has no capacity to tolerate. If hypnosis is to be useful with alcoholics, it must be seen as an adjunct to a broad-spectrum treatment protocol representing the current knowledge of habit disorders and addictive behaviors. Hypnobehavioral methods are sometimes useful in the context of a multimodal treatment plan.

Treatment begins with a detailed assessment of problem drinking. The Michigan Alcoholism Screening Test (MAST) (Selzer, 1971) or the Drinking Profile (Marlatt & Marques, 1977) are useful tools for assessment. The intake should focus on: the history of the patient's alcoholism (duration, course, current stage of alcoholism); periods of sobriety; coping styles in the life situations that contributed to the periods of sobriety; reasons for relapse; impact on life style (work and family interactions, self-esteem, sleep-wake cycle, and self-care); associated medical, psychiatric and neuro-psychological problems, and detoxification status.

The reinforcing effects of alcohol (Conger, 1956) cannot be denied. Alcohol serves many purposes for many people and different purposes at different stages of alcoholism. For example, it produces a state of physiological arousal, a "lift." It can be the drinker's sole means of relaxation or be a buffer for negative emotional states with which the alcoholic is unable to cope. It can release inhibitions and increase the patient's fantasies of personal power (Marlatt & Gordon, 1980), and in this sense enhance the patient's self-esteem. Miller and Muñoz (1976) help the patient identify the specific functions alcohol serves; then they help him find alternatives for producing the same effects. Hypnosis is sometimes useful in helping the patient discover substitutes (Wolberg, 1948).

Hypnosis has been used most extensively with alcoholics to teach relaxation (Blake, 1965; Byers, 1975; Gabrynowicz, 1977; Jacobson &

Silfverskiold, 1973; Langen, 1967; Smith-Moorhouse, 1969). The patient is hypnotized and taught some kind of relaxation, for example, tensing-relaxing of specific muscle groups or waves of relaxation while in trance.

Sometimes the alcoholic's attitudes toward drinking can be altered. Because of the overdetermined reinforcing effects of alcohol, alcohol may be positively valued despite the negative impact on the alcoholic's life. In the past, aversive conditioning methods and hypnoaversive psychotherapy were used as the main strategy in the treatment of the alcoholic (Abrams, 1964; Wolberg, 1948). The patient was hypnotized and asked to hallucinate a glass filled with fluid that smells and tastes like alcohol. Then suggestions were given that he relive the worst hangover of his life (Feamster & Brown, 1963) or that he become nauseated or sick (Kroger, 1942; Miller, 1959, 1976). After the patient experienced the sick and unpleasant feelings, posthypnotic suggestions were given that whenever he thought about drinking or was tempted to drink, he would feel nauseated. Hypnosis thus was used to condition the patient to become sick at the taste or smell of alcohol. Sometimes hypnoaversive methods still are used in conjunction with medication such as Antibuse and Metronidazole. Posthypnotic suggestions then attempt to reinforce the continuation of taking the medication (Hartman, 1976; Langen, 1967). While aversive methods have historical relevance, we do not recommend them as a general practice. They can be used for certain patients, especially at the onset of treatment (Smith-Moorhouse, 1969), but should not be employed generally. Aversive methods are not as useful as behavioral self-control training (Caddy & Lovibond, 1976; Miller, 1977) and are disrespectful of the patient; they contradict the patient's experience of pleasure or relief gained from drinking. An alternative method is to give graded posthypnotic suggestions evoking and increasing in the patient indifference to alcohol over time (Jacobson & Silfverskiold, 1973; Langen, 1967).

The alcoholic's current motivation for treatment should also be assessed, although the patient's reports are seldom reliable. To increase motivation, Gabrynowicz (1977) asked his patients to list problems resulting from excessive drinking and benefits of abstaining from excessive drinking. Hypnoprojective methods can uncover and reinforce unconscious reasons for reducing alcohol intake. The most reliable predictor of treatment outcome is a period of voluntary abstinence. Some hypnotherapists demand complete abstinence as a prerequisite to treatment (Gabrynowicz, 1977; Langen, 1967); others demand at least a desire for sobriety (Jacobson & Silfverskiold, 1973). We recommend abstinence wherever possible, although the demand for complete abstinence during treatment is not always realistic. If the alcoholic is unable to control his drinking, then that difficulty becomes the focus of preparatory, nonhypnotic behavioral treatment with the goal of increased control over problem drinking. Since hypnotizability may be associated with treatment outcome (Friend, 1957), it is advisable to assess hypnotizability by using standardized scales. Alcoholics do not differ from normal, nonalcoholics in hypnotic suggestibility (Lennox & Bonny, 1976), although when hypnotized they experience less fading of the GRO and greater impulsiveness than do nonalcoholics (Field & Scott, 1969).

The alcoholic who is unable to abstain is first taught behavioral self-monitoring. He must keep a daily record of every drink consumed and record the exact circumstances in which alcohol was consumed—the time, the situation, and his thoughts and feelings at the time of consumption (Gabrynowicz, 1977; Miller & Muñoz, 1976). In this way, the alcoholic can learn accurate daily self-monitoring of drinking, so that his reports of alcohol consumption are consistent with those of significant others (Miller, 1977). If the treatment goal is to increase the alcoholic's awareness of alcohol intake, diaries on daily alcohol consumption are sufficient. If the goal is to obtain an objective measurement of alcohol consumption, the patient can learn to monitor his own blood-alcohol content (BAC), using a breath test (Miller, 1977). In either case, the patient learns to track daily and weekly alcohol consumption.

The nonabstinent patient learns behavioral self-control (Miller, 1977; Miller & Muñoz, 1976). Using Miller and Muñoz's self-help manual for systematically reducing alcohol consumption, the patient learns to control the situation and location in which drinking occurs, the quantity of alcohol consumed at any given time, and the rate at which it is consumed. The therapist helps the patient set realistic goals to reduce alcohol consumption. Achieving these goals can be reinforced with posthypnotic suggestions (Gabrynowicz, 1977).

Approaches emphasizing the positive benefits of controlling problem drinking are generally more useful than aversive methods. The patient makes a list of benefits he expects to gain by abstaining from drinking (Gabrynowicz, 1977). While in trance, the patient is presented with a "general health formula" in which he is asked to imagine how his health and general well-being will improve (Smith-Moorhouse, 1969).

It is extremely important to enhance the patient's sense of self-efficacy in the course of the treatment. Wilson (1978) has criticized the well-known "disease" model of alcohol treatment (Jellinek, 1960) because it can interfere with the development of self-efficacy and foster unrealistic beliefs. The expectation of lifelong total abstinence is inconsistent with the behavior of most alcoholics. Most alcoholics are likely to drink again, and many go through periods of controlled drinking. A drink once in a great while does not inevitably lead to relapse. The disease view implies that the alcoholic is a passive victim of a progressive disease. While this view may be partially true, enthusiastic advocacy of it may undermine treatment.

The patient's perceived self-efficacy can be enhanced by examining those unrealistic beliefs and showing the patient concrete ways of increasing control over the drinking episodes (Wilson, 1978). Hypnotic ego-strengthening suggestions also aid this end (Byers, 1975; Edwards, 1966; Jacobson & Silfverskiold, 1973) and in some instances have been used as the primary treatment prevention (Gabrynowicz, 1967). Such suggestions include suggestions for increased well-being associated with sobriety or increased confidence to resist the temptation to drink.

The ability to stay sober is related to the alcoholic's involvement in a social network and the degree of social adjustment (Edwards, 1966). Many alcoholics show deficits in social skills (Miller, 1977). Furthermore, certain work settings (Roman & Trice, 1970) and family environments (Steinglass, 1979) reinforce drinking behaviors and contribute to continued drinking and relapse. Because of the significant impact of the social group on the alcoholic, group treatment and family treatment have had better success than individual treatment (Johnson, 1980; Vaillant, 1981). Patients are encouraged to attend AA meetings; posthypnotic suggestions have sometimes been used to reinforce attendance at AA meetings (Edwards, 1966). We recommend treatment of the alcoholic in educational *groups* wherever possible where patients can also be taught hypnotic relaxation (Byers, 1975). Discussion of problematic drinking can take place either before or after group hypnosis (Kroger, 1942). Group hypnotherapy, in which group interaction is fostered and directed under hypnosis, has also been used to enhance the alcoholic's social skills (Beahrs & Hill, 1971).

A major focus of alcoholic treatment is relapse prevention. Achieving sobriety or eliminating problematic drinking is only the first step in the overall treatment. Maintaining reduced alcohol consumption is the more important step. According to Hunt and his colleagues (1971), 50% to 60% of alcoholics relapse within 3 months of attaining sobriety, and only 25% maintain long-term sobriety (Costello, 1975). Wadden and Penrod (1981) are inconclusive about the efficacy of the existing hypnotic treatment approaches for the alcoholic and strongly recommend that hypnotic treatment should focus on relapse prevention in the following areas: (a) reducing withdrawal symptoms, (b) understanding the events that maintain problematic drinking, and (c) teaching the patient coping imagery with regard to alcohol-related situations.

The alcoholic suffers from a postacute withdrawal syndrome (Gorski & Miller, 1979), which begins 1 to 2 weeks after detoxification, peaks by the 2nd month, and then subsides over the next 3 months. The postalcoholic syndrome is characterized by autonomically mediated physical changes, cognitive impairments (decreased concentration and confused thinking), emotional lability, and a generalized apprehension regarding one's well-being. These changes increase the likelihood that the patient will return to drinking to "normalize" his condition. Training the patient in hypnotic relaxation helps reduce the withdrawal symptoms (Byers, 1975; Gabrynowicz, 1977; Paterson, 1974).

The patient must also be helped with the psychological craving associated with drinking (Ludwig & Stark, 1974). About 80% of alcoholics report such a craving (Donovan & Channey, 1985), which can be reduced by hypnotic desensitization. After deep hypnotic relaxation is induced, suggestions are given to intensify the cravings within tolerable limits, after which the patient is then told to return to a relaxed condition. By practicing these suggestions over time, the patient learns to tolerate more and more intense craving states. Posthypnotic suggestions reinforce the relaxation whenever such craving for alcohol occurs in daily life. Next, self-monitoring records are inspected to analyze the patterns of slips, that is, short-term return to problematic drinking.

The therapist helps the alcoholic recognize high-risk situations. According to Sanchez-Craig and Walker (1975), about 75% slips are associated with aversive social events (rejection and criticism) or their anticipation. When the alcoholic encounters difficult social situations, he readily returns to alcohol as a coping device. Difficulty in managing negative emotions is another contributor to relapse (Litman, Eiser, Rawson, & Oppenheim, 1979; Marlatt & Gordon, 1980). Alcohol initially helps the patient cope with negative emotions because of its biphasic pharmacological activity: Small amounts of alcohol elevate the patient's mood and relieve tension, yet continued use results in increased dysphoria (Solomon, 1980). The alcoholic persists in the belief that the alcohol will provide a pleasurable state, while the reality is that it is likely to exacerbate the negative emotional state.

Once the patient comes to understand his individual pattern of high-risk situations, the therapist adopts a problem-solving approach. The hypnotized patient can be reminded of the ill effects associated with drinking and the benefits associated with abstinence (Gabrynowicz, 1977). Hypnosis also can be used to teach the patient coping skills (Wadden & Penrod, 1981). Hypnoprojective methods are used to help the patient discover and enhance coping strategies. The hypnotized patient rehearses and fantasizes each high-risk situation, effectively applying the coping strategies. Any slips that do occur are reframed as learning experiences (Gabrynowicz, 1977). This cognitive approach to relapse prevention is, however, limited by the degree of neuropsychological impairment. Many alcoholics have undiagnosed neuropsychological impairments that prevent their understanding of complex cognitive treatment interventions. Every effort should be made to assess the degree of impairment before designing the approach.

Clinical Outcome. The utility of hypnosis in the treatment of alcoholics remains to be demonstrated. The literature is filled with anecdotal data and uncontrolled experimental studies, all claiming that hypnosis is quite effective. Two controlled studies (Edwards, 1966; Smith-Moorhouse, 1969) showed no difference between hypnotic and nonhypnotic treatment. Wadden and Penrod (1981) criticized these outcome studies for their failure to assess hypnotizability, for the brevity of the treatment, and for the failure to provide a coherent method of treatment. In other words, whether or not hypnosis offers an advantage to the treatment is yet unclear.

It is hoped that the future work will favor a multimodal approach like the one suggested here and elsewhere (e.g., Hartman, 1976) because it has been clearly demonstrated that (nonhypnotic) multimodal treatment protocols have achieved the highest success rates (Costello, 1975). It is also hoped that future work will focus more carefully on the type of alcoholic patient most likely to benefit from hypnotic treatment. The research suggests that hypnosis is most useful for hypnotizable alcoholics (Friend, 1957), who at least have the wish for sobriety (Jacobsen & Silfverskiold, 1969) and who are not at risk in terms of self-care (Costello, 1975) or social adjustment (Edwards, 1966). Most important, hypnosis is most useful only at the early stages in the overall course of alcoholism and is of little benefit once the disease has taken on a life of its own and has resulted in significant interruption in most areas of the patient's life.

THE TREATMENT OF SEXUAL DYSFUNCTIONS

An Integration of Hypnosis and Sex Therapy

Kaplan (1974) sets forth a triphasic model of human sexual response and its associated dysfunctions. Each of the three phases—desire, excitement, and orgasm—represent a unique physiological response pattern in both males and females. Specific physiological or psychological factors can impede the physiological response of each phase. For both males and females, there are three different types of sexual dysfunction: inhibition of sexual desire, dysfunction in the excitement phase (erectile dysfunction or impotence in the male and general sexual dysfunction or frigidity in the female), and dysfunction in the orgasmic phase (premature or retarded ejaculation in the male and anorgasmia in the female). Vaginismus in the female is an additional dysfunction independent of the three phases of sexual response.

The sex therapy techniques developed by Masters and Johnson (1970), Kaplan (1974), and others (Hartman & Fithian, 1974; LoPiccolo & LoPiccolo, 1978) have achieved impressive success. At least three out of four patients improve and gain or regain sexual functioning as a result of these therapeutic interventions. Effective treatment of sexual dysfunctions requires activation of the involuntary physiological processes of each phase of the total sexual response, as well as modification of cognitive processes that inhibit these physiological responses. Various negative emotional states (e.g., sexual anxiety and guilt), negative thought patterns (e.g., "spectatoring"), and defenses against erotic pleasure are the common immediate causes of inhibition of the sexual response. Conjoint treatment involves a progression of sexual tasks in which sexual partners learn to stimulate each other to produce the sexual response and also learn to overcome their inhibitions to do so.

Hypnosis, integrated with advances in the sex therapy field, can increase treatment efficacy even more. Extrapolating from Shor's (1962) classic paper on the three dimensions of hypnosis, Mosher (1980) has described the three dimensions of depth of involvement in the human sexual response: detachment from the generalized reality orientation and adoption of a specific sexual orientation; sexual role enactment; and depth of engagement with the sexual partner. The depth of sexual involvement requires the same capacities as involvement in hypnosis. Mosher's theory suggests that patients who are readily hypnotizable are more sexually responsive than less easily hypnotizable ones. Hypnosis used as an adjunct to sex therapy can improve sexual response at least in hypnotizable patients. The greater suggestibility in hypnosis allows for direct alteration of the sexual dysfunction at least for some patients (Dennerstein, 1980).

Hypnosis increases relaxation and thus alleviates some of the anxiety that otherwise inhibits the sexual response. Trance also increases access to imagery, since sexual arousal is positively correlated with the capacity for imagery (Harris, Lacoste, & Yulis, 1980), the heightened erotic fantasy in hypnosis leads to greater sexual arousal (Dennerstein, 1980). Furthermore, the hypnotized patient becomes more aware of unconscious thoughts and gains more control over cognitive processes. In hypnosis the patient is directly able to alter negative cognitions that heretofore inhibited the sexual response. According to Araoz (1982), hypnosis alters negative thought patterns, giving the autonomic nervous system a chance to function unimpeded in its production of the normal phases of the sexual response.

There are three hypnotic approaches in the treatment of sexual dysfunction: (a) direct and indirect suggestions to alter the symptoms, (b) brief hynobehavioral interventions conducted *in vitro* (in fantasy) or *in vivo* (with the sexual partner), and (c) hypnodynamic exploration of the conflicts contributing to the sexual dysfunction. The choice of approach depends on the patient. The quickest improvement is attained with direct and indirect suggestions (August, 1959; Doane, 1971; Erickson, 1973; Leckie, 1964). But suggestive methods work only for some patients (estimated at fewer than 25%). Most patients require brief hynobehavioral interventions (5–15 sessions). The majority of them respond well to treatment (Araoz, 1982; Kroger & Fezler, 1976). Another estimated 25% of patients reach a plateau beyond which they fail to improve. These patients require a combination of hynobehavioral and insight-oriented, uncovering techniques. In the latter, unconscious conflicts associated with the sexual dysfunction are identified and worked through hynotherapeutically or hynoanalytically (Crasilneck & Hall, 1975; Van Pelt, 1958b).

Assessment

Hypnotic treatment of sexual dysfunctions begins with a detailed assessment in which the patient's presenting problem, personal history, and family history are explored. The clinician should be alert for psychiatric complications associated with the sexual dysfunction—depression, phobic states and neurotic conflicts—because they affect both the prognosis and the treatment approach (Kaplan, 1974). The clinician should also rule out physical illness (diabetic, renal, and hepatic disease) and medications (anticholinergic, antihypertensive medication, atropine, alcohol, sedatives, and narcotics) that might cause the sexual dysfunction. Hypnotic intervention is designed primarily for sexual dysfunction not complicated by physical illnesses. The clinician should also assess the patient's overall relationship with the current sexual partner. Discord and failure in communication may contribute to the sexual dysfunction.

A detailed sexual history is also taken. This includes: religious attitudes and attitudes of the parents towards sexuality, the nature of childhood sexual play, evidence of unpleasant or traumatic sexual experiences, reactions to menarche or first ejaculation, type of sexual education given by the parents and others, initial sexual encounters, and current sexual adjustment. Because patients often distort the sexual history owing to the operation of defenses, Beigel (1972) recommends the use of a "hypnotic check-up" as a corrective measure. The patient's sexual history is reviewed in trance to determine discrepancies between the waking and trance history and to ascertain where memories of sexual experiences may be repressed.

A detailed account of current sexual activity is especially important in the treatment planning. Affects associated with the sexual dysfunction can be assessed with items from the Sex Anxiety Inventory (Janda & O'Grady, 1980) and the Sex Guilt Inventory (Mosher, 1965, 1966). Attitudes toward sexuality are equally important. Is sex seen as a performance? As an expression of playfulness? Of intimacy? Though attitudes are difficult to ascertain in an initial interview, the clinician should make every effort to help the patient become conscious of mental activities during sex. Araoz (1982) emphasizes, "Behind every sexual dysfunction lies a defective cognition" (p. 62). According to Walen (1980), the primary task of the sex therapist is "pinpointing the troublesome cognitive linkages between sexual stimuli and sexual responses" (p. 87). The patient is asked what typically goes through his mind during the act of sex and also how he sees himself during sex. Likewise, the patient is asked how he views his partner as a sexual provider—as gentle, crude, selfish, giving—and what type of sexual fantasies typically occur during sex. The clinician must determine whether these fantasies are used to excite the patient (Araoz, 1982) or to create distance from the partner (Hollender, 1963). The patient is also requested to detail the sequence of his usual sexual behavior through the three phases of the sexual response. What type of bodily sensations does he experience at each step? What does he do to increase his own sexual responsivness and that of his partner?

Some of the assessment can be made in hypnosis. Hypnoprojective methods can be used to explore strategies to cope with the sexual dysfunction. Suggestions can be given, for example, that the patient imagine a vivid sexual scene in which everything goes fine and there is no dysfunction (Araoz, 1982). In other suggested scenes, the patient discovers the most exciting sexual stimuli for him and his partner (Araoz, 1982), that is, those which would unblock the physiological responses representing the dysfunction. In his book, *Hypnosis and Sex Therapy,* Araoz gives a number of hypnotic procedures for uncovering conflicts associated with sexual dysfunctions. For instance, the patient visualizes himself naked before a mirror, describing the different areas of the body and evaluating each body part. With hypnoprojective techniques like the Theatre or Television Technique, the patient visualizes "a scene that has something to do with the problem of [name sexual dysfunction]." The patient also thinks about the sexual problem to become aware of whatever bodily sensations arise in association with the problem. To learn about the genetic roots of the sexual dysfunction, the patient imagines watching an old family movie or looking at a family picture album, observing everything that went on in the family.

Hypnotherapy of Sexual Dysfunction in Men

Treatment of Erectile Dysfunction.   Erectile dysfunction, or impotence, is a dysfunction of the parasympathetically controlled, local involuntary vasocongestive reflex, by which the blood vessels dilate and the penis becomes engorged and erect. Certain physical illnesses—notably diabetes, renal and hepatic disease—and certain substances (alcohol, sedatives, narcotics, and antihypertensive drugs) can disrupt the reflex. If, however, an erection can be obtained under any circumstances, it is likely that the vasocongestive reflex is intact and physical causes can be ruled out. The reflex is highly vulnerable to psychological influences, especially stress and anxiety. Anxieties associated with the sexual response—fear of failure, excessive demands by the partner for sexual performance, and inability to abandon oneself to sexual feelings—often contribute to impotence. Sometimes these anxieties have roots in deeper unconscious conflicts centering on castration. Cognitive processes also greatly influence the vasocongestive reflex, either facilitating or disrupting its functioning. Negative self-statements, obsessive ruminations regarding performance, and spectatoring have been shown to contribute to the erectile dysfunction (Araoz, 1982; Kaplan, 1974; Walen, 1980).

Direct and indirect hypnotic suggestions can be effective in the treatment of erectile dysfunction. Posthypnotic suggestions can be given that the patient will have firm, hard erections and will enjoy intercourse (Crasilneck & Hall, 1975). An alternative method is to suggest finger or limb catalepsy and posthypnotically transfer it to the penis during sex. The finger or arm becomes rigid and stiff during trance. Then the patient is told that his penis will become rigid and stiff just like the finger or arm each time he has sex (Araoz, 1982; Crasilneck & Hall, 1975). Sensations of warmth and pressure can be produced in the thighs by means of hypnotic imagery, for example, the heat of a fireplace, the pressure of a warm blanket of sand over the body while lying on the beach. Once the heat and pressure sensations are generated, they are transferred to the genital area. Kroger and Fezler (1976) claim such imagery directly activates the vasocongestive reflex. Paradoxical suggestions sometimes are used to counteract resistances. For example, as an antidote to the fear of losing an erection, Kroger and Fezler (1976) suggest that the patient explicitly try to lose the erection. The paradoxical effect is maintenance of the erection. While these forms of direct and indirect hypnotic suggestions are sometimes dramatically effective, it is difficult to know in advance for which patients they are indicated. If no response is obtained after several sessions, a switch to a hypnobehavioral approach is in order.

Hypnobehavioral treatment combines hypnosis with imagery conditioning and desensitization. Imagery conditioning distracts the patient from the characteristic negative cognitions that interfere with the vasocongestive reflex. Hypnotic recall and revivification of previous sexual experiences in which the patient was capable of producing and maintaining a normal erection (Kroger & Fezler, 1976; Nuland, 1978), revivification (Kroger & Fezler, 1976), or creation of past and fantasied sexually arousing encounters (Araoz, 1982) are examples of how hypnotically activated memories and fantasies can be used to enhance sexual arousal by replacing negative cognitions with sexually exciting fantasies and memories.

Hypnotic desensitization involves the rehearsal in fantasy of sexual play, leading to increased excitement and erection while in a deep state of relaxation. Fantasy desensitization, as an independent intervention, has limited efficacy in the treatment of erectile dysfunction (Kockott et al, 1975). It is better used as preparation for desensitization with the sexual partner. Having successfully imagined the steps of sexual play leading to and maintaining an erection, the patient is instructed to engage in a structured sequence of nondemanding sexual play with his partner (Kaplan, 1974). To dispel fears of losing the erection, the "squeeze method" is also helpful (Masters & Johnson, 1970). The partner squeezes the erect penis until it become flaccid. Then she stimulates the patient until it becomes erect again. Posthypnotic suggestions are also given for the patient to increasingly focus on erotic sensations and to engage in erotic fantasies during the sexual play. The sexual tasks are carried out until the patient is capable of maintaining an erection after penetration and up to ejaculation.

If the patient reaches a plateau with the progressive hypnobehavioral tasks, it is likely that the resistance to a change in the symptom represents deeper underlying conflict. The plateau is a signal to switch to a hypnodynamic approach. Uncovering methods are used to afford insight into the underlying conflicts, such as fear of punishment for masturbation, familial prohibitions regarding sexual expression, and oedipal conflicts (Deabler, 1976; Wolberg, 1948), and unconscious anger toward women (Crasilneck & Hall, 1975).

Nonhypnotic sex therapy has a 60% success rate with primary, and 74% with secondary, erectile dysfunctions, as compared to 45% for behavior modification (Cooper, 1960; Kaplan, 1974). Crasilneck and Hall (1975) claim an 80% success rate with hypnosis, using direct suggestions and dynamic hypnotherapy, but they do not distinguish between primary and secondary impotence. No outcome data are available yet for hynobehavioral methods. The outcome reports are consistent with what we might expect: Hypnosis modestly improves outcome in an area where treatment success is already well established. The advantage of hypnosis lies in its ability to address those patients who are responsive to direct and indirect suggestions for symptom alleviation. Hypnosis is used to enhance imagery, reinforce functional sexual behavior with posthypnotic suggestions as an adjunct to behavioral interventions, and identify underlying conflicts which can be worked through in brief hypnotherapy.

Orgasmic Dysfunction in Men.   Ejaculation is a different phase of the male sexual response. In contrast to erection, ejaculation is under the control of the sympathetic nervous system and is subject to facilitatory and inhibitory influences from the central nervous system. It consists of two phases: emission, the contraction of the internal organs; and ejaculation, the contraction of the striated bulbar muscles. At least this latter component is under voluntary control. The dysfunction of ejaculation represents a lack of normal voluntary control over the ejaculatory reflex. Most men with orgasmic dysfunction report deficient awareness of the sensations accompanying impending orgasm, what has been called "genital anesthesia" (Kaplan, 1974; Masters & Johnson, 1970).

Physical diseases and drugs seldom cause orgasmic dysfunction in the male; rather, psychological factors are typically implicated. Anxiety, defensive inhibition of the erotic sensations preceding orgasm (Kaplan, 1974), lingering effects of stressful first sexual experiences (Masters & Johnson, 1970), unconscious sadistic feelings toward women and power struggles with the partner (Kaplan, 1974) are the usual factors that disturb the orgasmic reflex.

Direct and indirect hypnotic suggestions are useful with certain patients to control premature ejaculation. Doane (1971) treated a patient with genital anesthesia by using direct hypnotic suggestions that all the feelings would return during sex. Erickson (1973) used a paradoxical suggestion to treat a patient with premature ejaculation. The patient's fear of failing to delay orgasm was transmuted into a hypnotically suggested failure for a specified time. Kroger and Fezler (1976) used hypnotically suggested time distortion, in which patients were led to believe that they had maintained an erection for a long time.

Most nonhypnotic sex therapy interventions have incorporated some version of the Seman's (1956) method into the treatment protocol. The Seman's method is a stop/start technique that fosters greater voluntary control over the orgasmic reflex. The patient is instructed to recognize the sensations while the partner stimulates the penis manually without intercourse. When the patient feels orgasm coming, stimulation is stopped until the sensations subside. The procedure is repeated three or four times. Each time the patient signals when to stop the stimulation. Once some control is achieved, it is repeated with the penis lubricated with vaseline. Finally, the procedure is repeated during intercourse with the female in the superior position. The patient signals his partner when to thrust and when to stop according to his awareness of the preorgasmic sensations. When voluntary control over the orgasmic reflex is achieved, coitus is repeated with the male in the side or superior position.

Hynobehavioral methods follow the same idea. Hypnobehavioral treatment of premature ejaculation places emphasis on the sensations preceding orgasm and those which foster voluntary control of the orgasmic reflex. Araoz (1982) suggests a sensation such as numbness of a finger to the patient in trance. Then the patient is given a posthypnotic suggestion that the numbness will go away at a self-induced signal, for example, blinking the eyes twice. In other words, the ability to feel or not to feel sensations in the fingers is under the patient's voluntary control. Next, posthypnotic suggestions are given to tranfer the numbness to the penis along with a release signal during intercourse. Ejaculation is delayed until the patient voluntarily blinks twice. To make this into a full stop/start technique, two signals can be given—one to produce numbness, one to release numbness—to be used by the patient to control the sensations and the orgasmic reflex. Kroger and Fezler (1976) used a form of stop/start imagery conditioning, with the hypnotized patient imagining both neutral and erotically stimulating scenes to dampen as well as foster sexual excitement. During intercourse the patient regulates the level of arousal by switching the imagery as needed.

A plateau reached in the hypnobehavioral treatment is a signal to the clinician to switch to a dynamic approach to treatment. The underlying causes of premature ejaculation are uncovered and worked through using hypnoprojective and hypnoanalytic methods (Erickson, 1935).

Direct suggestions are useful for some patients with retarded ejaculation. The hypnotized patient can be told he will enjoy the intense sensations reaching orgasm without thinking about it while becoming engrossed in these sensations. Hypnobehavioral treatment fosters greater voluntary control over the orgasmic reflex. To the patient in trance, Araoz (1982) suggests hypersensitivity of a finger, which is released upon a signal such as blinking twice. Through posthypnotic suggestion this hypersensitivity is transferred to the penis during intercourse, along with the release signal. During intercourse the patient has an increased awareness of the erotic sensations accompanying intercourse and voluntarily releases the orgasmic reflex through blinking. These suggestions can be accompanied by nonhypnotic conjoint sexual tasks in which the partner stimulates the patient to ejaculation in a series of steps (Kaplan, 1974). If the patient fails to respond to either the direct suggestions or the hypnobehavioral protocol, a hypnodynamic approach is used to help the patient gain insight into the unconscious conflicts associated with retarded ejaculation (Watkins, 1947).

Treatment of Sexual Dysfunction in Women

General Sexual Dysfunction/Frigidity.   In the female, general sexual dysfunction is a dysfunction of the local involuntary vasocongestive reflex, by which the blood vessels dilate and the vaginal walls become engorged with blood. The vagina expands and swells and the accompanying secretions serve as a lubricant during intercourse. The vasocongestive reflex in the female is less affected by illness and substances than in the male. The most common causes of inadequate physiological arousal are situational (inadequate stimulation or poor communication with the partner) or psychological (anxiety, stress, conflicts regarding sexual expression, or fear of rejection). Sometimes these conflicts have roots in deeper unconscious oedipal conflicts or are due to hostility toward the partner. The female vasocongestive reflex is especially influenced by thoughts and fantasies accompanying sexual excitement. Important factors contributing to frigidity are negative feelings about oneself; rigid, conscious control over sexual expression; spectatoring; and inhibitions in communicating what provides pleasure while going along with what the partner does (Kaplan, 1974).

Sometimes direct and indirect suggestions are effective in the treatment of frigidity. One approach is to condition the involuntary vasocongestive reflex to salivation. The patient is given an hypnotic suggestion to increase the flow of salivation in the mouth. Having succeeded, the patient is given a posthypnotic suggestion that a similar flow will occur in the vagina each time she feels sexually excited (Araoz, 1982). Further suggestions enable the patient to focus on the type of pleasurable bodily sensations and feelings accompanying sexual excitement (Leckie, 1964). In this sense, the hypnotic suggestions are comparable to Masters and Johnson's (1970) "sensate focus," which is designed to distract the patient from negative thoughts during sexual excitement by focusing on her pleasurable bodily sensations. Posthypnotic suggestions with sensate focus enhance the treatment effect for hypnotizable patients.

These hypnotic interventions can be combined with the standard conjoint sex therapy methods in which the couple engages in a sequence of sexual tasks: noncoital sensate focus, sensate focus with genital stimulation, sensate focus with nondemanding coitus with the female in the superior position (Beigel, 1972; Kaplan, 1974). Other hypnobehavioral treatment combines hypnosis with imagery conditioning and with *in vitro* and *in vivo* desensitization. Imagery conditioning helps distract the patient from the typical negative thinking that interferes with the vasocongestive reflex. Kroger and Fezler (1976) use "sensory imagery conditioning," in which the hypnotist suggests that the patient note the pleasurable sensations during imagined sex and posthypnotically transfers these to the clitoral area, first during masturbation and then during sexual activity with the partner. Araoz (1982) divides the hypnotic fantasy visualizations into several discrete steps:

1. The patient visualizes herself as wanted and loved by her partner while fully clothed.

2. The patient visualizes the mutual caring and the increased pleasurable bodily sensations while partially undressed with her partner.
3. The patient imagines herself undressed in the presence of her partner, experiencing the mutual caring and pleasurable bodily sensations, especially genital ones.
4. The patient is given a posthypnotic suggestion to experience pleasurable bodily sensations during intercourse with her partner.

The purpose of imagery conditioning is to enhance awareness of the bodily sensations during sexual excitement, which is believed to free the vasocongestive reflex from inhibition by negative cognitions and feelings. Hypnotic suggestions can also be given to desensitize the patient to the negative emotions previously associated with sexual excitement. The hypnotist and patient compose a list of reactions to sexual arousal. In a relaxed trance state, the patient imagines the steps of sexual arousal. Self-hypnosis reinforces the sense of pleasure associated with sexual arousal.

If the patient reaches a plateau with the progressive hypnobehavioral tasks, the clinician switches to a hypnodynamic approach, in which underlying conflicts are identified and worked through with hypnoprojective and hypnotherapeutic techniques (Leckie, 1964). Some of the conflicts that typically emerge are oedipal guilt with regard to sexual expression and unconscious hatred of men (Cheek & LeCron, 1968; Crasilneck & Hall, 1975; Ward, 1975).

Nonhypnotic sex therapy is approximately 80% successful (Masters & Johnson, 1970) for patients with general sexual dysfunction. Leckie (1964) claims a 75% success rate with hypnosis—25% with direct suggestions and 50% with other, mainly hypnodynamic, interventions. The scant outcome data are consistent with predictions. Some patients (25%) respond very quickly to direct suggestions to alleviate general sexual dysfunction, where hypnotically suggested sensate focus is the primary intervention. Other patients (estimated 50%) respond to brief hypnobehavioral interventions with imagery conditioning and densensitization with the sexual partner. The other 25% require insight-oriented uncovering of conflicts associated with the dysfunction. Though the success rates of sex therapy and hypnotherapy are comparable, treatment is often shorter with hypnosis, at least for the more hypnotizable patients.

Orgasmic Dysfunction in Women. Like the male sexual response, orgasm in the female sexual response is different from that of sexual excitement. Anorgasmia represents a lack of normal voluntary control over the orgasmic reflex (Kaplan, 1974; Masters & Johnson, 1970), a common condition among women. The usual causes of anorgasmia are inhibition of the orgasmic reflex due to negative cognitions and affects and inadequate clitoral stimulation during love making (Kaplan, 1974).

Direct hypnotic suggestions can increase awareness of bodily sensations and feelings accompanying excitement (Richardson, 1963), especially the sensations of impending orgasm. Hypnotically suggested time distortion can also be used so the patient is led to believe that a short interval of friction seems like a long period (Kroger & Fezler, 1976).

Some brief hypnobehavioral treatments emphasize increased awareness of sensations associated with orgasm. Cheek and LeCron (1968) begin by age-regressing the patient to childhood sensual experiences. The therapist revivifies positive sensual experiences, for example, being fondled by caregivers or early pleasurable feelings associated with masturbation. The therapist is also attentive to traumatic experiences and prohibitions associated with childhood sensuality. Subsequent sessions focus on enhancing the pleasure of current sexual experiences. The patient hallucinates various colored Christmas tree lights to represent the various areas of sexual pleasure in the body, associating certain colors with exquisite sensitivity of the genitalia, breasts, and other erogenous zones. The patient imagines a future date when she actually will be able to experience the imagined intensity of pleasurable sensations in these body zones and to report when this happens with her partner. Using a similar technique, Araoz (1982) has the patient take an imagined journey through the body to discover the areas where pleasure is generated. The patient specifically imagines herself inside the genitalia area, where she discovers which points respond with the most pleasurable sensations. In subsequent sessions the patient imagines her partner stimulating her in these most pleasurable areas.

A useful sequence of steps to heighten sensory awareness is: (a) the hypnotized patient first imagines sexually exciting scenes or recalls previously successful orgasmic sexual experiences; the patient next uses the sexual imagery while masturbating to climax; next, the patient imagines erotic scenes with the partner; finally, the patient engages in sexually exciting intercourse with the partner (Kroger & Fezler, 1976). The couple should be made aware of the importance of clitoral stimulation along with the value of heightened sensory awareness and erotic fantasy.

An alternative hypnobehavioral method is to employ stop/start imagery conditioning in which both neutral and erotic sexual imagery is used. By switching back and forth between the images as needed during intercourse, the patient learns to increase voluntary control over the orgasmic reflex. If the patient reaches a plateau, a hypnodynamic approach is used to uncover and work through the underlying conflicts. Kaplan (1974) reports a nearly 100% success rate for the treatment of anorgasmia with nonhypnotic conjoint sex therapy methods. In the only study available using hypnosis (Leckie, 1964), a 75% success rate is reported (25% by direct suggestions and 50 percent by dynamic interventions) (Leckie, 1964). No data on hypnobehavioral treatment are available. However, we feel confident that the outcome would improve and become comparable to the sex therapy data, the advantage being that results would be achieved more quickly in hypnotizable patients.

Vaginismus.   Vaginismus is the involuntary spasm of the muscles surrounding the vaginal entrance that makes penetration during intercourse impossible. Many women with vaginismus have a phobia about intercourse but not necessarily about sex, although some also try to avoid sexual situations. Vaginismus, sometimes attributed to physical causes, is typically attributed to psychological causes, notably misinformation about sex, restrictive attitudes regarding sex, traumatic sexual experiences, or unconscious hostility towards men.

Leckie (1964) used direct hypnotic suggestions to treat women with vaginismus. He suggested that the patient would find sexual intercourse to be a completely normal act, would lose all fear of intercourse, and would be able to relax the vaginal muscles. Schneck (1965) also used direct suggestions. Araoz (1982) has the patient imagine the muscles controlling the pelvic area to be like rubber bands. The patient then learns in trance to ease the tension of the bands.

Standard hypnobehavioral treatment combines fantasy and real-life desensitization (Fuchs et al., 1973; Hoch, Fuchs, & Paldi, 1972). Hypnosis relaxes the patient. Using a stimulus hierarchy, the clinician suggests that she imagine inserting a series of progressively larger dilators into the vagina while maintaining the relaxed state. Once the patient develops some degree of self-efficacy with the fantasy desensitization, she is instructed to use the same procedure with real, not imagined, stimuli,— Hegar dilators or one or more fingers. If the clinician uses a conjoint therapy approach, one of the husband's fingers, then a second, and finally the penis is used (Kaplan, 1974).

If the patient fails to respond to the hypnobehavioral treatment, a switch to a hypnodynamic approach is called for. Conflicts and resistances associated with the vaginismus are uncovered and worked through in hypnotherapy (Gottesfeld, 1978; Leckie, 1964; Richardson, 1963).

Outcome data on the treatment of vaginismus are impressive. Masters and Johnson report 100% success with progressive dilatation in conjoint therapy. Similar success rates have been reported for hypnosis: 87% by direct suggestion, 13% by dynamic hypnotherapy (Leckie, 1964).

Disorders of Desire

According to Kaplan (1979), disorders of desire represent a phase of the human sexual response different from sexual excitement or orgasm. While the latter two phases of sexual response pertain to involuntary physiological processes, the former is associated with voluntary control. The so-called lack of sexual desire in men or in women is due to the patient's active suppression of desire, not to an absence of desire. The patient voluntarily turns off the desire immediately upon registering it in consciousness. Typically, the patient switches attention away from the sexual stimulus toward negative thoughts. Often the pattern of negative thinking is accompanied by phobic avoidance of any sexual situations or of potential partners or at least of physical contact. Sometimes the sexual desire is transferred to less threatening objects, as is the case in perversions.

Direct hypnotic suggestions are sometimes useful in the treatment of disorders of sexual desire. The patient is told that sex is a normal, wonderful act (Leckie, 1964) and that as time passes, he will find sexuality to be more and more desirable. The patient is also told that the frequency of sexual desire will progressively become more harmonious with the desire of the partner (August, 1959) and that all sexual sensations will return during actual sexual intercourse (Doane, 1971). An alternative approach is to have the patient visualize the mind as a computer control room in which there is a dial that controls sexual desire. The patient imagines that the dial is not set correctly and is then told to set the dial at the right number. Posthypnotic suggestions reinforce the increased sexual desire (Araoz, 1982).

A hypnobehavioral approach combines sensory awareness training with either cognitive therapy or desensitization. The patient is first guided through awareness of various bodily sensations—heart beat, breathing, muscle and skin sensations—in order to feel the body as being more alive. Then the patient imagines in trance the most pleasurable sexual experience possible or is regressed to a previous period in life when sex was desirable. These pleasurable sexual experiences distract from negative thoughts about potential partners or sexual situations (Araoz, 1982). Hypnosis can also be combined with behavioral desensitization: the patient imagines a series of progressively more arousing sexual situations while maintaining hypnotic relaxation (Kraft & Al-Issa, 1968).

According to Kaplan (1979), most disorders of desire do not respond well to behavioral treatment. Resistances are often encountered because most disorders of desire are associated with psychological conflict: fear of sexuality (or of intimacy) as potentially dangerous, harmful, or too pleasurable; hostility toward the potential partner or rejection of the partner; or covert power struggles with the partner. Disorders of desire are likely, then, to require an uncovering approach. We recommend a trial treatment with direct suggestions, then hypnobehavioral treatment to offer quick relief to those patients who are responsive to these types of intervention. For the remainder, dynamic hypnotherapy designed to uncover and work through the conflicts or hypnoanalysis is indicated. Very few outcome data are available for either nonhypnotic or hypnotic treatment of disorders of desire. Kaplan's (1979) preliminary investigations suggest less optimism for those disorders than for disorders of excitement or orgasm.

SLEEP DISTURBANCES

Factors Contributing to the Development of Ideopathic Sleep Disturbances

A variety of disorders of initiating and maintaining sleep (DIMS) are classified together because various indices of sleep disturbance are highly consistent with one another. People with a sleep disturbance are likely to show a number of problems, such as taking more than 30 minutes to fall asleep, awakening frequently during the night, and having difficulty going back to sleep. All those who report difficulty with falling and remaining asleep, and complain of not being rested in the morning (Monroe, 1967), however, do not necessarily have a sleep disturbance. Many significantly overestimate the time it takes to fall asleep and underestimate the total hours they do sleep (Carskadon et al., 1976). The night-to-night variability across these parameters of sleep is usually very high for patients with sleep disturbances (Borkovec, 1982).

According to the DSM III (APA, 1980) there are nine types of disorders of initiating and maintaining sleep. Thirty-five percent of sleep disorders (SD) are associated with psychiatric disorders; 12% with drugs and alcohol; 15% psychophysiological SD; 9% subjective SD; 6% associated with sleep-induced respiratory impairment; and 15% of sleep disorders are associated with medical and environmental factors, myoclonus, or other conditions. Childhood onset of sleep disturbance is infrequent.

In each of the two most common types of sleep disturbance, the psychiatric disorder or the substance use is the primary problem, the SD secondary. If treatment of the primary problem is successful, the sleep disorder is usually alleviated. However, it is not always easy to determine whether the sleep disorder is primary or secondary, especially when the patient presents with depressive symptoms. On one hand, it may represent vegetative signs of depression, that is, symptoms secondary to depression. On the other hand, depression and anxiety are reactions commonly secondary to a chronic sleep disturbance. The anamnesis may be of some help in spotting patients who are primarily depressed, for they tend to show more early morning awakening than do patients with a primary sleep disturbance. If the diagnosis remains unclear, the clinician may use a sleep EEG. Analysis of the REM sleep patterns is a valid means to distinguish between depressive and primarily sleep-disturbed patients (Gillin, Duncan, Pettigrew, Franklin, & Snyder, 1979).

Idiopathic sleep disturbance (psychophysiological and subjective sleep disorder) is most amenable to hypnotic and behavioral interventions. Patients with psychophysiological sleep disorders have objectively measurable long sleep onset latencies; those with the subjective feeling of sleep disorder do not. Here again, a sleep EEG can distinguish between these two types of patients. The subjective insomniacs have a disturbed time sense. They overestimate the time it takes them to fall asleep—the sleep onset latencies of these patients, as measured by an EEG, are within normal limits. Regardless of the type, about 50% to 70% of idiopathic sleep disorder patients do well with short-term behavioral and hypnotic interventions (Borkovec, 1982). A portion of the remainder do well with dynamic psychotherapy and hypnotherapy aimed at resolving conflicts underlying the SD. Another portion improves with the resolution of life crises and situational stresses.

Figure 4.3 lists some of the mechanisms involved in idiopathic SD. On the subjective side, cognitive hyperactivity is usually involved in insomnia, psychological conflict is sometimes involved. Worry is implicated for 84% of patients with idiopathic insomnia (Borkovec, 1982). When those patients try to go to sleep, worries intrude into consciousness. Going to sleep creates a sensory-deprivation environment wherein worrisome events in the stream of consciousness become more salient and capture attention. Patients may preoccupy themselves with reviewing the incomplete projects of the day or with planning the next projects. They often complain that their minds race (Geer & Katkin, 1966). Sometimes patients worry about daily hassles and stressful life events (Roth, Kramer, & Lutz, 1976). They usually worry about daily problems, not deep, underlying conflicts, although some idiopathic insomniacs have deeper conflicts associated with their sleep disturbance. These are usually patients who internalize psychological conflicts rather than manifest conflicts in behavior. They become fearful of sleep, which becomes a state of "chronic emotional arousal" (Kales et al., 1976).

On the psychophysiological side, some patients have a deficient sleep system. Evoked potentials to certain waking stimuli are below the normal range (Borkovec, 1982), as are waking sensorimotor rhythms (Jordan, Havri, & Phelps, 1976). Insomniacs, who have a psychophysiological style of reducing responses to sensory stimuli during the day may at night have difficulty activating the sleep mechanism, which is triggered by the reduction in stimuli upon going to sleep.

The consequences of either the cognitive activity or the psychophysiological deficit is that the central nervous system remains activated and sleep-onset is delayed (Borkovec, 1982). For some patients, but not all, central nervous system activation is accompanied by activation of the autonomic nervous sytem and related increases in muscle tension and cardiac output (Johns, Gray, Masterson, & Bruce, 1971; Monroe, 1967). Being especially unrelaxed at the time of sleep onset is associated with excessive activity during the day (Marchini, Coates, Magistad, & Waldrum, 1983; Turner, 1984a).

Over time, the act of going to sleep becomes a loaded issue. Sleep-disturbed patients form poor sleep habits. Normally, sleep induction is

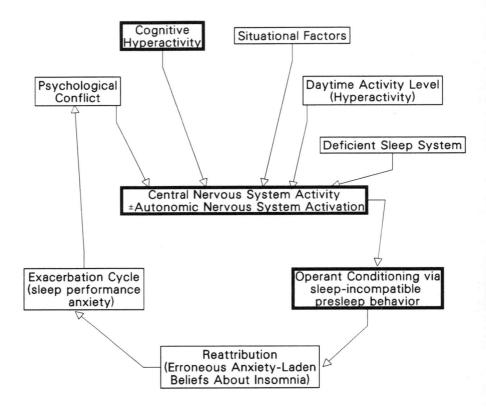

FIG. 4.3. The Causation and Maintenance of Ideopathic Sleep Disturbances. From Borkovec (1982), Kales et. al. (1976), and Turner (1984a).

facilitated by certain sensory cues: the bedroom, the bed, the clothing one wears to bed, the presleep routines, and the posture one adopts in going to sleep. Good sleepers develop consistent presleep routines and use consistent sensory cues (e.g., a desire to turn onto one side) as discriminatory signals for sleep. Poor sleepers, on the other hand, because they cannot sleep, bring into the bedroom activities that are incompatible with sleep (Bootzin, 1977) and thus operantly condition the continuation of the presleep-activated state, with its cognitive hyperactivity. This, of course, compounds the problem. People who are underactive during the day are especially prone to bring sleep-incompatible behaviors into the bedroom and thus to condition the sleep disturbance (Marchini et al., 1983; Turner, 1984b).

Patients whose arousal at bedtime is chronically too high develop a series of erroneous beliefs and misattributions about presleep arousal (Storms & Nisbett, 1970). If they become especially aware of their state of mind during the presleep period, they begin to develop beliefs about the harmful effects of not sleeping, they despair of their ability to exercise control over the sleep process, and they may misattribute to deep-seated emotional problems the persistent cognitive activity about daily events.

Once the sleep problem is well established, many patients begin an "exacerbation cycle" (Storms & Nisbett, 1970). Going to sleep becomes a major preoccupation. They try too hard and develop a kind of performance anxiety, whose end result is diminished control over the sleep process (Ascher & Efran, 1978).

The Hypnotic Treatment of Sleep Disturbances

The relative contribution of each of the aforementioned components to the overall sleep disturbance varies with each idiopathic insomniac patient. A careful assessment is necessary to determine which components need to be emphasized in the treatment planning. Many behavioral and hypnotic treatments of sleep disturbances are unidimensional, utilizing either direct suggestions, relaxation, desensitization, distraction, ego-strengthening, stimulus control, paradoxical intention, or dynamic hypnotherapy. Each of these approaches is successful for some insomniacs, perhaps comprising different subgroups of patients. Depending on the approach, successful outcome ranges from 25% (suggestion) to 75% (stimulus control) (Bootzin, 1977). A multidimensional treatment strategy is applicable to a larger portion of insomniacs across subgroups and is especially indicated for severe insomniacs (Ribordy & Denney, 1977).

Direct Suggestions and Imaginal Methods. We recommend three approaches for the hypnotic treatment of sleep disturbances: single-session directive suggestions, short-term hypnobehavioral therapy, and extended hypnodynamic therapy, in that order. First, one session in a directive hypnotic style can be tried (Vernon, 1961). The patient is hypnotized and told that he is becoming increasingly drowsy. The word "sleep" is avoided. A simple posthypnotic suggestion is given: "When you awaken from trance, you will feel so drowsy that you won't be able to keep your eyes open. You will close them and fall asleep." Once the patient responds, another posthypnotic suggestion is given: "Whenever you lie down at night to sleep, as soon as your body is in a horizontal position and you feel the touch of the pillow, your mind will wander off, and you will soon drift off into sleep without even knowing you have done so. You will have a full, uninterrupted sleep and will wake up feeling rested and refreshed."

Other, less directive hypnotic approaches have been designed for single- or several-session treatment of insomnia. Kroger and Fezler (1976) instruct the patient to visualize someone looking much like himself in a scene in which he is going to sleep. The patient imagines that person's breathing becoming deeper and more regular and the body becoming more and more relaxed. Soon the image becomes very drowsy and sleepy, and the patient visualizes the image in slow motion getting up from his bed or chair, approaching the patient, and merging with the patient so that the image and the patient become one and the same. Spiegel and Spiegel (1978) recommend creating a dissociation between the cognitive activity and the bodily state of the insomniac. The patient in trance projects thoughts, images, plans, ideas onto a screen and allows them to continue in their own way. Meanwhile, the patient imagines his body to be floating. The patient enjoys the relaxed, floating state while the cognitive activity continues on the screen. This dissociation is designed to produce bodily relaxation along with diminished preoccupation with thoughts. The instructions are reinforced by self-hypnosis and applied at the time of sleep. With less elaborate instructions, Wolberg (1948) gave his insomniac patients suggestions for relaxation and slow, deep breathing along with suggestions for letting the mind be passive while going to sleep. Some approaches use hypnotically suggested relaxation (Borkovec & Fowles, 1973), but in the treatment of insomnia hypnotic relaxation does not appear to be quite as effective as nonhypnotic progressive relaxation training (Graham, Wright, Toman, & Mark, 1975; Paul, 1969).

These short-term hypnotic approaches to insomnia have the advantage of providing quick relief for many patients with idiopathic insomnia. Although extensive outcome studies are not yet available, it is estimated that those brief hypnotic interventions are useful for fewer than 25% of patients (not counting patients who relapse). Because a good number of patients clearly respond to these approaches, sometimes dramatically so, we recommend utilizing them for the first session or two. If patients fail to show improvement, a multidimensional hypnobehavioral treatment is in order.

Hypnobehavioral Treatment.   Hypnobehavioral treatment begins with an assessment of situational life style and environmental stress factors that may contribute to the sleep disturbance. Stressful life events (Holmes & Rahe, 1967) and daily pressures (Kanner, Coyne, Schaefer, & Lazarus, 1981) are assessed. The patient's pattern of activity and thinking during the day may also contribute to the sleep disturbance (Marchini et al., 1983), especially if the patient is excessively over-or underactive. Substances that affect the autonomic nervous system (caffeine, nicotine, amphetamines) may also contribute to the sleep disturbance. The therapist attempts to identify such situational factors and counsels the patient on making the necessary changes. For example, those who are underactive during the day are advised to increase daily interactions with people so they are not tempted to bring the need for activity into the presleep period. Those who are overactive during the day are counseled to limit stimulating activities to the morning or afternoon and to integrate some form of relaxation practice into everyday routines (Turner, 1984b). The pattern of activity in the bedroom just prior to going to bed is especially relevant for ascertaining behaviors incompatible with sleep which may have conditioned the sleep disturbance (Bootzin, 1977).

The patient self-monitors behavior by keeping a daily sleep log (Kazarian, Howe, & Csapo, 1979; Monroe, 1967; Relinger & Bornstein, 1979), noting subjective estimates of number of minutes it takes to fall asleep, number of times awake during the night, total number of hours and minutes slept, and number of dreams. In addition, patients rate on a 5–point scale, the ease or difficulty in falling asleep and the degree to which they feel rested upon awakening. Even though subjective estimates are notoriously inaccurate, they nevertheless can be the basis for altering the patient's beliefs about his or her sleep disturbance. In fact, some patients show improvement after self-monitoring alone (Jason, 1975), although this phenomenon is probably limited to patients with mild sleep disturbance only (Shealy, 1979). The therapist helps the patient discover any relationship between day-to-day stress, waking activity level, and the like. Patients are encouraged to alter the situations as necessary. An example of a daily sleep chart is found in Fig. 4.4.

The next stage of treatment involves teaching the patient to relax. A number of studies have shown that simple hypnotic suggestions for relaxation are not as effective as progressive relaxation, although both work to some degree (Graham et al., 1975; Paul, 1969). Letting the patient alternately tense and relax the msucles in the various muscle groups of the body seems to be important (Borkovec & Fowles, 1973) and can be done

DATE: ____ ____ ____ ____ ____ ____ ____

(Rate the first five upon awakening and the last four *before* going to bed.)

How many minutes did it take you to fall asleep last night?

How many times did you awaken during the night?

Please rate the general level of difficulty falling back to sleep.
1---2---3---4---5
not very   extremely
difficult   difficult

Please rate how difficult it was for you to fall asleep last night.
1---2---3---4---5
not very   extremely

Please rate how rested you feel this morning.
1---2---3---4---5
very rested   poorly rested

Number of hours napping today:
Number of caffeine drinks today:
Level of activity during day.
1---2---3---4---5
very active   not at all

Level of activity just before sleep.
1---2---3---4---5
very active   not at all

Please keep track of other behaviors and activities you are monitoring on this and the reverse side of this sheet along with the date of their occurrence and your comments.

DATE   BEHAVIOR/ACTIVITY   COMMENTS

FIG. 4.4. Daily Sleep Chart

218

with or without hypnosis. Working with specific muscle groups, for example, the forehead muscle (frontalis muscle), has been shown in various biofeedback studies to be important for highly anxious patients (Borkovec, 1982). Nonhypnotic relaxation training alone helps from 59% to 71% of insomniacs (Borkovec, 1982); the improvement rate can be even greater when practice is reinforced by posthypnotic suggestions and self-hypnosis and integrated into a multidimensional treatment approach.

A major area of intervention is the cognitive–affective hyperactivity of the presleep state, of which a great majority of patients complain. Hypnotic suggestions are designed to distract the patient from the usual worrisome thoughts or to focus attention in ways that are incompatible with this cognitive hyperactivity (Borkovec & Fowles, 1973). It may be suggested, for example, that the patient involve himself in a pleasant, enjoyable fantasy, watch an imagined favorite movie or TV show, or listen to hypnotically hallucinated music. Because monotony is an important ingredient in the disruption of habitual cognitive hyperactivity (Montgomery, *et al.*, 1975), repetition of suggestions, with little variation in a lulling tone, helps. Sometimes imagery can increase monotony; the patient in trance can erase numbers in reverse sequence from an imaginary blackboard or listen to an imaginary metronome.

Geer and Katkin (1966) have devised a desensitization approach designed to reduce the anxiety associated with the presleep state. This approach can be adapted to hypnosis. The patient is first told to relax and then to imagine a scene in which he is lying in bed, trying to fall asleep. The patient imagines the usual difficulty falling asleep, and suggestions are given to amplify the discomfort. Then the patient returns to the relaxed condition until the discomfort fades. The instructions are repeated as necessary. The patient may also rehearse in fantasy the steps of falling asleep (Hinkle & Lutker, 1972). All these methods counteract cognitive activity, though it is unclear whether any method is more appropriate for certain types of patients than for others. Patients who continue to have difficulty with intrusive presleep cognitions can be assigned a specific time, well before bedtime, explicitly reserved for planning, reflection, and problem solving.

While the combination of self-monitoring and associated situation interventions, relaxation training, and cognitive interventions is designed to address the main contributors to the causes of insomnia, other techniques—namely, stimulus control, reattribution, and paradoxical intention—are designed to address factors that maintain the insomnia as a chronic habit. Since for most veteran insomniacs the sleep disturbance is learned, interventions that primarily counteract the continuation of the sleep disturbance are often more effective than those which solely address its original causes.

As a sole treatment intervention, stimulus control methods average about 70–75% reduction in sleep-onset latency; and relaxation training alone, 45% (Bootzin, 1977; Borkovec, 1982). Therefore, it is advisable to integrate stimulus control into the hypnotic treatment approach for chronic insomniacs. The basic nonhypnotic approach to stimulus control includes the following instructions (Bootzin, 1977): (1) do not engage in any activities in bed (watching TV, reading, eating) other than trying to sleep; (2) if you are unable to sleep after 20 minutes, get up and do something else; (3) go to bed only when sleepy; (4) set the alarm so you will awaken at the same time each morning; (5) avoid daytime naps. The purposes of instructions (1) and (2) is to make the bed a discriminatory cue for sleep-onset. The purpose of instructions (3), (4), and (5) is to develop consistent sleep rhythms (Bootzin, 1977).

For patients who are especially preoccupied with their state of mind during the presleep period and who attribute the source of their insomnia to emotional instability (Storms & Nisbett, 1970), self-monitoring is helpful. As patients discover the relationship between situational daily events and the vicissitudes of the sleep disturbance, they learn to reattribute the source of the insomnia, at least in part, to external situational factors. As the insomnia comes to be seen as caused by other than their own psychopathology, anxiety about having insomnia diminishes during the pre-sleep period. Another common tendency is for patients to despair about the sleep disturbance. The gradual hypnobehavioral approach is designed to develop self-efficacy; patients who learn to reattribute the process of sleeping to their own control have been shown to reduce delays in sleep-onset (Davison et al., 1973).

Paradoxical intention is used to disrupt the exacerbation cycle, which stems from trying too hard to sleep. To reverse the pattern of trying too hard to sleep, the patient is told to try intentionally to stay awake as long as possible after going to bed and closing his eyes (Cheek & LeCron, 1968). The patient should try to note bodily sensations (Ascher & Efran, 1978), external sounds (Kroger & Fezler, 1976), and defeatist thoughts (Relinger & Bornstein, 1979) as they occur in the stream of consciousness, while maintaining a happy feeling state (Turner, DiTomasso, & Giles, 1983). Some variations on this method are especially useful for patients who have a high performance anxiety about falling asleep. The effectiveness of the instructions seems somewhat dependent on the skill of the therapist (Turner & Ascher, 1982).

Dynamic Hypnotherapy. The systematic combination of these hypnobehavioral methods—self-monitoring, relaxation, training, cognitive interventions, stimulus control, reattribution, and paradoxical intention—over a number of sessions, in our estimation, is effective for about 70%–75% of idiopathic insomnias. The average treatment takes roughly 8 to 15 sessions. The largest number of the remaining idiopathic insomniacs can be treated with a hypnodynamic approach. Since it is difficult to tell in advance which patients should be treated by a hypnobehavioral and which by a hypnodynamic approach, the procedure we use is to start all patients with a hypnobehavioral approach and wait to see if a plateau develops. If it does not, the hypnobehavioral approach is used. If it is apparent by the fourth to sixth session that the hypnobehavioral approach brings no improvement, presumably intrapsychic conflict interferes with the onset of sleeping, and the therapist switches to hypnodynamic treatment. He uses hypnoprojective methods—Theatre Technique, hypnotic dreams about the concern with falling asleep, or age regression to a time when the insomnia started—to uncover the nature of the conflict and help the patient work it through (Van Pelt, 1954–55). Typical conflicts involve fear of loss of control, fear of death, fear of abandonment, or fear of sexual or aggressive impulses. Once the conflict is resolved, the sleep disturbance usually clears up. Sometimes the sleep disturbance improves immediately upon resolution. Sometimes it improves only after additional hypnobehavioral methods are used, especially those aimed at factors which maintain the sleep disturbance. The justification for resumption of the hypnobehavioral approach is that some sleep disturbances, which originally have dynamic causes, take on a secondary, overlearned dimension over time.

Skill development. As the patient shows some improvement, typically in the reduction of sleep-onset latency and in the number of nightly awakenings, the treatment emphasis shifts to skill development. The patient is taught self-hypnosis and is encouraged to practice self-hypnotic relaxation and cognitive interventions at home as part of his presleep routine. If the transition to self-hypnosis is difficult, the patient may be given a tape, although the use of tapes in general does not necessarily increase the effectiveness of the treatment (Lick & Heffler, 1977). Emphasis is also given to relaxing the body and the mind immediately upon lying down to sleep, that is, automatically, without the need of an extended or ritualized self-hypnotic procedure.

Symptom challenge suggestions may also enhance self-efficacy at the later stages of treatment. Hypnotic suggestions are given for the patient to use what he has been learning in hypnosis to fall asleep during the therapy session. Then hypnotic rehearsal in fantasy is used. The patient imagines himself trying to go to sleep after days which involve each of the typical situational factors which had previously been identified as contributing to the sleep disturbance. Such procedures help to innoculate the patient against relapse of the sleep disturbance upon encountering sleep-disturbing daily situations.

REFERENCES

Abboud, Francois M. (1976). Relaxation, autonomic control, and hypertension. *New England Journal of Medicine, 294,* 107–109.

Abrams, David B., & Wilson, G. Terence (1979). Self-monitoring and reactivity of cigarette smoking. *Journal of Counsulting and Clinical Psychology, 47,* 243–251.

Abrams, Stanley (1964). An evaluation of hypnosis in the treatment of alcoholism. *American Journal of Psychiatry, 120,* 1160–1165.

Abramson, Edward E. (1977). *Behavioral approaches to weight control.* New York: Springer.

Achterberg, Jeanne A. & Lawlis, G. Frank (1978). *Imagery of cancer: An evaluation tool for the process of disease.* Champaign, IL: Institute for Personality and Ability Testing.

Achterberg, Jeanne A. & Lawlis, G. Frank (1980). Rheumatoid arthritis: A psychological perspective. In *Bridges of the bodymind* (pp. 255–305). Champaign, IL: Institute for Personality and Ability Testing.

Achterberg, Jeanne A. McGraw, Phillip, & Lawlis, G. Frank (1981). Rheumatoid arthritis: A study of relaxation and temperature biofeedback as an adjunctive therapy. *Biofeedback and Self Regulation, 6,* 207–223.

Adams, Henry E., Feuerstein, Michael, & Fowler, Joanne L. (1980). Migraine headache: Review of parameters, etiology, and intervention. *Psychological Bulletin, 87,* 217–237.

Ader, Robert (1981). *Psychoneuroimmunology.* New York: Academic Press.

Ader, Robert, & Cohen, Nicholas (1975) Behaviorally conditioned immunosuppression. *Psychosomatic Medicine, 37,* 333–340.

Ad Hoc Committee on Classification of Headache (1962). Classification of headache. *Journal of the American Medical Association, 197,* 717–718.

Adler, Charles S., & Adler, Sheila M. (1976). Biofeedback-psychotherapy for the treatment of headaches: A five year follow-up. *Headache, 16,* 189–191.

Aja, Joaquin H. (1977). Brief group treatment of obesity through ancillary self-hypnosis. *American Journal of Clinical Hypnosis, 19,* 231–234.

Aleo, S. & Nicassio, P. (1978) Auto-regulation of duodenal ulcer disease: A preliminary report of four cases. *Proceedings of the Biofeedback Society of America* ((Abstract, pp. 278–281). Ninth Annual Meeting. Denver, CO.

Alexander, A. Barney, Miklich, Donald R., & Hershkoff, Helen (1972). The immediate effects of systematic relaxation on peak expiratory flow rates in asthmatic children. *Psychosomatic Medicine, 34,* 388–394.

Alexander, Franz (1939). Emotional factors in essential hypertension. *Psychosomatic Medicine, 1,* 173–179.

Alexander, Franz, & French, Thomas (1948). *Studies in psychosomatic medicine.* New York: Ronald Press.

Allington, H. V. (1952). Review of the psychotherapy of warts. *Archives of Dermatology, 66,* 316–326.

Almy, Thomas P., Kern, Fred, & Tulin, Maurice (1949). Alterations in colonic function in man under stress: Experimental production of sigmoid spasm in healthy persons. *Gastroenterology, 12,* 425–436.

Almy, Thomas P., & Tulin, Maurice (1947). Alterations in colonic function in man under stress: Experimental production of changes simulating the "irritable colon". *Gastroenterology, 8,* 616–626.

American Psychiatric Association (1980). *Diagnostic and statistical manual of mental disorders* (3rd ed.). Washington, DC: American Psychiatric Association.

Anderson, J. A. D., Basker, M. A., & Dalton, R. (1975). Migraine and hypnotherapy. *International Journal of Clinical and Experimental Hypnosis, 23*, 48–58.

Andreychuk, Theodore, & Skriver, Christian (1975). Hypnosis and biofeedback in the treatment of migraine headache. *International Journal of Clinical and Experimental Hypnosis, 23*, 172–183.

Anselmi, B., Del Bianco, P. L., de Vos, C. J., Galli, P., Lamar, J. C., Schonbaum, E., Sicuteri, F., Van der Veen, F. (1976). Clinical and animal pharmacology of migraine: New perspectives. *Monographs on Neural Science, 3*, 45–59.

Antonovsky, Aaron (1979). *Health, stress and coping.* San Francisco: Jossey-Bass.

Appenzeller, O. (1978). Reflex vasomotor function: Clinical and experimental studies in migraine. *Research & Clinical Studies in Headache, 6*, 160–166.

Araoz, Daniel L. (1982). *Hypnosis and sex therapy.* New York: Brunner/Mazel.

As, Arvid (1962a). Non-hypnotic experiences related to hypnotizability in male and female college students. *Scandinavian Journal of Psychology, 3*, 112–121.

As, Arvid (1962b). A note on distractibility and hypnosis. *American Journal of Clinical Hypnosis, 5*, 135–137.

As, Arvid (1967). Hypnosis as a subjective experience. In Jean Lassner (Ed.) *Hypnosis and psychosomatic medicine* (pp. 1–6). New York: Springer-Verlag.

As, Arvid, & Ostvold, Siri (1968). Hypnosis as subjective experience. *Scandinavian Journal of Psychology, 9*, 33–38.

Ascher, L. Michael, & Efran, Jay S. (1978). The use of paradoxical intention in a behavioral program for sleep onset insomnia. *Journal of Consulting and Clinical Psychology, 8*, 547–550.

Aston, E. E. (1959). Treatment of allergy by suggestion: An experiment. *American Journal of Clinical Hypnosis, 1*, 163–164.

Astor, Martin H. (1973). Hypnosis and behavior modification combined with psychoanalytic psychotherapy. *International Journal of Clinical and Experimental Hypnosis, 21*, 18–24.

August, Ralph V. (1959). Libido altered with the aid of hypnosis: A case report. *American Journal of Clinical Hypnosis, 2*, 88.

Badgley, Laurence E., Spiro, Howard M., & Senay, Edward C. (1969). Effect of mental arithmetic on gastric secretion. *Psychophysiology, 5*, 633–637.

Bahnson, Claus B., & Bahnson, Marjorie B. (1966). Role of the ego defenses: Denial and repression in the etiology of malignant neoplasm. *Annals of the New York Academy of Science, 125*, 827–845.

Bakal, Donald A. (1982). *The psychobiology of chronic headache.* New York: Springer.

Bakal, Donald A., & Kaganov, Judith A. (1977). Muscle contraction and migraine headache: Psychophysiologic comparison. *Headache, 17*, 208–215.

Bandura, Albert (1977). Self-efficacy: Toward a unifying theory of behavior change. *Psychological Review, 84*, 191–215.

Banyai, Eva I., & Hilgard, Ernest R. (1976). A comparison of active-alert hypnosis with traditional relaxation induction. *Journal of Abnormal Psychology, 85*, 218–224.

Barabasz, Areed F., & McGeorge, Christopher M. (1978). Biofeedback, mediated biofeedback and hypnosis in peripheral vasodilation training. *American Journal of Clinical Hypnosis, 21*, 28–37.

Barber, Theodore X. (1959). Toward a theory of pain: Relief of chronic pain by prefrontal leucotomy, opiates, placebos, and hypnosis. *Psychological Bulletin, 56*, 430–460.

Barber, Theodore X. (1961). Physiological effects of "hypnosis". *Psychological Bulletin, 58*, 390–419.

Barber, Theodore X., & Calverley, David S. (1962). "Hypnotic behavior" as a function of task motivation. *Journal of Psychology, 54*, 363–389.

Barber, Theodore X., & Calverley, David S. (1963). The relative effectiveness of task-motivating instructions and trance-induction procedure in the production of "hypnotic-like" behaviors. *Journal of Nervous & Mental Disease, 137*, 107–116.

Barber, Theodore X., & Cooper, B. J. (1972). Effects on pain of experimentally induced and spontaneous distraction. *Psychological Reports, 31*, 647–651.

Barber, Theodore X., & Hahn, Karl W. (1962). Physiological and subjective responses to pain producing stimulation under hypnotically suggested and waking-imagined "analgesia". *Journal of Abnormal and Social Psychology, 65*, 411–418.

Barkley, Russell A., Hastings, James E., & Jackson, Thomas L., Jr. (1977). The effects of rapid smoking and hypnosis in the treatment of smoking behavior. *International Journal of Clinical and Experimental Hypnosis, 25*, 7–17.

Barofsky, Ivan (1981). Issues and approaches to the psychosocial assessment of the cancer patient. In Charles K. Prokop & Lawrence A. Bradley (Eds.), *Medical Psychology: Contributions to Behavioral Medicine* (pp. 55–65). New York: Academic Press.

Barrios, Alfred H. (1973). Posthypnotic suggestion as higher-order conditioning: A methodological and experimental analysis. *International Journal of Clinical and Experimental Hypnosis, 21*, 32–50.

Bartlett, Kenneth A. (1970). Hypnotic treatment of a Novocain allergy. *American Journal of Clinical Hypnosis, 12*, 222–226.

Basker, M. A. (1970). Hypnosis in migraine. *British Journal of Clinical Hypnosis, 2*, 15–18.

Baumann, Franz (1970). Hypnosis and the adolescent drug abuser. *American Journal of Clinical Hypnosis, 13*, 17–21.

Beahrs, John O., & Hill, Marilyn M. (1971). Treatment of alcoholism by group-interaction psychotherapy under hypnosis. *American Journal of Clinical Hypnosis, 14*, 60–62.

Beaty, E. Thatcher (1976). Feedback-assisted relaxation training as a treatment for duodenal ulcers. *Biofeedback and Self-Regulation, 1*, 323–324 (Abstract).

Beck, Aaron T. (1976). *Cognitive therapy and the emotional disorders*. New York: International Universities Press.

Behrman, Howard T., Labow, Theodore A., & Rozen, Jack H. (1978). *Common skin diseases: Diagnosis and treatment*. New York: Grune & Stratton.

Beigel, Hugo G. (1972). The use of hypnosis in female sexual anesthesia. *Journal of the American Society of Psychosomatic Dentistry and Medicine, 19*, 4–14.

Bell, Iris R., & Schwartz, Gary E. (1975). Voluntary control and reactivity of human heart rate. *Psychophysiology, 12*, 339–348.

Bennet, E. A. (1955). Hypnotism in dermatology: Dermatologists group discussion. *British Medical Journal, 1*, 1214–1215.

Benson, Herbert (1975). *The relaxation response*. New York: Morrow.

Benson, Herbert, Rosner, Bernard A., Marzetta, Barbara R., & Klemchuk, Helen M. (1974). Decreased blood pressure in borderline hypertensive subjects who practice meditation. *Journal of Chronic Disease, 27*, 163–169.

Benson, Herbert, Shapiro, David, Tursky, Bernard, & Schwartz, Gary E. (1971). Decreased systolic blood pressure through operant conditioning techniques in patients with essential hypertension. *Science, 173*, 740–742.

Benson, Herbert, & Wallace, R. Keith (1972). Decreased blood pressure in borderline hypertensive subjects who practiced meditation. *Circulation, 46*, (Suppl. II), 130.

Bergman, Joel S., & Johnson, Harold J. (1971). The effects of instructional set and autonomic perception on cardiac control. *Psychophysiology, 8*, 180–190.

Berkowitz, Bernard, Ross-Townsend, Anita, & Kohberger, Robert (1979). Hypnotic treatment of smoking: The single treatment method revisited. *American Journal of Psychiatry, 136*, 83–85.

Bernstein, Dougals A. (1969). Modification of smoking behavior: An evaluative review. *Psychological Bulletin, 71*, 418–440.

Bernstein, Douglas A., & McAlister, Alfred (1976). The modification of smoking behavior: Progress and problems *Addictive Behaviors, 1*, 89–102.

Besedovsky, H. O., & Sorkin, E. (1981). Immunologic-neuroendocrine circuits: Physiological approaches. In Robert Ader (Ed.), *Psychoneuroimmunology* (pp. 545–574). New York: Academic Press.

Best, William R., Becktel, Jack M., Singleton, John W., & Kern, Fred Jr. (1976). Crohn's disease activity index. *Gastroenterology, 70,* 439–444.

Bethune, H. C., & Kidd, Cecil B. (1961). Psychophysiological mechanisms in skin diseases. *Lancet, 2,* 1419–1422.

Bieliauskas, Linus A., & Garron, David C. (1982). Psychological depression and cancer. *General Hospital Psychiatry, 4,* 187–195.

Birk, Lee (Ed.) (1973). *Biofeedback: Behavioral medicine.* New York: Grune & Stratton.

Björkhem, John (1956). Alcoholism and hypnotic therapy. *British Journal of Medical Hypnotism, 7,* 23–32.

Black, Stephen (1963a). Inhibition of immediate-type hypersensitivity response by direct suggestion under hypnosis. *British Medical Journal, 6,* 925–929.

Black, Stephen (1963b). Shift in dose-response curve of Prausnitz-Kustner reaction by direct suggestion under hypnosis. *British Medical Journal, 6,* 990–992.

Black, Stephen, & Friedman, Max (1965). Adrenal function and the inhibition of allergic responses under hypnosis. *British Medical Journal, 8,* 562–567.

Black, Stephen, Humphrey, J. H., & Niven, Janet S. F. (1963). Inhibition of Mantoux reaction by direct suggestion under hypnosis. *British Medical Journal, 6,* 1649–1652.

Blake, B. George (1965). The application of behavior therapy to the treatment of alcoholism. *Behavior Research & Therapy, 3,* 75–85.

Blanchard, Edward B., Miller, Stephen T., Abel, Gene G., Haynes, Mary R., & Wicker, Rebecca (1979). Evaluation of biofeedback in the treatment of borderline essential hypertension. *Journal of Applied Behavior Analysis, 12,* 99–109.

Blanchard, Edward B., Theobald, Dale E., Williamson, Donald A., Silver, Bernard , & Brown, Douglas A. (1978). Temperature biofeedback in the treatment of migraine headaches. *Archives of General Psychiatry, 35,* 581–588.

Blanchard, Edward B., Young, Larry D., Scott, Robert W., & Haynes, Mary R. (1974). Differential effects of feedback and reinforcement in voluntary acceleration of human heart rate. *Perceptual and Motor Skills, 38,* 683–691.

Blitz, Bernard, & Dinnerstein, Albert J. (1971). Role of attentional focus in pain perception: Manipulation of response to noxious stimulation by instructions. *Journal of Abnormal Psychology, 77,* 42–45.

Block, Jeanne, Jennings, Percy H., Harvey, Elinor, & Simpson, Elaine (1964). Interaction between allergic potential and psychopathology in childhood asthma. *Psychosomatic Medicine, 26,* 307–320.

Bloom, Alan A., Lo Presti, Philip., & Farrar, John T. (1968). Motility of the intact human colon. *Gastroenterology, 54,* 232–240.

Blumenthal, Lester S. (1963). Hypnotherapy of headache. *Headache, 2,* 197–202.

Bootzin, Richard R. (1977) Effects of self-control procedures for insomnia. In Richard B. Stuart (Ed.), *Behavioral self-management: Strategies, techniques and outcomes* (pp. 176–195). New York: Brunner/Mazel.

Borkovec, Thomas D. (1982). Insomnia. *Journal of Consulting and Clinical Psychology, 50,* 880–895.

Borkovec, Thomas D., & Fowles, Don C. (1973). Controlled investigation of the effects of progressive and hypnotic relaxation on insomnia. *Journal of Abnormal Psychology, 82,* 153–158.

Boudewyns, Patrick A. (1976). A comparison of the effects of stress vs. relaxation instruction on the finger temperature response. *Behavior Therapy, 7,* 54–67.

Boudewyns, Patrick A. (1982). Assessment of headache. In Francis J. Keefe, & James A. Blumenthal (Eds.), *Assessment strategies in behavioral medicine* (pp. 167–180). New York: Grune & Stratton.

Bourne, Peter G. (1975). Non-pharmacological approaches to the treatment of drug abuse. *American Journal of Chinese Medicine, 3,* 235–244.

Bowers, Kenneth S. (1968). Pain, anxiety, and perceived control. *Journal of Consulting and Clinical Psychology, 32,* 596–602.

Bowers, Kenneth S., & Brenneman, Heather A. (1979). Hypnosis and the perception of time. *International Journal of Clinical and Experimental Hypnosis, 27,* 29–41.

Bowers, Kenneth S., & Gilmore, J. Barnard (1969). Subjective report and credibility: An inquiry involving hypnotic hallucinations. *Journal of Abnormal Psychology, 74,* 443–451.

Bowers, Kenneth S., & Kelly, Paul (1979). Stress, disease, psychotherapy and hypnosis. *Journal of Abnormal Psychology, 85,* 490–505.

Bowers, Patricia (1982). The classic suggestion effect: Relationships with scales of hypnotizability, effortless experiencing, and imagery vividness. *International Journal of Clinical and Experimental Hypnosis, 30,* 270–279.

Brady, John Paul, Luborsky, Lester, & Kron, Reuben E. (1974). Blood pressure reduction in patients with essential hypertension through Metronome-conditioned relaxation: A preliminary report. *Behavior Therapy, 5,* 203–209.

Brady, Joseph V. (1958). Ulcers in "executive monkeys." *Scientific American, 199,* 95–100.

Brendstrup, P., Jesperson, K., & Asboe-Hanson, G. (1957). Morphologic and chemical connective tissue changes in fibrostic muscles. *Annals of the Rheumatic Diseases, 16,* 438–440.

Brener, Jasper (1977). Visceral perception. In Jackson Beatty & Heiner Legewie (Eds.). *Biofeedback and behavior* (pp. 235–259). New York: Plenum.

Brodie, Earle I. (1964). A hypnotherapeutic approach to obesity. *American Journal of Clinical Hypnosis, 6,* 211–215.

Brooks, Gary R., & Richardson, Frank C. (1980). Emotional skills training: A treatment program for duodenal ulcer. *Behavior Therapy, 11,* 198–207.

Brown, Daniel (1984). *A questionnaire study of pain coping strategies.* Unpublished manuscript.

Brown, Daniel P., & Engler, Jack (1980). The stages of mindfulness meditation: A validation study. *Journal of Transpersonal Psychology, 12,* 143–192.

Brown, Daniel, Forte, Michael, Rich, Philip, & Epstein, Gerald (1982–83). Phenomenological differences among self hypnosis, mindfulness meditation, and imaging. *Imagination, Cognition and Personality, 2,* 291–309.

Brown, Daniel, & Fromm, Erika (1986). *Hypnotherapy and hypnoanalysis.* Hillsdale, NJ: Lawrence Erlbaum Associates.

Brown, Ethan Allan (1965). The treatment of bronchial asthma as viewed by the allergist. *Journal of Asthma Research, 3,* 101–119.

Brownell, Kelly (1983, March). *The treatment of obesity in the clinic, community, and workplace.* Workshop Presentation at the Fourth Annual Meeting, The Society of Behavioral Medicine, Baltimore, MD.

Brownell, Kelly D., & Stunkard, Albert J. (1980). Physical activity in the development and control of obesity. In Albert J. Stunkard (Ed.), *Obesity* (pp. 300–324). Philadelphia: W. B. Saunders.

Bruyn, G. W. (1980). The biochemistry of migraine. *Headache, 20,* 235–246.

Bryan, William J. (1960). Hypnosis and hypertension. *The British Journal of Medical Hypnotism, 12,* 21–25.

Bryant, Maurice E. (1958). The treatment of alcoholics by hypnosis. *British Journal of Medical Hypnotism, 9,* 40–42.

Budzynski, Thomas H., Stoyva, Johann M., & Adler, Charles S. (1970). Feedback-induced muscle relaxation: Application to tension headache. *Journal of Behavior Therapy & Experimental Psychiatry, 1,* 205–211.

Budzynski, Thomas H., Stoyva, Johann M., Adler, Charles S., & Mullaney, Daniel J. (1973). EMG biofeedback and tension headache: A controlled outcome study. *Psychosomatic Medicine, 35,* 484–496.

Bueno-Miranda, Fernando, Cerulli, Maurice, & Schuster, Marvin M. (1976). Operant conditioning of colonic motility in irritable bowel syndrome (IBS). *Gastroenterology, 70,* 867 (Abstract).

Burnet, F. M. (1971). Immunological surveillance in neoplasia. *Transplant Review, 7,* 3–25.

Byers, Alvah P. (1975). Training and use of technicians in the treatment of alcoholism with hypnosis. *American Journal of Clinical Hypnosis, 18,* 90–93.

Byrne, Stephen (1973). Hypnosis and the irritable bowel: Case histories, methods and speculation. *American Journal of Clinical Hypnosis, 15,* 263–265.

Caddy, Glenn R., & Lovibond, S. H. (1976). Self-regulation and discriminated aversive conditioning in the modification of alcholics' drinking behavior. *Behavior Therapy, 7,* 223–230.

Cannon, Walter B. (1932). *The wisdom of the body.* New York: W. W. Norton.

Carrington, Patricia (1977). *Freedom in meditation.* New York: Anchor Press/Doubleday.

Carskadon, Mary A., Dement, William C., Mitter, Merrill M., Guilleminault, Christian, Zarcone, Vincent P., & Spiegel, Rene (1976). Self-reports versus sleep laboratory findings in 122 drug-free subjects with complaints of chronic insomnia. *American Journal of Psychiatry, 133,* 1382–1388.

Carter, Stephen K. (1976). Immunotherapy of cancer in man. *American Scientist, 64,* 418–423.

Cautela, Joseph R. (1970). Covert reinforcement. *Behavior Therapy, 1,* 33–50.

Cautela, Joseph R. (1975). The use of covert conditioning in hypnotherapy. *International Journal of Clinical and Experimental Hypnosis, 23,* 15–27.

Cedercreutz, Claes (1972). The big mistakes: A note. *International Journal of Clinical and Experimental Hypnosis, 20,* 15–16.

Chai, Hyman (1975). Management of severe chronic perennial asthma in children. *Advances in Asthma and Allergy, 2,* 1–12.

Chai, Hyman, Purcell, Kenneth, Brady, Kirk, & Falliers, C. J. (1968). Therapeutic and investigational evaluation of asthmatic children. *Journal of Allergy, 41,* 23–36.

Chapman, Loring F., Ramos, Armando, Goodell, Helen, & Wolff, Harold G. (1960). Neurokinin-A polypeptide formed during neuronal activity in man. *Transcripts of the American Neurological Association, 85,* 42–45.

Chappell, M. N., Steffano, J. J., Rogerson, J. S., & Pike, F. H. (1936). The value of group psychological procedures in the treatment of peptic ulcer. *American Journal of Digestive Diseases, 3,* 813–817.

Chaudhary, Nazir A., & Truelove, S. C. (1962). The irritable colon syndrome: A study of the clinical features, predisposing causes, and prognosis in 130 cases. *Quarterly Journal of Medicine, 31,* 307–322.

Chaves, John F., & Barber, Theodore X. (1974). Cognitive strategies, experimenter modeling, and expectation in the attenuation of pain. *Journal of Abnormal Psychology, 83,* 356–363.

Chaves, John F., & Brown, J. M. (1978). *Self-generated strategies for the control of pain and stress.* Paper presented at the annual meeting of the American Psychological Association, Toronto, Can.

Cheek, David B. (1965). Emotional factors in persistent pain states. *American Journal of Clinical Hypnosis, 8,* 100–110.

Cheek, David B., & LeCron, Leslie M. (1968). *Clinical hypnotherapy.* New York: Grune & Stratton.

Chong, Tong Mun (1966). Psychosomatic Medicine & Hypnosis. *American Journal of Clinical Hypnosis, 8,* 173–177.

Christensen, Edwin R., Jeffrey, D. Balfour, & Pappas, James P. (1977). A therapist manual for a behavior modification weight reduction program. In Edward E. Abramson (Ed.), *Behavioral approaches to weight control* (pp. 47–61). New York: Springer.

Citron, K. M. (1968). Hypnosis for asthma-A controlled trial. *British Medical Journal, 4,* 71–76.

Clark, G. H. V. (1965). The charming of warts. *Journal of Investigative Dermatology, 45,* 15–21.

Clark, Robert (1974). The "I can't" resistance to quitting smoking. *International Mental Health Research Newsletter, 16,* 9–10.

Clarke, J. Christopher, & Jackson, J. Arthur (1983). *Hypnosis and behavior therapy: The treatment of anxiety and phobias.* New York: Springer.

Clarkson, A. Kerr (1937). The nervous factor in juvenile asthma. *British Medical Journal, 2,* 845–850.

Cohen, Neal L., & Alpert, Murray (1978). Locus of control as a predictor of outcome in treatment of obesity. *Psychological Reports, 42,* 805–806.

Cohen, Samuel I., & Reed, John L. (1968). The treatment of "nervous diarrhea" and other conditioned autonomic disorders by desensitization. *British Journal of Psychiatry, 114,* 1275–1280.

Colgan, Michael (1977). Effects of binary and proportional feedback on bidirectional control of heart rate. *Psychophysiology, 14,* 187–191.

Collison, David R. (1968). Hypnotherapy in the management of asthma. *American Journal of Clinical Hypnosis, 11,* 6–11.

Collison, David R. (1970). Cardiological applications of the control of the autonomic nervous system by hypnosis. *American Journal of Clinical Hypnosis, 12,* 150–156.

Compagno, Lisete T., Leite, Jose V. P., & Krieger, Eduardo M. (1977). Continuous measurement of aortic caliber in conscious rats: Effect of acute hypertension. *Mayo Clinic Proceedings, 52,* 433–436.

Condiotte, Mark M., & Lichtenstein, Edward (1981). Self-efficacy and relapse in smoking cessation programs. *Journal of Consulting and Clinical Psychology, 49,* 648–658.

Conger, John J. (1956). Alcoholism: Theory, problem and challenge. II. Reinforcement theory and the dynamics of alcoholism. *Quarterly Journal of Studies on Alcohol, 17,* 296–305.

Connell, Alastair M. (1962). The motility of the pelvic colon II. Paradoxical motility in diarrhea and constipation. *Gut, 3,* 342–348.

Connell, Alistair M., Jones, F. A., & Rowlands, E. N. (1965). Motility of the pelvic colon. Part IV. Abdominal pain associated with colonic hypermotility after meals, *Gut, 6,* 105–112.

Conrad, S. W. (1954). The psychologic implications of overeating. *Psychiatric Quarterly, 28,* 211–224.

Cooper, Alan J. (1964). A case of bronchial asthma treated by behavior therapy. *Behavior Research & Therapy, 1,* 351–356.

Cooper, Alan J. (1969). Factors in male sexual inadequacy: A review. *Journal of Nervous and Mental Disease, 149,* 337–359.

Cooper, Cary L. (1984). The social psychological precursors to cancer. In Cary L. Cooper (Ed.), *Psychosocial stress and cancer* (pp. 21–33). New York: Wiley.

Cooper, Linn F., & Erickson, Milton H. (1959). *Time distortion in hypnosis: An experimental and clinical investigation* (2nd ed.). Baltimore: Williams & Wilkins.

Copemann, Chester D. (1977). Treatment of polydrug abuse and addiction by covert sensitization. *International Journal of the Addictions, 12,* 17–23.

Corson, Samuel A. (1966). Neuroendocrine and behavioral response patterns to psychologic stress and the problem of the target tissue in cerebrovisceral pathology. *Annals of the New York Academy of Science, 125,* 890–919.

Costello, Raymond M. (1975). Alcoholism treatment and evaluation: In search of methods. *International Journal of the Addictions, 10*, 251–275.

Cousins, Norman (1979). *The anatomy of an illness, as perceived by the patient.* New York: W. W. Norton.

Craighead, Linda W., Stunkard, Albert J., & O'Brien, Richard M. (1981). Behavior therapy and pharmacotherapy for obesity. *Archives of General Psychiatry, 38*, 763–768.

Crasilneck, Harold B., & Hall, James A. (1968). The use of hypnosis in controlling cigarette smoking. *Southern Medical Journal, 61*, 999–1002.

Crasilneck, Harold B., & Hall, James A. (1973). Clinical hypnosis in problems of pain. *American Journal of Clinical Hypnosis, 15*, 153–161.

Crasilneck, Harold B., & Hall, James A. (1975). *Clinical hypnosis: Principles and applications.* New York: Grune & Stratton.

Crasilneck, Harold B. (1979). Hypnosis in the control of chronic low back pain. *American Journal of Clinical Hypnosis, 22*, 71–78.

Creer, Thomas L. (1974). Biofeedback & asthma. *Advances in Asthma and Allergy, 1*, 7–12.

Creer, Thomas L. (1979). *Asthma therapy: A behavioral health care system for respiratory disorders.* New York: Springer.

Creer, Thomas L., Renne, Charles M., & Christian, Walter P. (1976). Behavioral contributions to rehabilitation and childhood asthma. *Rehabilitation Literature, 37*, 226–232.

Cruickshank, A. (1963). The anti-smoking clinic. *Lancet, 2*, 353-354.

Dalessio, Donald J. (1974). Mechanisms and biochemistry of headache. *Postgraduate Medicine, 56*, 55–62.

Dalessio, Donald J. (1980). *Wolff's headache and other pain.* New York: Oxford University Press.

Dalsgaard-Nielsen, T. (1965). Migraine and heredity. *Acta Neurologica Scandinavica, 41*, 287–300.

Dalton, Katharina (1973). Progesterone suppositories and pessaries in the treatment of menstrual migraine. *Headache, 12*, 151–159.

Daniels, Lloyd K. (1976). The effects of automated hypnosis and hand warming on migraine: A pilot study. *American Journal of Clinical Hypnosis, 19*, 91–94.

Daniels, Lloyd K. (1977). Treatment of migraine headache by hypnosis and behavior therapy: A case study. *American Journal of Clinical Hypnosis, 19, 241–244.*

Datey, K. K., Deshmukh, S. N., Dalvi, C. P., & Vinekar, S. L. (1969). "Shavasan": A yogic exercise in the management of hypertension. *Angiology, 20*, 325–333.

Davis, Margaret H., Saunders, David R., Creer, Thomas L., & Chai, Hyman (1973). Relaxation training facilitated by biofeedback apparatus as a supplemental treatment in bronchial asthma. *Journal of Psychosomatic Research, 17*, 121–128.

Davison, Gerald C., Tsujimoto, Richard N., & Glaros, Alan G. (1973). Attribution and the maintenance of behavior change in falling asleep. *Journal of Abnormal Psychology, 82*, 124–133.

Dawson, Arthur, & Simon, Ronald A. (1984). *The practical management of asthma.* Orlando, FL: Grune & Stratton.

De Gosseley, M., Konincky, N., & Lenfant, H. (1975). La recto-colite hémorragique: Training autogene à propos de quelques cas graves. *Acta Gastro-Enterologica Belgica, 38*, 454–462.

Deabler, Herdis L. (1976). Hypnotherapy of impotence. *American Journal of Clinical Hypnosis, 19*, 9–12.

Deabler, Herdis L., & Dillenkoffer, Robert L. (1973). Instrumental conditioning of diastolic blood pressure in essential hypertensive patients. *Journal of Applied Behavior Analysis, 6*, 377–382.

Deabler, Herdis L., Fidel, Edward, Dillenkoffer, Robert L., & Elder, S. Thomas (1973). The use of relaxation and hypnosis in lowering high blood pressure. *American Journal of Clinical Hypnosis, 16,* 75–83.

Dekker, E., & Groen, J. (1956). Reproducible psychogenic attacks of asthma. *Journal of Psychosomatic Research, 1,* 58–67.

Deeker, E., Pelser, H. E., & Groen, J. (1957). Conditioning as a cause of asthmatic attacks: A laboratory study. *Journal of Psychosomatic Research, 2,* 97–108.

Delprato, Dennis J. (1981). The constructional approach to behavioral modification. *Journal of Behavior Therapy and Experimental Psychiatry, 12,* 49–55.

Demjen, Stefan, & Bakal, Donald (1981). Illness behavior and chronic headache. *Pain, 10,* 221–229.

Dempster, Clifford R., Balson, Paul, & Whalen, Barbara Tate (1976). Supportive hypnotherapy during the radical treatment of malignancies. *International Journal of Clinical and Experimental Hypnosis, 24,* 1–9.

Dengrove, Edward (1968). Behavior therapy of headache. *Journal of the American Society of Psychosomatic Dentistry and Medicine, 15,* 41–48.

Dengrove, Edward (1970). A single-treatment method to stop smoking using ancillary self-hypnosis: Discussion. *International Journal of Clinical and Experimental Hypnosis, 18,* 251–256.

Dengrove, Edward (1973). The uses of hypnosis in behavior therapy. *International Journal of Clinical and Experimental Hypnosis, 21,* 13–17.

Dengrove, Edward (1976). *Hypnosis and behavior therapy.* Springfield, IL: Charles C. Thomas.

Dennerstein, Lorraine (1980). Hypnosis and psychosexual dysfunction. In Graham D. Burrows & Lorraine Dennerstein (Eds.), *Handbook of hypnosis and psychosomatic medicine* (pp. 341–358). New York: Elsevier/North-Holland Biomedical Press.

Devine, David A. (1978). Hypnosis and covert modeling in the treatment of obesity. Unpublished doctoral dissertation, University of Montana, 1977. *Dissertation Abstracts International, 38,* 3389b (University Microfilms, No. 77–28, 775).

Dexter, James D., Roberts, John, & Byer, John A. (1978). The five hour glucose tolerance test and effect of low sucrose diet in migraine. *Headache, 18,* 91–94.

Deyoub, Paul L. (1978). Relation of suggestibility to obesity. *Psychological Reports, 43,* 175–180.

Deyoub, Paul L. (1979a). Hypnosis in the treatment of obesity and the relation of suggestibility to outcome. *Journal of the American Society of Psychosomatic Dentistry, 26,* 137–149.

Deyoub, Paul L. (1979b). Hypnotizability and obesity. *Psychological Reports, 45,* 974.

Deyoub, Paul L., & Wilkie, Raymond (1980). Suggestion with and without hypnotic induction in a weight reduction program. *International Journal of Clinical and Experimental Hypnosis, 27,* 333–340.

Diamond, H. H. (1959). Hypnosis in children: The complete cure of forty cases of asthma. *American Journal of Clinical Hypnosis, 1,* 124–129.

Diamond, Seymour, & Dalessio, Donald J. (1978). *The practicing physician's approach to headache* (2nd ed.). Baltimore: Williams & Wilkins.

Diamond, Seymour, & Diamond-Falk, Judi (1982). *Advice from the Diamond Headache Clinic.* New York: International Universities Press.

Dias, Maury M. (1963). Hypnosis in irritable colon. *Revista Brasileira de Medicina, 20,* 132–134.

DiClemente, Carlo C. (1981). Self-efficacy and smoking cessation maintenance: A preliminary report. *Cognitive Therapy and Research, 5,* 175–187.

Dillon, Kathleen M., Minchoff, Brian, & Baker, Katherine H. (1985–86). Positive emotional states and enhancement of the immune system. *International Journal of Psychiatry in Medicine, 15,* 13–18.

Doane, William L. (1971). Report of a case of anesthesia of the penis cured by hypnotherapy. *Journal of the American Institute of Hypnosis, 12,* 165.

Dolovich, J., Hargreave, F. E., & Kerigan, A. T. (1973). Résponses asthmatiques tardives. *Medicine Moderne du Canada, 28,* 1075–1079.

Donovan, Dennis M., & Channey, Edmund F. (1985). Alcoholic relapse prevention and intervention: Models and methods. In G. Alan Marlatt & Judith R. Gordon (Eds.), *Relapse prevention: Maintenance strategies in the treatment of addictive behaviors* (pp. 351–416). New York: Guilford Press.

Draspa, Leon J. (1959). Psychological factors in muscular pain. *British Journal of Medical Psychology, 32,* 106–116.

Dukes, Herbert T., & Vieth, Roger G. (1964). Cerebral arteriography during migraine prodrome headache. *Neurology, 14,* 636–639.

Dunbar, Flanders (1943). *Psychosomatic diagnosis.* New York: Harper, Hoeber.

Dunn, William L., Jr. (1973). *Smoking behavior: Motives and incentives.* Washington, DC: Winston.

Edmondston, William E. (1977). Neutral hypnosis as relaxation. *American Journal of Clinical Hypnosis, 20,* 69–75.

Edwards, Griffith (1960). Hypnotic treatment of asthma: Real and illusory results. *British Medical Journal, 2,* 492–497.

Edwards, Griffith (1964). Hypnosis and lobeline in an antismoking clinic. *Medical Officer, 111,* 239–243.

Edwards, Griffith (1966). Hypnosis in treatment of alcohol addiction: Controlled trial, with analysis of factors affecting outcome. *Quarterly Journal of Studies on Alcohol, 27,* 221–241.

Eichorn, Ralph, & Tracktir, Jack (1955). The effect of hypnosis upon gastric secretion. *Gastroenterology, 29,* 417–421.

Eisen, Marlene R., & Fromm, Erika (1983). The clinical use of self-hypnosis in hypnotherapy: Tapping the functions of imagery and adaptive regression. *International Journal of Clinical and Experimental Hypnosis, 31,* 243–255.

Eissler, Kurt R. (1958). Remarks on some variations in psychoanalytic technique. *International Journal of Psychoanalysis, 39,* 222–229.

Elder, S. Thomas, Ruiz, Z. Rosalba, Deabler, Herdis L., & Dillenkoffer, R. L. (1973). Instrumental conditioning of diastolic blood pressure in essential hypertensive patients. *Journal of Applied Behavior Analaysis, 6,* 377–382.

Elliott, Rogers, & Tighe, Thomas (1968). Breaking the cigarette habit: Effects of a technique involving threatened loss of money. *Psychological Record, 18,* 503–513.

Ellis, Albert (1962). *Reason and emotion in psychotherapy.* New York: Lyle Stuart.

Elmore, Andrew M., & Tursky, Bernard (1981). A comparison of two psychophysiological approaches to the treatment of migraine. *Headache, 21,* 93–101.

Engel, George L. (1973). Ulcerative colitis. In Arthur E. Lindner (Ed.), *Emotional factors in gastrointestinal illness* (pp. 99–112). Amsterdam: Excerpta Medica.

Engstrom, David R. (1976). Hypnotic susceptibility, EEG-alpha, and self-regulation. In Gary E. Schwartz & David Shapiro (Eds.), *Consciousness and self regulation* (pp. 173–221). New York: Plenum Press.

Epstein, Gerald (1986). The image in medicine: Notes of a clinician. *Advances, 3,* 22–31.

Epstein, Leonard H., Hersen, Michel, & Hemphill, Diana P. (1974). Music feedback in the treatment of tension headache: An experimental case study. *Journal of Behavior Therapy & Experimental Psychiatry, 5,* 59–63.

Erickson, Milton H. (1935). Experimental neurosis hypnotically induced in a case of ejaculatio praecox. *British Journal of Medical Psychology, 15,* 34–50.

Erickson, Milton H. (1960). The utilization of patient behavior in the hypnotherapy of obesity: Three case reports. *American Journal of Clinical Hypnosis, 3,* 112–116.

Erickson, Milton H. (1964). The burden of responsibility in effective psychotherapy. *American Journal of Clinical Hypnosis, 6,* 269–271.

Erickson, Milton H. (1967). An introduction to the study and application of hypnosis for pain control. In Jean Lassner (Ed.), *Hypnosis and psychosomatic medicine* (pp. 83–90). New York: Springer-Verlag.

Erickson, Milton H. (1973). Psychotherapy achieved by a reversal of the neurotic processes in a case of ejaculatio precox. *American Journal of Clinical Hypnosis, 15,* 217–222.

Erickson, Milton H., Hershman, Seymour, & Sector, Irving I. (1961). *The practical application of medical and dental hypnosis.* New York: Julian.

Erickson, Milton H., & Rossi, Ernest L. (1979) *Hypnotherapy: An exploratory casebook.* New York: Irvington.

Esler, Murray, Zweifler, Andrew, Randall, Otelio, Julius, Stevo, & De Quattro, Vincent (1977). Agreement among three different indices of sympathetic nervous system activity in essential hypertension. *Mayo Clinic Proceedings, 52,* 379–382.

Evans, Frederick J. (1967). Suggestibility in the normal waking state. *Psychological Bulletin, 67,* 114–129.

Fahrion, Steven L. (1978). Autogenic biofeedback treatment for migraine. *Research and Clinical Studies in Headache, 5,* 1–11.

Fahrion, Steven L. (1980). *Etiology and intervention in essential hypertension: A biobehavioral approach.* Unpublished manuscript, The Menninger Foundation.

Falkner, Bonita, Onesti, Gaddo, & Hamstra, Barbara (1981). Stress response characteristics of adolescents with high genetic risk for essential hypertension: A five-year follow-up. *Clinical and Experimental Hypertension, 3,* 583–591.

Fauci, Anthony (1981). The revolution in clinical immunology. *Journal of the American Medical Association, 246,* 2567–2572.

Faulkner, William B. (1940). Severe esophageal spasm: An evaluation of suggestion-therapy as determined by means of the esophagoscope. *Psychosomatic Medicine, 2,* 139–140.

Faulkner, William B. (1941). Influence of suggestion on the size of the bronchial lumen. *Northwest Medicine, 40,* 367–368.

Fava, Giovanni A., & Pavan, Luigi (1976–77). Large bowel disorders. I. Illness configuration and life events. *Psychotherapy and Psychosomatics, 27,* 93–99.

Feamster, J. Harry, & Brown, John E. (1963). Hypnotic aversion therapy to alcohol: Three-year follow up of one patient. *American Journal of Clinical Hypnosis, 6,* 164–168.

Feldman, Gary M. (1976). The effect of biofeedback training on respiratory resistance of asthmatic children. *Psychosomatic Medicine, 38,* 27–34.

Fenichel, Otto (1945). *The psychoanalytic theory of neurosis.* New York: W. W. Norton.

Ferenczi, Sandor (1965). Comments on hypnosis. In Ronald E. Shor & Martin T. Orne (Eds.), *The nature of hypnosis: Selected basic readings* (pp. 177–182). New York: Holt, Rinehart & Winston.

Ferguson, James (1975). *Learning to eat: Behavior modification for weight control.* Palo Alto, CA: Bull.

Fernandez, G. R. (1955–56). Hypnotism in the treatment of the stress factor in dermatological conditions. *British Journal of Medical Hypnotism, 7,* 21–24.

Ferster, Charles B., Nurnberger, J. I., & Levitt, Eugene (1962). The control of eating. *Journal of Mathetics, 1,* 87–109.

Field, Peter B., & Palmer, R. D. (1969). Factor analysis: Hypnosis inventory. *International Journal of Clinical and Experimental Hypnosis, 17,* 50–61.

Field, Peter B., & Scott, Edward M. (1969). Experiences of alcoholics during hypnosis. *American Journal of Clinical Hypnosis, 12,* 86–90.

Finkelstein, Selig, & Howard, Marcia Greenleaf (1983). Cancer prevention—A three year pilot study. *American Journal of Clinical Hypnosis, 25,* 177–183.

Fischer, Roland (1971). A cartography of the ecstatic and meditative states. *Science, 174,* 897–904.

Flaxman, Judith (1978). Quitting smoking now or later: Gradual, abrupt, immediate, and delayed quitting. *Behavior Therapy, 9,* 260–270.

Flood, A. O. (1960). Slimming under hypnotism: The obese adolescent. *Medical World, 93,* 310–312.

Fordyce, Wilbert E. (1976). *Behavioral methods for chronic pain and illness.* St. Louis: Mosby.

Foss, Robert (1973). Personality, social influence and cigarette smoking. *Journal of Health and Social Behavior, 14,* 279–286.

Fox, Bernard H. (1981). Psychosocial factors and the immune system in human cancer. In Robert Ader (Ed.), *Psychoneuroimmunology* (pp. 103–157). New York: Academic Press.

Foxx, R. M., & Brown, Richard A. (1979). Nicotine fading and self-monitoring for cigarette abstinence or controlled smoking. *Journal of Applied Behavior Analysis, 12,* 111–125.

Francisco, John W. (1973). Modification of smoking behavior: A comparison of three approaches. (Doctoral dissertation, Wayne State University, 1972) *Dissertation Abstracts International, 33,* 5511b–5512b (University Microfilms, No. 73-12, 511).

Frank, Jerome (1962). *Persuasion and healing.* New York: Schocken Books.

Frankel, Fred H. (1976). *Hypnosis: Trance as a coping mechanism.* New York: Plenum Medical.

Frankel, Fred H., & Misch, Robert C. (1973) Hypnosis in a case of longstanding psoriasis in a person with character problems. *International Journal of Clinical and Experimental Hypnosis, 21,* 121–130.

Franks, C. M., & Leigh, D. (1959). The theoretical and experimental application of a conditioning model to a consideration of bronchial asthma in man. *Journal of Psychosomatic Research, 4,* 88–98.

Freeman, Edith H., Feingold, Ben F., Schlesinger, Kurt, & Gorman, Frank J. (1964). Psychological variables in allergic disorders: A review. *Psychosomatic Medicine, 26,* 543–575.

Freis, Edward D. (1978). A practical guide to help you manage your hypertensive patient. *Medical Times, 106,* 21–22.

Freytag, Fredericka (1965). The hallucinated unconscious body image. *American Journal of Clinical Hypnosis, 7,* 209–220.

Friar, Linda R., & Beatty, Jackson (1976). Migraine: Management by trained control of vasoconstriction. *Journal of Consulting and Clinical Psychology, 44,* 46–53.

Friedman, Arnold P. (1968). The migraine syndrome. *Bulletin of New York Academy of Medicine, 44,* 45–62.

Friedman, Howard, & Taub, Harvey A. (1977). The use of hypnosis and biofeedback procedures for essential hypertension. *International Journal of Clinical and Experimental Hypnosis, 25,* 335–347.

Friedman, Howard, & Taub, Harvey A. (1978). A six-month follow-up of the use of hypnosis and biofeedback procedures in essential hypertension. *American Journal of Clinical Hypnosis, 20,* 184–188.

Friedman, Meyer (1967). Behavior pattern and its relationship to coronary artery disease. *Psychosomatics, 8,* 6–7.

Friend, Merrill B. (1957). Group hypnotherapy treatment. In Robert S. Wallerstein (Ed.), *Hospital treatment of alcoholism.* New York: Basic Books.

Frischolz, Edward J., & Tryon, Warren W. (1980). Hypnotizability in relation to the ability to learn thermal biofeedback. *American Journal of Clinical Hypnosis, 23,* 53–56.

Frohlich, Edward D. (1977). The adrenergic nervous system and hypertension. *Mayo Clinic Proceedings, 52,* 361–368.

Fromm, Erika (1970). Age regression with unexpected reappearance of a repressed childhood language. *International Journal of Clinical and Experimental Hypnosis, 18,* 79–88.

Fromm, Erika (1977). Altered states of consciousness and hypnosis: A discussion. *International Journal of Clinical and Experimental Hypnosis, 25,* 325–334.

Fromm, Erika (1978–79). Primary and secondary process in waking and in altered states of consciousness. *Journal of Altered States of Consciousness, 4,* 115–128.

Fromm, Erika (1986, September). *Significant developments in clinical hypnosis during the past 25 years.* Paper presented at the annual meeting of the Society of Clinical and Experimental Hypnosis, Chicago.

Fromm, Erika, Brown, Daniel P., Hurt, Stephen W., Oberlander, Joab Z., Boxer, Andrew M. & Pfeifer, Gary (1981). The phenomena and characteristics of self-hypnosis. *International Journal of Clinical and Experimental Hypnosis, 29,* 189–246.

Fromm, Erika, & Hurt, Stephen W. (1980) Ego-psychological parameters of hypnosis and altered states of consciousness. In Graham D. Burrows & Lorraine Dennerstein (Eds.), *Handbook of hypnosis and psychosomatic medicine* (pp. 13–27). New York: Elsevier/North Holland Biomedical Press.

Fromm, Erika, & Shor, Ronald E. (Eds.) (1979). *Hypnosis: Developments in research and new perspectives* (2nd ed.). New York: Aldine.

Fromm-Reichman, Frieda (1937). Contribution to the psychogenesis of migraine. *Psychoanalytic Review, 24,* 26–33.

Frumkin, Kenneth, Nathan, Robert J., Prout, Maurice F., & Cohen, Miriam C. (1978). Nonpharmacologic control of essential hypertension in man: A critical review of the experimental literature. *Psychosomatic Medicine, 40,* 294–320.

Fry A. (1957). The scope for hypnosis in general practice. *British Medical Journal, 1,* 1323–1328.

Fuchs, K., Hoch, Z., Paldi, E., Abramovici, H., Brandes, J. M., Timor-Tritsch, I., & Kleinhaus, M. (1973). Hypno-desensitization therapy of vaginismus: Part I. "In vitro" method. Part II. "In vivo" method. *International Journal of Clinical and Experimental Hypnosis, 21,* 144–156.

Furman, Seymour (1973). Intestinal biofeedback in functional diarrhea: A preliminary report. *Journal of Behavior Therapy and Experimental Psychiatry, 4,* 317–321.

Gabrynowicz, Jan (1977). Hypnosis in a treatment programme for alcoholism. *Medical Journal of Australia, 64,* 653–656.

Galanter, Marc (1976). The "intoxication" state of consciousness: A model for alcohol and drug abuse. *American Journal of Psychiatry, 133,* 635–640.

Gardner, G. Gail, & Lubman, Alison (1983). Hypnotherapy for children with cancer: Some current issues. *American Journal of Clinical Hypnosis, 25,* 135–142.

Geer, James H., & Katkin, Edward S. (1966). Treatment of insomnia using a variant of systematic desensitization: A case report. *Journal of Abnormal Psychology, 71,* 161–164.

Gellhorn, Ernst (1967). *Autonomic-somatic integrations.* Minneapolis: University of Minnesota Press.

Gerbert, Barbara (1980). Psychological aspects of Crohn's disease. *Journal of Behavioral Medicine, 3,* 41–58.

Germana, Joseph (1969). Central efferent processes and autonomic-behavioral integration. *Psychophysiology, 6,* 78–90.

Ghory, Joseph E. (1975). Exercise and asthma: Overview and clinical impact. *Pediatrics, 56,* 844–846.

Gibbons, Don E. (1974). Hyperempiria, a new "altered state of consciousness" induced by suggestion. *Perceptual and Motor Skills, 39,* 47–53.

Gibbons, Don E. (1979). *Applied hypnosis and hyperempira.* New York: Plenum Press.

Giles, Stephen L. (1978). Separate and combined effects of biofeedback training and brief individual psychotherapy in the treatment of gastrointestinal disorders. (Doctoral dissertation. University of Colorado, Boulder, 1978). *Dissertation Abstracts International, 39,* 2495b (University Microfilms No. 7820511).

Gill, Merton M., & Brenman, Margaret M. (1959). *Hypnosis and related states: Psychoanalytic studies in regression.* New York: International Universities Press.

Gillin, Christian J., Duncan, Wallace, Pettigrew, Karen D., Frankel, Bernard L., & Snyder, Frederick (1979). Successful separation of depressed, normal and insomniac subjects by EEG sleep data. *Archives of General Psychiatry, 36,* 85–90.

Gilmore, J. Bernard (1968). Toward an understanding of imitation. In E. C. Simmel, R. A. Hoppe, & G. A. Milton (Eds.), *Social facilitation and imitative behavior* (pp. 217–238). Boston: Allyn & Bacon.

Ginsburg, Genevieve, & Baker, Jean (1977). Exercise management. In Edward E. Abramson (Ed.), *Behavioral approaches to weight control* (pp. 123–129). New York: Springer.

Glad, Wayne R., Tyre, Timothy E., & Adesso, Vincent J. (1976). A multidimensional model of cigarette smoking. *American Journal of Clinical Hypnosis, 19,* 82–90.

Glad, Wayne, & Adesso, Vincent J. (1976). The relative importance of socially induced tension and behavioral contagion for smoking behavior. *Journal of Abnormal Psychology, 85,* 119–121.

Glover, Edward (1932). On the etiology of drug addiction. *International Journal of Psychoanalysis, 13,* 298–328.

Glover, F. Scott (1961). Use of hypnosis for weight reduction in a group of nurses. *American Journal of Clinical Hypnosis, 3,* 250–251.

Glucksman, Myron L., Rand, Colleen, S., & Stunkard, Albert J. (1978). Psychodynamics of obesity. *Journal of the American Academy of Psychoanalysis, 6,* 103–115.

Gold, W. M., Kessler, G. F., & Yu, D. Y. C. (1972). Role of vagus nerves in experimental asthma in allergic dogs. *Journal of Applied Physiology, 33,* 719–725.

Goldfried, Marvin R. (1977). The use of relaxation and cognitive relabeling as coping skills. In Richard B. Stuart (Ed.), *Behavioral self-management: Strategies, techniques and outcomes* (pp. 82–116). New York: Brunner/Mazel.

Goodfriend, Theodore L. (1983). *Hypertension essentials: Current concepts of cause and control.* New York: Grune & Stratton.

Goodman, H. Philip (1962). Hypnosis in prolonged resistant eczema: A case report. *American Journal of Clinical Hypnosis, 5,* 144–145.

Gordon, Hugh (1955). Hypnotism in dermatology. *British Medical Journal, 1,* 1214–1215.

Gorski, Terence T., & Miller, Merlene (1979). *Counseling for relapse prevention.* Hazel Creste, IL: Alcoholism Systems Associates.

Gottesfeld, Mary L. (1978). Treatment of vaginismus by psychotherapy with adjunctive hypnosis. *American Journal of Clinical Hypnosis, 20,* 272–277.

Gottlieb, Harold, Strite, Laban, C., Koller, Rueben, Madorsky, Arthur, Hockersmith, Virgil, Kleeman, Michael, & Wagner, Jeffrey (1977). Comprehensive rehabilitation of patients having chronic low back pain. *Archives of Physical Medical Rehabilitation, 58,* 101–108.

Gottschalk, Louis A., Serota, Herman M., & Shapiro, Louis B. (1950). Psychologic conflict and neuromuscular tension. I. Preliminary report and a method, as applied to rheumatoid arthritis. *Psychosomatic Medicine, 12,* 315–319.

Gould, William L. (1953). Use of a lozenge to curb smoking appeal. *General Practitioner, 7,* 53–54.

Grace, William J., Pinsky, Ruth H., & Wolff, Harold G. (1954). The treatment of ulcerative colitus II. *Gastroenterology, 26,* 462–468.

Graff, Harold, Hammett, Van Buren O., Bash, Nicholas, Fackler, William, Yanovski, Alexander, & Goldman, Arnold (1966). Results of four antismoking therapy methods. *Pennsylvania Medical Journal, February,* 39–43.

Graham, Charles (1970). The allocation of attention in a simultaneous audio-visual monitoring task in hypnotically susceptible and insusceptible subjects. (Doctoral dissertation, Pennsylvania State University).

Graham, George Wayne (1975). Hypnotic treatment for migraine headaches. *International Journal of Clinical and Experimental Hypnosis, 23,* 165–171.

Graham, J. R., & Wolff, H. G. (1938). Mechanism of migraine headache and action of ergotamine tartrate. *Archives of Neurological Psychiatry, 39,* 737–763.

Graham, Kenneth R., & Greene, Lawrence D. (1981). Hypnotic susceptibility related to an independent measure of compliance-alumni annual giving. *International Journal of Clinical and Experimental Hypnosis, 29,* 351–354.

Graham, Kenneth R., Wright, Gail W., Toman, Wendy J., & Mark, Charles R. (1975). Relaxation and hypnosis in the treatment of insomnia. *American Journal of Clinical Hypnosis, 18,* 39–42.

Green, Elmer, & Green, Alyce (1979). General and specific applications of thermal biofeedback. In John V. Basajian (Ed.), *Biofeedback: Principles and practice for clinicians* (1st ed.) (pp. 153–169). Baltimore, MD: Williams & Wilkins.

Green, Elmer E., Green, Alyce M., & Norris, Patricia A. (1980). Self-regulation training for control of hypertension. *Primary Cardiology, 6,* 126–137.

Green, Elmer E., Green, Alyce M., & Walters, E. Dale (1970). Voluntary control of internal states: Psychological and physiological. *Journal of Transpersonal Psychology, 1,* 1–26.

Greene, Robert J. (1973). Combining rational-emotive and hypnotic techniques: A review and preliminary study. *Psychotherapy: Theory, Research and Practice, 10,* 71–73.

Greenwald, Harold (1970). *Hypnotic LSD trips.* Philadelphia: American Academy of Psychotherapists Tape Library. Vol. 42.

Greer, S., & Morris, Tina (1975). Psychological attributes of women who develop breast cancer: A controlled study. *Journal of Psychosomatic Research, 19,* 147–153.

Gritz, Ellen R., & Jarvik, Murray E. (1973). A preliminary study: Forty eight hours of abstinence from smoking. *Proceedings of the 81st Annual Convention of the American Psychological Association, 1,* 1039–1040.

Groen, J., & Bastiaans, J. (1951). Psychotherapy of ulcerative colitis. *Gastroenterology, 17,* 344–352.

Grosz, Hanus J. (1979). Hypnotherapy in the management of terminally ill cancer patients. *Journal of the Indiana Medical Assocation, 72,* 126-129.

Guyton, Arthur C. (1980). *Arterial pressure and hypertension.* Philadelphia: Saunders.

Guyton, Arthur C., Coleman, Thomas G., Bower, John D., & Granger, Harris J. (1970). Circulatory control in hypertension. *Circulation Research, 26* (Suppl. II), 135–147.

Hall, Howard R. (1983). Hypnosis and the immune system: A review with implications for cancer and the psychology of healing. *American Journal of Clinical Hypnosis, 25,* 92–103.

Hall, James A., & Crasilneck, Harold B. (1970). Development of a hypnotic technique for treating chronic cigarette smoking. *International Journal of Clinical and Experimental Hypnosis, 18,* 283–289.

Hamburger, Robert N. (1976). Allergy and the immune system. *American Scientist, 64,* 157–164.

Hanley, F. W. (1967). The treatment of obesity by individual and group hypnosis. *Canadian Psychiatric Association, 12,* 549–551.

Hanley, F. W. (1974). Individualized hypnotherapy of asthma. *American Journal of Clinical Hypnosis, 16,* 275–279.

Harburg, Ernest, Erfurt, John C., Havenstein, Louise S., Chape, Catherine, Schull, William J., & Schork, M. A. (1973). Socio-ecological stress, suppressed hostility, skin color, and black-white male blood pressure: Detroit. *Psychosomatic Medicine, 35,* 276–296.

Harding, H. Clagett (1961). Hypnosis and migraine or vice versa. *Northwest Medicine, February,* 168–172.

Harm, Deborah L., Marion, Richard J., Kotses, Harry, & Creer, Thomas L. (1984). Effect of subject effort on pulmonary function measures: A preliminary investigation. *Journal of Asthma, 21*, 295–298.

Harris, Mary B. (1969). Self-directed program for weight control: A pilot study. *Journal of Abnormal Psychology, 74*, 263–270.

Harris, Mary B., & Hallbauer, Erin S. (1973). Self-directed weight control through eating and exercise. *Behavior Research and Therapy, 11*, 523–529.

Harris, Ron, Lacoste, Diane, & Yulis, Sergio (1980). Relationships among sexual arousability, imagery ability, and introversion-extroversion. *Journal of Sex Research, 16*, 72–86.

Harrison, Robert H. (1975). Psychological testing in headache: A review. *Headache, 14*, 177–185.

Hart, Henry H. (1961). A review of the psychoanalytic literature on passivity. *Psychiatric Quarterly, 35*, 331–352.

Hartland, John (1965). The value of "ego-strengthening" procedures prior to direct symptom-removal under hypnosis. *American Journal of Clinical Hypnosis, 8*, 89–93.

Hartland, John (1971). *Medical and dental hypnosis and its clinical applications.* Baltimore, MD: Williams & Wilkins.

Hartman, B. J. (1976). Hypnotherapeutic approaches to the treatment of alcoholism. *Journal of the National Medical Association, 68*, 101–103; 147.

Hartman, William E., & Fithian, Marilyn A. (1974). *Treatment of sexual dysfunction.* New York: Aronson.

Haynes, Stephen N., Griffin, Philip, Mooney, Dean, & Parise, Mario (1975). Electromyographic biofeedback and relaxation instructions in the treatment of muscle contraction headaches. *Behavior Therapy, 6*, 672–678.

Hedberg, Allan G. (1973). The treatment of chronic diarrhea by systematic desensitization: A case report. *Journal of Behavior Therapy and Experimental Psychiatry, 4*, 67–68.

Helig, Robert, & Hoff, Hans (1925). Beitrage zur hypnotischen beeinflussung der magenfunklion. *Mediziniche Klinik, 21*, 162–163.

Hendin, Herbert (1974). Students on heroin. *Journal of Nervous & Mental Diseases, 158*, 240–255.

Henry. P. Y., Vernhiet, J., Orgogozo, J. M., & Caille, J. M. (1978). Cerebral blood flow in maigraine and cluster headache. *Research & Clinical Studies in Headache, 6*, 81–88.

Henryk-Gutt, Rita, & Rees, W. Linford (1973). Psychological aspects of migraine. *Journal of Psychosomatic Research, 17*, 141–153.

Herberman, Ronald B., & Holden, Howard T. (1979). Natural killer cells and antitumor effector cells. *Journal of the National Cancer Institute, 62*, 441–445.

Herman, C. Peter, & Polivy, Janet (1980). Restrained eating. In Albert J. Stunkard (Ed.), *Obesity* (pp. 208–225). Philadelphia: Saunders.

Hershman, Seymour (1955). Hypnosis in the treatment of obesity. *Journal of Clinical and Experimental Hypnosis, 3*, 136–139.

Hershman, Seymour (1956). Hypnosis and excessive smoking. *Journal of Clinical and Experimental Hypnosis, 4*, 24–29.

Herxheimer, H., & Prior, F. N. (1952). Further observations on induced asthma and bronchial hyposensitization. *International Archives of Allergy and Applied Immunology, 3*, 189–207.

Hilgard, Ernest R. (1965). *Hypnotic susceptibility.* New York: Harcourt, Brace & World, Inc.

Hilgard, Ernest R. (1969). Pain as a puzzle for psychology and physiology. *American Psychologist, 24*, 103–113.

Hilgard, Ernest R. (1974). Toward a neo-dissociation theory: Multiple cognitive controls in human functioning. *Perspectives in Biology and Medicine, 17*, 301–316.

Hilgard, Ernest R. (1975). The alleviation of pain by hypnosis. *Pain, 1*, 213–231.

Hilgard, Ernest R. (1977). *Divided consciousness: Multiple controls in human thought and action*. New York: Wiley.

Hilgard, Ernest R., & Hilgard, Josephine R. (1975). *Hypnosis in the relief of pain*. Los Altos, CA: Kaufmann.

Hilgard, Josephine R. (1970). *Personality and hypnosis: A study of imaginative involvement*. Chicago: The University of Chicago Press.

Hilgard, Josephine R., & Hilgard, Ernest R. (1979). Assessing hypnotic responsiveness in a clinical setting: A multi-item clinical scale and its advantages over single-item scales. *International Journal of Clinical and Experimental Hypnosis, 27*, 134–150.

Hinkle, John, & Lutker, Eric R. (1972). Insomnia: A new approach. *Psychotherapy: Theory, Research, and Practice, 9*, 236–237.

Hirsch, Jules, & Knittle, Jerome L. (1970). Cellularity of obese and non-obese human adipose tissue. *Federation Proceedings, 29*, 1516–1521.

Hoch, Z., Fuchs,. K., & Paldi, E. (1972). Hypno-behavioral approach for the non-consummated marriage. *Journal of the American Society of Psychosomatic Dentistry and Medicine, 19*, 129–136.

Hodge, James R., & Wagner, Edwin E. (1964). The validity of hypnotically induced emotional states. *American Journal of Clinical Hypnosis, 7*, 37–41.

Holden, Constance (1978). Cancer and the mind: How are they connected? *Science, 200*, 1363–1369.

Holland, Jimmie, Masling, Joseph, & Copley, Donald (1970). Mental illness in lower class, normal, obese, and hyperobese women. *Psychosomatic Medicine, 32*, 351–357.

Hollander, Mark B. (1959). Excoriated acne controlled by post-hypnotic suggestion. *American Journal of Clinical Hypnosis, 1*, 122–123.

Hollender, Marc H. (1963). Women's fantasies during sexual intercourse. *Archives of General Psychiatry, 8*, 102–106.

Holmes, Thomas H., & Rahe, Richard H. (1967). The social readjustment rating scale. *Journal of Psychosomatic Research, 11*, 213–218.

Holroyd, Jean (1980). Hypnosis treatment for smoking: An evaluative review. *International Journal of Clinical and Experimental Hypnosis, 28*, 341–357.

Holroyd, Kenneth A., & Andrasik, Frank (1978). Coping and the self-control of chronic tension headache. *Journal of Consulting and Clinical Psychology, 46*, 1036–1045.

Holt, Robert (1964). Imagery: The return of the ostracized. *American Psychologist, 19*, 254–264.

Horan, John S. (1950). Management of neurodermatitis by hypnotic suggestion. *British Journal of Medical Hypnotism, 2*, 43–46.

Horan, John S. (1953). Hypnosis and recorded suggestions in the treatment of migraine: Case report. *Journal of Clinical and Experimental Hypnosis, 1*, 7–10.

Horton, Douglas J., Suda, William L., Kinsman, Robert A., Souhrada, Joseph, & Spector, Sheldon L. (1977). *Bronchoconstrictive suggestion in asthma: A role for airways in hyperactivity and emotions*. Unpublished manuscript. National Jewish Hospital and Research Center.

Hull, Clark L. (1933). *Hypnosis and suggestibility: An experimental approach*. New York: Appleton-Century-Crofts.

Hunt, William A., Barnett, L. Walker, & Branch, Laurence G. (1971). Relapse rates in addiction programs. *Journal of Clinical Psychology, 27*, 455–456.

Hunt, William A., & Bespalec, Dale A. (1974). An evaluation of current methods of modifying smoking behavior. *Journal of Clinical Psychology, 30*, 431–438.

Hunt, William A., & Matarazzo, Joseph D. (1970). Habit mechanisms in smoking. In William A. Hurt (Ed.), *Learning mechanisms in smoking* (pp. 65–90). Chicago: Aldine.

Hutchings, Donald F., & Reinking, R. H. (1976). Tension headaches: What form of therapy is most effective? *Biofeedback and Self-Regulation, 1*, 183–190.

Ikard, Frederick F., Green, Dorothy E., & Horn, Daniel (1969). A scale to differentiate between types of smoking as related to the management of affect. *International Journal of Addictions, 4,* 649–659.

Ikemi, Yujiro (1967). *Psychological desensitization in allergic disorders, hypnosis and psychosomatic medicine.* New York: Springer-Verlag.

Ikemi, Yujiro (1978). Premorbid psychological factors as related to cancer incidence. *Journal of Behavioral Medicine, 1,* 45–133.

Ikemi, Yujiro, Minoru, Akagi, Maeda, Jyoji, Fukumoto, Shiro, Kawate, Kazumoto, Hirakwa, Kazuhiro, Gondo, Shigeo, Nakagawa, Tetsuya, Honda, Tatsuki, Sakamoto, Asahi, & Kumagai, Masahiro (1959). Hypnotic experiments on the psychosomatic aspects of gastrointestinal disorders. *International Journal of Clinical and Experimental Hypnosis, 7,* 139–150.

Jacobs, Martin A., Friedman, Sidney, Franklin, Morton J., Anderson, Luleen S., Muller, James J., & Eisman, Howard D. (1966). Incidence of psychosomatic predisposing factors in allergic disorders. *Psychosomatic Medicine, 28,* 679–695.

Jacobson, Edmund (1927). Spastic esophagus and mucous colitis. *Archives of Internal Medicine, 39,* 433–445.

Jacobson, Edmund (1938). *Progressive relaxation* (2nd ed.). Chicago: University of Chicago Press.

Jacobson, Edmund (1939). Variation of blood pressure with skeletal muscle tension and relaxation. *Annals of Internal Medicine, 12,* 1194–1212.

Jacobson, Nils O., & Silfverskiold, N. Peter (1973). A controlled study of hypnotic method in the treatment of alcoholism, with evaluation by objective criteria. *British Journal of Addiction, 68,* 25–31.

James, William (1961). *Psychology: The briefer course.* Gordon Allport (Ed.), New York: Harper & Row (Original Version 1892).

Jana, H. (1967). Effect of hypnosis on circulation and respiration. *Indiana Journal of Medical Research, 55,* 591–598.

Janda, Louis H., & O'Grady, Kevin F. (1980). Development of a sex anxiety inventory. *Journal of Consulting and Clinical Psychology, 48,* 169–175.

Janet, Pièrre (1925). *Psychological healing: A historical and clinical study.* English translation (Eden Paul & Cedar Paul, Trans.), New York: Macmillan (French Original) (Vols. 1–2).

Jason, Leonard (1975). Rapid improvement in insomnia following self-monitoring. *Journal of Behavior Therapy & Experimental Psychiatry, 6,* 349–350.

Jeffery, Robert W., Wing, Rena R., & Stunkard, Albert J. (1978). Behavioral treatment of obesity: The state of the art 1976. *Behavior Therpy, 9,* 189–199.

Jellinek, Elvin Morton (1960). *The disease concept of alcoholism.* New Haven, Ct: Hillhouse Press.

Jessup, Barton A., Neufeld, Richard W. J., & Merskey, Harold (1979). Biofeedback therapy for headache and other pain: An evaluative review. *Pain, 7,* 225–270.

Johns, M. W., Gray, T. J., Masterson, J. P., & Bruce, D. W. (1971). Relationship between sleep habits, adreno cortical activity and personality. *Psychosomatic Medicine, 33,* 499–508.

Johnson, Richard F. Q., & Barber, Theodore X. (1978). Hypnosis, suggestions, and warts: An experimental investigation implicating the importance of "believed-in efficacy". *American Journal of Clinical Hypnosis, 20,* 165–174.

Johnson, Vernon E. (1980). *I'll quit tomorrow* (revised ed.). San Francisco: Harper & Row.

Johnston, Edwin, & Donaghue, John R. (1971). Hypnosis and smoking: A review of the literature. *American Journal of Clinical Hypnosis, 13,* 265–272.

Jordan, James B., Hauri, Peter, & Phelps, Patricia J. (1976). The sensorimotor rhythm (SMR) in insomnia. *Sleep Research, 5,* 175, (Abstract).

Julius, Steve, & Esler, Murray (1975). Autonomic nervous cardiovascular regulation in borderline hypertension. *American Journal of Cardiology, 36,* 685–696.

Justesen, Don R., Braun, Edward W., Garrison, Robert G., & Pendleton, R. B. (1970).

Pharmacological differentiation of allergic and classically conditioned asthma in guinea pigs. *Science, 170*, 864–866.

Kales, Anthony, Caldwell, Alex B., Preston, Terry Anne, Healy, Shevy, & Kales, Joyce D. (1976). Personality patterns in insomnia. *Archives of General Psychiatry, 33*, 1128–1134.

Kanfer, Frederick H. (1977). The many faces of self-control, or behavior modification changes its focus. In Richard B. Stuart (Ed.), *Behavioral self-management: Strategies, techniques and outcomes* (pp. 1–48). New York: Brunner/Mazel.

Kanfer, Frederick H., & Grimm, Lawrence G. (1977). Behavioral analysis: Selecting target behaviors in the interview. *Behavior Modification, 1*, 7–28.

Kanfer, Frederick H., & Phillips, Jeanne S. (1970). *Learning foundations of behavior therapy.* New York: Wiley.

Kannel, William B., & Dawber, Thomas R. (1973). Hypertensive cardiovascular disease: The Framingham study. In Gaddo Onesti, Kwan E. Kim, & John H. Moyer (Eds.), *Hypertension: Mechanisms and management* (pp. 93–110). New York: Grune & Stratton.

Kanner, Allen D., Coyne, James C., Schaefer, Catherine, & Lazarus, Richard S. (1981). Compairson of two models of stress measurement: Daily hassles and uplifts versus major life events. *Journal of Behavioral Medicine, 4*, 1–37.

Kaplan, Harold I., & Kaplan, Helen Singer (1957). The psychosomatic concept of obesity. *Journal of Nervous Mental Disorders, 125*, 181–201.

Kaplan, Helen Singer (1974). The new sex therapy: Active treatment of sexual dysfunctions. New York: Brunner/Mazel.

Kaplan, Helen Singer (1979). Disorders of sexual desire and other new concepts and techniques in sex therapy. New York: Simon & Schuster.

Karush, Aeron, Daniels, George, Flood, Charles, O'Connor, John F., Druss, Richard, & Sweeting, Joseph (1977). *Psychotherapy in chronic ulcerative colitis.* Philadelphia: W. B. Saunders Co.

Katz, David H. (1978). The allergic phenotype: Manifestation of allergic breakthrough and imbalance in normal damping if IgE antibody production. *Immunology Review, 41*, 78.

Katz, Norman W. (1980). Hypnosis and the addictions: A critical review. *Addictive behaviors, 5*, 41–47.

Kavanagh, T., Shephard, R. J., & Doney, H. (1974). Hypnosis and exercise—A possible combined therapy following myocardial infarction. *American Journal of Clinical Hypnosis, 16*, 160–165.

Kavanagh, T., Shephard, R. J., Pandit, V., & Doney, H. (1970). Exercise and hypnotherapy in the rehabilitation of the coronary patient. *Archives of Physical Medicine & Rehabilitation, 51*, 578–587.

Kazarian, Shahe S., Howe, Margaret G., & Csapo, Kalman G. (1979). Development of the sleep behavior self-rating scale. *Behavioir Therapy, 10*, 412–417.

Kazdin, Alan E. (1974). Self-monitoring and behavior change. In Michael J. Mahoney & C. E. Thoresen (Eds.), *Self-control: Power to the person* (pp. 218–246). Monterey, CA: Brooks-Cole.

Keefe, Francis J., Block, A. R., & Williams, Redford B. (1980). *Behavioral treatment of the prechronic vs. chronic pain patient.* Paper presented at the American Pain Society, New York.

Keefe, Francis J., & Blumenthal, James A. (1982). *Assessment strategies in behavioral medicine.* New York: Grune & Stratton.

Keefe, Francis J., & Gardner, E. Ty (1979). Learned control of skin temperature: Effects of short and long-term biofeedback training. *Behavior Therapy, 10*, 202–210.

Keefe, Francis J., & Rosenstiel, Anne K. (1980). *Development of a questionnaire to assess cognitive coping strategies in chronic pain patients.* Paper presented at the 14th annual convention of the Association for Advancement of Behavior Therapy, New York.

Keegan, David L. (1973). Psychosomatics: Toward an understanding of cardiovascular disorders. *Psychosomatics, 14*, 321–325.

Keesey, Richard E. (1980). A set-point analysis of the regulation of body weight. In Albert J. Stunkard (Ed.), *Obesity* (pp. 144–165). Philadelphia: Saunders.

Kennedy, Alexander (1957). The medical use of hypnotism. *British Medical Journal, 1*, 1317–1319.

Kentsmith, D., Strider, F., Copenhaver, J., & Jacques, D. (1976). Effects of biofeedback upon suppression of migraine symptoms and plasma dopamine-B-hydroxylase activity. *Headache, 16*, 173–177.

Keutzer, Carolin S., Lichtenstein, Edward, & Mees, Hayden L. (1968). Modification of smoking behavior: A review. *Psychological Bulletin, 70*, 520-533.

Khantzian, Edward J. (1975). Self selection and progression in drug dependence. *Psychiatric Digest, 36*, 19–22.

Kiecolt-Glaser, Janice N., Garner, Warren, Speicher, Carl, Penn, Gerald M., Holliday, Jane S., & Glaser, Ronald (1984). Psychosocial modifiers of immunocompetence in medical students. *Psychosomatic Medicine, 46*, 7–14.

Kirsner, Joseph B., & Palmer, Walter L. (1958). The irritable colon. *Gastroenterology, 34*, 491–501.

Kirsner, Joseph B., & Shorter, Roy G. (1982). Recent developments in "nonspecific" inflammatory bowel disease. *New England Journal of Medicine, 306*, 775–785; 837–848.

Kissen, David M. (1966). The significance of personality in lung cancer in men. *Annals of the New York Academy of Science, 125*, 820–826.

Kline, Milton V. (1953). Delimited hypnotherapy: The acceptance of resistance in the treatment of a long standing neurodermatitis with a sensory-imagery technique. *Journal of Clinical and Experimental Hypnosis, 1*, 18–22.

Kline, Milton V. (1954). Psoriasis and hypnotherapy: A case report. *Journal of Clinical and Experimental Hypnosis, 2*, 318–322.

Kline, Milton V. (1970). The use of extended group hypnotherapy sessions in controlling cigarette habituation. *International Journal of Clinical and Experimental Hypnosis, 18*, 270–282.

Knapp, Peter H., Michael, Charles, & Wells, Harriet (1963). Addictive aspects in heavy cigarette smoking. *American Journal of Psychiatry, 119*, 966–972.

Knudson, Alfred G., Jr. (1977). Genetics and etiology of human cancer. *Advances in Human Genetics, 8*, 1–66.

Kockott, G., Dittmar, F., & Nusselt, L. (1975). Systematic desensitization of erectile impotence: A controlled study. *Archives of Sexual Behavior, 4*, 493–500.

Koenig, Karl P., & Masters, John (1965). Experimental treatment of habitual smoking. *Behavior Research & Therapy, 3*, 235–243.

Kohler, Peter F., & Vaughan, John (1982). The autoimmune diseases. *Journal of the American Medical Association, 248*, 2646–2657.

Kohut, Heinz (1971). *The analysis of self.* New York: International Universities Press.

Kolata, Gina (1986). Obese children: A growing problem. *Science, 232*, 20–21.

Kondo, Charles, & Canter, Arthur (1977). True and false electromyogram feedback: Effect on tension headache. *Journal of Abnormal Psychology, 81*, 93–95.

Kraft, Tom, & Al-Issa, Ihsan (1968). The use of methohexitone sodium in the systematic desensitization of premature ejaculation. *British Journal of Psychiatry, 114*, 351–352.

Kraus, Herbert H., Katzell, Raymond, & Krauss, Beatrice J. (1974). Effect of hypnotic time distortion upon free-recall learning. *Journal of Abnormal Psychology, 83*, 140–144.

Kristt, Donald A., & Engel, Bernard T. (1975). Learned control of blood pressure in patients with high blood pressure. *Circulation, 51*, 370–378.

Kroger, William S. (1942). The conditioned reflex treatment of alcoholism. *Journal of the*

American Medical Association, 120, 714.

Kroger, William S. (1963). Hypnosis in the removal of habit patterns. *Journal of Clinical and Experimental Hypnosis,* 274–276.

Kroger, William S. (1963). Hypnotherapeutic management of headache. *Headache, 3,* 50–62.

Kroger, William S. (1964). Current status of hypnosis in allergy. *Annals of Allergy, 22,* 123–129.

Kroger, William S. (1970). Comprehensive management of obesity. *American Journal of Clinical Hypnosis, 12,* 165–176.

Kroger, William S. (1980). Hypnotherapy and behavior modification. In Graham D. Burrows & Lorraine Dennerstein (Eds.), *Handbook of hypnosis and psychosomatic medicine* (pp. 509–516). Amsterdam: Elsevier/North-Holland Biomedical Press.

Kroger, William S., & Fezler, William D. (1976). *Hypnosis and behavior modification: Imagery conditioning.* Philadelphia: J. B. Lippincott.

Kroger, William S., & Libott, Robert Y. (1967). *Thanks doctor I've stopped smoking.* Springfield, IL: Charles C. Thomas.

Krystal, Henry (1962). The study of withdrawal from narcotics as a state of stress. *Psychiatric Quarterly Supplement, 36,* 53–65.

Krystal, Henry (1975). The opiate-withdrawal syndrome as a state of stress. *Annals of Psychoanalysis, 3,* 179–219.

Krystal, Henry, & Raskin, Herbert A. (1970). *Drug dependence: Aspects of ego function.* Detroit: Wayne State University Press.

Kunzendorf, Robert G. (1980). Imagery and consciousness: A scientific analysis of the mind-body problem. (Doctoral dissertation, The University of Virginia). *Dissertation Abstracts International, 40,* 3448B–3449B.

Lance, James W. (1973). *Mechanisms and management of headache.* London: Butterworth.

Lando, Harry A. (1977). Successful treatment of smokers with a broad-spectrum behavioral approach. *Journal of Consulting and Clinical Psychology, 45,* 361–366.

Lang, Peter J., Troyer, William G., Jr., Twentyman, Craig T., & Gatchell, Robert J. (1975). Differential effects of heart rate modification training on college students, older males, and patients with ischemic heart disease. *Psychosomatic Medicine, 37,* 429–446.

Langen, D. (1967). Modern hypnotic treatment of various forms of addiction, in particular alcoholism. *British Journal of Addiction, 62,* 77–81.

Latimer, Paul R. (1978). Crohn's disease: A review of the psychological and social outcome. *Psychological Medicine, 8,* 649–656.

Latimer, Paul R. (1983). *Functional gastrointestinal disorders: A behavioral medicine approach.* New York: Springer.

Lawton, M. Powell (1967). Group methods in smoking withdrawal. *Archives of Environmental Health, 14,* 258–265.

Lazarus, Arnold A. (1973). "Hypnosis" as a facilitator in behavior therapy. *International Journal of Clinical and Experimental Hypnosis, 21,* 25–31.

Lazarus, Richard S. (1966). *Psychological stress and the coping process.* New York: McGraw Hill.

Leckie, Hamilton F. (1964). Hypnotherapy in gynecological disorders. *International Journal of Clinical and Experimental Hypnosis, 12,* 121–146.

LeBaw, Wallace, Holton, Charlene, Tewell, Karen, and Eccles, Doris (1975). The use of self-hypnosis by children with cancer. *American Journal of Clinical Hypnosis, 17,* 233–238.

LeCron, Leslie M. (1959). Group hypnosis in the treatment of obesity. *American Journal of Clinical Hypnosis, 1,* 114–117.

Lehman, Robert E. (1978). Brief hypnotherapy of neurodermatitis: A case with four-year follow up. *American Journal of Clinical Hypnosis, 21,* 48–51.

Lenox, John R., & Bonny, Helen (1976). The hypnotizability of chronic alcoholics. *International Journal of Clinical and Experimental Hypnosis, 24,* 419–425.

LeShan, Lawrence (1964). The world of the patient in severe pain of long duration. *Chronic Diseases, 17,* 119–126.

LeShan, Lawrence, & Worthington, Richard E. (1955). Some psychologic correlates of neoplastic disease: Preliminary report. *Journal of Clinical & Experimental Psychopathology, 16,* 281–288.

LeShan, Lawrence, & Worthington, Richard E. (1956). Some recurrent life history patterns observed in patients with malignant disease. *Journal of Nervous & Mental Diseases, 124,* 460–465.

Levendula, Dezso (1962). A contemporary view of hypnosis. *Headache, 1,* 15–19.

Leventhal, Howard, & Everhart, D. (1979). Emotion, pain, and physical illness. In Carroll E. Izard (Ed.), *Emotions in personality and psychopathology* (pp. 261–299). New York: Plenum Press.

Lichenstein, Edward, Harris, Darrel E., Birchler, Gary R., Wahl, James M., & Schmahl, David P. (1973). Comparison of rapid smoking, warm, smoky air, and attention placebo in the modification of smoking behavior. *Journal of Consulting and Clinical Psychology, 40,* 92–98.

Lick, John R., & Heffler, David (1977). Relaxation training and attention placebo in the treatment of severe insomnia. *Journal of Consulting and Clinical Psychology, 45,* 153–161.

Liss, Jay L., Alpers David, & Woodruff, Robert A. (1973). The irritable colon syndrome and psychiatric illness. *Diseases of the Nervous System, 34,* 151–157.

Litman, Gloria K., Eiser J. Richard, Rawson, Nigel S. B., & Oppenheim, A. N. (1979). Differences in relapse precipitants and coping behavior between alcohol relapsers and survivors. *Behavior Research & Therapy, 17,* 89–94.

Lo Piccolo, J., & Lo Piccolo, L. (Eds.) (1978). *Handbook of sex therapy.* New York: Plenum Press.

Lombard, Lisa, Kahn, Stephen, & Fromm, Erika. (in press) The role of imagery in self-hypnosis: Its relationship to personality characteristics and gender. *International Journal of Clinical and Experimental Hypnosis.*

Luckhardt, Arno B., & Johnston, Robert L. (1924). Studies in gastric secretion. I. The psychic secretion of gastric juice under hypnosis. *American Journal of Physiology, 70,* 174–182.

Ludwig, Arnold M. (1966). Altered states of consciousness. *Archives of General Psychiatry, 15,* 225–234.

Ludwig, Arnold M., & Lyle, W. H. (1964). The experimental production of narcotic drug effects and withdrawal symptoms through hypnosis. *International Journal of Clinical and Experimental Hypnosis, 12,* 1–17.

Ludwig, Arnold M., Lyle, W. H., & Miller, J. S. (1964). Group hypnotherapy techniques with drug addicts. *International Journal of Clinical and Experimental Hypnosis, 12,* 53–66.

Ludwig, A. M., & Stark, L. H. (1974). Alcohol craving: Subjective and situational aspects. *Quarterly Journal of Studies on Alcohol, 35,* 899–905.

Lutker, Eric R. (1971). Treatment of migraine headache by conditioned relaxation: A case study. *Behavior Therapy, 2,* 592–593.

MacMahon, Brian, Cole, Philip, & Brown, James (1973). Etiology of breast cancer: A review. Journal of the National Cancer Institute, 50, 21–43.

Magonet, A. Philip (1960). Hypnosis in asthma. *International Journal of Clinical and Experimental Hypnosis, 8,* 121–127.

Maher-Loughnan, G. P. (1970). Hypnosis and autohypnosis for the treatment of asthma. *International Journal of Clinical and Experimental Hypnosis, 18,* 1–14.

Maher-Loughnan, G. P. (1975). Intensive hypno-autohypnosis in resistant psychosomatic disorders. *Journal of Psychosomatic Research, 19,* 361–365.

Maher-Loughnan, G. P., MacDonald, N., Mason, A. A., & Fry, Lionel (1962). Controlled trial of hypnosis in the symptomatic treatment of asthma. *British Medical Journal, 2,* 371–376.

Mahoney, Michael J. (1974). Self-reward and self-monitoring techniques for weight control. *Behavior Therapy, 5,* 48–57.

Mahoney, Michael J. (1978). Behavior modification in the treatment of obesity. *Psychiatric Clinics of North America, 1,* 651–660.

Mahoney, Michael J., & Mahoney, Kathryn (1976). *Permanent weight control: A total solution to the dieter's dilemma.* New York: W. W. Norton.

Malmo, Robert B., Boag, Thomas J., & Raginsky, Bernard B. (1954a). Electromyographic study of hypnotic deafness. *International Journal of Clinical and Experimental Hypnosis, 2,* 305–317.

Mann, Herbert (1953). Group hypnosis in the treatment of obesity. *American Journal of Clinical Hypnosis, 1,* 114–116.

Marchesi, Carlo (1949). The hypnotic treatment of bronchial asthma. *British Journal of Medical Hypnotism, 1,* 14–19.

Marchini, Evelyn J., Coates, Thomas J., Magistad, John G., & Waldum, Shirley J. (1983). What do insomniacs do, think, and feel during the day? A preliminary study. *Sleep, 6,* 147–155.

Margolis, Clorinda G. (1983). Hypnotic imagery with cancer patients. *American Journal of Clinical Hypnosis, 25,* 128–134.

Marlatt, G. Alan, & Gordon, Judith R. (1980). Determinants of relapse: Implications for the maintenance of behavior change. In Park O. Davidson & Sheena M. Davidson (Eds.), *Behavioral medicine: Changing health lifestyles* (pp. 410–452). New York: Brunner/Mazel.

Marlatt, G. Alan, & Gordon, Judith R. (1985). *Relapse prevention: Maintenance strategies in the treatment of addictive behaviors.* New York: Guilford Press.

Marlatt, G. Alan, & Marques, Janice K. (1977). Meditation, self-control and alcohol use. In Richard B. Stuart (Ed.), *Behavioral self-management* (pp. 117–153). New York: Brunner/Mazel.

Marshall, John (1978). Cerebral blood flow in migraine without headache. *Research & Clinical Studies in Headache, 6,* 1–5.

Maslach, Christina, Marshall, Gary, & Zimbardo, Philip G. (1972). Hypnotic control of peripheral skin temperature: A case report. *Psychophysiology, 9,* 600–605.

Mason, A. A. (1963). Hypnosis and allergy. *British Medical Journal, 6,* 1675–1676.

Mason, A. A., & Black, Stephen (1958). Allergic skin responses abolished under treatment of asthma and hayfever by hypnosis. *Lancet, 1,* 877–880.

Mason, Russell E. (1961). *Internal perception and bodily functioning.* New York: International Universities Press.

Masters, William H., & Johnson, Virginia E. (1970). *Human sexual inadequacy.* Boston: Little, Brown.

Masuda, Minoru, & Holmes, Thomas H. (1967). The social readjustment rating scale. *Journal of Psychosomatic Research, 11,* 227–237.

Matarazzo, Joseph D., & Saslow, George (1960). Psychological and related characteristics of smokers and nonsmokers. *Psychological Bulletin, 57,* 493–513.

Matefy, Robert E. (1973). Behavior therapy to extinguish spontaneous recurrences of LSD effects: A case study. *Journal of Nervous & Mental Diseases, 156,* 226–231.

Mathe, Aleksander A., & Knapp, Peter H., (1971). Emotional and adrenal reactions to stress in bronchial asthma. *Psychosomatic Medicine, 33,* 323–340.

Mathew, Ninan T., Hrastnik, Franc, & Meyer, John S. (1976). Regional cerebral blood flow in the diagnosis of vascular headache. *Headache, 15,* 252–260.

Mausner, Bernard (1966). Report on a smoking clinic. *American Psychologist, 21,* 251–255.

Mausner, Bernard (1973). An ecological view of cigarette smoking, *Journal of Abnormal Psychology, 81,* 115–126.

McClelland, David C. (1979). Inhibited power motivation and high blood pressure in men. *Journal of Abnormal Psychology, 88,* 182–190.

McClelland, David C., Alexander, Charles, & Marks, Emilie (1982). The need for power, stress, immune function, and illness among male prisoners. *Journal of Abnormal Psychology, 91,* 61–70.

McCord, Hallack (1967). Hypnotic treatment of alcoholism: Brief case history. *Journal of the American Society of Psychosomatic and Dental Medicine, 14,* 104–105.

McDowell, Mehl (1949). Juvenile warts removed with the use of hypnotic suggestion. *Bulletin of the Menninger Clinic, 13,* 124–126.

McDowell, Mehl (1959). Hypnosis in dermatology. In Jerome M. Schneck (Ed.), *Hypnosis in modern medicine.* Springfield, IL: Charles C. Thomas.

McFall, Richard M. (1977). Parameters of self-monitoring. In Richard B. Stuart (Ed.), *Behavioral self-management: Strategies, techniques and outcomes* (pp. 196–214). New York: Brunner/Mazel.

McGlashen, Thomas H., Evans, Frederick J., & Orne, Martin T. (1969). The nature of hypnotic analgesia and the placebo response to experimental pain. *Psychosomatic Medicine, 31,* 227–246.

McKegney, F. Patrick, & Williams, Redford B., Jr. (1967). Psychological aspect of hypertension: II. The differential influence of interview variables on blood pressure. *American Journal of Psychiatry, 123,* 1539–1545.

McKinney, Mark E., Hofschiro, Philip J., Buell, James C., & Eliot, Robert S. (1984). Hemodynamic and biochemical responses to stress: The necessary link between Type A behavior and cardiovascular disease. *Behavioral Medicine Update, 6,* 16–21.

Meares, Ainslie (1968). Psychological mechanisms in the relief of pain by hypnosis. *American Journal of Clinical Hypnosis, 11,* 56–57.

Meares, Ainslie (1979). Mind and cancer. *Lancet, 1,* 1978.

Meares, Ainslie (1983). A form of intensive meditation associated with the regression of cancer. *American Journal of Clinical Hypnosis, 25,* 114–121.

Meichenbaum, Donald (1974). *Cognitive behavior modification.* Morristown, NJ: General Learning Press.

Meichenbaum, Donald (1978). *Cognitive behavior modification: An integrative approach.* New York: Plenum.

Melzack, Ronald (1973). *The puzzle of pain.* New York: Basic Books.

Melzack, Ronald (1975). The McGill Pain Questionnaire: Major properties and scoring methods. *Pain, 1,* 277–299.

Melzack, Ronald, & Perry, Campbell (1975). Self-regulation of pain: The use of alpha-feedback and hypnotic training for the control of chronic pain. *Experimental Neurology, 46,* 452–469.

Mendelson, C. G., & Kligman, Albert M. (1961). Isolation of wart virus in tissue culture. *Archives of Dermatology, 83,* 559–562.

Metropolitan Life Insurance Company (1960). Statistical Bulletin No. 41. New York.

Milkman, Harvey, & Frosch, William A. (1973). On the preferential abuse of heroin and amphetamine. *Journal of Nervous & Mental Disease, 156,* 242–248.

Miller, Jeffrey E. (1974). Hypnotic susceptibility, achievement motivation, and the treatment of obesity. Unpublished doctoral dissertation, University of Southern California. *Dissertation Abstracts International,* 1975, *35,* 3026b–3027b (University Microfilms, No. 74-28, 456).

Miller, Michael M. (1959). Treatment of chronic alcoholism by hypnotic aversion. *Journal of the American Medical Association, 171,* 1492–1495.

Miller, Michael M. (1965). Hypnoaversion treatment of nicotinism. *Journal of the National Medical Association, 66,* 480–482.

Miller, Michael M. (1974). Hypnoaversion in the treatment of obesity. *Journal of the National*

Medical Association, 66, 480–481.

Miller, Michael M. (1976). Hypnoaversion treatment in alcoholism, nicotinism, and weight control. *Journal of the National Medical Association, 68,* 129–130.

Miller, Milton L. (1948). Psychodynamic mechanisms in a case of neurodermatitis. *Psychosomatic Medicine, 10,* 309–316.

Miller, Neil E. (1969). Learning of visceral and glandular responses. *Science, 163,* 434–445.

Miller, Neal E. (1975). Applications of learning and biofeedback to psychiatry and medicine. In Alfred M. Freedman, Harold I. Kaplan & Benjamin J. Sadock (Eds.), *Comprehensive textbook of psychiatry* (2nd ed.) (pp. 349–365). Baltimore: Williams & Wilkins.

Miller, Neal E. (1975). Clinical applications of biofeedback: Voluntary control of heart rate, rhythm, and blood pressure. In H. I. Russek (Ed.), *New horizons in cardiovascular practice* (pp. 245–246). Baltimore: University Park Press.

Miller, Neal E., DiCara, Leo V., Solomon, Henry, Weiss, Jay M., & Dworkin, Barry (1970). Learned modifications of autonomic functions: A review and some new data. *Circulation Research Supplement I, 16 & 17,* I–3, I–11.

Miller, Peter M., & Sims, Karen L. (1981). Evaluation and component analysis of a comprehensive weight control program. *International Journal of Obesity, 5,* 57–65.

Miller, R. J. (1980). The Harvard Group Scale of Hypnotic Susceptibility as a predictor of nonhypnotic suggestibility. *International Journal of Clinical and Experimental Hypnosis, 28,* 46–52.

Miller, William R. (1977). Behavioral self-control training in the treatment of problem drinkers. In Richard B. Stuart (Ed.), *Behavioral self-management* (pp. 154–175). New York: Brunner/Mazel.

Miller, William R., & Muñoz, Ricardo F. (1976). *How to control your drinking.* Englewood Cliffs, NJ: Prentice-Hall.

Millikin, Lester A. (1964). Arthritis and Raynaud's syndromes-As psychosomatic problems successfully treated with hypnotherapy. *British Journal of Medical Hypnotism, 15,* 37–44.

Mills, Walter W., & Farrow, John T. (1981). The Transcendental Meditation technique and acute experimental pain. *Psychosomatic Medicine, 43,* 157–164.

Milsum, John H. (1980). Lifestyle changes for the whole person: Stimulation through health hazard appraisal. In Park O. Davidson & Sheena M. Davidson (Eds.), *Behavioral medicine: Changing health lifestyles* (pp. 116–150). New York: Brunner/Mazel.

Mitch, Paul S., McGrady, Angele, & Iannone, Anthony (1976). Autogenic feedback training in migraine: A treatment report. *Headache, 15,* 267–274.

Mitchell, Kenneth R. (1978). Self-management of spastic colitis. *Journal of Behavioral Therapy & Experimental Psychiatry, 9,* 269–272.

Mitchell, Kenneth R., & White, Ronald G. (1977). Behavioral self-management: An application to the problem of migraine headaches. *Behavior Therapy, 8,* 213–221.

Mittleman, Bela (1947). Psychoanalytic observations on skin disorders. *Bulletin of the Menninger Clinic, 11,* 169–176.

Moeller, Theodore A., & Love, William A. (1974). *A method to reduce arterial hypertension through muscular relaxation.* Unpublished manuscript. Nova University, Ft. Lauderdale, FL.

Monjan, Andrew A. (1981). Stress and immunologic competence: Studies in animals. In Robert Ader (Ed.), *Psychoneuroimmunology* (pp. 185–228). New York: Academic Press.

Monroe, Lawrence J. (1967). Psychological and physiological differences between good and poor sleepers. *Journal of Abnormal Psychology, 72,* 255–264.

Montgomery, Iain, Perkin, Graham, & Wise, Deirdre (1975). A review of behavioral treatments for insomnia. *Journal of Behavior Therapy, 6,* 93–100.

Moody, Hamilton (1953). An evaluation of hypnotically induced relaxation for the reduction of peptic ulcer symptoms. *British Journal of Medical Hypnotism, 5,* 23–30.

Moore, J. G., & Schenkenberg, T. (1974). Psychic control of gastric acid: Response to anticipated feeding and biofeedback training in a man. *Gastroenterology, 66,* 954–959.

Moore, Norah (1965). Behavior therapy in bronchial asthma: A controlled study. *Journal of Psychosomatic Research, 9,* 257–276.

Moorefield, C. W. (1971). The use of hypnosis and behavior therapy in asthma. *American Journal of Clinical Hypnosis, 13,* 162–168.

Moses, Ferris M. (1964). Treating smoking habit by discussion and hypnosis. *Diseases of the Nervous System, 25,* 184–188.

Moses, Leon, Daniels, George E., & Nickerson, John L. (1956). Psychogenic factors in essential hypertension: Methodology and preliminary report. *Psychosomatic Medicine, 18,* 471–485.

Mosher, Donald L. (1965). Interaction of fear and guilt in inhibiting unacceptable behavior. *Journal of Consulting Psychology, 29,* 161–167.

Mosher, Donald L. (1966). The development and multitrait-multimethod matrix analysis of three measures of three aspects of guilt. *Journal of Consulting Psychology, 30,* 25–29.

Mosher, Donald L. (1980). Three dimensions of depth of involvement in human sexual response. *Journal of Sex Research, 16,* 1–42.

Mott, Thurman (1979). The clinical importance of hypnotizability. *American Journal of Clinical Hypnosis, 21,* 263–269.

Mott, Thurman, & Roberts, Jean (1979). Obesity and hypnosis: A review of the literature. *American Journal of Clinical Hypnosis, 22,* 3–7.

Murrell, T. G. C., & Deller, D. J. (1967). Intestinal motility in man: The effects of bradykinin on the motility of the distal colon. *American Journal of Digestive Disease, 12,* 568–576.

Nelson, Rosemary O. (1977). Methodological issues in assessment via self-monitoring. In John D. Cone & Robert P. Hawkins (Eds.), *Behavioral assessment: New directions in clinical psychology* (pp. 217–240). New York: Brunner/Mazel.

Nerenz, David R., & Leventhal, Howard (1983). Self-regulation theory in chronic illness. In Thomas G. Burish & Lawrence A. Bradley (Eds.), *Coping with chronic disease: Research and applications* (pp. 13–37). New York: Academic Press.

Nestel, P. J. (1969). Blood pressure and catecholamine excretion after mental stress in labile hypertension. *Lancet, 1,* 692–694.

Newton, Bernauer W. (1983). The use of hypnosis in the treatment of cancer patients. *American Journal of Clinical Hypnosis, 25,* 104–113.

Nisbett, Paul D. (1973). Smoking, physiological arousal, and emotional response. *Journal of Personality and Social Psychology, 25,* 137–144.

Nisbett, Richard E. (1972). Hunger, obesity, and the ventromedial hypothalamus. *Psychological Review, 79,* 433–453.

Nolan, J. Dennis (1968). Self-control procedures in the modification of smoking behavior. *Journal of Consulting and Clinical Psychology, 32,* 92–93.

Nuland, William (1978). The use of hypnosis in the treatment of impotence. In Fred H. Frankel & Harold S. Zamansky (Eds.), *Hypnosis at its bicentennial-Selected papers* (pp. 221–227). New York: Plenum.

Nuland, William, & Field, Peter B. (1970). Smoking and hypnosis: A systematic clinical approach. *International Journal of Clinical and Experimental Hypnosis, 18,* 290–306.

O'Brien, M. D. (1971). Cerebral blood changes in migraine. *Headache, 10,* 139–143.

O'Brien, J. S., Raynes, A. E., & Patch, V. D. (1972). Treatment of heroin addiction with aversion therapy, relaxation training and systematic desensitization. *Behavior Research & Therapy, 10,* 77–80.

Oakley, R. P. (1960). Hypnosis with a positive approach in the management of "problem" obesity. *Journal of the American Society of Psychosomatic Dentistry & Medicine, 7,* 28–40.

Oliver, George W. (1983). A cancer patient and her family: A case study. *American Journal of*

Clinical Hypnosis, 25, 156–160.

Olness, Karen (1981). Imagery (self-hypnosis) as adjunct therapy in childhood cancer: Clinical experience with 25 patients. *American Journal of Pediatric Hematology/Oncology, 3,* 313–321.

Olton, David S., & Noonberg, Aaron R. (1980). *Biofeedback: Clinical applications in behavioral medicine.* Englewood Cliffs, NJ: Prentice-Hall.

Orleans, Carole S., & Shipley, Robert H. (1982). Assessment in smoking cessation research: Some practical guidelines. In Francis J. Keefe & James A. Blumenthal (Eds.), *Assessment strategies in behavioral medicine* (pp. 261–294). New York: Grune & Stratton.

Orne, Martin T. (1959). The nature of hypnosis: Artifact and essence. *Journal of Abnormal and Social Psychology, 58,* 277–299.

Orne, Martin T. (1977). The construct of hypnosis: Implications of the definition for research and practice. *Annals of the New York Academy of Science, 296,* 14–33.

Ornstein, Robert E. (1970). *On the experience of time.* Baltimore, MD: Penguin Books.

Ottenberg, Perry, Stein, Marvin, Lewis, Jerry, & Hamilton, Charles (1958). Learned asthma in the guinea pig. *Psychosomatic Medicine, 20,* 395–400.

Patel, Chandra (1973). Yoga and bio-feedback in the management of hypertension. *Lancet, 2,* 1053–1055.

Patel, Chandra (1975). Twelve-month follow-up of yoga and biofeedback in the management of hypertension. *Lancet, 2,* 62–65.

Patel, Chandra, & North, W. R. S. (1975). Randomised controlled trial of yoga and biofeedback in management of hypertension. *Lancet, 2,* 93–95.

Paterson, Arthur Spencer (1974). Hypnosis as an adjunct to the treatment of alcoholics and drug addicts. *International Journal of Offender Therapy and Comparative Criminology, 18,* 40–45.

Patterson, B. R., Hawkins, Nancy, McNeal, Shirley, & Phelps, Richard (1967). Reprogramming the social environment. *Journal of Child Psychology and Psychiatry, 8,* 181–195.

Paul, Gordon J. (1969). Physiological effects of relaxation training and hypnotic suggestion. *Journal of Abnormal Psychology, 74,* 425–437.

Paulley, J. W., & Haskell, D. A. L. (1975). The treatment of migraine without drugs. *Journal of Psychosomatic Research, 19,* 367–374.

Pavlov, Ivan P. (1927). *Conditioned reflexes.* London: Oxford University Press.

Paykel, E. S., & Rao, B. M. (1984). Methodology in studies of life events and cancer. In Cary L. Cooper (Ed.), *Psychosocial stress and cancer* (pp. 73–89). New York: Wiley.

Peck, Connie L., & Kraft, George H. (1977). Electromyographic biofeedback for pain related to muscle tension. *Archives of Surgery, 112,* 889–895.

Pederson, Linda L., Scrimgeour, William G., & Lefcoe, Neville M. (1975). Comparison of hypnosis plus counseling, counseling alone, and hypnosis alone in a community service smoking withdrawal program. *Journal of Consulting & Clinical Psychology, 43,* 920.

Pederson, Linda L., Scrimgeour, William G., & Lefcoe, Neville M. (1979). Variables of hypnosis which are related to success in a smoking withdrawal program. *International Journal of Clinical and Experimental Hypnosis, 27,* 14–20.

Penick, Sydnor B., Filion, Ross, Fox, Sonja, & Stunkard, Albert J. (1971). Behavior modification in the treatment of obesity. *Psychosomatic Medicine, 33,* 49–55.

Pennebaker, James W. (1982). *The psychology of physical symptoms.* New York: Springer-Verlag.

Perloff, Milton M., & Spiegelman, Jay (1973). Hypnosis in the treatment of a child's allergy to dogs. *American Journal of Clinical Hypnosis, 15,* 269–272.

Perry, Campbell, Gelfand, Robert, & Marcovitch, Phillip (1979). The relevance of hypnotic susceptibility in the clinical context. *Journal of Abnormal Psychology, 88,* 592–603.

Perry, Campbell, & Mullen, Grace (1975). The effect of hypnotic susceptibility on reducing smoking behavior treated by an hypnotic technique. *Journal of Clinical Psychology, 31,* 498–505.

Peterson, Linda Gay, Popkin, Michael K., Hall, Richard C. W. (1981). Psychiatric aspects of cancer. *Psychosomatics, 22,* 774–789.

Philips, C. (1977). A psychological analysis of tension headache. In Stanley Rachman (Ed.), *Contributions to medical psychology* (vol. 1) (pp. 91–113). New York: Pergamon Press.

Pomerleau, Ovide F., & Brady, Joseph V. (Eds.) (1979). *Behavioral medicine: Theory and practice.* Baltimore: Williams & Wilkins.

Pomerleau, Ovide F., & Pomerleau, Cynthia S. (1977) *Break the smoking habit: A behavioral program for giving up cigarettes.* Champaign, IL: Research Press Company.

Povorinsky, Y. A. (1961). Psychotherapy of smoking. In Ralph B. Winn (Ed.), *Psychotherapy in the Soviet Union* (pp. 144–152). New York: Philosophical Library.

Powell, Douglas H. (1980). Helping habitual smokers using flooding and hypnotic desensitization techniques: A brief communication. *International Journal of Clinical and Experimental Hypnosis, 28,* 192–196.

Pozniak-Patewicz, Ewa (1976). "Cephalic" spasm of head and neck muscles. *Headache, 15,* 261–266.

Price, Kenneth P., & Clarke, Lewis K. (1979). Classical conditioning of digital pulse volume in migraineurs and normal controls. *Headache, 19,* 328–332.

Purcell, Kenneth (1963). Distinctions between subgroups of asthmatic children: Children's perceptions of events associated with asthma. *Pediatrics, 31,* 486–494.

Purcell, Kenneth, & Weiss, Jonathan H. (1970). Asthma. In Charles G. Costello (Ed.), *Symptoms of psychopathology* (pp. 597–623). New York: Wiley.

Pyke, Sandra, MckAgnew, Neil, & Kopperud, Jean (1966). Modification of an overlearned maladaptive response through a relearning program: A pilot study on smoking. *Behavior Research & Therapy, 4,* 197–203.

Raab, W. (1966). Emotional and sensory stress factors in myocardial pathology: Neurogenic and hormonal mechanisms in pathogenesis, therapy, and prevention. *American Heart Journal, 72,* 538–564.

Rado, Sandor (1926). The psychic effects of intoxicants: An attempt to evolve a psychoanalytical theory of morbid cravings. *International Journal of Psychoanalysis, 7,* 396–413.

Rado, Sandor (1933). The psychoanalysis of pharmacothymia (Drug addiction). *Psychoanalytic Quarterly, 2,* 1–23.

Raginsky, Bernard B. (1962). The investigation of allergy through hypnotic techniques. *Psychosomatics, 3,* 137–147.

Rand, Colleen S., & Stunkard, Albert J. (1977). Psychoanalysis and obesity. *Journal of the American Academy of Psychoanalysis, 5,* 459–497.

Rand, Colleen S., & Stunkard, Albert J. (1978). Obesity and psychoanalysis. *American Journal of Psychiatry, 135,* 547–551.

Rapaport, David (1967). Some metapsychological considerations concerning activity and passivity (published originally in 1961). In M. M. Gill (Ed.), *The collected papers of David Rapaport* (pp. 631–664). New York: Basic Books.

Reeves, John L. (1976). EMG-biofeedback reduction of tension headache: A cognitive skills-training approach. *Biofeedback & Self-Regulation, 1,* 217–225.

Reif, Arnold E. (1981). The causes of cancer. *American Scientist, 69,* 437–447.

Reinherz, Ellis L., Rubenstein, Arye, Geha, Raif S., Strelkauskas, Anthony J., Rosen, Fred S., & Schlossman, Stuart F. (1979). Abnormalities of immunoregulatory T cells in disorders of immune function. *New England Journal of Medicine, 301,* 1018–1022.

Reisel, J. H. (1969). Epidemiological and psychosomatic aspects in essential hypertension. *Psychotherapy and Psychosomatics, 17,* 169–177.

Reiser, Morton F., Brust, Albert A., & Ferris, Eugene B. (1951). Life situations, emotions, and the course of patients with arterial hypertension. *Psychosomatic Medicine, 13,* 133–139.

Relinger, Helmut, & Bornstein, Philip H. (1979). Treatment of sleep onset insomnia by paradoxical instruction: A multiple baseline design. *Behavior Modification, 3,* 203–222.

Renne, Charles, & Creer, Thomas L. (1976). The effects of training on the use of inhalation therapy equipment by children with asthma. *Journal of Applied Behavior Analysis, 9,* 1–11.

Ribordy, Sheila C., & Denney, Douglas R. (1977). The behavioral treatment of insomnia: An alternative to drug therapy. *Behavior Research & Therapy, 15,* 39–50.

Richardson, T. A. (1963). Hypnotherapy in frigidity. *American Journal of Clinical Hypnosis, 5,* 194–199.

Rickes, W. H., Cohen, M. J., & McArthur, D. L. (1977). *A psychophysiologic study of autonomic nervous system response patterns in migraine headache patients and their headache-free friends.* Presentation at the 19th Annual Meeting. American Association for the Study of Headache, San Francisco.

Riley, Vernon M., Fitzmaurice, M.A., & Spackman, Darrel H. (1981). Psychoneuroimmunologic factors in neoplasia: Studies in animals. In Robert Ader (Ed.), *Psychoneuroimmunology* (pp. 31–102). New York: Academic Press.

Ritchie, James (1973). Pain from distension of the pelvic colon by inflating a balloon in the irritable colon syndrome. *Gut, 14,* 125–132.

Roberts, Alan, Kewman, Donald G., & MacDonald, Hugh (1973). Voluntary control of skin temperature: Unilateral changes using hypnosis and feedback. *Journal of Abnormal Psychology, 82,* 163–168.

Roberts, Alan H., Schuler, Joanne, Bacon, Jane R. Zimmerman, Robert L., & Patterson, Robert (1975). Individual differences and autonomic control: Absorption, hypnotic susceptibility, and the unilateral control of skin temperature. *Journal of Abnormal Psychology, 84,* 272–279.

Rodin, Judith (1980a). The externality theory today. In Albert J. Stunkard (Ed.), *Obesity* (pp. 226–239). Philadelphia: W.B. Saunders.

Rodin, Judith (1980b). *The Yale weight control program.* Unpublished manuscript, Yale University.

Rodolfa, Emil R., Kraft, William A., & Reilley, Robert R. (1985). Current trends in hypnosis and hypnotherapy: An interdisciplinary assessment. *American Journal of Clinical Hypnosis, 28,* 20–26.

Roman, Paul M., & Trice, Harrison M. (1970). The development of deviant drinking behavior: Occupational risk factors. *Archives of Environmental Health, 20,* 424–435.

Romanczyk, Raymond G. (1974). Self-monitoring in the treatment of obesity: Parameters of reactivity. *Behavior Therapy, 5,* 531–540.

Romancyzk, Raymond G., Tracey, Dorothy A., Wilson, G. Terence, & Thorpe, Geoffrey . (1973). Behavioral techniques in the treament of obesity: A comparative analysis. *Behavior Research & Therapy, 11,* 629–640.

Rosch, Paul J. (1979). Stress and cancer: A disease of adaptation? In Jean Toche, Hans Seyle & S.B. Day (Eds.), *Cancer, stress and death* (pp. 187–212). New York: Plenum Press.

Rosch, Paul J. (1984). Stress and cancer. In Cary L. Cooper (Ed.), *Psychosocial stress and cancer* (pp. 3–19). New York: Wiley.

Rose, Stanley (1967). A general practitioner approach to the asthmatic patient. *American Journal of Clinical Hypnosis, 10,* 30–32.

Rosenthal, Barbara S., & Marx, Robert D. (1981). Determinants of initial relapse episodes among dieters. *Obesity/Bariatric Medicine, 10,* 94–97.

Roskies, Ethel, & Lazarus, Richard S. (1980). Coping theory and the teaching of coping skills. In Park O. Davidson & Sheena M. Davidson (Eds.), *Behavioral medicine: Changing health lifestyles* (pp. 38–69). New York: Brunner/Mazel.

Roth, Thomas, Kramer, Milton, & Lutz, Thomas (1976). The nature of insomnia: A descriptive summary of a deep sleep clinic population. *Comprehensive Psychiatry, 17,* 217–220.

Rubin, Jesse, Nagler, Richard, Spiro, Howard M., & Pilot, Martin L. (1962). Measuring the effect of emotions on esophageal motility. *Psychosomatic Medicine, 24,* 170–176.

Rubinfeld, A.R., & Pain, M.C.F. (1976). Perception of asthma. *Lancet,* April 24, 882–884.

Rubinfeld, A.R., & Pain, M.C.F. (1977a). Bronchial provocation in the study of sensations associated with disordered breathing. *Clinical Science and Molecular Medicine, 52,* 423–428.

Rubinfeld, A.R., & Pain, M.C.F. (1977b). Conscious perception of bronchospasm as a protective phenomenon in asthma. *Chest, 72,* 154–158.

Russell, M.A.H. (1974). Realistic goals for smoking and health: A case for safer smoking. *Lancet, 2,* 254–257.

Sacerdote, Paul (1965). Hypnotherapy in neurodermatitis: A case report. *American Journal of Clinical Hypnosis, 7,* 249–253.

Sacerdote, Paul (1970). Theory and pratice of pain control in malignancy and other protracted or recurring painful illness. *International Journal of Clinical and Experimental Hypnosis, 18,* 160–180.

Sachar, Edward J., Cobb, Jeremy C., & Shor, Ronald E. (1966). Plasma cortisol changes during hypnotic trance. *Archives of General Psychiatry, 14,* 482–490.

Sachar, Edward J., Fishman, Jacob R., & Mason, John W. (1965). Influence of the hypnotic trance on plasma 17-hydroxycorticosteroid concentration. *Psychosomatic Medicine, 27,* 330–341.

Sachs, Lewis B., Feuerstein, Michael M., & Vitale, John H. (1977). Hypnotic self-regulation of chronic pain. *American Journal of Clinical Hypnosis, 20,* 106–113.

Salber, Eva J., Welsh, B., & Taylor, S.V. (1963). Reasons for smoking given by secondary school children. *Journal of Health and Human Behavior, 4,* 118–129.

Sanchez-Craig, Martha, & Walker, Keith O. (1975). I may be lonely but that doesn't mean I have to drink. *Addictions, 22,* 3–17.

Sanders, Shirley (1977). Mutual group hypnosis and smoking. *American Journal of Clinical Hypnosis, 20,* 131–135.

Sarbin, Theodore R., & Coe, William C. (1972). *Hypnosis: A social psychological analysis of influence communication.* New York: Holt, Rinehart & Winston.

Sarbin, Theodore, R., Slagle, Robert W. (1979). Hypnosis and psychophysiological outcomes. In Erika Fromm & Robert E. Shor (Eds.), *Hypnosis: Developments in research and perspectives* (2nd ed.) (pp. 273–303). Chicago: Aldine.

Sargent, Joseph D., Green, Elmer E., & Walters, E. Dale (1972). The use of autogenic feedback training in a pilot study of migraine and tension headaches. *Headache, 12,* 120–124.

Sargent, Joseph D., Walters, E. Dale, & Green, Elmer E. (1973). Psychosomatic self-regulation of migraine headaches. *Seminars in Psychiatry, 5,* 415–428.

Savitt, Robert A. (1963). Psychoanalytic studies on addiction: Ego structure in narcotic addiction. *Psychoanalytic Quarterly, 32,* 43–57.

Schachter, Stanley (1967). Some extraordinarly facts about obese humans and rats. *American Psychologist, 26,* 129–144.

Schachter, Stanley, & Singer, Jerome E. (1962). Cognitive, social, and physiologial determinants of emotional state. *Psychological Review, 69,* 379–399.

Schneck, Jerome M. (1958). Hypnotherapy for achalasia of the esophagus (cardiospasm). *American Journal of Psychiatry, 114,* 1042–1043.

Schneck, Jerome M. (1965). Hypnotherapy for vaginismus. *International Journal of Clinical and Experimental Hypnosis, 13,* 92–95.

Schneck, Jerome M. (1966a). A study of alterations in body sensations during hypnoanalysis. *International Journal of Clinical and Experimental Hypnosis, 24,* 216–231.

Schoenberg, Bernard, & Carr, Arthur C. (1963). An investigation of criteria for brief psychotherapy of neurodermatitis. *Psychosomatic Medicine, 25,* 253–263.

Schowalter, Joseph M. (1959). A case of allergy cured by hypnotic suggestion the modern way. *British Journal of Medical Hypnotism, 10,* 29–30.

Schuster, Marvin M. (1983). Disorders of the esophagus: Applications of psychophysiological methods of treatment. In Rupert Hözl & William Whitehead (Eds.), *Psychophysiology of the gastrointestinal tract: Experimental and clinical applications* (pp. 33–42). New York: Plenum Press.

Schuster, Marvin M. (1983). Irritable bowel syndrome: Applications of psychophysiological methods of treatment. In Ruper Hözl & William E. Whitehead (Eds.), *Psychophysiology of the gastrointestinal tract: Experimental and clinical applications* (pp. 289–297). New York: Plenum Press.

Schuster, Marvin M., Nikoomanesh, P., & Wells, D. (1973). Biofeedback control of lower esophageal sphincter contraction. *Rondiconti di Gastroenterologia, 5,* 14–18.

Schwartz, Gary E. (1977). Biofeedback and the self-management of disregulation disorders. In Richard B. Stuart (Ed.), *Behavioral self-management: Strategies, techniques and outcomes* (pp. 49–70). New York: Brunner/Mazel.

Schwartz, Gary E. (1979). Disregulation and systems theory: A biobehavioral framework for biofeedback and behavioral medicine. *Biofeedback and behavioral medicine,* 27–56.

Schwartz, Gary E., & Weiss, Stephen M. (1978). Yale conference on behavioral medicine: A proposed definition of statement of goals. *Journal of Behavioral Medicine, 1,* 3–14.

Schwartz, Gary E., & Weiss, Stephen M. (1980). Behavioral medicine revisited: An amended definition. *Journal of Behavioral Medicine, 1,* 249–251.

Schwartz, Wynn (1978). Time and context during hypnotic involvement. *International Journal of Clinical and Experimental Hypnosis, 26,* 307–316.

Sclafani, Anthony (1980). Dietary obesity. In Albert J. Stunkard (Ed.), *Obesity* (pp. 166–181). Philadelphia: W. B. Saunders.

Scott, Donald S., & Barber, Theodore X. (1977). Cognitive control of pain: Effects of multiple cognitive strategies. *Psychological Record, 2,* 373–383.

Scott, Michael J. (1960). *Hypnosis in skin and allergic diseases.* Springfield: Charles C. Thomas.

Seer, Peter (1979). Psychological control of essential hypertension: Review of the literature and methodological critique. *Psychological Bulletin, 86,* 1015–1043.

Selby, George, & Lance, James W. (1960). Observations on 500 cases of migraine and allied vascular headache. *Journal of Neurology, Neurosurgery, and Psychiatry, 23,* 23–32.

Seligman, Martin E.P. (1975). *Helplessness: On depression, development & death.* New York: Freedman.

Selzer, Melvin L. (1971). The Michigan Alcoholism Screening Test: The quest for a new diagnostic instrument. *American Journal of Psychiatry, 127,* 1653–1658.

Semans, James H. (1956). Premature ejaculation, a new approach. *Southern Medical Journal, 49,* 353–358.

Shapiro, Alvin P. (1978). Behavioral and environmental aspects of hypertension. *Journal of Human Stress, 4,* 9–17.

Shapiro, Alvin P., Schwartz, Gary E., Ferguson, Donald C. E., Redmond, Donald P., & Weiss, Stephen M. (1977). Behavioral methods in the treatment of hypertension. *Annals of Internal Medicine, 86,* 626–636.

Shapiro, Arnold (1983). Psychotherapy as adjunct treatment for cancer patients. *American Journal of Clinical Hypnosis, 25,* 150–155.

Shapiro, Deane H. (1978). Meditation and psychotherapeutic effects: Self-regulation strategy and altered state of consciousness. *Archives of General Psychiatry, 35,* 294–302.

Shealy, Clayton R. (1979). The effectiveness of various treatment techniques on different degrees and durations of sleep-onset insomnia. *Behavior Research & Therapy, 17,* 541–546.

Sheehan, Peter W., & McConkey, Kevin M. (1982). *Hypnosis and experience: The exploration of phenomena and process.* Hillsdale, NJ: Lawrence Erlbaum Associates.

Shewchuk, L. A., Dubren, R., Burton, D., Forman, M., Clark, R. R., & Jaffin, A. R. (1977). Preliminary observations on an intervention program for heavy smokers. *International Journal of the Addictions, 12,* 323–336.

Shibata, Joseph Izuru (1967). Hypnotherapy of patients taking unbalanced diets. *American Journal of Clinical Hypnosis, 10,* 81–83.

Shiffman, Paul M., & Jarvik, Murray E. (1976). Smoking withdrawal symptoms in two weeks of abstinence. *Psychopharmacology, 50,* 35–39.

Shiffman, Saul, Read, Laura, Maltese, Joan, Rapkin, David, & Jarvik, Murray E. (1985). Preventing relapse in ex-smokers: A self-management approach. In G. Alan Marlatt & Judith R. Gordon (Eds.), *Relapse prevention: Maintenance strategies in the treatment of addictive behaviors* (pp. 472–520). New York: Guilford Press.

Shoemaker, James E., & Tasto, Donald L. (1975). The effects of muscle relaxation on blood pressure of essential hypertensives. *Behavior Research and Therapy, 13,* 29–43.

Shor, Ronald E. (1959). Hypnosis and the concept of the generalized reality-orientation. *American Journal of Psychotherapy, 13,* 582–602.

Shor, Ronald E. (1962). Three dimensions of hypnotic depth. *International Journal of Clinical and Experimental Hypnosis, 10,* 23–38.

Shor, Ronald E. (1979). A phenomenological method for the measurement of variables important to an understanding of the nature of hypnosis. In Erika Fromm & Ronald E. Shor (Eds.), *Hypnosis: Developments in research and new perspectives* (pp. 105–135). New York: Aldine.

Shor, Ronald E., & Orne, Emily C. (1962). *The Harvard Group Scale of Hypnotic Susceptibility, Form A.* Palo Alto, CA: Consulting Psychologists Press.

Shorter, R. G., Huizenga, K. A., & Spencer, R. J. (1972). A working hypothesis for the etiology and pathogenesis of nonspecific inflammatory bowel disease. *American Journal of Digestive Diseases, 17,* 1024–1032.

Shturman, Ellstein R., Zeballos, R. J., & Buckley, J. M. (1978). The beneficial effect of nasal breathing on exercise-induced bronchoconstriction. *American Review of Respiratory Diseases, 118,* 65–73.

Sicuteri, F., Fanciullacci, M., & Michelacci, S. (1978). Decentralization supersensitivity in headache and central panalgesia. *Research & Clinical Studies in Headache, 6,* 19–33.

Silver, Bernard V., & Blanchard, Edward B. (1978). Biofeedback and relaxation training in the treatment of psychophysiological disorders: Or are the machines really necessary? *Journal of Behavioral Medicine, 1,* 217–239.

Simon, Ronald A. (1984). Environmental control and dust abatement. In Arthur Dawson & Ronald A. Simon (Eds.), *The practical management of asthma* (pp. 133–135). Orlando, FL: Grune & Stratton.

Simonton, O. Carl, Matthews-Simonton, Stephanie, & Creighton, James (1978). *Getting well again: A step-by-step self help guide to overcoming cancer for patients and their families.* Los Angeles: Tarcher.

Simonton, O. Carl, Matthews-Simonton, Stephanie, & Sparks, T. Flint (1980). Psychological intervention in the treatment of cancer. *Psychosomatics, 21,* 226–233.

Sinclair-Gieban, A. H. C. (1960). Treatment of status asthmaticus by hypnosis. *British Medical Journal, 2,* 1651–1652.

Sinclair-Gieban, A. H. C., & Chalmers, Derek (1959). Evaluation of treatment of warts by hypnosis. *Lancet, 2,* 480–482.

Singer, Jerome L. (1974). *Imagery and daydream methods in psychotherapy and behavior modification.* New York: Academic Press.

Sirota, Alan D., & Mahoney, Michael J. (1974). Relaxing on cue: The self regulation of asthma. *Journal of Behavioral Therapy and Experimental Psychiatry, 5,* 65–66.

Sirota, Alan D., Schwartz, Gary E., & Shapiro, David (1974). Voluntary control of human heart rate. Effect on reaction to aversive stimulation. *Journal of Abnormal Psychology, 83,* 261–267.

Sirota, Alan D., Schwartz, Gary E., & Shapiro, David (1976). Voluntary control of human heart rate: Effect on reaction to aversive stimulation: A replication and extension. *Journal of Abnormal Psychology, 85,* 473–477.

Skinhøj, E., & Paulson, O. B. (1969). Regional blood flow in internal carotid distribution during migraine attack. *British Medical Journal, 3,* 569–570.

Skinner, B. F. (1953). *Science in human behavior.* New York: Macmillan.

Sklår, Lawrence S., & Anisman, Hymie (1981). Stress and cancer. *Psychological Bulletin, 89,* 369–406.

Smith, David E., & Wesson, Donald R. (1974). *Diagnosis and treatment of adverse reactions to sedative-hypnotics.* Washington, DC: National Institute on Drug Abuse.

Smith, J. M., & Burns, C. L. C. (1960). The treatment of asthmatic children by hypnotic suggestion. *British Journal of Diseases of the Chest, 54,* 78–81.

Smith, Shirley J., & Balaban, Alvin B. (1983). A multidimensional approach to pain relief: Case report of a patient with systemic lupus erythematosus. *International Journal of Clinical and Experimental Hypnosis, 31,* 72–81.

Smith-Moorhouse, P. M. (1969). Hypnosis in the treatment of alcoholism. *British Journal of Addiction, 64,* 47–55.

Smyth, Larry D., & Lowy, Doug (1983). Auditory vigilance during hypnosis: A brief communication. *International Journal of Clinical and Experimental Hypnosis, 31,* 67–71.

Snape, William J., Jr., Carlson, Gerald M., & Cohen, Sidney (1976). Colonic myoelectric activity in the irritable bowel syndrome. *Gastroenterology, 70,* 326–330.

Snape, William J., Jr., Matarazzo, Stephen A., & Cohen, Sidney (1978). Effect of eating and gastrointestinal hormones on human colonic myoelectrical and motor activity. *Gastroenterology, 75,* 373–378.

Solomon, George Freeman (1981). Emotional and personality factors in the onset and course of autoimmune disease, particularly rheumatoid arthritis. In Robert Ader (Ed.), *Psychoneuroimmunology* (pp. 159–182). New York: Academic Press.

Solomon, George F., Amkraut, A. A., & Kasper, P. (1974). Immunity, emotions and stress. *Annals of Clinical Research, 6,* 313–322.

Solomon, George F., & Moos, Rudolf H. (1964). Emotions, immunity and disease: A speculative theoretical integration. *Archives of General Psychiatry, 11,* 657–674.

Solomon, Richard L. (1980). The opponent-process theory of acquired motivation: The costs of pleasure and the benefit of pain. *American Psychologist, 35,* 691–712.

Sovak, M., Kunzel, M., Sternbach, R. A., & Dalessio, D. J. (1978). Is volitional manipulation of hemodynamics a valid rationale for biofeedback therapy of migraine? *Headache, 18,* 197–202.

Spanos, Nicholas P. (1982). Hypnotic behavior: A cognitive, social psychological perspective. *Research Communications in Psychology, Psychiatry and Behavior, 7,* 199–213.

Spanos, Nicholas, P., Radtke-Bodorik, H. Lorraine, Ferguson, John D., & Jones, Bill (1979). The effects of hypnotic susceptibility, suggestions for analgesia, and the utilization of cognitive strategies on the reduction of pain. *Journal of Abnormal Psychology, 88,* 282–292.

Spanos, Nicholas P., Rivers, Steven M., & Ross, Stewart (1977). Experienced involuntariness and response to hypnotic suggestions. In William E. Edmondston, Jr. (Ed.), Conceptual and investigative approaches to hypnosis and hypnotic phenomena. *Annals of The New York Academy of Science, 296,* 208–221.

Spanos, Nicholas P., Stam, Henderikus J., Rivers, Stephen M., & Radtke, H. Lorraine (1980). Meditation, expectation and performance on indices of nonanalytic attending. *International Journal of Clinical and Experimental Hypnosis, 28,* 244–251.

Spector, Sheldon, Luparello, Thomas J., Kopetzky, Michael J., Souhrada, Joseph, & Kinsman, Robert A. (1976). Response of asthmatics to Methacholine and suggestions. *American Review of Respiratory Disease, 113,* 43–50.

Spiegel, Herbert (1970). A single treatment method to stop smoking using ancillary self-hypnosis. *International Journal of Clinical and Experimental Hypnosis, 18,* 235–250.

Spiegel, Herbert, & DeBetz, Barbara (1978). Restructuring eating behavior with self-hypnosis. *International Journal of Obesity, 2,* 287–288.

Spiegel, Herbert, & Linn, L. (1969). The "ripple effect" following adjunct hypnosis in analytic psychotherapy. *American Journal of Psychiatry, 126,* 53–58.

Spiegel, Herbert, & Spiegel, David. (1978). *Trance and treatment: Clinical uses of hypnosis.* New York: Basic Books.

Stacher, George (1983). The responsiveness of the esophagus to environmental stimuli. In Rupert Hözl & William E. Whitehead (Eds.), *Psychophysiology of the gastrointestinal tract: Experimental and clinical applications* (pp. 22–31). New York: Plenum Press.

Stacher, G., Schuster, P., Bauer, P., Lahoda, R., & Schulze, D. (1975). Effect of suggestion of relaxation or analgesia on pain threshold and pain tolerance in the waking and in the hypnotic state. *Journal of Psychosomatic Research, 19,* 259–265.

Stalonas, Peter M., Johnson, WIlliam G., & Christ, Maryann (1978). Behavior modification for obesity: The evaluation of exercise, contingency management, and program adherence. *Journal of Consulting and Clinical Psychology, 46,* 463–469.

Stambaugh, Edward E., & House, Alvin E. (1977). Multimodality treatment of migraine headache: A case study utilizing biofeedback, relaxation, autogenic and hypnotic treatments. *American Journal of Clinical Hypnosis, 19,* 235–240.

Stankler, L. (1967). A critical assessment of the cure of warts by suggestion. *The Practitioner, 198* (April–June), 690–694.

Stanton, H. E. (1975). Weight loss through hypnosis. *American Journal of Clinical Hypnosis, 18,* 34–38.

Stanton, H. E. (1976). Fee-paying and weight loss: Evidence for an interesting interaction. *American Journal of Clinical Hypnosis, 19,* 47–49.

Stanton, H. E. (1978). A one-session hypnotic approach to modifying smoking behavior. *International Journal of Clinical and Experimental Hypnosis, 26,* 22–29.

Stein, Calvert (1964). A displacement and reconditioning technique for compulsive smokers. *International Journal of Clinical and Experimental Hypnosis, 12,* 230–238.

Stein, Marvin, Schleifer, Steven J., & Keller, Steven E. (1981). Hypothalamic influences on immune responses. In Robert Ader (Ed.), *Psychoneuroimmunology* (pp. 429–447). New York: Academic Press.

Steinglass, Peter (1979). Family therapy with alcoholics: A review. In Edward Kaufman & Pauline N. Kaufman (Eds.), *Family therapy and alcohol abuse.* New York: Gardner Press.

Stephens, Joseph H., Harris, Alan H., Brady, Joseph B., & Shaffer, John W. (1975). Psychological and physiological variables associated with large magnitude voluntary heart rate changes. *Psychophysiology, 12,* 381–387.

Sternbach, Richard A. (1974). *Pain patients: Traits and treatment.* New York: Academic Press.

Sternberg, Barbara (1985). Relapse in weight control: Definitions, processes, and prevention strategies. In G. Alan Marlatt & Judith R. Gordon. *Relapse prevention: Maintenance strategies in the treatment of addictive behaviors* (pp. 521–545). New York: Guilford Press.

Stevenson, Donald D., Simon, Ronald A., & Mathison, David A. (1980). Aspirin sensitive asthma: Tolerance to aspirin after positive oral aspirin challenge. *Journal of Allergy and Clinical Immunology, 66,* 82–88.

Stevenson, Ian, & Ripley, Herbert S. (1952). Variations in respiration and in respiratory symptoms during changes in emotion. *Psychosomatic Medicine, 14,* 476–490.

Stewart, H. (1957). Some uses of hypnosis in general practice. British Medical Journal, 1, 1320–1322.

Stilson, Donald W., Matus, Irwin, & Ball, Gary (1980). Relaxation and subjective estimates of muscle tension: Implications for a central efferent theory of muscle control. *Biofeedback and Self-Regulation, 5,* 19–36.

Stone, Richard A., & De Leo, James (1976). Psychotherapeutic control of hypertension. *New England Journal of Medicine, 294,* 80–84.

Storms, Michael D., & Nisbett, Richard E. (1970). Insomnia and the attribution process. *Journal of Personality and Social Psychology, 16,* 319–328.

Stoyva, Johann M., & Budzynski, Thomas H. (1974). Cultivated low arousal: An antistress response. In L. V. DiCara (Ed.), *Research advances in limbic and autonomic nervous systems research* (pp. 370–394). New York: Plenum Press.

Straits, B. C. (1966, August). *The discontinuation of cigarette smoking: A multiple discriminant analysis.* Paper presented at the Annual Meeting of The American Sociological Association. Miami Beach, FL.

Strauss, Richard H., McFadden, E. R., Ingram, R. H., & Jaeger, James J. (1977). Enhancement of exercise-induced asthma by cold air. *New England Journal of Medicine, 297,* 743–747.

Stuart, Richard B. (1967). Behavioral control of overeating. *Behavior Research & Therapy, 5,* 357–365.

Stuart, Richard B. (1971). A three-dimensional program for the treatment of obesity. *Behavior Research & Therapy, 9,* 177–186.

Stuart, Richard B., & Davis, Barbara (1972). *Slim chance in a fat world: Behavioral control of obesity.* Champaign: IL: Research Press.

Stunkard, Albert J. (1972). New therapies for the eating disorders. *Archives of General Psychiatry, 26,* 391–398.

Stunkard, Albert J. (1976). *The pain of obesity.* Palo Alto, CA: Bull.

Stunkard, Albert J. (1977). Behavioral treatment of obesity: Failure to maintain. In Richard B. Stuart (Ed.), *Behavioral self-management: Strategies, techniques and outcomes* (pp. 317–350). New York: Brunner/Mazel.

Stunkard, Albert J. (1978). Behavioral treatment of obesity: The current status. *International Journal of Obesity, 2,* 237–248.

Stunkard, Albert J. (1978). *Obesity.* Philadelphia: W. B. Saunders.

Stunkard, Albert, & Mendelson, Myer (1967). Obesity and the body image: I. Characteristics of disturbances in the body image of some obese persons. *American Journal of Psychiatry, 123,* 1296–1300.

Stunkard, Albert J., & Penick, Sydnor B. (1979). Behavior modification in the treatment of obesity. *Archives of General Psychiatry, 36,* 801–806.

Stunkard, Albert J., & Rush, John (1974). Dieting and depression reexamined: A critical review of reports of untoward responses during weight reduction for obesity. *Annals of Internal Medicine, 81,* 526–533.

Suinn, R. M. (1974). Behavior therapy for cardiac patients. *Behavior Therapy, 5,* 569–571.

Surman, Owen S., Gottlieb, Sheldon K., & Hackett, Thomas P. (1972). Hypnotic treatment of a child with warts. *American Journal of Clinical Hypnosis, 15,* 12–14.

Surman, Owen S., Gottlieb, Sheldon K., Hackett, Thomas P., & Silverberg, Elizabeth L. (1973). Hypnosis in the treatment of warts. *Archives of General Psychiatry, 28,* 439–441.

Surwitt, Richard S., Williams, Redford B., & Shapiro, David (1982). *Behavioral approaches to cardiovascular disease.* New York: Academic Press.

Swanson, David W., Swenson, Wendell M., Maruta, Toshihiko M., & McPhee, Malcolm (1976). Program for managing chronic pain. 1. Program description and characteristics of patients. *Mayo Clinic Proceedings, 51*, 401–408.

Swinehart, James W., & Kirscht, John P. (1966). Smoking: A panel study of beliefs and behavior following the PHS report. *Psychological Reports, 18*, 519–528.

Szasz, Thomas S. (1968). The psychology of persistent pain. In Andre Soulairac (Ed.), *Pain*. London: Academic Press.

Szentivanyi, Andor (1968). The Beta adrenergic theory of the atopic abnormality in bronchial asthma. *Journal of Allergy, 42*, 203–232.

Taplin, Paul S., & Creer, Thomas L. (1978). A procedure for using peak expiratory flow rate data to increase the predictability of asthma episodes. *Journal of Asthma Research, 16*, 15–18.

Tart, Charles T. (Ed.) (1969). *Altered states of consciousness: A book of readings*. New York: Wiley.

Tart, Charles T. (1971). *On being stoned: A psychological study of marijuana intoxication*. Palo Alto, CA: Science & Behavior Books.

Tart, Charles T. (1975). *States of consciousness*. New York: E. P. Dutton.

Tasini, Miriam F., & Hackett, Thomas P. (1977). Hypnosis in the treatment of warts in immunodeficient children. *American Journal of Clinical Hypnosis, 19*, 152–154.

Tasto, Donald L., & Hinkle, John E. (1973). Case histories and shorter communications. *Behavior Research & Therapy, 11*, 347–349.

Taylor, C. Barry, Farquhar, John W., Nelson, Eliot, & Agras, Stewart (1977). Relaxation therapy and high blood pressure. *Archives of General Psychiatry, 34*, 339–342.

Taylor, C. Barry, Ferguson, James M., & Reading, James C. (1978). Gradual weight loss and depression. *Behavior Therapy, 9*, 622–625.

Taylor, H. L., Buskirk, E. R., & Remington, R. D. (1973). Exercise in controlled trials of the prevention of coronary heart disease. *Federation Proceedings, 32*, 1623–1627.

Taylor, I., Darby, C., Hammond, P., & Basu, P. (1978). Is there a myoelectrical abnormality in the irritable colon syndrome? *Gut, 19*, 391–395.

Tellegen, Auke, & Atkinson, Gilbert (1974). Openness to absorbing and self-altering experiences ("absorption"), a trait related to hypnotic susceptibility. *Journal of Abnormal Psychology, 83*, 268–277.

Temoshok, Lydia, & Heller, Bruce W. (1984). On comparing apples, oranges and fruit salad: A methodological overview of medical outcome studies in psychosocial oncology. In Cary L. Cooper (Ed.), *Psychosocial stress and cancer* (pp. 231–260). New York: Wiley.

Tenzel, James H., & Taylor, Robert L. (1968). An evaluation of hypnosis and suggestion as treatment for warts. *Psychosomatics, 10*, 252–257.

Thorne, D. Eugene, Rasmus, Carolyn, & Fisher, A. Garth (1976). Are "fat-girls" more hypnotically susceptible? *Psychological Reports, 38*, 267–270.

Tighe, Thomas J., & Elliot, Rogers (1968). A technique for controlling behavior in natural life settings. *Journal of Applied Behavior Analysis, 1*, 263–266.

Tilker, Harvey A., & Meyer, Robert G. (1972). The use of covert sensitization and hypnotic procedures in the treatment of an overweight person: A case report. *American Journal of Clinical Hypnosis, 15* 15–19.

Tomkins, Silvan S. (1966). Psychological model for smoking behavior. *American Journal of Public Health, 56*, 17–20.

Travell, Janet G. (1976). Myofascial trigger points: Clinical review. *Advances in Pain Research, 1*, 919–926.

Tullis, I. Frank (1973). Rational diet construction for mild and grand obesity. *Journal of the American Medical Association, 226*, 70–71.

Turk, Dennis C. (1975). *Cognitive control of pain: A skills-training approach*. Unpublished master's thesis, The University of Waterloo.

Turk, Dennis C., Meichenbaum, Donald, & Genest, Myles (1983). *Pain and behavioral medicine: A cognitive-behavioral perspective.* New York: Guilford.

Turnbull, John W. (1962). Asthma conceived as a learned response. *Journal of Psychosomatic Research, 6,* 59–70.

Turner, Ralph M. (1984a). Behavior self-control procedures for disorders of initiating and maintaining sleep (DIMS). *Clinical Psychology Review,* 1-30.

Turner, Ralph M. (1984b, May 24) *Sleep disorders: Physiology, diagnosis, and treatment.* Workshop presentation, Fifth Annual Scientific Session, Society of Behavioral Medicine, Philadelphia.

Turner, Ralph M., & Ascher, Michael L. (1982). Therapist factor in the treatment of insomnia. *Behavior Research & Therapy, 20,* 33–40.

Turner, Ralph M., DiTomasso, R., & Giles, T. (1983). Failures in the treatment of insomnia: A plea for differential diagnosis. In E. B. Fóa (Ed.), *Failures in behavior therapy.* New York: Wiley.

Turner-Warwick, Margaret (1966). Diagnosis and management of asthma. *British Medical Journal,* 403–404.

Twerski, Abraham J., & Naar, Ray (1974). Hypnotherapy in a case of refractory dermatitis. *American Journal of Clinical Hypnosis, 16,* 202–205.

Ullman, Montague (1947). Herpes simplex and second degree burn induced under hypnosis. *American Journal of Psychiatry, 103,* 828–830.

Ullman, Montague (1959). On the psyche and warts. I. Suggestion and warts: A review and comment. *Psychosomatic Medicine, 21,* 474–488.

Ullman, Montague, & Dudek, Stephanie (1960). On the psyche and warts. II. Hypnotic suggestion and warts. *Psychosomatic Medicine, 22,* 68–76.

Vachon, Louis, & Rich, Edwin S. (1976). Visceral learning in asthma. *Psychosomatic Medicine, 38,* 122–130.

Vaillant, George E. (1981). Dangers of psychotherapy in the treatment of alcoholism. In Margaret H. Bean & Norman E. Zinberg (Eds.), *Dynamic approaches to the understanding and treatment of alcoholism* (pp. 36–54). New York: Free Press.

Van Itallie, Theodore B., & Kral, John G. (1981). The dilemma of morbid obesity. *Journal of the American Medical Association, 246,* 999–1003.

Val Pelt, S. J. (1949). Hypnotherapy in medical practice. *British Journal of Medical Hypnotism, 1,* 8–13.

Van Pelt, S. J. (1953). Asthma, emotion and hypnotherapy. *British Journal of Medical Hypnotism, 5,* 20–24.

Van Pelt, S. J. (1954). Migraine, emotion and hypnosis. *British Journal of Medical Hypnotism, 6,* 22–24.

Van Pelt, S. J. (1954–55). Waking hypnosis and insomnia. *British Journal of Medical Hypnotism, 6,* 17–19.

Van Pelt, S. J. (1958a). Alcoholics limited and hypnosis. *British Journal of Medical Hypnotism, 9,* 25.

Van Pelt, S. J. (1958b). *Secrets of hypnotism.* North Hollywood, CA: Wilshire.

Van Pelt, S.J. (1958c). The control of the heart rate by hypnotic suggestion. In Leslie M. LeCron (Ed.), *Experimental Hypnosis* (pp. 266–275). New York: Macmillan.

Van Pelt, S.J. (1961). Hypnotism, "rheumatism" and fibrositis. *British Journal of Medical Hypnotism, 12,* 19–21.

Vaughn, Richard, Pall, Michael L., & Haynes, Stephen N. (1977). Frontalis EMG response to stress in subjects with frequent muscle-contraction headaches. *Headaches, 16,* 313–317.

Vernon, R.D. (1961). A brief technique for the treatment of insomnia. *British Journal of Medical Hypnotism, 12,* 4–7.

Vogel, Victor H. (1937). Suggestibility in narcotic addicts. *Public Health Report, 16* (Suppl.), 1–7.

Von Dedenroth, T.E.A. (1964). The use of hypnosis with "tobaccomaniacs". *American Journal of Clinical Hypnosis, 6,* 326–331.

Von Dedenroth, T.E.A. (1965). Some newer ideas and concepts of alcoholism and the use of hypnosis. Part I. *British Journal of Medical Hypnotism, 16,* 27–31.

Von Dedenroth, T.E.A. (1968). The use of hypnosis in 1000 cases of "tobaccomaniacs". *American Journal of Clinical Hypnosis, 10,* 194–197.

Wadden, Thomas A., & Anderton, Charles H. (1982). The clinical use of hypnosis. *Psychological Bulletin, 91,* 215–243.

Wadden, Thomas A., & Flaxman, Judith (1981). Hypnosis and weight loss: A preliminary study. *International Journal of Clinical and Experimental Hypnosis, 29,* 162–173.

Wadden, Thomas A., & Penrod, James H. (1981). Hypnosis in the treatment of alcoholism: A review and appraisal. *American Journal of Clinical Hypnosis, 24,* 41–47.

Waingrow, Selwyn M., Horn, Daniel, & Ikard, Frederick F. (1968). Dosage patterns of cigarette smoking in American adults. *American Journal of Public Health, 58,* 54–70.

Walen, Susan R. (1980). Cognitive factors in sexual behavior. *Journal of Sex and Marital Therapy, 6,* 87–101.

Walker, Barbara B. (1983). Treating stomach disorders: Can we reinstate regulatory processes? In Rupert Hözl & William E. Whitehead (Eds.), *Psychophysiology of the gastrointestinal tract: Experimental and clinical applications* (pp. 209–233). New York: Plenum Press.

Walker, Barbara B., Lawton, Cheryl A., & Sandman, Curt A. (1978). Voluntary control of electrogastric activity. *Psychosomatic Medicine, 40,* 610–619.

Walker, Barbara, & Sandman, Curt A. (1977). Physiological response patterns in ulcer patients: Phasic and tonic components of the electrogastrogram. *Psychophysiology, 14,* 393–400.

Wallace, Robert K. (1970). Physiological effects of transcendental meditation. *Science, 167,* 1751–1754.

Walton, D. (1960). The application of learning theory to the treatment of a case of bronchial asthma. In Eysenck (Ed.), *Behavior therapy and the neuroses* (pp. 188–189). New York: Pergamon Press.

Wangel, Anders G., & Deller, Donald J. (1965). Intestinal motility in man. III. Mechanisms of constipation and diarrhea with particular reference to the irritable colon syndrome. *Gastroenterology, 48,* 69–84.

Ward, W. O. (1975). Successful treatment of frigidity through hypnosis. *Virginia Medical Monthly, 102,* 223–228.

Warner, G., & Lance, J. W. (1975). Relaxation therapy in migraine and chronic tension headache. *Medical Journal of Australia, 1,* 298–301.

Waters, W. E. (1974). The Pontypridd headache survey. *Headache, 14,* 81–90.

Watkins, John G. (1947). The hypoanalytic treatment of a case of impotence. *Journal of Clinical Psychopathology, 8,* 453–480.

Watkins, Helen H. (1976). Hypnosis and smoking: A five-session approach. *International Journal of Clinical and Experimental Hypnosis, 24,* 381–390.

Watson, John B., & Raynor, Rosalie (1920). Conditioned emotional reactions. *Journal of Experimental Psychology, 3,* 1–14.

Weiner, H. (1970). Psychosomatic research in essential hypertension: Retrospect and prospect. In M. Koster, H. Musaph, & P. Visser (Eds.), *Psychosomatics in essential hypertension bibliography psychiatry* (pp. 164–189). New York: Karger.

Weinstock, S. Alexander (1976). The reestablishment of intestinal control in functional colitis. *Biofeedback and Self-Regulation, 1,* 324–325.

Weiss, Jay M., Pohorecky, Lorissa A., Salmon, Sherry, & Gruenthal, Michael (1976). Attenuation of gastric lesions by psychological aspects of aggression in rats. *Journal of Comparative & Physiological Psychology, 90,* 252–259.

Weitzenhoffer, André M. (1957). *General techniques of hypnotism.* New York: Grune & Stratton.

Weitzenhoffer, André (1974). When is an "instruction" an "instruction"? *International Journal of Clinical and Experimental Hypnosis, 22,* 258–269.

Weitzenhoffer, André M., & Hilgard, Ernest R. (1959). *Stanford Hypnotic Susceptibility Scale, Forms A & B.* Palo Alto, CA: Consulting Psychologists Press.

Weitzenhoffer, André M., & Hilgard, Ernest R. (1962). *Stanford Hypnotic Susceptibility Scale, Form C.* Palo Alto, CA: Consulting Psychologists Press.

Weitzenhoffer, André M., & Hilgard, Ernest R. (1963). *Stanford Profile Scales of Hypnotic Susceptibility, Forms I & II.* Palo Alto, CA: Consulting Psychologists Press.

Welgan, Peter R. (1974). Learned control of gastric acid secretion in ulcer patients. *Psychosomatic Medicine, 36,* 411–419.

Wells, David T. (1973). Large magnitude voluntary heart rate changes. *Psychophysiology, 10,* 260–269.

Wentworth-Rohr, Ivan (1984). *Symptom reduction through clinical biofeedback.* New York: Human Sciences Press.

Whatmore, George B., & Kohli, Daniel R. (1974). *The physiopathology and treatment of functional disorders.* New York: Grune & Stratton.

White, Benjamin V., Jr., & Jones, Chester M. (1938). Effect of irritants and drugs affecting autonomic nervous system upon the mucosa of the normal rectum and rectosigmoid, with especial reference to "mucous colitis". *New England Journal of Medicine, 218,* 791–797.

White, H. C. (1961). Hypnosis in bronchial asthma. *Journal of Psychosomatic Research, 5,* 272–279.

White, Robert W. (1941). A preface to the theory of hypnotism. *Journal of Abnormal and Social Psychology, 36,* 477–505.

Whitehead, William E. (1984). Psychotherapy and biofeedback in the treatment of irritable bowel syndrome. In Nicholas W. Read (Ed.), *Irritable bowel syndrome* (pp. 245–256). London: Grune & Stratton.

Whitehead, William E., Engel, Bernard T., & Schuster, Marvin M. (1980). Irritable bowel syndrome: Physiological and psychological differences between diarrhea-predominant and constipation-predominant patients. *Digestive Diseases and Sciences, 25,* 404–413.

Whitehead, William E., Renault, Pierre F., & Goldiamond, Israel (1975). Modification of human gastric acid secretion with operant-conditioning procedures. *Journal of Applied Behavior Analysis, 8,* 147–156.

Whitehead, William E., & Schuster, Marvin M. (1985). *Gastrointestinal disorders: Behavioral and physiological basis for treatment* (pp. 125–154). New York: Academic Press.

Whitehead, William E., Winget, Carolyn, Fedoravicius, Al S., Wooley, Susan, & Blackwell, Barry (1982). Learned illness behavior in patients with irritable bowel syndrome and peptic ulcer. *Digestive Diseases and Sciences, 27,* 202–207.

Whorwell, P. J., Prior, Alison, & Faragher, E. B. (1984). Controlled trial of hypnotherapy in the treatment of service refractory irritable-bowel syndrome. *Lancet, 2,* 1232–1233.

Wick, Erika, Sigman, Robert, & Kline, Milton V. (1971). Hypnotherapy and therapeutic education in the treatment of obesity: differential treatment factors. *Psychiatric Quarterly, 45,* 234–254.

Wickramaskera, Ian E. (1973a). Temperature feedback for the control of migraine. *Journal of Behavior Therapy & Experimental Psychiatry, 4,* 343–345.

Wickramasekera, Ian (1973b). The application of verbal instructions and EMG feedback training to the management of tension headache-Preliminary observations. *Headache, 13,* 74–76.

Wieder, Herbert, & Kaplan, Eugene H. (1969). Drug use in adolescents: Psychodynamic meaning and pharmacogenic effect. *Psychoanalytic Study of the Child, 24,* 399–431.

Williams, Redford B. (1975). Heart rate and forearm blood flow feedback in the treatment of a case of severe essential hypertension. *Psychophysiology, 12,* 237 (Abstract).

Williams, Redford B. (1981). Behavioral factors in cardiovascular disease: An update. In John Willis Hurst (Ed.), *Update V: The Heart* (pp. 219–230). New York: McGraw-Hill.

Wilson, G. Terence (1978). Booze, beliefs, and behavior: Cognitive processes in alcohol use and abuse. In Peter E. Nathan, G. Alan Marlatt & T. LoBerg (Eds.), *Alcoholism: New directions in behavioral research and treatment.* New York: Plenum Press.

Wilson, G. Terence (1980). Behavior modification and the treatment of obesity. In Albert J. Stunkard (Ed.), *Obesity* (pp. 325–344). Philadelphia: W.B. Saunders.

Wilson, G. Terence (1980). Cognitive factors in lifestyle changes: A social learning perpsective. In Park O. Davidson & Sheena M. Davidson (Eds.), *Behavioral medicine: Changing health lifestyles* (pp. 3–37). New York: Brunner/Mazel.

Winkelstein, L.B. (1959). Hypnosis, diet, and weight reduction. *New York State Journal of Medicine, 59,* 1751–1756.

Wolberg, Lewis R. (1948). *Medical hypnosis. Volume I: The principles of hypnotherapy.* New York: Grune & Stratton.

Wolf, Steward, & Almy, Thomas P. (1949). Experimental observations on cardiospasm in man. *Gastroenterology, 13,* 401–421.

Wolff, Harold G., & Wolf, Stewart (1951). The management of hypertensive patients. In Elexious Thompson (Ed.), *Hypertension* (pp. 457–489). Minneapolis: University of Minnesota Press.

Wollersheim, Janet P. (1970). ... on learning principles ... *ology, 76,* 462–474.

... In Edward E. Abram-... New York: Springer.

... *Clinical Hypnosis, 4,*

..., CA: Stanford Uni-

... indelic acid in cases

... *npulsive drug use.*

... ilar manifestations

... Robert A. (1976).

... ations for the pri-

... *pain. International*

... skin tests. *Annals of*

... ient. In Ralph B. Winn ... (pp. 178–181). New York: Philosophical Li-

Zinberg, Norman E., Harding, Wayne M., Stelmack, Shirley M., & Marblestone, Robert A. (1978). Patterns of heroin use. *Annals of the New York Academy of Science, 311,* 10–24.

Zisook, S., & De Vaul, R. A. (1977). Emotional factors in inflammatory bowel disease. *Southern Medical Journal, 70, 716–719.*

Author Index

Subject Index